Complete
Mental Health

The Go-to-Guide for
Clinicians and Patients

Complete Mental Health

The Go-to-Guide for Clinicians and Patients

JOHN INGRAM WALKER, MD

W. W. NORTON & COMPANY

NEW YORK • LONDON

NOTE: The quizzes in this book are not standardized.

Copyright © 2010 by John Ingram Walker, MD

616.89
W15C
2010

All rights reserved
Printed in the United States of America
First Edition

For information about permission to reproduce selections from this book, write to
Permissions, W. W. Norton & Company, Inc.
500 Fifth Avenue, New York, NY 10110

For information about special discounts for bulk purchases, please contact
W. W. Norton Special Sales at
specialsales@wwnorton.com or 800-233-4830

Manufacturing by RR Donnelley, Bloomsburg
Book design by Gilda Hannah
Production manager: Leeann Graham

Library of Congress Cataloging-in-Publication Data

Walker, J. Ingram (John Ingram), 1944–
Complete mental health: the go-to guide for clinicians and patients / John Ingram Walker. — 1st ed.
    p. cm.
"A Norton Professional Book."
Includes bibliographical references and index.
ISBN 978-0-393-70623-9 (pbk.)
1. Mental health. 2. Mental illness. I. Title.
  RA790.W225 2010
  616.89—dc22   2009039282

ISBN: 978-0-393-70623-9 (pbk.)

W. W. Norton & Company, Inc., 500 Fifth Avenue, New York, N.Y. 10110
www.wwnorton.com
W. W. Norton & Company Ltd., Castle House,
75/76 Wells Street, London W1T 3QT

1 2 3 4 5 6 7 8 9 0

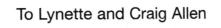
To Lynette and Craig Allen

Contents

Acknowledgments

Highest praise goes to wordsmith Wende Whitus, who wove the words of a patchwork manuscript into a comprehensible pattern of information. Deepest appreciation and gratitude goes to Dave and Reba Campbell, without whose help I may have never made it through medical school; to Binford Weaver, who taught selfless sacrifice for the growth of others; to my mentor, the late Leonard Coleman, MD, for modeling compassionate commitment for every patient. Thanks to H. Keith H. Brodie, MD, President of Duke University from 1985 to 1993, for introducing me to academic medicine. My deepest love goes to my grandfather, grandmother, mother, and the Weaver uncles and aunts, who, around the dinner table, taught the magic of life-long learning. A case of gold stars goes to my second family, the staff at the Behavior Health Unit Grimes-St. Joseph Medical Center, especially Jeff Baker, Susan Bice, Felicia Carmouche, Jan Childress, Michelle Comeaux, Barb Courser, Shirley Higginbotham, Carrol Johnson, Kelly Kyle, Doris Redman, Carol Davis-Rios, Norma Rivas, Luke Scamardo, MD, Lyne' Taylor, and Brigitte Turner, whose warm humor and spiritual sustenance kept us focused on serving the harassed and the helpless. Those times spent on the BHU will forever be a treasure to recall. Appreciation goes to the staff at St. Albans Hospital, Carilion New River Valley Medical Center for their acceptance and encouragement. I especially want to thank Mark D. Kilgus, MD, PhD, Chair, Department of Psychiatry and Behavioral Medicine, Carilion Clinic, as without his introduction of me to Deborah Malmud, Director of Norton Professional Books, this book would not have come to be. Deborah immediately understood the book's unique concept and polished and broadened its appeal. Thanks to the staff at W. W. Norton: Kristen Holt-Browning, Libby Burton, invaluable copy editor Kathleen Brown, and Kelvin Olsen, who brought fun to writing a book. Thanks, Brad, for your encouragement. Finally, all my love, admiration, and warmhearted praise go to my wife, Vicki, who paves the road of life with bricks of gold.

Preface

After completing a rotating internship and serving 2 years as a flight surgeon in the U.S. Air Force, I became a general practitioner in a medium-size Texas town. I soon noticed that many of my patients might have either primary or underlying emotional problems. These problems seemed to interfere with their getting the most out of life and in some cases were apparent contributors to physical disease. Although I enjoyed my practice and the relationships I had with my professional associates, I found myself becoming increasingly interested in emotional illnesses. After many hours of consideration, I decided to apply to Duke Medical Center for a psychiatric residency.

Fortunately, I was accepted. After completing my residency, I accepted a joint appointment in the Department of Medicine and the Department of Psychiatry to become director of the Combined Medical Specialties Unit dedicated to the treatment of psychosomatic illnesses. The last 20 years of my career have been spent practicing psychiatry in the rural areas of Texas and, most recently, Virginia. In these small town settings, I have seen firsthand that a lack of psychiatrists underscores the need for more comprehensive psychiatric training for those in clinical care.

Because of the high incidence of mental and emotional disorders, I believe that it is imperative that clinicians understand psychiatric diagnosis and treatment. Consider the statistics: A survey by the National Institute of Mental Health indicated that 46% of Americans will suffer from a neuropsychiatric or behavior disorder in their lifetime. In any given year, 26%—a little over a fourth of the population—meet criteria for a mind disorder. These numbers fail to reflect the impact that neuropsychiatric illness has on families, friends, and work productivity. Mind-related illness in the United States exceeds $300 billion in health care costs annually. This figure represents more than the cost of heart disease, cancer, and AIDS combined.

The neuroscience of mental health, covering a wide range of knowledge from molecular events to social phenomena, has emerged as one of the most exciting areas of medical research. Advances in the understanding of brain function have repaired the damaging division between emotional and physical health.

With advances come challenges. More than any other area of medicine, the mental health field is beset by inequities in access to care. The shrinking availability of psychiatrists mandates that primary care clinicians utilize the advances in mental health research to treat the millions of Americans who otherwise would be without care.

It is my hope that my many years of practice, both in primary care and in psychiatry, will prove helpful to clinicians who wish to apply neuroscientific advances in treating their patients.

John Ingram Walker, MD

CHAPTER 1

What Is Normal?

Behind the Wizard's Curtain

Life is about as predictable as a matchbook boat spinning down a drainage ditch. You never know where you will end up or what you'll encounter along the way.

I was reminded of the unpredictability of life on a recent outing with my granddaughter. Following a thunderous rain, my granddaughter, Lori, and I left the house to play. Strolling to a neighborhood creek, we put two matchbook boats side by side in the stream. We ran as quickly as we could to the footbridge crossing the creek and watched the progress of the two little boats. Although these boats were identical in size and structure, one boat quickly sailed under our footbridge, while the other boat bumped along slowly, was caught in a hydraulic force, and spit into an eddy, where it stalled.

"Pop, how come that boat kept going and the other one got stuck?" Lori asked.

Wanting Lori to be the smartest kid in gym class, I said, "According to scientists studying chaos theory, it's due to deterministic nonperiodic flow" (Lorenz, 1963).

"I thought you would say something like that. I think I'll go ask Mimi. She gives simpler answers," replied Lori as she smiled and skipped away.

I never discovered what her grandmother, Mimi, answered, but Lori's dilemma presents some difficult questions: Why did one boat sail swiftly with the current, while the other boat floundered in shallow waters? In somber times, we sometimes ask a similar question about our lives. Does the outcome of our life depend on the currents of fate, the structure of our life, or something else? Are our actions determined? Do we have free will to sail the streams of our choosing?

Watch two bits of paper flowing side by side at the bottom of a waterfall. What can you guess about how close they were at the top? Nothing. Watch two people sitting side by side at church. What can you guess about the experiences they have had? Nothing.

Why do matchbook boats sail erratically? Why are our lives so unpredictable? Why does the kid voted most likely to succeed spend his life under a park bench while the class clown wins the Nobel Prize?

Tiny differences in input can quickly become overwhelming disparities in output. A butterfly stirring the air in Mule Shoe, Texas can transform storm systems in London the next month. A man pushes the snooze button on his alarm clock. He leaves his house in the morning 30 seconds later than usual. Walking from the parking garage, a falling wrench from a construction site knocks him dead. Little did he know that 30 seconds was a half a minute too late. Just as there exist too many butterflies for the weather predictor to make an accurate forecast all the time, psychiatrists have a difficult time predicting how an individual will respond to the alarm clock (Lorenz, 1996). Thus, there is no definite psychiatric explanation for why some lead successful lives and others develop emotional problems.

A Work in Progress

The study of behavior development is a work in progress that has spawned numerous theories. Abraham Maslow's well-known hierarchy of needs provides one framework. According to Maslow (1954), we are motivated by both biological and psychological needs. The most basic of all needs are those for water, food, shelter, sleep, and other conditions necessary for life. Certainly, we want to avoid pain and discomfort. Most of us want sexual gratification. After these basic biological needs are met, we seek those things that make us human. We need to feel adequate, competent, and secure. We wish to love and to be loved. We want to feel good about ourselves and to earn respect from others. We seek meaning in life. We strive to express ourselves and to become all we can be. Think of this hierarchy of needs as a pyramid with biological needs at the base of the pyramid, followed by avoidance of pain, the need for love and approval, the quest for self-esteem and identity, while at the top of the pyramid, fulfillment beckons.

Normal behavior development leads to emotional stability as we grow and mature. But, what defines "normal" anyway? We examine the spectrum of normal behavior in this chapter, but first it is important to take a look at some of the ingredients that influence behavior.

Obviously, many factors along life's journey contribute to the end result. Among those variables are genetics, upbringing, environment, culture, personality type, and psychological factors, not to mention the numerous experiences and events that fill our days. Unlike a recipe, by which ingredients blend together to create the same casserole time after time, staggering numbers of possible combinations yield an infinite number of potential outcomes. The unpredictability of our lives is what makes human behavior so interesting and exciting—and so difficult to forecast.

Nature Versus Nurture: Trading Places With Mortimer and Randolph

Remember the movie *Trading Places*? A snooty investor and a crafty con artist find their positions reversed as part of a bet by two heartless millionaires. Louis Winthorpe III is a successful Philadelphia commodity broker. Billy Ray Valentine is a shrewd vagabond. Winthorpe's employers, the elderly Duke brothers—Mortimer and Randolph—make a wager that switching the lifestyle of the two will cause Louis to turn to a life of crime and transform Billy Ray into a law-abiding citizen. The shenanigans begin when Louis and Billy Ray join forces to get rich . . . and get revenge.

Mortimer and Randolph debate the age-old question of nature versus nurture: What's more important in a person's life: genetic endowment, or environmental conditioning? They bet a dollar that they know the answer to a question that has puzzled the greatest minds since money was first coined. That dollar bet costs the Duke brothers their entire fortune. They learn that the nature or nurture question cannot be answered with a simple "yes" or "no." Environmental conditions and genetic endowments are equally important in human development.

We are what we are because of nature (in computer lingo, our hard drive) *and* nurture (our software). Our genetic inheritance interacts with environmental conditions to make us who we are.

Cultural Influences

Our cultural climate plays a significant role in making us who we are. Two psychologists gave American and Japanese elementary school students the same impossible math problems to solve (Stigler & Hiebert, 1999). The American kids struggled briefly with the problem and then quit. In contrast, the Japanese kids kept trying so long that the experiment was stopped.

This experiment illustrated a difference between the two cultures. The Japanese students believed that if they kept working, they would eventually solve the problem. Americans think that solving problems has more to do with talent than with tenacity. To a Japanese student, the inability to find a solution to a problem results from failing to work hard enough. To an American student, failure results from lack of talent.

Americans typically think that inborn ability is more important than effort and persistence. We often think that the more effort required to succeed, the less talented we must be. In reality, an integration of talent, effort, emotional stability, and persistence leads to successful behavior.

Personality

Personalities are like faces: They are all different, but at the same time they can be clustered into categories—redhead, blond, brunette, gray haired; blue, brown, green, hazel eyes; large nose, small nose, round nose, flat nose. We could continue this for hundreds of pages. Describing personality types could be just as robust.

A simple system for understanding people, developed by William Moulton Marston (1928) in the 1920s, divides behavior into four personality styles. The original research has been incorporated into the DISC® profile (Kulkin, 2002), a simple pen-and-paper or online test that identifies four styles: dominant, influential, steady, and conscientious. It is fun to take these kinds of tests, but the derived data obviously paint an incomplete picture, just as a police sketch does not show depth of detail compared to a color photograph.

Personality Types

1. **D** = **D**ominant—decisive and driven, these people enjoy challenges. They quickly take action and seek immediate results.
   - Driver, direct, decisive
   - Focus on facts and ideas
   - Fast and to the point
   - Accomplishment oriented
   - Action driven
   - Independent and dominant
   - Persistent and determined
   - Tell rather than ask

2. **I** = **I**nfluential—enthusiastic and extroverted, these individuals entertain and energize others.
   - Expressive
   - Flamboyant, talkative
   - Interesting, interacting
   - Friendly and sociable
   - Optimistic and outgoing
   - Big plans, poor follow-through

- Colorful dress, loud laugh
- Enjoyment in being around others as the life of the party

3. **S** = **Steady**—friendly and supportive, these people prefer being behind the scenes while helping others.
   - Amiable
   - Submissive, stable, shy
   - Peace-seeking
   - Friendly and neighborly
   - Like supporting others
   - Like stability
   - Consistent
   - Accommodating
   - Good listeners
   - Ask rather than tell

4. **C** = **Conscientious**—perfectionistic and logical, these individuals focus on details and quality.
   - Analytical
   - Cautious, careful, contemplative, correct
   - Slow and critical thinker
   - Logical, fact based
   - Organized, follows rules
   - Doesn't show feelings
   - Private
   - Few friends, but good ones

Psychological Factors

Attitudes, fears, and expectations all influence behavior as well. People who see the glass half empty may unwittingly "program" negative thoughts into reality. Individuals with irrational fears avoid situations that bring discomfort and therefore short-circuit experiences that might have otherwise brought richness to their lives. Individuals who expect something good to happen often create an environment that fosters success. Obviously, these three examples highlight just a few of the many psychological indicators of behavior.

Values

Legend tells us that "Honest Abe" Lincoln, while working as a young sales clerk, once walked 3 miles to return 6 cents to a customer he had accidentally shortchanged. Contrast this with the story of Bernie Madoff, the Wall Street crook who robbed billions of dollars from investors in an elaborate

Ponzi scheme. One man valued integrity, while the other valued money. Values can be a crucial barometer of conduct.

Values can be especially challenging to analyze, though, because they often change as a person matures. For example, an adolescent may willingly follow his parent's religious or political leanings, but when grown he may take an entirely different position on careful examination of his own core beliefs. Values also vary by degree. What may be a mere opinion for one person could be a strongly held conviction for someone else.

Flawed Formulas

So, predicting behavior is as easy as plugging all of these variables—values, genetics, culture, personality, and psychological factors—into a formula, right? Nope. There hasn't been a computer built yet that can forecast how an individual will behave 100% of the time. However, it is true that careful examination of each of these areas can increase understanding of what a person might choose to do. Let's explore this by looking at a fictional case study.

Jane was a 24-year-old woman who lived with her parents. She had a job as a department store clerk but quit when the job got too stressful. Jane had always been extremely quiet and reserved. She chose to take easy classes in school and never pursued sports or other extracurricular activities. Jane's few friends occasionally came over to watch a movie or play a video game, but Jane rarely went out of the house to socialize. Most nights, their family time consisted of sitting in front of the TV and eating take-out meals. Jane admitted that she was "addicted" to several daytime and evening soap operas, often rearranging appointments and work schedules to be home to follow her favorite shows. When asked, Jane said she enjoyed her lifestyle and did not see any reason to change what she is doing. Recently, a friend invited Jane and several others to go on a weekend beach trip. Jane chose not to go.

After reading the case study, it's not surprising to us that Jane declined the invitation. We expected this reaction because we knew a little bit about some of the variables. If Jane not only accepted the beach trip invitation but also went parasailing, waterskiing, and barhopping all weekend, that would be totally unexpected given her personality and background. We view her choice not to go as normal under these circumstances. But, defining *normal* is tricky indeed.

Inside the White Lines

How can we distinguish eccentric behavior from normal conduct? Perhaps there exists no proper standard for normal behavior. Is normal behavior a

TABLE 1-1	
Theories of Normal Behavior	
THEORIES OF THINKERS	**WHAT THEY THINK**
Humanist theory	Those who develop their talents are normal.
Behaviorist theory	Normal behavior can be molded and shaped using a variety of conditioning techniques.
Interpersonal theory	Those who have satisfying relationships with others are normal.
Psychodynamic theory	Those who channel aggressive and sexual drives into love and work are normal.
Cognitive theory	Positive thoughts generate normal behavior.

lack of significant deviation from the average? Is the person who develops innate gifts normal? Would one who achieves satisfactory relationships be considered normal? "Am I normal?" depends on who's asking **(Table 1-1).**

Using definitions from statistical norms places a genius among the abnormal. Using personal adjustment as a norm ignores the individual's role in society. On the other hand, those who adjust to the rules of society might be haunted by personal discomfort.

Defining *normal* as one who conforms to social expectations generates problems. Using that designation, a person who drives the speed limit would be considered abnormal. After all, don't most of us travel 5 or 10 miles per hour over the speed limit?

What words define *normal behavior?* Normal behavior has alternatively been described as "mainstream," "in touch with reality," "in equilibrium," "stable," "maintaining a healthy lifestyle," or "having a peaceful demeanor." Would "average" be considered a synonym for normal?

In reality, normal behavior covers a wide range of patterns. Some of us are so normal that we are almost boring. Others live on the fringe. People might consider us "weird" or idiosyncratic, but from a psychiatric viewpoint, we would still be normal. Some of us are normal in all aspects of our lives except for one tiny deviation. This deviation might be strange enough that psychiatrists would classify us as abnormal.

A practical definition for normal behavior is based on function. A normal person, according to function theory, is one who can love, work, and enjoy recreation while allowing others to pursue happiness. In contrast, abnormal people would be defined as those who cannot function effectively in society. They are unable to have healthy, loving relationships with others. They cannot produce work that benefits self or society. They are limited in their capacity to enjoy life.

Normal does not mean a life free from problems. Everyone experiences periods of dysfunction from time to time. Conflict, which is a normal event in life, encourages emotional growth, but when ill timed, severe stress can foster psychiatric symptoms in even the most well-adjusted individual.

Certain biological emotional illnesses—schizophrenia, bipolar disorder, major depressive disorder, panic disorder, to name a few—require medication for remission of symptoms. Patients with primary psychiatric illnesses do best when they take medicine to correct the biochemical problem and work with a counselor to modify behavior that contributes to their biological illness. Subsequent chapters of this book shed light on various psychiatric ailments and their treatments.

We typically think of abnormal people as those who need a psychiatrist's care. But, what about the other extreme side of the behavior continuum? High achievers can hardly be described as ordinary. It's important to note, though, that "success" does not equal "normal," just as "failure" cannot be necessarily equated with "abnormal." Those who are extremely successful in one arena may lack balance in all other areas of life.

Living Smart

We all have heard stories of someone who aced the Scholastic Aptitude Test (SAT) and flunked out of college by the second semester. That's because success in college, and in life, has little to do with raw intelligence. IQ predicts success about 20% of the time. Behavioral scientists have discovered that 80% of success depends on emotional factors.

Harvard students from the 1940s—a time when there was a wider range of IQ at that school—were tracked into middle age (Goleman, 1995). The men with high IQ were not any more successful than those lower in intelligence. Similarly, 450 boys from Boston slums were followed into middle age. Success in this social group was not dependent on intelligence. Ten years after 81 valedictorians and salutatorians graduated from their high school, only 4 were at the highest level of young people of comparable age in their chosen profession. Academic intelligence fails to predict how one will react to the vicissitudes of life.

Psychologists gave college freshmen tests to measure optimism. Four years later, the psychologists found that optimism was a better predictor of college grades than SAT scores or high school grades (Seligman, 2006).

In a Met-Life Insurance Company study, insurance executives hired a special group of applicants who failed the standard aptitude test but scored high on optimism (Seligman, 2006). The first year on the job, the "dumb" optimists sold 21% more insurance than the "smart" pessimists. The second year, the optimists sold 57% more insurance than the pessimists. Dumb optimists sold more insurance than smart pessimists.

Daniel Goleman (1995), a former brain sciences editor of *The New York Times*, wrote a follow-up book to his enormously popular *Emotional Intelligence*. The sequel, *Working With Emotional Intelligence* (Goleman, 1998), was based on studies done by dozens of experts in 500 corporations, government agencies, and nonprofit organizations worldwide. An examination of these studies indicated that emotional intelligence is twice as important as either IQ or technical expertise in predicting career success.

Here's good news for all of us with average IQ scores: Unlike IQ, emotional intelligence continues to grow with life experiences. Because emotional intelligence is essential to career success and leadership potential, let's look at those areas that define emotional intelligence.

Know Thyself

Knowing our internal states—our emotional strengths and weaknesses—can help us develop our talents while minimizing our defects. For example, if we understand that we have a weakness for impulsive decision making, we can train ourselves to sleep on a decision or wait through a weekend before making a determination. On the other hand, waiting until we have enough facts to be confident that we have covered all the bases causes deal-defeating delay. Taking action when we have 50–60% of the information prevents "analysis paralysis."

Cool Under Pressure

Those with high emotional intelligence know that they have control over one factor—their internal state. While we are unable to control other people or events, we can control our feelings by changing our beliefs about people and events. We can also learn to manage our disruptive emotions—to control our temper, our pessimism, and our cynicism.

Moved by Action

Many talented people waste their abilities because they remain inactive. Productive action comes from the desire for pleasure, the urge to avoid pain, and the belief that goals can be accomplished. Motivation comes from craving success multiplied by the belief that we can accomplish our desires. Belief in ourselves is enhanced when we see others accomplishing their goals.

Winning With People

The art of getting along with people is more important than raw intelligence. Studies at the Carnegie Institute of Technology proved that even in the technical areas of science and engineering, 85% of success depended on skill with managing people, and 15% of financial success was due to technical knowledge (Carnegie, 1938). John D. Rockefeller said, "The ability to deal with people is as purchasable a commodity as sugar or coffee. And I will pay more for that ability than for any other under the sun."

Persistence

In the 1940s, pediatrician Benjamin Spock (1946) advised parents to give children confidence by responding lovingly to their needs and feelings. Brandeis University psychologist Abraham Maslow taught that self-esteem ranked highest among the basic human needs. A sense of being loved and "unconditional positive regard" (Rogers, 1951) became more valued than hard work and achievement. Positive feedback and praise became the standard teaching method that has persisted until the present day.

The self-esteem myth has produced a narcissistic society that values innate talent, luck, and social status over effort. Advertisers have told us that a particular possession can provide self-esteem that will fill our lives with friends and fun. In our Wonderland World, we acknowledge the declaration proclaimed by Alice: "All have won, and all will receive prizes."

Parents have been taught that compliments for effortless achievement will encourage children to try tasks that are more difficult. Just the opposite occurs. After all, why work harder when the humdrum brings praise?

Encouragement, optimism, positive feedback, and confidence have tremendous value. The usefulness of failure, the fun of challenge, the values of persistence, and the lessons learned from hard work have even more value.

Oatmeal Cookies

Walking home from the creek where Lori and I had sailed our matchstick boats, my thoughts centered on the ideas her question had generated. As soon as I stepped over the threshold of our home, the aroma of freshly baked cookies wafted from the kitchen, where I found Mimi and Lori taking the first batch from the oven. "Have a cookie," Lori said.

Sometimes when we try to explain the unexplainable—nature and nurture, genetics and environment, normal and abnormal—we can thank God for oatmeal cookies. And, fortunately, when there aren't any cookies, we can still find reassurance in a warm hug, an act of kindness, a word of encouragement, or the gentle touch of a loving hand, not to mention, sailboats, basketballs, violins, butterflies, and reading *The Chronicles of Narnia* to grandchildren before bedtime prayers. These and other simple pleasures, the nuances, the incongruities, the subtleties, are what give life value. They are the unadorned enchantments that frame our lives. That's the best I can do to explain the wonder of human behavior. And so it is that a simple question from a child gives me the hopeful assurance of life's richness for us all.

Are You Confident and Personable?				
Make Check Mark (✓) in Appropriate Column	Little of the Time 1 point each ✓	Some of the Time 2 points each ✓	A Lot of the Time 3 points each ✓	Most of the Time 4 points each ✓
I am open-minded when making decisions with my loved ones.				
I feel good about myself and treat myself kindly.				
I have a friend I can count on when the chips are down.				
I treat others the way I like to be treated.				
Relationships with my family give me pleasure.				
I accept my limitations and deficiencies.				
I have an intimate and trusting relationship with someone I love.				
I assert myself without being aggressive even when my opinions may be unpopular.				
I feel empathy for those less fortunate than I am.				
I keep my promises to others and myself.				
Multiply ✓ by the value given in each column.				

Add the total for each column to get the **Grand total** = _____

SCORING

10–14 points = Lonely and insecure

15–24 points = Few friends and little influence

25–34 points = Likable and understanding

35–40 points = Confident friend and lover

How Flexible Are You?				
Make Check Mark (✓) in Appropriate Column	Little of the Time 1 point each ✓	Some of the Time 2 points each ✓	A Lot of the Time 3 points each ✓	Most of the Time 4 points each ✓
I manage my disappointment when someone tells me "no."				
I learn from my mistakes.				
I accept responsibility for my behavior.				
I tolerate defeat and disappointment.				
I don't have to get everything I want immediately.				
I am forgiving.				
I avoid a grudge when people treat me unfairly.				
I learn from the ideas and thoughts of others.				
I have learned to deal with slow highway drivers or long lines without getting angry.				
I tolerate change.				
Multiply ✓ by the value given in each column.				

Add the total for each column to get the **Grand total** = _____

SCORING

10–14 points = Lonely and insecure

15–24 points = Few friends and little influence

25–34 points = Likable and understanding

35–40 points = Confident friend and lover

Rate Your Maturity Level				
Make Check Mark (✓) in Appropriate Column	Little of the Time 1 point each ✓	Some of the Time 2 points each ✓	A Lot of the Time 3 points each ✓	Most of the Time 4 points each ✓
I help those in need without the expectation of something in return.				
I feel comfortable being alone and being around others.				
Except for my mortgage, I am debt free.				
I am patient with the frailties of others.				
I use my credit card only for convenience and pay my bills on time.				
I treat others the way I would like to be treated.				
I have a satisfying spiritual life.				
I can have sexual intimacy without being promiscuous.				
I save 10% of my income.				
I avoid negative talk and gossip.				
Multiply 3 by the value ✓given in each column.				

Add the total for each column to get the **Grand total** = _____

Scoring

10–14 points = Diaper dandy

15–24 points = Kindergarten kid

25–34 points = Growing-up

35–40 points = Worldly wise

A Clinician's Quiz

(There is no answer key. The answers are found in the text.)

1. List Maslow's hierarchy of needs.
2. Regarding how cultural influences shape behavior, Americans typically think that _____ is more important than _____.
3. List the four personality types developed by William Moulton Marston.
4. According to function theory a normal person is one who can _____, _____, and _____.
5. Several studies have shown that _____ is a better predictor of success than _____.
6. List five factors that define emotional intelligence.
7. Define analysis paralysis.
8. What three factors promote productive action?
9. What percent of success depends on skill with managing people?
10. Explain the self-esteem myth.

CHAPTER 2

An Overview of Psychiatric Diagnosis and Treatment

Bedlam Classified

Vincent Van Gogh, unrecognized as a great artist until long after his death, was sensitive, withdrawn, paranoid, and suffered severe mood swings. He believed that people were trying to poison him. On one occasion, he attacked his friend with a razor; later, he cut off his own ear and presented it to a prostitute. He died of a self-inflicted gunshot wound. Edgar Allen Poe was depressed and intoxicated most of his short life. The composer Robert Schumann wrote passionately during episodes of high energy, but he once tried to drown himself in the Rhine River (Jamison, 1994).

If these celebrated individuals had lived in the 15th century, they may have been residents at Bedlam. Records show that as early as 1403, St. Mary's of Bethlehem—the shortened name became Bedlam—served patients with mental disorders. The inmates, as they were called, slept on damp floors. There was no fresh air, no light. Their food provided scant nutrition. Treated little better than wild animals, they were whipped and beaten for misbehavior. The most unruly were chained to walls. The public visited the hospital and paid an entertainment fee to watch the patients. Bedlam became synonymous with uproar and confusion. The mentally ill, accused of having succumbed to spells and incantations, were charged with committing sinful offenses with the devil, sorcerers, and other demons (Walsh, 1907).

Since the beginning of written history, people have attempted to define and understand mental disorders. The Assyrians, Babylonians, and Israelites initiated the belief that demons caused abnormal behavior. In the Middle Ages, the mentally ill became regarded as dangerous people who had no control over their impulses. The 16th century marked the beginning of imprisoning disturbed individuals. In the 18th century, "insane asylums" became popular (Alexander & Selesnick, 1996).

More or Less Touched

In writing of authors and other artists, Lord Byron remarked, "We of the craft are all crazy. Some are affected by gaiety, others by melancholy, but all are more or less touched" (Jamison, 1994, p. 2). All of us, from artists to zookeepers, are, by degrees, a little "touched."

Fast-forward to the 21st century and we trade the romance of the 19th century poet Byron for Ambien in print—*The Diagnostic and Statistical Manual*

TABLE 2-1	
It's All Greek to Me	
Ancient Egyptians	The heart was responsible for mental symptoms. Loss of status or money caused mental illness. Treatment consisted of "talking it out" and turning to religion and faith.
Old Testament	Despair caused mental illness— faith was the cure.
Early Greeks	Depression resulted from an excess of "black bile."
Hippocrates	Both melancholia and natural medical causes contributed to mental illness. He advised abstinence of various types, a natural vegetable diet, and exercise as treatment.
Homer	Mental illness resulted from the Gods taking the mind away. He offered no treatment.
Galen	Brain dysfunction caused mental illness. Treatment consisted of confrontation, humor, and exercise.

TABLE 2-2	
Who's Abnormal?	
CLASSIFICATION OF ABNORMAL	**POINT OF VIEW**
Deviation from statistical norms	This definition makes a brilliant person abnormal.
Maladaptive behavior	Behavior that affects a person's well-being, such as excessive drinking or overeating.
Personal distress	Abnormality depends on subjective feelings such as anxiety or depression.
Legal definition of abnormal	This definition is the inability to judge between right and wrong.
The medical view	Abnormal behavior is diagnosed through symptoms and cured through treatment.
The behavior model	Abnormal behavior results from faulty learning.
The psychodynamic viewpoint	Abnormal behavior is produced by unresolved, unconscious conflicts.
The cognitive element	Abnormal behavior is caused by thoughts often based on false assumptions.
The social-cultural outlook	Abnormal behavior is learned within a social context of family, community, and culture.
The complete therapy view	Abnormal behavior is characterized by significant difficulties with love, work, or enjoying recreation.

- Order a double cheeseburger, fries, and a diet soda
- Work out on an exercise bike while watching the Food Channel
- Buy the most expensive golf clubs available then throw them in the water
- Look for our eyeglasses while wearing them
- Yell at each other all the way to church then smile beatifically when entering the sanctuary
- Buy a best-selling book and never read past the first chapter
- Turn the dial on the exercise bike to the most difficult level when someone passes then dial it to the easiest level when they're gone
- Come home more tired from a vacation than when returning from work
- Attend a sales meeting while a customer is waiting
- Text message someone when attending a listening skills conference
- Every year make New Year's resolutions that are never kept
- Telephone someone at midnight and ask if they were awake
- Join a club to get to know new people and spend all the time visiting with old friends
- Watch reality shows instead of having a "real" life
- Wear weird costumes to football games.

of Mental Disorders, Fourth Edition, Text Revision (DSM-IV-TR; American Psychiatric Association, 2000). Written by committee, *DSM-IV-TR* is a pretentious affair, slow and sleepy, a lethargy of lists that give the signs and symptoms of every emotional disorder a committee of scholarly psychiatrists can conceive.

Using the *DSM-IV-TR* (American Psychiatric Association, 2000) as a guide, the diagnosis of a mental disorder can be made by counting symptoms. Suspect panic disorder? Turn to page 432. If a patient has 4 (or more) of 13 symptoms, the diagnosis is confirmed—*if* these symptoms "developed abruptly and reached a peak within 10 minutes." The manual does not say what the diagnosis would be if these abrupt symptoms reached a peak within 11 minutes.

Want to argue the finer points of diagnosis? Turn to page 323 (American Psychiatric Association, 2000) and read some of the confusing nomenclature regarding the diagnosis of schizoaffective disorder. To make the diagnosis, one must find "an uninterrupted period of illness during which, at some time, there is either a Major Depressive Episode, a Manic Episode, or a Mixed Episode concurrent with symptoms that meet Criterion A for Schizophrenia." One must also have "symptoms that meet criteria for a mood episode which are present for a substantial portion of the total duration of the active and residual periods of the illness." Wouldn't a more practical definition for schizoaffective disorder be "a condition in which symptoms of schizophrenia and a mood disorder coexist"? The diagnosis is a little more complicated than my simple definition, but not much.

Despite the cookbook approach to mental illness, these sallies into signs and symptoms have enormous clinical value. Every clinician uses this gold standard of psychiatric classification (American Psychiatric Association, 2000), and it, more or less, takes the guesswork out of diagnosis while leaving plenty of room for debate and argument.

The Mutiaxial Assessment

The *DSM-IV-TR* contains five diagnostic categories that the book calls "Multiaxial Assessment." Here they are with an example for each in parentheses:

- Axis I = Psychiatric illnesses (major depression, recurrent, severe)
- Axis II = Personality disorders and mental retardation (dependent personality disorder)
- Axis III = Physical illnesses (migraine headaches, hypertension)
- Axis IV = Social and environmental problems (lost job, impending divorce, relocation to a new city)
- Axis V = Global Assessment of Functioning (GAF = 50)

Axis I, II, and III are self-explanatory. Let's look at Axis IV and Axis V, which are not. Axis IV contains social and environmental problems that affect the outcome of treatment, including the following categories:

- Problems with the primary support group such as, but not limited to, death of a family member, divorce or marital separation, family discord, physical or sexual abuse.
- Social problems, including living alone, inadequate recreational outlets, retirement.
- School problems such as poor reading skill, dyscalculia, teacher discord.
- Work problems, including job dissatisfaction, unemployment, and job change.
- Housing problems such as homelessness, unsafe neighborhood, hurricane damage.

- Financial problems, including credit card debt, checking account overdrawn, low-income job inadequate to meet basic family needs.
- Inadequate health care services such as insufficient medical insurance, health care services unavailable, unavailability of psychiatric care.

Axis V, GAF is a fancy term for a performance rating scale. The *DSM-IV-TR* (American Psychiatric Association, 2000) rating scale goes from 0 to 100 with zero equal to, you guessed it, the worst possible result and 100 equal to top performance. This rating scale can be simplified by omitting all ratings not divisible by 10:

10 = Persistent danger of severely hurting self/others or inability to maintain minimal personal hygiene—think Paris Hilton on an out-of-control rampage.

20 = Some danger of hurting self/others or gross impairment in communication—think drugged and besotted Lindsey Lohan in a police lineup.

30 = Delusions/hallucinations or seriously strange behavior—think the late Michael Jackson.

40 = Some impairment in communication or major impairment in work, school, thinking, mood, family life—think Homer Simpson.

50 = Serious symptoms in social/school or work impairment—think Dick Cheney on a hunting trip.

60 = Moderate difficulties in school or social/occupational functioning—think of the characters in the television show The Office.

70 = Mild symptoms, but usually functioning well—think "Can you hear me now?" in the Verizon Wireless television commercial.

80 = Transient symptoms or expectable reactions to psychosocial stressors—think Chicago Cub baseball fan in October.

90 = Good function in all areas of life—think happy-ever-after theme in most Walt Disney movies.

100 = Superior functioning in all areas of life—think Superman.

Do you get the idea? This rating scale is subjective. The examples I chose prove the point. Which is worse, a missed call or failing to make it to the World Series again? Who would you rather be, Dick Cheney with a shotgun or Homer Simpson without one? Who has the most problems, Paris Hilton or Lindsey Lohan? The GAF rating scale has more to do with the person doing the rating than the person being rated.

Diagnostic Categories

An overview of *DSM-IV-TR* (American Psychiatric Association, 2000) diagnostic categories can be compared to a 747 pilot getting a glimpse at the runway on a cloudy day while circling the terminal at 25,000 feet. This high-flying look at psychiatric nomenclature can be referred to from time to time to clarify questions regarding symptom clusters.

Disorders of Infancy, Childhood, or Adolescence

A separate section for psychiatric illnesses in childhood reflects the time, in general, that these disorders first appear and is not meant to suggest a vast difference between childhood and adult disorders (American Psychiatric Association, 2000).

- Mental retardation includes categories for mild (IQ below 70), moderate (IQ below 50), severe (IQ below 40), and profound (IQ below 25) intellectual impairment.
- Learning disorders are diagnosed when academic skills are two standard deviations below expectations.
- Motor skills disorders are diagnosed when physical impairments interfere with academic achievement or activities of daily living.
- Communication disorders include language and articulation difficulties. Stuttering is included in this category.
- Pervasive developmental disorders characterized by severe impairment in social interaction skills include autism, Asperger's disorder, and those disorders in which there exists a significant loss of acquired skills.
- Attention deficit/hyperactivity disorders can be diagnosed when persistent patterns of inattention or hyperactivity-impulsivity exist. DSM-IV-TR uses nine pages to describe the idiosyncratic differences in symptom clusters in this diagnostic category.
- Conduct disorders exist when the rights of others are repetitively violated. Diagnostic divisions are particularly complex: There are four main groupings, two subtypes, and three severity specifiers in this diagnostic cluster.
- Oppositional defiant disorder is characterized by negative, insubordinate, and hostile behavior. These symptoms are not as severe as those found in conduct disorders and generally fail to include aggression toward others, deceit, or the destruction of property.
- Eating disorders include pica (a persistent pattern of eating nonnutritive substances—dirt, cloth, leaves, etc.) and rumination disorder

(repeated regurgitation and rechewing of food). Anorexia nervosa usually begins in mid- to late adolescence, while bulimia typically begins in late adolescence or early adult life.

- Recurrent stereotyped motor movements or vocalizations mark tic disorders.
- Encopresis and enuresis are elimination disorders not due to medical conditions.
- Separation anxiety is marked by excessive anxiety over separation from home or loved ones.

Cognitive Disorders

Memory regression can be divided into three major categories: Delirium (change in cognition over a short time period); dementia (long-lasting cognitive deficits); and amnestic disorders (memory impairments generally caused by psychological factors).

Substance-Related Disorders

Substance-related disorders include conditions related to taking a drug of abuse, the toxic exposure to a drug, or medication side effects. This huge diagnostic category, which includes abuse, dependence, intoxication, withdrawal, delirium, dementia, amnesia, psychosis, mood, anxiety, sleep disorders, and sexual dysfunction related to drug or alcohol use takes up 104 pages of *DSM-IV-TR* (American Psychiatric Association, 2000).

Schizophrenia

Schizophrenia, marked by delusions, hallucinations, poverty of speech, inability to participate in goal-directed activities, and restriction of emotions, is a persistent psychotic condition that interferes with social, occupational, and personal well-being. There are five types of schizophrenia: paranoid, disorganized, catatonic, undifferentiated, and residual. *Schizophreniform disorder* is the developmental stage of schizophrenia. *Schizoaffective disorder* occurs when a manic or depressive episode is associated with symptoms compatible with schizophrenia.

Delusional Disorder

Delusional disorder, a false belief that cannot be reasoned or reckoned with, consists of erotomanic (belief another person loves the individual); grandiose (delusions of inflated worth); jealous (belief that the person's sexual partner is unavailable); persecutory (delusions that the person is being malevolently treated); somatic (delusions that the person has some medical condition); and mixed (more than one of the above) delusions.

Brief psychotic disorder is marked by delusions, hallucinations, disorganized speech, or bizarre behavior lasting more than 1 day but less than 1 month.

Depressive Disorders

There are several types of depression, including

- Major depression—depression associated with loss of interest and pleasure that lasts for more than 2 weeks.
- Dysthymia—mildly depressed mood lasting longer than 2 years.
- Postpartum depression—depression following childbirth.
- Depression secondary to a medical condition.
- Depression associated with bipolar illness.

Bipolar Disorders

Bipolar disorders, marked by mood swings of depression and elevated mood, are divided into three types:

- Bipolar I—episodes of depression alternating with episodes of mania (persistently elevated, expansive, or irritable mood lasting for at least 1 week).
- Bipolar II—recurrent episodes of depression with at least one episode of hypomania (mild episodes of elevated, expansive, or irritable mood lasting at least 4 days).
- Cyclothymia—mild mood swings lasting for at least 2 years.

Anxiety Disorders

Anxiety disorders of pesistent worry, dread, fearfulness, and apprehension consist of several distinct disorders:

- Panic disorder—episodes of shortness of breath, palpitations, sweating, and racing pulse associated with a fear of impending doom.
- Panic disorder with agrophobia—panic associated with fear of situations from which escape might be difficult or embarrassing.
- Phobia—anxiety provoked by exposure to a feared object.
- Social phobia—anxiety associated with exposure to groups of people or performance situations.
- Obsessive-compulsive disorder—anxiety associated with repetitive thoughts and behaviors.
- Post-traumatic stress disorder—flashbacks, intrusive thoughts, and nightmares associated with a past traumatic event.
- Generalized anxiety disorder—persistent trepidation, dread, apprehension, uneasiness, fretfulness, and fearfulness.

1. Schizophrenia: "Do You Hear What I Hear?"
2. Multiple personality disorder: "We Three Kings Disoriented Are"
3. Dementia: "I Think I'll Be Home for Christmas"
4. Narcissism: "Hark the Herald Angels Sing About Me"
5. Mania: "Deck the Halls and Walls and House and Lawn and Streets and Stores and Office and Town and Cars and Buses and Trucks and Trees and . . ."
6. Paranoia: "Santa Claus Is Coming to Town to Get Me"
7. Borderline personality disorder: "You Better Watch Out, I'm Gonna Cry, I'm Gonna Pout, Maybe I'll Tell You Why"
8. Attention deficit disorder: "Silent Night, Holy . . . oooh look at the Froggy—can I have a chocolate, why is France so far away?"
9. Obsessive-compulsive disorder: "Jingle Bells, Jingle Bells, Jingle Bells, Jingle Bells, Jingle Bells, Jingle Bells, Jingle Bells, Jingle Bells, Jingle Bells . . ."

Somatoform Disorders

Somatoform disorder, characterized by physical symptoms that suggest a medical condition but are caused instead by emotional factors, can be divided into several categories:

- Somatization disorder—a history of numerous physical complaints beginning before age 30. The physical symptoms must consist of four pain symptoms, two gastrointestinal symptoms, one sexual symptom, and one neurological symptom that occur at any time during the course of the illness.
- Conversion disorder—an illness in which anxiety is converted into a physical symptom.
- Acute or chronic pain disorder associated with psychological factors— an illness in which anxiety is converted into a chronic pain or physical illness in which anxiety exacerbates chronic pain.
- Hypochondriasis—preoccupation with fear of having a serious disease, based on the person's misinterpretation of physical symptoms in which the conviction of a having a disease persists despite a normal physical evaluation and reassurance.

- Body dysmorphic disorder—preoccupation with an imagined defect in appearance.
- Factitious disorders—physical or psychological symptoms are intentionally produced or feigned to assume the sick role.
- Depersonalization disorder—feeling of being detached from one's body or mental processes caused by or associated with stress and anxiety.

Sexual Disorders

Sexual dysfunctions caused by psychological factors include the following:

- Disorders in sexual desire.
- Paraphilias characterized by sexual urges involving unusual activities.
- Gender identity disorders (characterized by persistent distress with one's assigned sex).

Sleep Disorders

Sleep disorders are divided into the following:

- Primary sleep disorders—sleep disturbances complicated by emotional conditioning factors are divided into dyssomnias (poor quantity or quality of sleep) and parasomnias (abnormal behavior associated with sleep).
- Narcolepsy—irresistible attacks of sleep.
- Sleep apnea—excessive daytime sleepiness secondary to temporary suspension of breathing during nighttime sleep.

MENTAL HEALTH TELEPHONE INSTRUCTIONS FROM CYBERSPACE

- If you are obsessive-compulsive, press 1 repeatedly.
- If you are codependent, please ask someone to press 2 for you.
- If you are paranoid, we know who you are and what you want; stay on the line so we can trace your call.
- If you are depressed, it doesn't matter which number you press; nothing will make you happy anyway.
- If you have short-term memory loss, press 9; if you have short-term memory loss, press 9; if you have short-term memory loss, press 9.
- If you have low self-esteem, please hang up; our operators are too busy to talk with you.
- If you are menopausal, put the gun down, hang up, turn on the fan, lie down, and cry. It won't last forever.

TABLE 2-3	
Those Who Treat Emotional Problems	
Psychiatrist	A medical doctor with 4 years of specialized training in brain disorders who provides comprehensive skill in diagnosis and management of psychiatric illness with special emphasis on psychotherapy, neuroscience, and psychopharmacology. A well-trained psychiatrist has a working knowledge of psychodynamic theory, psychotherapy, and communication techniques and has a comprehensive understanding of clinical medicine, genetics, and molecular biology.
Psychoanalyst	A psychiatrist or clinician with advanced training who studies in analytic institutes and learns the techniques first taught by Sigmund Freud.
Clinical psychologist	Someone who studies human behavior in order to provide psychotherapy for patients suffering from emotional disorders. Advanced practitioners have earned a PhD in clinical psychology.
Nurse Practitioner	A registered nurse who has special training in medical and psychiatric care. Nurse practioners can have advanced degrees to the doctoral level.
Physician Assistant	A health professional licensed to practice medicine under the supervision of a physician.
Primary care physician	A medical doctor who provides first contact with patients, offers continued care, and imparts referral to medical specialists when necessary. Primary care physicians are the major providers for psychiatric care.

- Circadian rhythm sleep disorder—sleep disruption due to interruption of the normal sleep-wake cycle.
- Nightmare disorder—repeated awakenings secondary to frightening dreams.
- Sleep terror disorder—abrupt awakening from sleep associated with intense fear, unresponsiveness to comforting efforts by others, amnesia for the episode, and no dream recall.
- Sleepwalking disorder.

Impulse Control Disorders
Illnesses caused by failure to resist an impulse include intermittent explosive disorder, kleptomania, pyromania, pathological gambling, and trichotillomania (recurrent pulling out of one's hair).

Psychiatric Symptoms Related to Medical Conditions
Psychotic, mood, anxiety, sleep, sexual, and delusion disorders can be caused by endocrine, electrolyte, traumatic, neoplastic, nutritional, inflammatory, infectious, vascular, and other medical conditions, as well as substance abuse.

Personality Disorders
Marked by excuse making, blaming, and failure to assume responsibility for one's behavior, personality disorders can be divided into three clusters: odd or eccentric behavior, dramatic or emotional behavior, or behaviors associated with anxiety.

The Challenge of Diagnostic Labels
In the course of a lifetime, just under 50% of Americans will experience a mental illness that to some extent impairs function. Although milder mental illnesses sometimes abate without treatment, severe cases of mental illness require professional treatment.

The challenge of contemporary psychiatry comes from assessing the extent of impairment that merits a diagnostic label. At best, such labels have value in recommending particular treatments and giving an estimation of clinical outcome. In many cases, diagnostic labels serve only to give the false belief that in naming something, we have gained control over a particular malady.

Notwithstanding the diagnostic label, clinical responsibility mandates that we attempt to resolve conflict by helping our patients overcome misfortune and the adverse conditions of illness. We can strive to work positively in whatever situation we find ourselves, never judge those we are called to help, and work diligently toward the greater good of all.

Are You on the Border of Sanity?

Make Check Mark (✓) in Appropriate Column	Little of the Time 1 point each ✓	Some of the Time 2 points each ✓	A Lot of the Time 3 points each ✓	Most of the Time 4 points each ✓
My life seems to be filled with chaos.				
I am sensitive to rejection and rebuff.				
I feel that people tend to abandon me.				
When I meet certain people, I think they are terrific, but they turn out to be total jerks.				
I feel empty inside.				
I lose my temper quickly.				
I get terribly depressed over things that seem insignificant to others.				
I cut myself or burn myself to take away tension and stress.				
When I get depressed or angry, I bounce back fast.				
I hate people who threaten to leave me or abandon me.				
Multiply ✓ by the value given in each column.				

Add the total for each column to get the **Grand total** = _____

SCORING

10–14 points = Totally centered

15–24 points = A few flaws

25–34 points = Psychotherapy may be able to help you think and feel better

35–40 points = Beyond the pale

Complete Mental Health

A Clinician's Quiz

1. In DSM-IV-TR, Axis IV contains_____and _____problems.
2. In DSM-IV-TR, what is the performance rating scale known as?
3. What well-known illness of childhood is listed as a pervasive development disorder?
4. What are the three major divisions of illness that are found in the cognitive disorder category?
5. What disorder marked by delusions and hallucinations interferes with social, occupational, and personal well-being?
6. What disorder marked by delusions and hallucinations lasts for more than one day, but less than one month?
7. List five types of depression.
8. What disorder consists of recurrent episodes of depression with at least one episode of hypomania?
9. What disorder is marked by episodes of shortness of breath, palpitations, sweating, and racing pulse associated with the fear of impending doom?
10. In the course of a lifetime what percentage of the population will experience a mental illness that to some extent impairs function?

CHAPTER 3

The Diagnosis and Treatment of Depression

Despair's Pit

Depression is ubiquitous. It has no limits, no borders, and no confines. It affects all ages, all ethnic groups, all occupations, rich and poor, young and old, doctors and dentists, psychologists and psychiatrists.

Ellen DeGeneres, comedian and actor, developed a yearlong depression shortly after the cancellation of her show "The Ellen DeGeneres Show." Actress Drew Barrymore has had severe depressive episodes resulting in a suicide attempt and hospitalization. Television and movie star Rosie O'Donnell had symptoms of depression as a child that continued episodically into adulthood, until she began to improve with treatment at age 37. In the early 1990s, Elton John battled depression. He improved and then became depressed again, when his friend, Princess Diana, who had suffered from postpartum depression, died. Even actresses who play psychiatrists can become depressed. Lorraine Bracco, who played the psychiatrist on the television show "The Sopranos," overcame her depression with medication and psychotherapy and now works toward ending the stigma of emotional illness (depression-help-resource.com, 2009) **(Table 3-1)**.

Almost everyone experiences occasional feelings of mild depression. There are days when we all ask the question, "What's the use?" A slowed gait, gloomy expression, and a slumped posture tell the world, "I'm miserable." These low periods attack even the most exuberant optimist at times, but they rarely persist. In millions of other people, however, symptoms of depression may linger for months or even years.

TABLE 3-1	
Famous Depressed People	
Terry Bradshaw	After leading the Pittsburg Steelers to four Super Bowl wins and divorcing his third wife, he became depressed—characterized by weight loss, crying spells, insomnia, and anxiety.
Jim Carrey	Comedian and movie star, he is best known for his rubber-like facial expressions and his over-the-top physical comedy. Although he became successful, he continued to suffer from depression that began when Carrey was 16 years old when his father lost his job.
Brooke Shields	Actress and model, she wrote a book—*Down Came the Rain*—that documented her postpartum depression.
Billy Joel	Winner of six Grammys, he attempted suicide by drinking furniture polish.

Surveys indicate that major depression occurs in 5–10% of patients visiting a primary care physician and in 10–14% of patients hospitalized for medical reasons (Schulberg, 1992). When all depressive disorders are included, as many as 20% of patients have depression as one of their diagnoses, making depression the most common psychiatric illness in primary care (McDaniel, Musselman, & Proter, 1995) **(Table 3-2, Table 3-3)**.

Types of Depression
Depression can be divided into 10 types:

- Adjustment disorder with depressed mood—depressive reaction resulting from an environmental stress.
- Major depression, single episode—severe depression that occurs for the first, and perhaps, only time.
- Major depression, recurrent—repeat episodes of severe depression.
- Depression with melancholic features.
- Dysthymic disorder—chronic low-grade depression.
- Psychotic depression—depression associated with loss of reality.
- Involutional depression—depression occurring late in life.
- Postpartum depression—depression following childbirth.
- Bipolar depression—depression alternating with episodes of mania.
- Atypical depression—depression with an unusual presentation.

TABLE 3-2	
Red Flag: Don't Miss These Warnings	
SIGNS AND SYMPTOMS OF DEPRESSION	**ILLNESSES OFTEN MISTAKEN FOR DEPRESSION**
Dysphoric mood or loss of pleasure in usual activities At least four of the following: Change in appetite Sleep difficulty Loss of energy Psychomotor agitation Decrease in sexual drive Inappropriate guilt Indecisiveness Suicidal thoughts Psychomotor retardation Duration of symptoms for at least 2 weeks No evidence of schizophrenia or organic brain disease	Thyroid disease and other endocrine diseases Parkinson's disease Sleep apnea Nutritional illnesses Drugs or drug withdrawal Cerebral tumors Coronary artery disease Renal or hepatic failure AIDS Syphilis Mononucleosis Tuberculosis Hepatitis Pneumonia Cancer of the head or of the pancreas Complex partial seizures Multiple sclerosis Left frontal stroke Dementia Alcoholism

Adjustment Disorder With Depressed Mood

Adjustment disorder with depressed mood, marked by loss of pleasure in usual activities, lack of motivation, and other symptoms of depression, occurs in response to a significant stress such as loss of a job, marital problems, termination of a romantic relationship, or a home foreclosure. The symptoms of depression are not severe enough to meet the criterea for a major depression. Adjustment disorder with depressed mood is separate from bereavement characterized by the "normal" grieving that occurs following the death of a loved one. By definition, an adjustment disorder resolves within 6 months, but may last longer than 6 months if a significant stressor continues, such as joblessness or homelessness. Supportive psychotherapy helps the patient progress through the crisis. Occasionally behavior therapy that provides visualization, practice techniques, and specific assignments to

TABLE 3-3

Types of Depression	
CLASSIFICATION	**CHARACTERISTICS**
Adjustment disorder with depressed mood	Depressive reaction resulting from an environmental stress; self-limiting; resolves without treatment or with brief psychotherapy
Dysthymic disorder	Depressive symptoms lasting at least 2 years; symptoms fail to be sufficiently severe to be classified as a major depressive disorder
Major depression, single episode	Periods of normal mood separating episodes of dysphoric mood associated with other symptoms of the depressive syndrome
Major depression, recurrent	Periods of normal mood separating episodes of dysphoric mood associated with other symptoms of the depressive syndrome
Bipolar depression	Depression associated with mood swings
Postpartum depression	Depression following the birth of a child, often associated with bipolar illness that may develop later in life
Psychotic depression	Depression associated with critical auditory hallucinations and persecutory or somatic delusions
Atypical depression = "masked" depression or "pseudodementia"	Depression "hidden" by physical symptoms; decreased appetite, sleep disturbance, and lack of sexual drive attributed to physical problems; depressed mood may be "masked" by these physical symptoms; occasionally an elderly person will claim memory problems when poor concentration and slow thinking secondary to a "masked" depression will be the cause for worries about memory impairment— so-called pseudodementia
Involutional depression	Late-life depression frequently associated with debilitating illnesses or with cerebrovascular disease

Depression

actively work through the crisis (techniques that can help the patient get a new job, for example) can be helpful.

> A 34-year-old married man with two children became depressed, lethargic, and hopeless after he lost his job as an assembly line worker at a Volvo plant when 1500 employees were laid off. The behavior therapist had the patient make a list of 10 jobs he would enjoy and be qualified for. He helped the patient visualize success and then gave him a homework assignment to call 5 businesses a day in hopes of getting at least one interview. The therapist continued to encourage and guide him through disappointment after disappointment until the patient finally found a job 9 weeks after his layoff working in manufacturing mass spectrometers in a chemical plant.

Major Depression

To meet the criteria of the *Diagnostic and Statistical Manual of Mental Disorders, Fourth Edition, Text Revision* (*DSM-IV-TR*; American Psychiatric Association, 2000) for major depression characterized by five or more of a list of symptoms (a daily depressed mood or lack of pleasure in activities for 2 weeks and significant appetite and weight changes, sleep disturbance, fatigue, poor concentration, recurrent thoughts of death, feelings of worthlessness or excessive guilt), the symptoms cannot be due to a medical condition, substance abuse, or bipolar illness. The unrelenting course of the illness and the intractable nature of the depressive symptoms can contribute to suicidal thoughts and, sometimes, suicide attempts.

Following an initial episode of major depression, 60% of patients develop a second episode (American Psychiatric Association, 2000). Each depressive episode increases the risk of another. After a third episode of depression, for example, the risk for a fourth is 90% (Thase, 1990).

> Elizabeth had a downcast gaze, her hands did not move from her lap, and the normal posture shifts were absent. She cried easily and reported poor sleep and no energy. After a few weeks of medication, her depressive symptoms began to lift. Following a full 8-month course of antidepressants, Elizabeth remained symptom free for almost 2 years before she became incapacitated by another major depression. Psychotherapy failed to help her fight off the depressive symptoms. After her third depression, Elizabeth decided she would be better off taking antidepressants for the rest of her life.

Pervasive negative thinking may contribute to recurrent major depression (Beck, Rush, Shaw, & Emery, 1979). Depressed patients, who often possess rigid, all-or-nothing thinking ("Because I burned the toast, I'm a totally incompetent person"), attribute unfortunate events to personal inadequacies ("A hit-and-run driver put a dent in my car because I'm so stupid that I didn't park close enough to the curb"). Robust medication treatment fails to prevent recurrence of major depression in patients beleaguered by unremitting self-criticism. Omnipresent negative thinking mandates aggressive cognitive-behavior therapy (CBT) to prevent irreversible joylessness.

Major Depression Disorder, Recurrent

Major depressive disorder, recurrent is simply the presence of two or more episodes of major depressive disorder. There must be an interval of more than two months in which there are no signs of depression. The clinician must closely review the patient's history to make certain there have been no episodes of hypomania or mania. If either of these symptoms has been present in the past, bipolar disorder would be the correct diagnosis. Major depressive disorder, recurrent is treated exactly as major depressive disorder, single episode.

Depression With Melancholic Features

The term melancholic features describes a severe form of depression that is most likely to respond to medications or may, on occasion, require electrocon-vulsive therapy for full remission of symptoms. (Andreasen & Black, 2006). Using "melancholic features" as a qualifier, the diagnosis would be coded as major depression, single episode with melancholic features; or major depres-sion, recurrent with melancholic features. According to the DSM-IV-TR (American Psychiatric Association, 2000), to meet the diagnostic criteria for melancholia the patient must have one of the following two symptoms: the patient has lost pleasure in all, or almost all, activities, or the patient does not feel better when something good happens. In addition, three of the following six symptoms must be present:

1. A profound depressed mood
2. Depression regularly worse in the morning and improved slightly as the day progresses
3. Terminal sleep disturbance (early morning awakenings)
4. Severe psychomotor slowing or extreme agitation
5. Significant weight loss or anorexia
6. Inappropriate or excessive feelings of guilt

A successful 62-year-old widowed woman changed jobs almost on a whim, moving from Texas to Montana without considering all of the conse-quences. She rationalized that because she could retire in a few years, she would move before retirement so she could live closer to her children and grandchildren. Arriving at her new destination, she began to realize that the job she took was much more difficult than the one she left; furthermore, she was making less money. She sank into a profound depression. Nothing gave her pleasure. Even visiting her grandchildren failed to perk her up. Early each morning, she would wake suddenly. Tossing in bed (she did not have enough energy or willpower to get up), she would ruminate about the mistake she had made, feeling guilty about her impulsive decision. After she had lost 15 pounds, her son insisted that she seek help. She responded fairly quickly to an antidepressant medication and although the job got no easier, she no longer worried about mistakes she had made and applied her new-found energy to productive work and enjoyment of her family.

Dysthymia

Dysthymics, the Eeyores of the world, are chronically depressed. Dysthymia comes from two Greek words: *dys* (bad) and *thymia* (mood). Dysthymics are the type of people who could curdle milk. They look as if they were weaned on a pickle. They walk into a room, and the room dims. They have no fun, and they are no fun to be around. Chronically tired and socially inadequate, dysthymics, powered by a pessimistic outlook, leave a brooding crankiness in their wake. The *DSM-IV-TR* (American Psychiatric Association, 2000) committee insisted that a person with dysthymia has had a depressed mood every day for at least 2 years, but those who experience the misfortune of a long-term association with a dysthymic will discover that this illness often persists for a lifetime.

Although these individuals may respond to activating antidepressants and aggressive CBT, these patients are, in many ways, much more difficult to treat than those with a major depression because they would rather suffer pity than risk the responsibility of a life fully lived.

Doubly daunting is the so-called double depression—dysthymia associated with a coexisting major depression. As many as 9 of 10 dysthymic patients may experience at least one major depressive episode (Thase, 1992). From 25% to 50% of those with a major depression have a concomitant dysthymic disorder (Dubovsky, Davies, & Dubovsky, 2003) **(Table 3-4)**.

Psychotic Depression

Tortured by critical hallucinations and delusions of being evil or cancer ridden, those with a psychotic depression also possess the cluster of symptoms associated with a major depression. Reports of the number of patients with serious depression who exhibit psychotic symptoms are wide ranging. Dubovsky and Thomas (1992) reported epidemiological studies that found from 16% to 54% of depressed patients possessed psychotic symptoms.

TABLE 3-4

Diagnostic Differences of Selected Depressive Syndromes

ADJUSTMENT DISORDER WITH DEPRESSED MOOD	DYSTHYMIC DISORDER	MAJOR DEPRESSION	MASKED DEPRESSION
Results from acute environmental stress or grief over a loss	Lifetime depression	Loss of pleasure in usual activities	Physical symptoms predominate
Self-limiting symptoms that last for a few weeks or months	Pessimistic whiner; help-rejecting complainer	Inappropriate guilt and feelings of inadequacy	May complain of poor memory and answers questions with "I don't know"
Usually good premorbid social life and friendships	No social life; few friends; few recreational outlets that give pleasure	Usually premorbid perfectionist and obsessive personality traits	Often precipitated or exacerbated by a loss or financial difficulties
No biological markers	Complains of poor sleep but generally sleeps fairly well	Early morning awakenings with difficulty returning to sleep, change in appetite and decreased libido	Sleep disturbance, decreased appetite, and changes in sex life will be attributed to physical illness
Responds to supportive therapy, environmental change, rest, and relaxation	Medications cause side effects	Responds to medications and cognitive psychotherapy	Responds to antidepressants and low-dose antipsychotics

There are two types of psychotic depression: mood-congruent psychotic depression and mood-incongruent psychotic depression. Depression with mood-congruent psychotic features includes hallucinations or delusions whose content is consistent with the depressive themes of guilt, shame, personal inadequacy, or deserved punishment. The belief that worms are eating the spine as punishment for "doing bad things" or hearing the accusatory voice of the devil are mood-congruent psychotic features. Mood-incongruent psychotic features include hallucinations or delusions whose content does not involve typical depressive themes of personal inadequacy, shame, guilt, or deserved punishment. Delusions of mind control or auditory hallucinations beamed in from the Andromeda galaxy are mood-incongruent psychotic features. The course and outcome of the illness will help distinguish depression with mood-incongruent psychotic features from schizophrenia. Both mood-incongruent psychotic depression and mood-congruent psychotic depression as in the following case are treated with a combination of antidepressants plus antipsychotic medication.

> Leon was admitted to the psychiatric unit because he heard voices telling him to kill himself because he had been unfaithful to his wife. Convinced that a silicon chip had been implanted in his brain as punishment for an extramarital affair, Leon thought his wife had programmed the chip to afflict him with poor sleep, weight loss, and lack of energy. A computed tomographic scan ruled out a brain tumor. His depression responded to a combination of antipsychotic and antidepressant medications.

Involutional Depression

The onset of depression in older patients is often associated with loss of health, family, and friends.

> An 83-year-old lady had taken a full bottle of digoxin and turned on the gas jets of her oven. She had not called anyone about her suicide plans. She was serious about dying. Fortunately, the postal worker delivering the mail smelled gas, broke in, and called 911. At the hospital, whenever a nurse or physician walked into her room, she turned away and faced the wall. Her daughter reported that her mother had spoken no more than two or three sentences since entering the hospital. When she did speak, she talked about worms eating a hole in her stomach. At night, she could see the worms crawling out of her abdomen. She failed to respond to several different medications and medication combinations. Nothing worked. Her family decided against electroconvulsive therapy. She died a few months later in a nursing home, malnourished but in keeping with her wishes.

Postpartum Depression

Following the birth of a child, 85 of 100 mothers experience irritability, crying spells, and mood swings known as the postpartum blues (O'Hara, 1995). This temporary condition begins spontaneously during the month following delivery. The symptoms generally fade in less than 10 days. Dysphoria following delivery is so common that postpartum blues could be considered a "normal" response.

During the first 4 weeks following childbirth, 10 of 100 women experience postpartum depression (Cox, Murray, & Chapman, 1993). Those women who have a history of depression are 24% more likely to have a postpartum depression (O'Hara, 1995). Those with a history of postpartum depression are 50% more likely to have another postpartum depression (Wisner & Wheeler, 1994).

Symptoms of postpartum depression are similar to those of a major depression, and treatment is the same. Neglect of the infant is a great concern. Children of women with postpartum depression are at risk for behavior problems unless their father or extended family becomes closely involved in their care.

Postpartum psychosis, occurring in 1 of 1,000 births, is characterized by confusion, hallucinations, delusions, irritability, sleep and appetite disturbance, and disorganized thinking (O'Hara, 1995). Because postpartum psychosis may lead to suicide or infanticide, hospitalization is required. Women with postpartum psychosis are at risk for developing bipolar illness. Antipsychotics and mood stabilizers are the medications of choice in treating postpartum psychosis.

A few days after delivering a healthy infant, a mother of four whose husband had left for Iraq a few weeks earlier began to see witches in the house and hear voices telling her to poison her children. She became acutely agitated, wringing her hands and pacing back and forth in her bedroom. She could not remember her children's names. Her mother flew from Wisconsin to take care of the children. Her husband was given emergency leave. She was hospitalized and treated successfully with antipsychotics and mood stabilizers.

Bipolar Depression

Bipolar depression is characterized by mood swings alternating with periods of normal behavior. Manic episodes are associated with an elevated mood, unexplained temper outbursts, surplus energy, sleeplessness, excessive talking, distractibility, and indiscriminate behavior **(Table 3-5)**. (A word on nomenclature here: Recurrent depressions without episodes of elevated mood are known by researchers as unipolar depressions—for example, a major depression, recurrent without any "highs," would be a unipolar depression. I believe that a great deal of these so-called unipolar depressions could be classified as bipolar depressions. The psychiatrists just do not ask enough questions to look for episodes of elevated mood.)

Atypical Depression

Atypical depression can be diagnosed when the depressed mood brightens with the occurrence of positive events (mood reactivity). In addition, two of the following symptoms must be present: 1) Weight gain; 2) Excessive sleep; 3) A heavy feeling in the arms or legs; 4) Longstanding sensitivity to rejec-

TABLE 3-5		
The Bipolar Spectrum		
CLINICAL MANIFESTATION	**DEPRESSIVE SYMPTOMS**	**MANIC SYMPTOMS**
Mood changes	Depression; anxiety; crying spells or the complaint of being unable to cry; pain or physical complaints substitute for mood changes	Irritability, anger, elation, euphoria
Cognitive/emotional disturbance	Low self-esteem, guilty ruminations, self-reproach, poor concentration, indecisiveness, loss of interest in usual activities, anhedonia, negative ruminations	Grandiosity, bluster, feelings of superiority, racing thoughts, flight of ideas, gregariousness, buying sprees, foolish business investments, sexual indiscretions
Biological expression	Psychomotor retardation, fatigue, decreased energy, and changes in appetite, sleep, and sex drive	Psychomotor hyperactivity, decreased need for sleep, excessive sexual behavior, high levels of energy
Psychotic features	Delusions of worthlessness, persecution, physical illness, critical auditory hallucinations	Delusions of grandeur or omnipotence

tion (American Psychiatric Association, 2000). Atypical depression is probably more common than it is diagnosed and may be confused with Borderline Personality Disorder because borderlines also have rejection hypersensitivity and brightening of mood when exposed to positive events. Personal experience indicates that these patients may respond best to MAOIs or SSRIs.

Causes of Depression

Multiple factors contribute to depression, including psychological issues and emotional conflicts, genetic predisposition, neurochemical influences, and stress.

Psychological contributors to depression include the following:

- Loss
- Failure, perceived or real

- Learned helplessness
- Childhood experiences
- Anger turned inward
- Negative thinking

Loss

Loss through separation, divorce, death, or loss of a job or prestige can produce depression (Dubovsky et al., 2003). While social support mitigates the effects of loss, little or no support system results in a higher rate of depression. Loss of the father or the mother during the first 5 years of life or the loss of the father between the ages of 10 and 14 increases the risk of depression in adulthood (Kilgus & Criss, 2009).

Failure, Perceived or Real

Failure, whether perceived or real, may result in a diminution of an individual's self-esteem, contributing to depression (Whybrow, Akiskal, & McKinney, 1984). Depression-prone individuals beleaguered by unrealistic expectations develop a hypersensitivity to failure (Dubovsky et al., 2003). When achievements fail to reach high expectations of excellence, depression sets in.

A high school basketball coach became clinically depressed when his team failed to win the state championship for an unprecedented third consecutive year. He felt that the loss of the championship game proved that he was an inferior coach and forever precluded his coaching in college, a goal that he had coveted to "show that I'm man enough to make it in the big time."

Occasionally, individuals become depressed after promotions, outstanding accomplishments, or successful organ transplants or other life-saving surgeries. This paradoxical depression can occur for three reasons (MacKinnon & Michels, 1971; O'Conner, Berry, & Weiss, 2002):

1. The individual may feel guilty about success, equating successful assertion with hostile aggression.
2. The individual may believe that he or she is inadequate to cope with the increased responsibility of success.
3. After working diligently toward a goal, emptiness may follow an outstanding achievement.

Soon after being promoted to the largest church in the district, a 41-year-old Methodist pastor became depressed. He felt that his small-town background did not equip him to deal with the pressures of a city congregation.

His depression led to a failure to capitalize on his promotion, and he was transferred back to a smaller church, where he felt more comfortable.

Learned Helplessness

The theory of learned helplessness provides a model for explaining depression. Chronically depressed people, as the theory goes, remain depressed because over the years they have come to believe that they have no control over their destiny (Seligman, 1975).

> Scientists put an animal in a cage, and applied a mild electrical shock all over the floor of the cage. When the animal discovered that escape was impossible, the animal lay down and passively accepted the shock. Next, the electrical shock was applied only to the area where the animal was lying. The rest of the cage was made shock free. However, the animal continued to stay in the corner. Humans who are constantly exposed to poverty or any other negative environment situation from which there appears to be no escape will eventually give up and surrender to the situation. Not many therapists find value in dragging their patients toward a courageous life.

Childhood Experiences

Emotional, physical, or sexual abuse increases vulnerability to adult depression and other psychiatric illnesses (Kilgus & Criss, 2009). Some depression-prone individuals have experienced real or perceived parental loss of love during early childhood, resulting in frustration or anger (Whybrow et al., 1984). The child then attempts to win approval through achievement. The depression-prone individual learns to isolate and deny uncomfortable feelings through hard work and determination. With perceived failure, or the loss of loved ones or valued possessions, depression becomes likely.

> Ralph, a 33-year-old dentist, was success oriented. When he was a child, his father would drive him incessantly to achieve. His father insisted on Ralph being the best in everything, and Ralph, because he was talented, was able to perform well in athletics and academics. Ralph became conflicted. He both hated his father and, at the same time, longed for his father's approval. Ralph blossomed into a high school athlete whom recruiters courted. He played first string for the state university, graduated from college with honors, and through hard work, finished dental school in 3 years. Following graduation, he quickly established a lucrative practice, married a beautiful woman, and became the country club golf champion. Ralph's self-esteem was based entirely on achievement. He was highly successful but felt miserable: His success was not enough. Although a

winner, Ralph always considered himself to be a loser because he could never gain what he desired most—unconditional love from his father.

Anger Turned Inward

According to psychoanalytic theory, depression is "anger turned inward" (Abraham, 1911). As the theory goes, depression-prone individuals have a difficult time expressing anger. Because they base their self-worth on the opinion of others and bend over backward to please others, depression-prone individuals turn the anger they feel toward others against themselves. Treatment involves helping the depressed person understand the conflicts that engender anger, demonstrating how unexpressed anger causes problems, and teaching the individual to become appropriately assertive.

Thinking

Cognitive therapists believe that feelings are in large part determined by thoughts (Beck et al., 1979). According to cognitive-behavior theory, depressed individuals make negative generalizations. They tend to magnify negative experiences, disqualify prior positive experiences, and selectively recall negative material at the expense of positive memories. They frequently make "should," "ought," and "must" statements. "Shoulda, oughta, musta" is their credo. These sweeping negative generalizations about oneself, the world, and the future contribute to a depression-prone personality.

Genetic Aspects of Depression

Just as there exists no single cause for depression, there is no single gene that causes depression. Depression is caused by a combination of genetic factors, environmental influences, personality characteristics, and emotional stress. One person might have a high level of emotional stress and very little genetic predisposition to precipitate a depression, while another may carry a high genetic risk and little environmental stress and become depressed. (Kilgus & Criss, 2009). Nonetheless, family studies have repeatedly shown that mood disorders have a genetic component (Gershon, 1990). Concordance rates for mood disorder in monozygotic twins are around 60% while concordance rates for dizygotic twins are about 15% (Kilgus & Criss, 2009).

Inherited Factors of Depression

- Relatives of patients with a mood disorder are two to three times more likely to have depression than the normal population.
- If one parent has a bipolar mood disorder, the risk that a child will suffer from a depression or a bipolar disorder is 28%.
- If both parents have a mood disorder, the risk of a child having a mood disorder is two to three times as great as the normal population.

- In twins with a mood disorder, an identical twin has a two to three times greater chance of depression than a nonidentical twin.
- An adoptee with depression is more likely to have a biological parent with a depression than an adoptee that has an adoptive parent with depression.

Neurochemical Causes of Depression

Research indicates that, in at least some depressions, chemical imbalances may contribute to depression. Some depressed individuals seem to be deficient in chemicals (called *neurotransmitters*) that facilitate the spread of impulses across central nervous system connections. A decrease in the activity of the transmitters seems to be related to depression, while an increase in activity is related to mania. Neurotransmitters implicated in depression include the following:

- Serotonin—because at least 15 distinct serotonin subtypes exist, many of which have more than one function, serotonin plays many roles as a neurotransmitter. A serotonin inequity contributes to depression, self-destructive behavior, anger, irritability, and sleep and appetite dysfunction. Serotonin also plays a part in panic disorder,anxiety, and obsessive behavior (Dubovsky et al., 2003).
- Norepinephrine—both relative excesses and deficiencies of norepinephrine seem to play a part in depression, creating a hypothesis that uneven responsiveness of norepinephrine may be the actual contributor to depression (Siever & Davis, 1985).
- Dopamine—decreased levels of dopamine contribute to depression, poor motivation, lack of pleasure, and decreased concentration (Brown, Steinberg, & van Praag, 1994).
- GABA (gamma-aminobutyric acid)—a decrease in GABA may contribute to anxiety and depression by influencing serotonin function (Dubovsky et al., 2003).
- Acetylcholine—excessive amounts of this neurotransmitter may contribute to depression (Poland et al., 1997).
- Second messengers—enzymes and electrolytes inside the cell can contribute to mood changes. For example, brisk but subtle changes in calcium ions may produce rapid cycling between depression and mania (Dubovsky, Murphy, Christiano, & Lee, 1992).
- Messenger RNA—antidepressants may regulate the gene expression of depressive traits by sending messages to DNA inside the nucleus of nerve cells (Stahl, 2008).

Tests for Depression

Thus far, no test for depression beats a good clinical interview (Dubovsky et al., 2003). Magnetic resonance imaging (MRI) sometimes shows enlarged brain ventricles in some depressed patients. Positron emission tomography (PET) and single-photon emission computed tomography (SPECT) show reduced metabolic activity in the frontal lobes of the brain in some depressed patients. In patients with major depression, abnormalities in the dexamethasone suppression test occur about 40–60% of the time (Kilgus & Criss, 2009). The dexamethasone suppression test, a blood test to measure brain stimulation of steroid activity in the body, sometimes indicates increased steroid activity in severely depressed patients. The thyrotropin-releasing hormone stimulation test fails to stop release of the thyroid hormone in one third of severely depressed individuals (Dubovsky et al., 2003). The inconsistencies of these tests limit their usefulness in the diagnosis of depression. They interest researchers but have limited clinical usefulness.

Clinical Pearls: Tips for Uncovering a "Masked" Depression (Depression Without the Typical Signs and Symptoms)

About half the patients who present with depression fail to report its symptoms. Instead, they complain of physical symptoms or have vague, nonspecific presentations. The lack of a laboratory test for depression mandates that the clinician possess good clinical interviewing skills. Here are some questions a physician can ask to uncover depressive symptoms. "If you rate your pain on a scale of 0–10, with a 10 being the most severe pain you have ever experienced, is your pain so severe that you . . ."

- wake in the middle of the night, which keeps you from being able to return to sleep?
- no longer have desire for sex?
- have no desire to eat, so much so that you have lost weight?
- feel like crying, but you can't?
- have lost pleasure in usual activities?
- have lost enthusiasm for sports and hobbies?
- avoid your friends because you are in so much pain?
- are irritable a great deal of the time?
- have difficultly concentrating?
- have thought life just wasn't worth living?

If the patient answers affirmatively to most of these questions, the physician can respond as follows:

"I'm afraid you have been in so much pain that you have depleted some of the chemicals in your brain. These so-called neurotransmitters help fight off pain. You've been trying to fight this pain so much that you have no more transmitters left. You are running on empty. I am going to give you some medicine to increase these neurotransmitters. Some people call these medicines antidepressants, but these medicines, no matter what they are called help build up those neurotransmitters that you have lost. Now, this medicine may not get rid of all your pain, but it should help you feel better and thus help you deal with your pain better and if all goes well you should do much, much better than you have in the past." [Note: the repeated use of the word "better" reinforces a positive response as does carefully explaining how and why the medications work. The repeated use of the word "should" is a qualifier in case the medication fails to meet expectations.]

Although there are no specific tests for depression, the prudent clinician will perform a series of tests to rule out illnesses that may mimic depression:

- Complete blood count to rule out anemia or blood diseases.
- Thyroid-stimulating hormone level to rule out thyroid disease.
- Comprehensive metabolic panel to rule out liver disease, kidney disease, protein abnormalities, and electrolyte deficiencies.
- Urine drug screen.
- Pregnancy test in women of child-bearing age.

Course and Outcomes of Depression

Approximately twice as many females as males will have a depressive disorder. The average age of onset of major depression is in the mid-20s, but depression may occur at any age, including childhood. Education, income, marital status, or ethnicity seem unrelated to the prevalence rates of major depression. There is an increased risk of alcohol dependence and anxiety dis-

---

COURSE OF MAJOR DEPRESSION
(VERY ROUGH EXTRAPOLATION OF NUMEROUS STUDIES)

- 20% of depressed people recover or have a partial remission.
- 60% of depressed people recover but have subsequent episodes.
- 20% of depressed people are continuously depressed or commit suicide.
- Inadequate treatment increases the risk of a relapse fourfold.
- The greater the number of previous recurrences of depression, the higher the risk of future recurrences.

Complete Mental Health

TABLE 3-6			
Red Flags for Suicide Risk			
SOCIAL SIGNS	**WARNING CUES**	**PAST EVENTS**	**ALARMING SIGNS**
Male sex	Severe depression	Previous suicide attempts	A specific plan
Recent loss	Panic attacks	Family history of suicide	Has access to lethal weapon
Never married, no friends, loner	Expresses feelings of hopelessness	Drug abuse; excessive drinking	Selling or giving away property
Excessively troubled about aging; joyless retirement	Hearing voices urging suicide; delusions of being unloved	Intractable severe pain; deteriorating health	Repeated hospitalizations for depression

orders in first-degree biological relatives of those with major depression (American Psychiatric Association, 2000).

Suicide

Every 16 minutes someone in the United States commits suicide. In 2004, 32,559 people in the United States took their lives. Probably twice that number were incorrectly reported. Suicide ranks as the eighth leading cause of death for males in the United States and is the third leading cause of death in the group aged 15–24 years. White males are more likely to commit suicide than any other group. Women attempt suicide three times as often as men, but men are four times more likely to die from suicide than women. Suicide rates increase with age (Centers for Disease Control and Prevention, 2005). About half of suicide completers were clinically depressed at the time of the suicide. Not everyone who commits suicide is depressed. Drugs, alcohol, psychosis, and other psychiatric illness contributed to suicide in 40% of cases (Andreasen & Black, 2006) **(Table 3-6)**.

Although many factors determine when suicidal thoughts become suicidal plans, a threat must be taken seriously. Sometimes, suicide gestures turn deadly.

A handsome, womanizing Air Force lab tech read in a medical journal that no one had ever died from an overdose of Valium. Whenever the lab tech Lothario got into a bind with his jealous girlfriends, he swallowed a few Valium in a suicide gesture. His lovelorn would gather around his hospital bed sobbing hysterically. As he "miraculously" recovered from his "coma," his indiscretions were forgiven. Once again caught in flagrante delicto, he reached for the Valium. The bottle was empty. No matter—he substituted a handful of barbiturates. His funeral reinforced the saying, "There is nothing more pathetic than a good-looking, dumb man."

Treatment Medications

A variety of antidepressants that seem to work by changing the levels of certain neurotransmitters has been extensively studied—the monoamine oxidase inhibitors (MAOIs); tricyclic antidepressants (such as Elavil [amitriptyline] and Tofranil [imipramine]); selective serotonin reuptake inhibitors (SSRIs), serotonin-norepinephrine reuptake inhibitors (SNRIs); Wellbutrin (bupropion), which seems to work on dopamine and norepinephrine; and many others.

Tradition indicates that all antidepressants are equally effective. The heterogeneity of the medications makes this concept implausible. The idea that antidepressants give equal results comes from 6-week clinical trials that define efficacy as a 50% improvement, or to put the statement in the vernacular, a medication is deemed effective if it gets the patient "half-well." In short clinical trials, 30% of patients taking a placebo get half-well; 50–70% of patients taking an "effective" antidepressant get half-well. Medications with more complex neurotransmitter effects such as the SNRIs Effexor (venlafaxine) and Cymbalta (duloxetine), the tricyclics, and the MAOIs may better induce a full remission—a complete cure. This hypothesis is being investigated (Schatzberg, Cole, & DeBatista, 2007).

Side effects and safety are major considerations in choosing an antidepressant. Tricyclic antidepressants cause dry mouth, blurred vision, constipation, urinary hesitancy, hypotension, and heart block. The most common side effect of MAOIs is dizziness secondary to orthostatic hypotension. Activation and sedation are potential problems depending on the particular medication. Hypertensive crisis when MAOIs are combined with cheese and other foods and drugs containing tyramine is the most fearful side effect. The SSRIs are better tolerated and much safer than their predecessors. The most common side effects are GI distress, insomnia, agitation, sedation, and sexual dysfunction. The SNRIs (Effexor and Cymbalta) can cause nausea, sexual dysfunction, and, in high doses, a slightly elevated diastolic blood pressure. Wellbutrin can cause insomnia, dry mouth, and tremor (Schatzberg, Cole & DeBattista 2007).

An antidepressant can also be chosen based on target symptoms. For example, depressed people with anxiety can be given an SSRI. Those with pain can be prescribed Effexor XR or Cymbalta. Those with lack of pleasure and motivation may receive Wellbutrin. Understanding the mechanism of action of the antidepressants can help with the choice of medication. The dose of the antidepressant and the duration of treatment are other important choices, all of which are discussed in the chapter on psychopharmacology.

Psychotherapy

To achieve optimal results, everyone who takes antidepressant medications should be involved in some type of psychotherapy. As a broad general statement, this rule holds: Antidepressant medications improve about 50% of depressive symptoms, and psychotherapy improves the other 50%. Although there are several psychotherapy options that work, two therapies were specifically designed for treating depression. These are discussed extensively in the chapter on psychotherapy.

Cognitive Therapy

Research studies have shown that cognitive therapy (CT) is just as effective as antidepressant medications in mild-to-moderate depressions (Elkin et al., 1989). CBT augments the effectiveness of antidepressant medication in severe depressions (Thase, 1990).

Based on the theory that depression results from global negative thinking and attitudes, the therapist teaches the patient to recognize and correct common errors in information processing (Beck et al., 1979). For example:

- Overgeneralization—I made a B in freshman composition; therefore, I am a poor writer. But Michael Crichton made so many Cs in English that he decided to become a medical doctor.
- All-or-nothing thinking—There are flaws in my book even though I worked hard on it; therefore, I produced nothing of value. But Margaret Mitchell worked 8 years on *Gone with the Wind*, and it still had flaws.
- Excessive personalization—My editor didn't return my call, therefore she doesn't like my book. In fact, the editor was in meetings all day long.

Interpersonal Therapy

Interpersonal therapy (IPT) has been found as effective as CT and the antidepressant imipramine in treating depression (Elkin et al., 1989). Using a written protocol, the therapist helps the patient work through structured assignments dealing with problems in relationships. Usually conducted in weekly sessions for 12–16 weeks, the therapist helps the patient identify four basic problems that interfere with self-esteem and relationships—unresolved grief, disputes with others, transitions to new roles, and social skills deficits. After identifying specific conflicts, the therapist teaches improved communi-

TABLE 3-7	
Treatments for Depression Syndromes	
TYPE OF MOOD DISORDER	**TREATMENT OF FIRST CHOICE**
Adjustment disorder with depressed mood	Psychotherapist suggests practical approaches for dealing with the precipitating stress
Dysthymic disorder	CBT or IPT
Major depression, single episode	Antidepressants + cognitive or IPT psychotherapy
Major depression, recurrent	Antidepressant + lithium or Lamictal + CBT or IPT
Bipolar depression	Mood stabilizers
Postpartum depression	Antidepressants and supportive psychotherapy; antipsychotic if depression is severe enough to cause loss of reality; mood stabilizer if a bipolar component exists
Psychotic depression	Antidepressants + antipsychotics
Atypical depression	Consider MAO inhibitors or antidepressants in combination with a low-dose antipsychotic
Involutional depression	Pamelor or Celexa indicated by evidence-based studies

cation skills and new interaction techniques (Andreasen & Black, 2006) **(Table 3-7)**.

Practical Advice for Patients

CBT teaches the patient three commonsense lessons: the power of words, the power of optimism, and the power of practical living. Often, cognitive-behavior therapists will provide the patient with a list of commonsense instructions, such as the following:

- **Rid yourself of negative thinking.** Expunge "should," "ought," and "must" from your vocabulary. Remember your successes; forget your failures. Visualize the good things that have happened to you. Concentrate on the positive things you have done.

- **Exercise.** Vigorous exercise—20 to 30 minutes of jogging, swimming, brisk walking, cycling, or aerobic dance—improves circulation, increases metabolic rate, and enhances a sense of well-being. Exercise increases brain neurotransmitters that help boost energy and enthusiasm. The exhaustion that depressed people experience is caused by mental fatigue, not physical fatigue. Physical exercise enhances mental alertness.
- **Eat right.** Complex carbohydrates—fruits, vegetables, and grains—stimulate brain serotonin, a neurotransmitter that improves mood. Protein—found in eggs, chicken, fish, and lean beef—improves alertness and mental energy.
- **Rest.** Overwork contributes to a depressed mood.
- **Don't take yourself too seriously.** Develop a cosmic sense of humor—the ability to laugh at yourself and your mistakes.
- **Stay active.** Activity cures misery by releasing endorphins. Plus, when we are busy, we don't have time to feel sorry for ourselves. I know that if I don't have anything to do on the weekends, I get restless and dysphoric. That's why I'm working feverishly on this manuscript at 11:01 P.M. on Saturday night (that and an almost impossible deadline). So if you can't get motivated, find an editor with a fiendish sense of time. Or find a friend who will keep you accountable.
- **Confront problems.** When a conflict occurs, deal with the difficulty immediately. Avoiding a problem increases depression and frustration. Speak up. Don't bottle your feelings or nurse grudges.
- **Wear brightly colored clothes.** Reds, yellows, and oranges enhance mood. These are good colors for women to wear. But, men, if you wear a red suit they will think you are manic and lock you up, which would be very depressing. Wear a red tie instead.
- **Do your best.** Give up the quest for perfection and appreciate your best effort. Know your limitations, as well as your capabilities, and feel good about your attempt. Just do your best. That's all anyone can do.
- **Change.** Life is too short to be miserable. Be receptive to new ideas. Take risks. Step out and step up. Follow your bliss.

Make Check Mark (✓) in Appropriate Column	Little of the Time 1 point each ✓	Some of the Time 2 points each ✓	A Lot of the Time 3 points each ✓	Most of the Time 4 points each ✓
Are You Depressed?				
I have trouble sleeping at night.				
My current eating habits are different from my normal eating habits.				
My current sex habits are different from my normal sex habits.				
I have less energy than I used to.				
I have more trouble concentrating than I used to.				
I have more difficulty making decisions than I used to.				
I feel less hopeful about the future than I used to.				
I don't enjoy things that I used to enjoy.				
I feel less useful and needed than I used to feel.				
I feel others would be better off if I were dead.				
Multiply ✓ by the value given in each column.				

Add the total for each column to get the **Grand total** = _____

SCORING

10–14 points = Sunshine all the time

15–24 points = Partly cloudy

25–34 points = Cloudy and cold

35–40 points = 100% chance of rain

A Clinician's Quiz

1. What type of depression is characterized by loss of pleasure in almost all activities, feeling worse in the morning, terminal sleep disturbance, significant weight loss, and inappropriate guilt?

2. What type of depression is characterized by mood reactivity, significant weight gain, hypersomnia, rejection hypersensitivity, and leaden feelings in the arms and legs?

3. What is the term for those people who believe they have no control over their lives?

4. What emotion do most depression prone people have difficulty expressing?

5. Which therapy is based on the theory that feelings come from thoughts?

6. Enzymes and electrolytes inside the cells can contribute to mood changes. What are these enzymes and electrolytes called?

7. Theoretically, the lack of a certain neurotransmitter can contribute to depression by causing poor motivation, lack of pleasure, and decreased concentration. What is the name of this neurotransmitter?

8. What group is more likely to commit suicide than any other group?

9. In research studies, efficacy is defined as _____ percent improvement.

10. Which therapy deals with unresolved grief, disputes with others, transitions to new roles, and social skill deficits?

CHAPTER 4

The Bipolar Spectrum
Up the Down Escalator

Meriwether Lewis, famous for the Lewis and Clark Expedition (1804–1806) that blazed a trail to the Pacific Ocean, was an American explorer, soldier, and naturalist. At times, his boundless energy produced prodigious accomplishments. Then, without warning, he would retreat to his tent, disconsolate and unproductive. A few weeks later, he would rush ahead of the group, make voluminous botanical recordings in his journal, climb mountains, and navigate rivers, exhausting his fellow explorers. Returning from the expedition as a living legend, he soon slipped into a depression. When he was 35 years old, at a tavern about 70 miles from Nashville, Tennessee, he died from self-inflicted wounds (Ambrose, 1996).

Vivian Leigh, an award-winning actress who played Scarlet O'Hara in the film *Gone With the Wind*, suffered from terrible bouts of extreme mania and depression following a miscarriage. Her husband, the great English actor Laurence Olivier, nursed Leigh through the disease for years before their eventual divorce. He often stayed awake with her for hours after midnight because she required little sleep during manic episodes. Poor health exacerbated by her bipolar illness precipitated her early death at age 53 (A. Walker, 1987).

Bipolar disorder, also known as "manic-depressive illness," is character-ized by dramatic mood swings—from elevated mood to depressed mood and then back again, often with periods of normal mood in between. Perhaps because great volumes of creative work can be achieved during the "highs" of mania, several well-known artists and musicians have suffered from bipolar disorder. The well-researched list of famous and accomplished people with symptoms of bipolar illness includes Tolstoy, Virginia Woolf, Robert Lowell, Henry James, Victor Hugo, Tchaikovsky, Coleridge, Hemingway, Byron, Blake, Balzac, Goethe, Gauguin, Gorky, Handel, Schumann, Dickens, Barrie, Berlioz, Beethoven, and a host of others (Jamison, 1993). One can find a volu-minous list of contemporary artists, athletes, and entrepreneurs presumed to have bipolar illness. The celebrities most commonly mentioned include Robert Downey Jr., Patty Duke, Ben Stiller, Ted Turner, and golfer John Daly.

In her book *Touched With Fire*, psychologist Kay Redfield Jamison (1993) studied the lives of distinguished writers and artists, finding in Britain that 38% had been treated for mood disorder. Creative people are 18 times more likely to commit suicide and 10–20 times more likely to have bipolar disorder than the general population (Jamison, 1996). During times of high levels of energy, creative people are most productive. Depressive episodes cause them to be more sensitive to the vicissitudes of life. There is no evidence, however, that bipolar illness enhances creativity.

Although not famous or particularly artistic, he was well liked by just about everyone he met. They called him "Hap" or sometimes "Happy" because of his boyhood exuberance and love of life. Men enjoyed being around him; women adored him. Born and raised in the Big Thicket of Texas—a vast array of virgin woods, briars, and swamps—he lacked culture and sophistication, but his enthusiastic personality attracted all who met him. A high school graduate, he married a refined schoolteacher who had grad-uated from college when she was 19. He "just swept me off my feet," she said. Soon they had two children, both boys.

When Hap returned from World War II after serving as a tail gunner on B-24 bombers, he was different. He had crying spells, nightmares, intrusive thoughts of air battles, and flashbacks. His wife and friends thought he was suffering from "combat fatigue," as post-traumatic stress disorder was then called. As the years passed, the nightmares and flashbacks abated, but he still had episodic crying spells accompanied by loss of pleasure, feelings of hopelessness, guilty ruminations, decreased energy, and sleep disturbance. Although he was hospitalized in Veterans Affairs facilities on several occasions for suicidal thoughts, family and friends still considered these depressive episodes secondary to his war experiences.

When free of depressive symptoms, he was like the Hap of old—laughing, joking, gregarious, and outgoing. At times, he was more talkative than usual; he had an overabundance of energy, thoughts raced through his mind, and he began spending more money than he could afford to. One day without warning, he picked up his wife after school in a bright red Cadillac convertible. "Jump in," he said. "We're going to Carlsbad Caverns for a vacation."

Before she could protest or ask where he had gotten the money for the Cadillac, they were on the road to New Mexico. He placed blankets in the back seat and floorboard, makeshift beds on which the boys could sleep. With an exhilarated sense of freedom from all cares and responsibilities, he drove the big red Cadillac down the winding roads of east Texas, through the black land prairies, over the mountains of the hill country, across the Llano Escatado, and through the immense Texas desert onto the Jornada del Muerto, arriving in Carlsbad, New Mexico, after stopping only for gas, snacks, and bathroom breaks. He had too much energy to stop, he said as he laughed, sang, told stories from his Big Thicket days, and announced that as soon as they returned from their vacation, the family was moving to Kilgore, Texas, where a new oil boom promised lucrative jobs.

The job proved less than the promise, so they moved again and again as Hap searched for some lasting satisfaction. Gratification came only in bursts and with it came more foolish spending and risky living that spawned drifts into deep-seated depression and hospitalizations. Tiring of bill collectors and unexpected moves, his wife finally left him. But no matter, he found another wife, and another after that as he continued his whirlwind life from grandiosity to grief and back again, until on a crisp October night, at age 63, he shot himself with "Ole Rem," his favorite .12-gauge shotgun.

Diagnosis of Bipolar Disorder

In the early 20th century, renowned pioneer of psychiatry Emil Kraepelin (1921) differentiated schizophrenia, marked by gradual brain deterioration, from episodic mood swings that he called "manic-depressive insanity." Since that time, different intensities and varying frequencies of bipolar disorder have been recognized. The emotions of bipolar illness can range from cyclothymia—mild mood swings—to severe, life-threatening psychoses.

Psychiatrists have categorized bipolar disorder into several types based on intensity, scope, and duration of the symptoms. Are the "highs" severe or mild? Does the mood rapidly change from highs to lows? Are there mixed symptoms of depression and mania at the same time? How severe are the symptoms? How often do the cycles occur? These are questions that clinicians must ask when determining a proper diagnosis.

Before looking at the different types of bipolar illness, it is important to define the symptoms. What distinguishes mania from simply a "good mood"? How does bipolar depression differ from other types of depression?

Manic Symptoms

The passions of manic individuals transcend their judgment. While blessed with unbounded enthusiasm that allows the mania-prone individual to pursue tasks with gusto and gaiety, their energy imperceptibly can escalate to pathological proportions: a warm and friendly manner turns into an elevated, irritable mood; engaging conversation converts to senseless talk; vigor turns to wasteful hyperactivity. The manic patient may telephone acquaintances regardless of the time of day or inappropriately share intimate personal secrets with complete strangers. Buying sprees, foolish business ventures, and reckless driving add to the personality disruption.

During an acute manic attack, the individual dresses outlandishly; the person may be wearing two or three watches or several hats, necklaces, or belts. Occasionally, the manic may be delusional—the individual may believe that he or she is a special emissary from God or a secret agent from the Federal Bureau of Investigation. Sometimes, the manic condition may escalate into a delirious state characterized by incoherent speech, purposeless activity, and confusion.

A farmer with bipolar illness did well when he took his medication. During harvest season, he failed to take his medicine for 3 weeks. One day, he began walking to the clinic to get a new prescription. To entertain himself on his 30-mile walk, he sang hymns. He began to disrobe as the day grew hotter. When the police picked him up, he was walking along the side of the highway singing hosannas, clad only in his work boots.

The symptoms of elevated mood can be remembered by using the by the acronym BIPOLAR:

B = **B**lemished behavior—buying sprees, sexual indiscretion, recklessness

I = **I**nsomnia—an overabundance of energy that makes sleep difficult

P = **P**ressured speech—speech that is fast, interrupting, and excessive

O = **O**mnipotent feelings—grandiose, invincible, powerful feelings

L = **L**oss of attention—poor concentration, distractibility

A = **A**ctivity in unexplained bursts of energy

R = **R**acing thoughts—thoughts that come fast and furious

Depressive Symptoms

Although many symptoms of bipolar depression are similar to those of unipolar depression—sleep disturbance, appetite and libido changes, loss of pleasure in usual activities, guilty ruminations, thoughts of unworthiness, and feelings of hopelessness or helplessness—the risk of drug abuse tends to be more frequent in bipolar depression than in unipolar depression (American Psychiatric Association, 2000). Psychomotor retardation, hypersomnia, irritability, and extreme fatigue are also more widely reported by patients with bipolar depression (Kilgus & Criss, 2009).

Clinical Types of Bipolar Disorder

In 1976, Dunner and colleagues proposed the two major categories of bipolar disorder: bipolar I disorder and bipolar II disorder (Hadjipavlou, Mok, & Yatham, 2004). Both bipolar I and bipolar II patients have depressive spirals. The difference between the two disorders is that patients with bipolar I exhibit severe or psychotic mania, while patients with bipolar II have lower levels of mania.

Other subtypes of bipolar disorder are cyclothymia (mild mood swings), mixed bipolar states (manic and depressive symptoms occurring simultaneously), and bipolar NOS (not otherwise specified), which includes those conditions that fit none of the other categories. Rapid cycling, by which episodes

TABLE 4-1	
Clinical Types of Bipolar Disorder	
TYPE	**DISTINGUISHING FEATURE**
Bipolar I	Severe or psychotic mania
Bipolar II	Mild forms of mania (hypomania)
Mixed bipolar	Symptoms of depression and mania or hypomania occur concurrently
Cyclothymia	Lifelong episodes of mild depression and mild hypomania
Bipolar NOS	Fails to meet the criteria for other bipolar illnesses
Rapid cycling	A subcategory of bipolar illness characterized by four episodes of a mood disturbance occurring in a 12-month period

of mania and depression alternate quickly, conveys a symptom description rather than a specific type of bipolar illness **(Table 4-1).**

Bipolar I Disorder

Patients with bipolar I disorder have episodes of mania—a severely elevated mood that causes work and social impairment, often requires hospitalization, and frequently produces psychotic symptoms. The distinctive feature of bipolar I disorder, as compared to other mood disorders, is the presence of at least one manic episode. Although the illness typically begins in early adulthood, the episodic nature of the disorder may go unrecognized, causing needless suffering for years. Nine of ten who have a single manic episode have another one (or several) if left untreated. Usually, these manic episodes immediately precede or follow a depressive episode, although each individual has a unique pattern of mood cycles that, once identified, is predictable. Retroactive studies have shown that without lithium, on the average, four episodes occurred every 10 years, with the intervals between episodes decreasing with age. The majority of patients experience a leveling of mood after each manic episode, but about 60% of patients continue to have problems with relationships and difficulties at work between acute episodes of depression or mania (American Psychiatric Association, 2000).

Bipolar II Disorder

Bipolar II disorder is characterized by depressive episodes alternating with mild episodes of mania, called *hypomania* (hypo = below mania). The hypomanic symptoms are less severe and persist for a shorter time. During episodes of hypomania, almost all patients have intermittent irritability. A hypomanic episode is not severe enough to cause marked impairment in daily living skills, is not associated with psychotic features, and does not lead to hospitalization. Instead, a hypomanic episode is characterized by a 4-day (or more) period of persistently elevated, expansive, or irritable mood. A hypomanic episode is marked by:

- Decreased need for sleep
- Inflated self-esteem
- Unusual talkativeness
- Racing thoughts
- Easy distractibility
- Hyperactivity
- An increase in pleasure-seeking or risky behavior

Because they often demonstrate several episodes of depression before an initial hypomanic episode, patients with bipolar II depression may be falsely diagnosed as having recurrent unipolar depression. When compared to unipolar depressed patients, patients with bipolar II depression are more likely to have the following characteristics (American Psychiatric Association, 2000):

- Family history of mania, bipolar illness, or substance abuse
- Earlier age of onset of depression (adolescence or early 20s)
- A higher number of depressive episodes
- Mood swings
- Nonresponse or agitation on antidepressants

Rapid cycling, defined as the presence of four or more affective episodes in a year, is much more prevalent in patients with bipolar II than bipolar I. Brief, frequent episodes of depression are highly suggestive of rapid-cycling bipolar II disorder. Because antidepressants can exacerbate rapid cycling, current guidelines recommend antidepressants be used for a limited time and only adjunctively with mood stabilizers in treating bipolar disorder.

Research and clinical experience since 1976 have debunked the original idea that, in terms of disability and ease of treatment, bipolar I disorder was the most severe form on the bipolar spectrum. In studies indicating the severity of the illness, patients with bipolar II illness actually rated their illness as significantly more disruptive than did those with bipolar I. Individuals with bipolar II experience greater functional impairment in health, recreation, and finances than bipolar I patients (MacQueen & Young, 2001) **(Table 4-2)**.

Mixed Bipolar States
Just under half of bipolar patients will have concurrent symptoms of depression and mania. When these synchronous symptoms are observed, the official diagnosis contains a subcategory, for example, "bipolar II, mixed." This condition may be confused with rapid cycling. Some cases may result from chronic use of antidepressants (Dubovsky et al., 2003).

Cyclothymic Disorder
Cyclothymic disorder is a chronic condition marked by numerous cycles of mild depression and hypomania. Some believe this condition acts more like a personality disorder than a primary mood disorder. This pervasive, lifelong pattern of behavior is difficult to treat.

Bipolar NOS
Sometimes, patients clearly show signs of a bipolar illness, but their symptoms do not meet the official requirements listed in the *Diagnostic and Statistical Manual of Mental Disorders, Fourth Edition, Text Revision* (*DSM-IV-TR*;

TABLE 4-2

Differences Between Mania and Hypomania

	MANIA	HYPOMANIA
Diagnostic differences	Found in bipolar I disorder	Found in bipolar II disorder
Mood	Expansive or irritable mood	Same as mania
Symptom complex	At least three of the following symptoms: 1. Grandiosity 2. Decreased sleep 3. Excessive talking 4. Racing thoughts 5. Distractibility 6. Hyperactivity 7. Excessively harmful activities such as buying sprees, sexual indiscretion, poor decisions	Same as mania
Work/social impairment	Yes	No
Requires hospitalization	Often	No
Psychotic symptoms	Frequent	Never
Duration of symptoms	One week	Four days
Prevalence	1% of population	4–6% of population
Episodes of depression	Yes—depressive episodes three times more frequent than elevated mood	Same as mania
Prescriptions for elevated mood	Mood stabilizers—Lithium, Depakote, Lamictal	Same as mania
Length of treatment with mood stabilizer	Lifetime	Same as mania
Prescriptions for depressed mood	Antidepressant always in conjunction with mood stabilizer to prevent manic episodes	Same as mania
Use of antipsychotic	During episodes of manic or depressive psychosis	Use if patient has a psychotic depression

The Bipolar Spectrum

American Psychiatric Association, 2000). Such a patient would then receive a diagnosis of "bipolar NOS." According to *DSM-IV-TR*, examples of bipolar NOS include:

- Extremely rapid alteration of typical manic and depressive symptoms, occurring within days of each other
- Recurrent hypomanic episodes without depressive episodes
- Conditions in which the clinician is unable to determine whether the manic-depressive symptoms are due to cyclothymia, a superimposed psychotic disorder, a general medical condition, or a substance-induced disorder

Conditions Confused With Bipolar Illness

Considerable symptom overlap between bipolar disorder and attention deficit/hyperactivity disorder (ADHD) may lead to diagnostic confusion. More than half of patients with childhood bipolar disorder meet criterea for ADHD and 20 to 25% of children with ADHD fulfill the criterea for bipolar disorder (Popper et al., 2003). Key distinguishing features of ADHD include inattention, hyperactivity, and impulsivity; diagnostic features of bipolar disorder include elation, grandiosity, racing thoughts, decreased need for sleep, and severe mood instability (Dubovsky et al., 2003). When there is significant clinical overlap between bipolar disorder and ADHD, the clinician would do well to add a mood stabilizer to prevent the psychostimulants from precipitating a full-blown manic episode.

Medical illnesses, street drugs, and medications can cause manic or depressive symptoms. Patients with cancer often have depression. Cardiovascular conditions, hypothyroidism, and many neurological illnesses can cause symptoms of depression. A huge textbook of psychiatry lists two pages of substances that can cause mania or depression (Hales & Yudofsky, 2003). Because many patients with bipolar disorder abuse alcohol and drugs, it is often difficult to decide which came first, the bipolar illness or the drug use. Many illicit drugs cause ups and downs in mood similar to bipolar illness.

Anxiety, depression, and mania have considerable overlap. Individuals with borderline, histrionic, antisocial, and narcissistic personality disorders share some of the same symptoms with bipolar patients. Some believe that personality disorders may contribute to the development of mood disorders in those patients who have a genetic predisposition (Dubovsky et al., 2003).

Epidemiology

Prevalence surveys vary. At any given time, from 1% to 2.5% of the population has bipolar I disorder, depending on the study (Akiskal, 1995). The rates for the entire bipolar spectrum range from 3% to 6.5% (Akiskal, 1995; Angst,

1995). In 1989 about one third of patients with major depression met the criteria for the bipolar spectrum (Cassano et al., 1989). Over the years that percentage has grown. If a clinician takes a detailed history from a close relative of a patient with depression and continues to care for that patient for at least 10 years, almost half of those patients will have had symptoms or will have symptoms of mania or hypomania. That means that almost half the patients with a unipolar depressive disorder will eventually be diagnosed as having a bipolar spectrum disorder (Stahl, 2008).

Since 1910, all industrial countries in the world have shown an increase in depression, suicide, and bipolar spectrum disorders. An abrupt jump in the rate of these illnesses has occurred since 1940. Not only are these illnesses becoming more common, but they also appear at an earlier age. One might attribute the rate increase to improved recognition or the availability of treatment, but cross-cultural studies failed to substantiate this theory (Weissman et al., 1996). Perhaps stress has something to do with the increase. No one knows.

Causes Of Bipolar Illness

Most scientists agree that there is no single cause for bipolar disorder. Rather, many factors likely act together to produce the illness or increase risk.

Bipolar illness can be influenced by genetics, neurotransmitters, and psychological factors. These are discussed next.

Genetics

Bipolar disorder tends to run in families, so researchers are looking for genes that may increase a person's chance of developing the illness. Children with a parent or sibling who has bipolar disorder are 4 to 6 times more likely to develop the illness, compared with children who have no family history of bipolar disorder (NIMH, 2009). Although identical twins share all of the same genes, studies of identical twins show that the twin of a person with bipolar illness does not always develop the disorder (NIMH, 2009). Identical twin studies surveyed by the National Institute of Mental Health (2009) suggest factors besides genes are also at work. Stress, emotional loss, debilitating illness, trauma, drug use, or psychological factors interact with genetic influences to produce the illness (Jamison, 1993) **(Table 4-3)**.

Neurotransmitters

Abnormal functions of the systems that control neurocircuits in the brain—serotonin, dopamine, acetylcholine, norepinephrine, glutamate, and GABA (gamma-aminobutyric acid)—are implicated as causative factors of bipolar illness. To oversimplify a complex theory, the basic hypothesis is that these so-called neurotransmitters (because they regulate the flow of nerve impulses in one nerve cell across a gap in the cells to the adjacent nerve cells) are

TABLE 4-3	
The Genetics of Bipolar Disorder	
EXPOSURE	**RISK**
General population for bipolar I	1%
Bipolar spectrum	4–6%
One parent	15–30%
Both parents	50–75%
Siblings and fraternal twins	15–25%
Identical twins	70%

From "What Role Does Genetics or Family History Play in Bipolar Disorder?" Depression-guide.com. n.d. Retrieved July 22, 2009, from http://www.depression-guide.com/bipolar-disorder-history.htm.

decreased when a person is depressed and increased during a manic episode. Just as depression is thought to be caused by a deficiency of neurotransmitters, mania may be caused by an increase in these chemicals. Some forms of mania may be related to an imbalance of sodium and potassium and other electrolytes in the body.

Modulators, known as *second messengers*, inside the nerve cell—cAMP (cyclic adenosine monophosphate), G protein, and calcium—can influence symptoms of manic-depressive illness. Messenger RNA can also contribute to bipolar illness by regulating genetic expression (Dubovsky et al., 2003).

Psychological Factors

Losses of loved ones, jobs, self-esteem, or prestige can precipitate a depressive episode. A psychoanalytic theory proposes that anger toward a loved one or about a situation can be turned against the self, causing depression; this explanation is a theory of "anger turned inward" (Whybrow, Akiskal, & McKinney, 1984). Unresolved grief, disputes between loved ones, and transitions to a new job or geographical area can also precipitate a depressive episode (Dubovsky et al., 2003). Stress can also produce manic symptoms.

Psychodynamic theory postulates that a desire to avoid mature responsibilities in life produces a manic response, thus allowing the individual to escape into the pleasurable, uninhibited, and expansive aspects of life. A flight into fantasy can act as a defense against inner emotional pain.

Treatment Medications

Medications known as mood stabilizers are used to treat bipolar illness by preventing swings of mood. The best-studied antimanic drug, lithium, treats and prevents manic episodes, reduces bipolar and recurrent depressive episodes, augments antidepressant medications in the treatment of depression, and reduces the risk of suicide in patients with a mood disorder (Stahl, 2005). The usual oral dose range for acute illness is 600 mg three times daily and 300 mg three or four times daily for a maintenance dose (Stahl, 2005). Because lithium takes up to 10 days to work, benzodiazepines for agitation/anxiety and antipsychotics for agitation/psychosis can be used for faster action (Kilgus & Criss, 2009). Haldol 5–10 mg and Ativan 2 mg IM can calm manics less than an hour after injection.

Side effects include a mild tremor, moderate leukocytosis, acne, weight gain, and, in 3% of patients, thyroid goiter. A severe tremor, nausea and vomiting, ataxia, slurred speech, and memory problems generally indicate toxicity (Stahl, 2005). Because toxic blood levels that may begin around 1.5 mEq/L are close to therapeutic levels (0.5–1.2 mEq/L), frequent blood level monitoring becomes essential.

Depakote (valproic acid), a versatile anticonvulsant especially useful for mixed states (patients who simultaneously show signs of depression and mania) and rapid cycling bipolar disorder, can be used to treat mania, agitation/aggression secondary to dementia, irritability/agitation in personality disorders, and mood changes from a closed head injury (Stahl, 2005).

For mania the usual starting dose for extended release Depakote (Depakote ER) = 10 x body weight (a patient weighing 150 pounds would require a starting dose of 1500 mg). If necessary for severe mania, the starting dose may be repeated two times within the first 24 hours of treatment if not precluded by complications. The maximum dose for mania is 30 x body weight within the first 24 hours. Maintenance doses to achieve therapeutic plasma levels (50–100µg/ml) vary widely, often between 750–3000 mg/day. Plasma drug levels up to 125 µg/ml may be required in some acutely manic individuals (Stahl, 2005).

The most common side effects are sedation, tremor, dizziness, ataxia, alopecia, abdominal pain, and heartburn. Depakote ER has fewer gastrointestinal side effects and thus is preferred over immediate release divalproex or generic valproate; Depakote is contraindicated in pancreatitis, liver disease, and thrombocytopenia. The clinician must be alert for symptoms of hepatotoxicity—malaise, lethargy, edema, and jaundice. Depakote can cause pancreatitis marked by acutely severe abdominal pain, vomiting, and anorexia.

Lamictal (lamotrigine), an anticonvulsant, has emerged as a popular medication for treating bipolar depression and maintenance treatment of bipolar disorder, probably because this medication has fewer side effects than the traditional medications used to treat bipolar illness. The usual dose for bipolar disorder, 100–200 mg daily, must be reduced to 100 mg daily when combined with Depakote, and increased to 400 mg daily in combination with enzyme-inducing drugs—Tegretol, Dilantin, phenobarbital, and most antidepressants. To prevent Stevens-Johnson Syndrome the dose must be gradually increase to therapeutic levels: 25 mg daily for two weeks; 50 mg daily for two weeks; 100 mg daily for one week; and, if necessary, 200 mg daily.

Lamictal rarely causes side effects. The most common side effects include a benign rash (found in approximately 10% of patients), sedation, blurred vision, dizziness, ataxia, headache, tremor, and GI symptoms. Lamictal must be stopped immediately if there is a confluent, purpuric, or tender rash with prominent involvement of the neck, eyes, and mouth associated with fever, malaise, or lympadnopathy to prevent multi-organ failure associated with Stevens-Johnson Syndrome (Stahl, 2005).

In reviewing the literature, Licht (1998) found that all antipsychotics have antimanic properties. Treatment of agitation found in acute manic episodes has often required the use of antipsychotic medications, usually delivered intramuscularly. Most of the atypical antipsychotics have been approved for maintenance therapy.

The use of antidepressants alone in bipolar disorder has been discouraged because antidepressants may precipitate manic episodes and contribute to the rapid-cycling mood swings. When treating a depressive episode with antidepressants, a mood stabilizer should be used concurrently to prevent precipitating a manic episode or engendering rapid cycling.

Psychotherapy

Although the melancholic side of bipolar illness, a source of unendurable misery, indolent anguish, heartache, torpor, despondency, decay, and death, may motivate the bipolar patient to seek psychotherapy, the exhilaration of mania discourages it. Manics fear that treatment will transform them into dreary, stale, monotonous, tedious, uninteresting, lackluster, bland, and lifeless bores.

In addition to fearing the loss of euphoria engendered by the elevated mood, the manic fears other losses—loss of perceived power; loss of control; loss of loved ones who have been have been emotionally, verbally, and, perhaps, physically abused; and loss of self-esteem resulting from embarrassing behavior during a manic episode. Identifying these fears will help engage the bipolar patient in therapy.

For bipolar patients, lifestyle changes rarely transpire without irresistible motivation. Usually, a tragedy has to occur: jobs are repeatedly lost, a spouse leaves, or children rebel. Something must happen to cause the bipolar patient to become disgusted. "What have I done to myself and my family?" becomes a signal that the patient is willing to start the process toward health.

Psychotherapy for bipolar illness proves difficult in most cases because manic and hypomanic patients enjoy the exuberance and sense of well-being that the illness produces. Only when manic patients come down from their "highs" can they begin to work in psychotherapy on correcting some of the damaging fallout from a manic episode. Building a therapeutic alliance with the bipolar patient begins with taking into account the severity and consequences of untreated illness.

Traditional therapies include cognitive psychotherapy, which can help patients deal with the remorse engendered by manic behavior and help them reduce the expression of negative emotion. Interpersonal therapy can aid the patient in empathetically treating others more kindly while enhancing sensitivity to the needs of others. Family therapy can improve understanding of the illness and help family members repair emotional wounds inflicted when the patient was manic or hypomanic.

Psychoeducation, as prosaic as episodes of mania are colorful, can be divided into three parts:

- Improving compliance with medications
- Problem solving
- Relapse prevention

While psychoeducation consists of teaching the patient the signs and symptoms of bipolar disorder, the natural course of the illness, treatment outcomes, and potential side effects of the medication, a great deal of time should also be spent educating the patient on the usefulness of medications.

Patients may resist taking medications because they believe that drugs may dampen their zest for living, impede creativity, and diminish energy; to the contrary, medications improve work, learning, and ingenuity by enhancing focus and consistency. Bipolar individuals, who fear being robbed of the grandiosity they experience during the manic state, must be reminded of the pain their omnipotent feelings generate when regrets for their impulsive behavior become manifest following a manic episode.

Noncompliance to medical treatment—forgetting to take medications, misunderstanding instructions, and the inability to make recommended lifestyle changes or ignoring medical advice—looms large in bipolar illness. The main reason for noncompliance is that manics love their emotional highs and do not want them to be taken away. They often say, "I don't want to be a zombie" or "I don't want to be doped up like the rest of those people." They also enjoy the volume of productive work engendered during a manic episode. Clinicians must work hard to educate their bipolar patients on the importance of maintaining their prescription use.

Because side effects of mood stabilizers appear to be directly related to the drug levels of the medication, the lowest possible dose to control mood swings should be used. The typical side effects mandate lowering the dose or stopping the medication. The clinician who lowers the dose of the medication when patients complain of more subjective side effects—indifference, malaise, passivity, and decreased environmental responsiveness—not only enhances the likelihood of patients continuing medication but also builds the therapy alliance so that clinician and patient can work together to find the correct dose that prevents relapse while allowing enthusiasm and initiative to flourish.

Because complex pharmacological jargon intimidates patients, language describing the usefulness of medications must be adjusted to the level of the patient's education and sophistication. Showing respect for the patient improves the clinician–patient relationship, which in turn improves compliance.

Likewise, encouraging the patient to do personal research regarding medication treatment enhances the therapeutic alliance, while preventing mushrooming misconceptions regarding the medication by enabling the clinician to counter misunderstandings of literature twaddle and Internet gabble. Proper interpretation of scientific data augments compliance.

Another subtype of psychoeducation—problem solving—empowers the bipolar patient by discussing ways to cope with the problems of daily living. This includes teaching the patient techniques for stress management and learning to resolve work and social problems. Family therapy is a beneficial venue for educating loved ones who are affected by the patient's bipolar illness.

Relapse prevention helps the patient recognize events and feelings that can trigger a manic episode. Recognizing prodromal symptoms can abort a full-blown manic episode. In addition, prevention of mood cycles includes helping the patient regulate habits. Sleep, hygiene, proper diet, regular exercise, and meditation techniques are emphasized. Ways to avoid substance abuse are discussed. Early warning signs of a manic or depressive episode are identified.

No other psychiatric illness reflects the infinite variety and complexity of life than does bipolar disorder. In treating bipolar illness, the clinician must walk the fine line between detracting from the mind's labyrinthine complexity while strengthening the romance, mystery, and beauty of a life fully lived.

Are You Manic?				
Make Check Mark (✓) in Appropriate Column	Little of the Time 1 point each ✓	Some of the Time 2 points each ✓	A Lot of the Time 3 points each ✓	Most of the Time 4 points each ✓
People can't get me to stop talking.				
I have special powers and talents that may go unrecognized by others.				
I can stay up for days on end without sleep.				
I have so much energy others can't keep up with me.				
My excitement has disrupted my social relationships or my job.				
I can get angry and become irritable easily.				
I spend money freely on investments, projects, or gambling ventures.				
I am much more interested in sex than most people I know.				
I am greatly interested in being around others.				
My thoughts race through my mind, or I become distracted.				
Multiply ✓ by the value given in each column.				

Add the total for each column to get the **Grand total** = _____

SCORING

10–14 points = No way

15–24 points = Energetic, but not manic

25–34 points = Tiresome to others

35–40 points = Over-the-top manic

Are You a High-Energy and Enthusiastic Person?				
Make Check Mark (✓) in Appropriate Column	Little of the Time 1 point each ✓	Some of the Time 2 points each ✓	A Lot of the Time 3 points each ✓	Most of the Time 4 points each ✓
People consider me a chatterbox, and I dominate conversations.				
I feel I have accomplished a lot more than most people I know.				
I don't need as much sleep as others.				
I have an abundance of energy.				
I am optimistic and hopeful.				
I am easily bored and impatient.				
I spend more money than I should and overextend my credit.				
I have a lot of sexual energy.				
I prefer being with others rather than doing things alone.				
My mind seems to fill up with ideas.				
Multiply ✓ by the value given in each column.				

Add the total for each column to get the **Grand total** = _____

SCORING

10–14 points = Turtle

15–24 points = Slow off the blocks

25–34 points = Energetic and engaging

35–40 points = You are hypomanic. Your high energy and bubbly personality may wear most people out. If you see your friends panting, sweating, and flushed, take a deep breath, go to your room, close the door, and read a dull book.

Are You Bipolar?				
Make Check Mark (✓) in Appropriate Column	Little of the Time 1 point each ✓	Some of the Time 2 points each ✓	A Lot of the Time 3 points each ✓	Most of the Time 4 points each ✓
I have episodes of crying and irritability.				
I have episodes of feeling excited and depressed at the same time.				
I have episodes alternating between high and low sexual arousal.				
People have trouble predicting how I will respond to stressful situations.				
My self-confidence ranges from doubt to overconfidence.				
I have tremendous swings in my mood.				
I have times of mental dullness alternating with creative thinking.				
I alternate from pessimism to optimism.				
My work productivity varies tremendously.				
I range from excessively talkative to very quiet.				
Multiply ✓ by the value given in each column.				

Add the total for each column to get the **Grand total** = _____

SCORING

10–14 points = As firm and stable as granite

15–24 points = Everyone enjoys a ride on the back yard tree swing

25–34 points = You are twirling so fast you can't see the tree

35–40 points = The rope broke

A Clinician's Quiz

1. What distinguishes mania from a "good mood?"
2. Give the symptoms of hypomania and discuss how hypomania differs from mania.
3. The symptoms of an elevated mood can be remembered by using the acronym BIPOLAR. What symptom of bipolar illness does each letter represent?
4. Describe the differences between bipolar I disorder and bipolar II disorder.
5. What is a mixed bipolar state?
6. Define cyclothymia.
7. What mood stabilizer has been found to reduce the risk of suicide in patients with a mood disorder?
8. What mood stabilizer has a therapeutic blood level that is close to the toxic level? Give the range for the therapeutic blood level of lithium. Give the blood level that usually borders on a toxic level. In using lithium, what is the best indicator of successful treatment, the blood level or the clinical response? (I know this is a four-part question but I wanted to give you a chance to get extra credit. Give yourself ten points for each correct answer.)
9. What is the most dangerous side effect of Depakote?
10. What is the most dangerous side effect of Lamictal?

CHAPTER 5

Schizophrenia and Other Psychotic Disorders

The Mind Besieged

After my second year of medical school, I spent time as an extern at a state hospital. Every Thursday afternoon, we had grand rounds for presentation of interesting cases or diagnostic dilemmas. We sat in a huge semicircular amphitheater, the seats rising up at an 80-degree angle. We hovered right over the patients, looking down. Our first patient for grand rounds was a middle-aged woman, who told the interviewing doctor that she came to the hospital to get away from the men who kept driving by her house in hopes that they could have sex with her. It became so bad, she said, that she put a sign out on her lawn reading, "My bones are not turning." She said this without any emotion. From that case study, we learned about Eugen Bleuler's (1911) four As of schizophrenia: a flat *affect*—powerful words spoken without sentiment or emotion; loose *associations*—thoughts that were disconnected (how was "bones turning" related to men driving by the house?); *ambivalence*—her complete interview showed that she had some attraction to men despite her apparent disgust for them; and *autism*—social isolation and preoccupation with her own thoughts.

These 4 As—affect, associations, ambivalence, and autism—became widely accepted as the defining criteria of schizophrenia for decades following Bleuler's (1911) publication of his textbook, *Dementia Praecox or the Group of Schizophrenias*. Bleuler, a Swiss psychiatrist, was the first to coin the term *schizophrenia*—the roots of which literally mean "split mind" (not designating split personalities, a common misconception, but instead describing fragmented mental capacities). Bleuler's criteria failed to give a complete picture of the disease, however, and a more precise definition evolved that we see today in the *Diagnostic and Statistical Manual of Mental Disorders, Fourth Edition, Text Revision* (*DSM-IV-TR*; American Psychiatric Association, 2000). Diagnostic criteria for schizophrenia includes delusions, hallucinations, disorganized speech (e.g., frequent derailment or incoherence), grossly disorganized or catatonic behavior, and negative symptoms (such as affective flattening, alogia, and avolition). Other criteria include work, interpersonal relations, or self-care markedly below the level achieved prior to the onset, continuous signs of the disturbance persisting for at least 6 months, and symptoms not due to drug of abuse, medication, or medical condition, including pervasive developmental disorder, schizoaffective disorder, or mood disorder (American Psychiatric Association, 2000).

These criteria can be clearly evidenced in notable examples of schizophrenia, including the case of John Nash (Nasar, 1998). Dr. Nash, an eccentric mathematical genius whose 30-year battle against schizophrenia ended in a career victory—winning the 1994 Nobel Prize in economics—became well known after he was portrayed in the Oscar-winning film *A Beautiful Mind*.

Just after *Fortune* magazine named him America's brilliant young mathematics star, schizophrenia overwhelmed the personal and professional life of Dr. Nash. He began writing bizarre, rambling papers that lacked coherence and were filled with unfathomable cryptograms that he thought would dissuade Russian spies determined to probe his mind for national secrets. In the classroom, he skipped from subject to subject, leaving his students perplexed. He spent hours gazing at magazine articles plastered on his office walls that he was convinced would reveal a pattern spelling out plans for destroying the American government. In 1959, he lost his academic post at the Massachusetts Institute of Technology due to his bizarre behavior. Within months, at age 30, Dr. Nash was committed to McLean Hospital, a psychiatric facility. A series of readmissions followed.

Dr. Nash suffered from fearful paranoid delusions and failed treatments. He wandered around Europe for a while. He spent time in Roanoke, Virginia, near the homes of his mother and sister. Later, he returned to Princeton where he had received his PhD in 1950. The once-rising star became known as the phantom of Fine Hall, a misunderstood figure who babbled about magic numbers and scribbled unintelligible equations on blackboards.

Almost three decades after his illness began, Dr. Nash gradually began to recover. He came out of isolation. He made friends with a few graduate students. He talked to other mathematicians. He learned to use computers for his research. His work on mathematical problems began to make sense. Then came the telephone call from Stockholm. He, with two other pioneers of game theory, had won the Nobel Prize for economics.

Characteristics of Schizophrenia

Schizophrenia, a disabling brain disease of uncertain causation, manifests recognizable symptom clusters with both positive and negative signs. Positive symptoms—hallucinations, delusions, illusions, disordered thinking, and bizarre behavior—signal an excess or distortion of normal functions.

Schizophrenics can have bizarre delusions (e.g., because the moon goddess has taken over the world's car washes, we can't water golf courses). Their thinking becomes scrambled; their speech and ideas disconnected and illogical. Schneiderian first rank symptoms, named from the German psychiatrist who first described them, help confirm the diagnosis of schizophrenia (Kilgus & Noga, 2009):

- Thought broadcast—the schizophrenic's thoughts can be heard by everyone.
- Thought insertion—thoughts are ascribed to other people who put them in the schizophrenic's mind.
- Thought withdrawal—thoughts have been removed from the schizophrenic's mind.
- Third person hallucinations—voices conversing about the schizophrenic, commenting on the schizophrenic's actions, or demanding actions (command hallucinations).
- Delusional perceptions—falsely attributing a bizarre meaning to a common perception (A honking horn indicates the world is being taken over by ants).

Visual and olfactory hallucinations, rare in schizophrenics, more commonly denote dementia, delirium, or general medical conditions. Tactile hallucinations associated with delusions (e.g., bugs crawling on the skin prove that the devil is breaking the patient's bones) signify schizophrenia, whereas non-delusion tactic hallucinations more commonly reflect delirium.

Negative symptoms reflect a loss of normal mental functioning. A flat affect—a constriction of feeling tone, a restricted emotional expression, a loss of spirit, a lack of empathy—bestows an impenetrable coldness on the schizophrenic that is almost always diagnostic of the illness. With signs, confidence in the diagnosis rises; without them, the diagnosis becomes less certain. Poverty of speech, poor social skills, lack of pleasure, paucity of thought, loss of motivation, poor grooming, and neglect of hygiene are other negative symptoms of schizophrenia. Most of these negative symptoms can be remembered by using the so-called "5-As" mnemonic (Stahl, 2008):

- Alogia—restrictions in thought and speech
- Affective flattening—emotional restrictions
- Asociality—reduced social drive

- Avolition—reduced motivation
- Anhedonia—lack of pleasure

Patterns of Schizophrenia
- A constricted, flat, hollow-eyed expression. When you attempt to interact with a schizophrenic, an emotional connection fails to exist. You feel as if you are looking into a bottomless pit. Schizophrenics seem to look beyond you—they just are not "there."
- Social isolation. Schizophrenics detach themselves from others. They have no friends, no shared interests, and no recreational pursuits.
- Bizarre speech patterns. Schizophrenics often give monosyllabic responses to questions, or they may go on tangential, disconnected, and fragmented rambles that are difficult to comprehend. Their conversation just does not make much sense.

Schizophrenia usually begins just as young adults are learning to become independent and productive. Because the illness typically strikes people when they are between the ages of 17 and 28, relatively few celebrated people have been diagnosed with schizophrenia. There are a handful of well-known exceptions. Nijinsky, the Russian dancer, made his mark as a genius before the disease struck. Meera Popkin, known for her entrancing performances in Andrew Lloyd Weber's *Cats, Starlight Express,* and *Miss Saigon,* went from a show-stopping star to a Wendy's french-fry cook until small doses of Haldol and supportive psychotherapy returned her to the stage (Schizophrenia.com, 2009).

For a significant group, medications, compassion, and receptivity allow the schizophrenic to become independent again. Some return to work, cultivate friendships, and marry. Occasionally, a remarkable remission occurs. Often, though, treatment is ineffective. Even with the best of medications, most schizophrenics almost never return to their previous level of function.

We see her every 2 or 3 months on our hospital unit. Gayleen enters filthy, foul breathed, and malodorous, her hair disheveled and lice-eaten. Until we can give her an antipsychotic injection, she scratches and tries to bite the nurses. The aides spend hours bathing and scrubbing her, while all the time she babbles incoherently. Within a few days, she is cooperative and docile, but she tends to isolate herself and speaks in monosyllables. Our short-term unit lacks the capacity to keep Gayleen more than a week or so. The state hospital refuses to take her because their beds are filled, and they have a long waiting list. Her family abandoned her long ago. Public housing is scarce. We finally get her a place in a shelter. Outside the hospital, Gayleen refuses to take her medications. She never keeps her appointments with the community mental health center. The clinic is too overwhelmed to give her the attention she requires. Within a few days, she wanders away from the shelter and begins sleeping on park benches or, when it's raining, under bridges.

Causes of Schizophrenia

Like diabetes, heart disease, and thyroid illness, schizophrenia is a biological disorder caused by a combination of contributing risk factors, including genetic predisposition. Biological, environmental, and psychological elements all play a role, but the exact cause of the disease remains unknown.

Autopsies, genetic studies, and technology that permits pictures of the living brain cause scientists to believe that schizophrenia results from impaired circuit functioning in several regions of the brain. While the exact reason remains a mystery, the illness seems to be linked to certain chemicals in the brain. When these chemicals are out of balance, schizophrenic symptoms emerge.

Techniques for Measuring Brain Activity

- **Computed tomography (CT scan)** presents a major advance from the flat, two-dimensional X-ray. CT scanners produce a series of successive pictures taken as the patient, lying down, moves through a scanning ring. Schizophrenic patients have larger fluid-filled spaces (ventricles) than normal individuals, indicating that schizophrenics may have less brain tissue for performing cognitive functions.
- **Magnetic resonance imaging (MRI)** measures the changes in the body's natural magnetic field as patients are exposed to various radio frequencies. A computer can compile a three-dimensional view of the brain, making the smallest brain structures visible. MRI images have shown that schizophrenics have smaller brains than those without the illness. They also have smaller frontal lobes, the section of the brain responsible for decision making, learning, and emotional control.
- **Positive emission tomography (PET)** uses radioactive tracers to give a picture of the brain in action. Brain regions of schizophrenics communicate poorly with one another.
- **Functional magnetic resonance (fMR)** monitors changes in brain oxygen consumption. Schizophrenic patients activate the same regions of the brain as normal subjects but with less blood flow and less intensity.
- **Magnetoencephalography (MEG)** measures nerve cell firing by detecting magnetic signals in brain neurons. Schizophrenic brains activate more slowly than normal brains.

Scientists also believe genetic factors play a role. While 1% of the general population has schizophrenia, 10% of those with a close family relative who has the disease will develop the illness. Although schizophrenics seem to have a genetic vulnerability for the illness, people do not acquire schizophrenia directly, like they inherit the color of their eyes or hair. Because brain structure and biochemistry change dramatically in teen and young adult years, schizophrenia appears to lie dormant during childhood. As the brain develops, schizophrenic symptoms begin to appear, subtly at first. A full-blown psychotic breakdown erupts when the stresses of young adulthood become less manageable (National Institute of Mental Health, 1999).

Some scientists believe that one gene may be responsible for triggering schizophrenia; others put their chips on the multiple-gene card. Family and twin studies militated against genetic factors as the lone cause of schizophrenia. In studies of identical twins, if one sibling had schizophrenia, the other identical twin developed the disorder only half of the time (Torrey, 2001).

Scientists continue to look for the particular genetic combination that produces schizophrenia. Genetically determined factors could interrupt the response of the brain to sensory information (National Institute of Mental Health, 1999). Perhaps schizophrenics, for genetic reasons, fail to produce a certain enzyme or other biochemical. Possibly, specific nerves fail to develop correctly. Nobody knows for sure.

A viral infection, in combination with genetics and an autoimmune response, may cause schizophrenia. Following a viral infection, activated abnormal genes may influence the body's immune system to attack brain function. Some scientists suspect that schizophrenia could be an autoimmune disease—a disease caused by the body's immune system attacking itself (National Institute of Mental Health, 1999).

We do know that genetic mutations may trigger abnormal levels of certain neurotransmitters in schizophrenics. Successful use of antipsychotic medications implicates the neurotransmitter dopamine as a contributing factor in schizophrenic symptoms. Antipsychotics reduce the brain's response to dopamine, indicating that schizophrenic patients produce an excessive amount of dopamine. Perhaps the brains of schizophrenics are extraordinarily sensitive to dopamine (Gottesman, 1999).

Almost certainly, a combination of factors contributes to the development of schizophrenia. A genetic predisposition, prenatal complications, viral infections, childhood emotional conflicts, sexual or physical abuse, an unsupportive home environment, drug use, poverty, and environmental stressors form a constellation of features that all contribute to the development of schizophrenia. These negative stressors can be moderated by protective factors—academic or athletic success, financial blessings, an emotionally sustaining childhood, and emotional support from friends and family, to name a few (Torrey, 2001).

Types of Schizophrenia

Particular schizophrenia types designating the most recent evaluation may change over time (American Psychiatric Association, 2000). Differentiation of the following types of schizophrenia is discussed next: catatonic, disorganized, paranoid, residual, and undifferentiated.

Catatonic Schizophrenia

A relatively rare condition, catatonia is characterized by excessive purposeless activity, mutism, bizarre posturing, or statue-like stupors. An intramuscular injection of a benzodiazepine rapidly clears the psychomotor disturbances. Prior to modern antipsychotic medications, these bizarre postures may have lasted days or weeks.

> A patient with chronic schizophrenia was found sitting on the floor of his room with his legs folded underneath his body, his left arm akimbo, and his right arm extended at a 90-degree angle from his torso. Mute and rigid, he made no eye contact. He resisted movement in proportion to the force applied by the psychiatrist (gegenhalten—"counterhold"). Within 30 minutes, an intramuscular injection of 5 mg Haldol and 2 mg Lorazepam relieved all of the patient's symptoms.

The Disorganized Type

The disorganized type of schizophrenia, characterized by silly, inappropriate behavior, neglect of personal habits, and odd grimacing, reflects a regressed, childlike orientation.

> A formerly quiet and rather socially withdrawn student began to show bizarre behavior on entering college. He would interrupt classes with inappropriate laughter and gesturing. His roommate noticed him standing before the mirror for hours posturing and grimacing. On hospital admission, the patient was incoherent and excited. The next day, he stared vacantly at the floor, at times breaking into a silly giggle.

Paranoid Schizophrenia

Paranoid schizophrenia is typified by delusions of persecution associated with signs and symptoms of schizophrenia. Occasionally, paranoid schizophrenia presents in the fourth decade of life.

A 36-year-old college graduate became convinced that people thought he was a homosexual, and he felt that the club members where he worked as a tennis instructor were mocking him. He began going to church regularly and began praying and reading the Bible continuously. Soon, he started preaching to the club members about the sin of persecution. He believed he was being persecuted just like Jesus. In an attempt to gain spiritual purity, he decided to blind himself by dipping his head into a bucket of Lysol.

Residual Schizophrenia

Individuals with residual schizophrenia include those patients who have a history of a schizophrenic episode but whose clinical picture fails to show prominent psychotic symptoms in the present. Certain signs of schizophrenia persist, such as emotional blunting, social withdrawal, and a mild communication disorder.

An unmarried woman had suffered an acute catatonic episode when she was 24 years old. At that time, she entered the hospital, babbling incoherently and imitating the actions and words of the psychiatrist. She responded to high doses of antipsychotics. The patient has been free of prominent psychotic symptoms for almost 8 years, although she seldom leaves her home except to shop for groceries with her mother. She never smiles and only occasionally speaks. Her behavior is regarded as "strange" by her neighbors.

Undifferentiated Schizophrenia

The undifferentiated subtype includes all those schizophrenic patients who fail to meet the diagnostic criteria for the other schizophrenic subtypes.

A sullen and shiftless 48-year-old unmarried man spent most of his days wandering the streets. Frequently, he would stand on the street corner yelling, "My name is Smithy, and I'm looking for trouble." His attorney, whose office was on the 14th floor of a downtown office building, reported that on a clear, windless day, he could hear the patient shouting on the streets below. Occasionally, the patient would enter the bank where he received money from a family trust fund and would shout obscenities. The clerks and tellers, accustomed to his behavior, never looked up from their work. The patient would report hearing voices calling him "bad names" and occasionally would put a sign in front of his house that stated, "This house is free of sin." The patient was tolerated by the community as a harmless crank and was regarded as somewhat of a local landmark.

Illnesses Confused With Schizophrenia

Although schizophrenia has well defined signs and symptoms, differentiating schizophrnia from other illnesses sometimes challenges both the neophyte and the most skilled clinician. Bipolar disorder, schizoaffective disorder, delusional disorder, and brief psychotic disorder are the illnesses most commonly confused with schizophrenia, and are discussed next.

Bipolar Illness

Although schizophrenics have distinct signs and symptoms, schizophrenia can be confused with bipolar illness, the disease that afflicted Vincent Van Gogh, Charles Dickens, Beethoven, and a host of other geniuses (Jamison, 1994). Bipolar illness, primarily a disorder of mood rather than of thinking, typically arrives later in life. Blessed with a high level of energy and active minds, manic-depressives often hold high-level jobs and are astoundingly creative between episodes. Bipolar disorder is discussed in Chapter 4.

Schizoaffective Disorder

People with schizoaffective disorder have symptoms of a thought disorder like schizophrenia and symptoms of a mood disorder like bipolar illness. Many persons with a diagnosis of schizoaffective disorder have had, at a prior time, inaccurate diagnoses of either of these two illnesses. Frequently, this previous diagnosis is revised to schizoaffective disorder when it becomes clear, over time, that the person has sometimes experienced manic or depressive symptoms without psychotic symptoms while on other occasions has experienced hallucinations or delusions when the mood is neither depressed nor elevated. The diagnosis is easier to corroborate when schizoaffective disorder presents with schizophrenic-type symptoms and mood symptoms at the same time.

> A 27-year-old physics graduate believed he had powers that connected him to the Milky Way Galaxy through spider webs because the webs of spiders were sticky like spilled milk. This discovery thrilled him so much that he spent days and nights trying to contact journal editors to let him write an article about his theories. He talked incessantly about his grandiose ideas. His mood was exuberant and his enthusiasm contagious, although his theories were plainly psychotic. His rapid-fire staccato speech and laughter were characteristic of mania, while his disconnected thoughts resembled the loose associations of a schizophrenic as he described his discovery: "The first time I swung from the moon to mars with silk spinning spinnerets from little Miss Muffett who sat on a tuffet made from cream and whey, which is why I was way-far out right not way out wrong but write a letter to the dean."

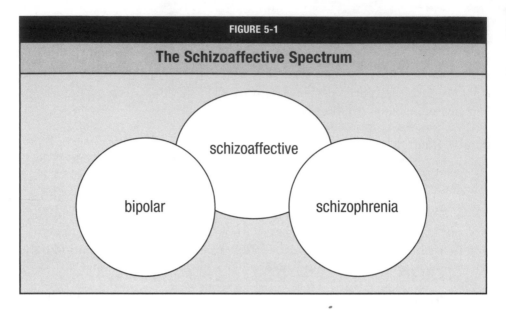

FIGURE 5-1

The Schizoaffective Spectrum

schizoaffective

bipolar

schizophrenia

Schizoaffective disorder is a fascinating disease. It may be best to consider these psychotic disorders as part of a spectrum, with schizoaffective disorder in the middle of the spectrum, bipolar disorder on one end, and schizophrenia on the other end. A history of bipolar illness in the families of schizoaffectives and a better outcome for schizoaffective disorder than schizophrenia indicate that schizoaffective disorder is more a disorder of mood than a form of schizophrenia. On the other hand, better response to antipsychotic medication than to mood stabilizers make schizoaffective disorder seem more like schizophrenia than a mood disorder **(Figure 5-1)**.

Delusional Disorder
In contrast to the offbeat delusions of schizophrenics, those with a delusional disorder have false beliefs that are not bizarre and, to the uninitiated, could be considered plausible. There are several types of delusions (American Psychiatric Association, 2000):

- The erotomanic—the delusion that another person is in love with the delusional person
- Jealous type—the belief that a spouse or lover is unfaithful
- Persecutory type—the belief of being conspired against
- Grandiose type—the conviction of having a great, but unrecognized, talent

Don Juan DeMarco, one of the most delightful overlooked romantic comedies of all time, depicts a delusional disorder better than any case history. In the film, a young man (Johnny Depp) believes he is the legendary Don Juan.

He comes to New York in search of his lost love. The psychiatrist (Marlon Brando) assigned to treat him begins to believe the young man's story of love won and romance lost. Written by Jeremy Levin, a psychologist trained at Yale Medical School, the witty dialogue shows how closely a delusion can mimic reality when the patient, Don Juan DeMarco, met, for the first time, the psychiatrist in his office:

"Women react to me the way that they do, Don Octavio, because they sense that I search out the beauty that dwells within until it overwhelms everything else. And then they cannot avoid their desire, to release that beauty and envelop me in it. So, to answer your question, I see as clear as day that this great edifice in which we find ourselves is your villa. It is your home. And as for you, Don Octavio DeFlores, you are a great lover like me, even though you may have lost your way . . . and your accent."

Brief Psychotic Disorder

Stress can cause a brief psychotic disorder characterized by delusions, hallucinations, disorganized speech, and bizarre behavior that closely mimics schizophrenia. The difference is that schizophrenia is a lifelong illness, while a brief psychotic disorder lasts for only a few days.

A 23-year-old college senior, who had recently failed to get into medical school and whose girlfriend had recently left him, became convinced that his former lover had conspired with his premed advisor to poison him. He barricaded himself in his apartment and called the local newspaper to tell the editor that he would continue his hunger strike until his girlfriend confessed her "dastardly deeds" or he died of thirst, whichever came first. He initially repelled the mental health workers who came to help him by throwing water balloons on them from his third-floor apartment, yelling, "Drink the vile poison from a false lover and die." Committed to the psychiatric ward, the patient returned to normal behavior following a few days of antipsychotic medication.

Treatment of Schizophrenia

The current treatment methods discussed next and based on both clinical research and experience reduce the symptoms of schizophrenia and lessen the chances that symptoms will return.

Medications

When the antihistamine Thorazine (chlorpromazine) was discovered to be effective for schizophrenics in 1952, the back wards of mental institutions were emptied of their schizophrenic patients. The fierce lion of psychiatry had been tamed. All but the sickest of the sick recovered and were discharged. Thorazine morphed into Mellaril and Mellaril into Stelazine and Stelazine into Haldol. But, these medicines had side effects: terrible motor problems. Muscles would stiffen and twitch. Tongues would protrude and writhe, snake-like. Eyeballs would roll back into the head.

A second wave of inpatient releases came with the development of Clozaril (clozapine) in 1989. This medication released the most uncontrollable of patients but caused drooling and massive weight gain. Blood samples had to be taken weekly to make certain that the bone marrow continued to produce blood cells. Clozaril gave way to Risperdal (1993), then along came Zyprexa (1996), Seroquel (1997), Geodon (2001), and Abilify (2002), medications that had less-debilitating side effects, but side effects nonetheless. Because these medications were newer, they cost more—a lot more. The back wards had emptied, but the sidewalks had filled up with schizophrenics who failed to take their medications regularly and refused to comply with aftercare. Medicine was an improvement, but it was no cure-all.

The precept that patients respond better to recently developed drugs than to more established ones generates the dictum: "Hurry, use the new drug before it stops working." The introduction of an innovative drug often engenders self-fulfilling high expectations. Over time, as adverse side effects and limitations become apparent, the medication's popularity wanes. Ironically, a U.S. study involving 1,460 patients confirmed that newer drugs might be less desirable than the older medications (Lieberman et al., 2005). A British study using clinical and economic data compared the cost difference between atypical and conventional antipsychotics in routine practice. The research team found that conventional antipsychotics had lower costs and higher quality adjusted life-years than atypical antipsychotics. The study indicated that conventional antipsychotics were more than 50% likely to be cost-effective and their use resulted in an improved quality of life when compared with atypical antipsychotics (Davies, et al., 2007).

When choosing an antipsychotic medication, the cost–benefit ratio and the side effect profile must be considered. The most severe side effect of the older antipsychotics, tardive dyskinesia, characterized by buccal-facial masticatory movements, can occur in about 8% of patients. The newer antipsychotics can cause massive weight gain, diabetes mellitus, hyperlipidemia, and metabolic syndrome. These side effect profiles force the clinician and the informed patient to make difficult choices **(Table 5-1)**.

The vast majority of people with schizophrenia show substantial improvement when treated with antipsychotic drugs. Some patients, however, fail to benefit from medications. Response is unpredictable. Side effects still prevail. Treatment of schizophrenia must consist of more than adjusting brain chemistry.

Evidence-Based Psychotherapy for Schizophrenia

Because of the overall success of antipsychotic medications (side effects notwithstanding), few psychiatrists venture into psychotherapy—it is too time consuming; psychiatrists are too scarce. Psychoanalysis has given way to "med checks." Common treatment for schizophrenia centers on antipsychotic medications and case management. Psychotherapy for schizophrenia is virtually nonexistent except in some academic medical centers where research supports the idea that certain types of psychotherapy may be beneficial in the treatment of schizophrenia. Interpersonal therapy (IPT), compliance therapy, acceptance and commitment therapy (ACT), and supportive therapy show some promise (Dickerson & Lehman, 2006).

Interpersonal Therapy

Interpersonal therapy focuses on the ability to adapt to stressors of the illness, communication skills, and getting along with other people. When compared with family therapy and supportive therapy, no significant differences were shown in returning to hospitals, but those who received IPT showed improved social skills and a decrease in negative symptoms (Dickerson & Lehman, 2006).

Compliance Therapy

The main goal of compliance therapy is getting the patient to continue taking medication following discharge from the hospital. Compliance therapy does not seem to work very well. One study showed that 18% of patients never filled their prescriptions (Kripalani et al., 2006). Between 30% and 40% were noncompliant at any given time, and 2 years following hospitalization, 75% of schizophrenics had stopped taking their medications for 1 week or longer (Ho, Black, & Andreason, 2003). Injections of long-acting medications such as Haldol Decanoate or Risperdal Consta work better than compliance psychotherapy.

Acceptance and Commitment Therapy

Acceptance and commitment therapy eliminates stress associated with delusions or hallucinations by encouraging the patient to become aware of his or her delusions and hallucinations while not acting on them. The stress of acting on the instructions of delusions and hallucinations can add to the increase of perceptual abnormalities. Two small research studies have shown that ACT lowers the rates for relapse and the return to hospitalization (Dickerson & Lehman, 2006).

Supportive Therapy

Supportive therapy helps schizophrenics deal with their disorder with reas-

TABLE 5-1

Cost of Antipsychotics
(Derived July 2009 in U.S. Dollars)

MEDICATION	RETAIL COST FOR *ONE* PILL OR *ONE* INJECTION
Newer, unconventional antipsychotics	
Risperdal	0.25 mg = $4.15 1 mg = $5.33 3 mg = $10.62 Risperdal Consta 25-mg injection = $307.28
Geodon	Geodon 40-mg oral = $6.62 Geodon 20-mg injection = $14.49
Zyprexa	2.5 mg = $7.55 10 mg = $13.75 15 mg = $19.60
Seroquel	25 mg = $2.55 100 mg = $4.56 300 mg = $11.06
Abilify	15 mg = $14.01
Older, traditional antipsychotics	
Haldol	5-mg oral = $0.28 5-mg injection = $7.49 Haldol Decanoate 50 mg = $18.50
Stelazine	1 mg = $0.43 5 mg = $0.58
Thorazine	100 mg = $0.27

Data collected by Stephen Ingram, RPh, BCPP, Clinical Pharmacy Specialist in Psychiatry, July 2009.

surance, clarifications, and general assistance. Supportive therapy seems to have the best outcome (Dickerson & Lehman, 2006).

Cognitive-Behavior Therapy
Cognitive-behavior therapy focuses on the implementation of natural coping strategies. Rather than cure the illness, CBT helps patients develop rational

thoughts and perspectives about their delusions and hallucinations. Schizo-phrenics have shown significant and long-standing improvements in positive symptoms (delusions and hallucinations), but no significant improvements were found with social functioning (Ho et al., 2003). The main problem is the same for medications: noncompliance and dropout rates.

A combination of illness education, cognitive therapy to change beliefs about delusions and hallucinations, social skills training, and emotional sup-port accompanied with compliance to medication regimes provides the best treatment for schizophrenia (Dickerson & Lehman, 2006).

Treatment Outcomes

Loosely constructed research and empirical findings led investigators to describe a rule of thirds: Approximately one third of schizophrenics live rel-atively normal lives; one third can function in society despite significant symptoms; and recalcitrant symptoms leave one third terribly impaired. Approximately 10% of the most severely impaired require long-term institu-tional care (Sadock & Sadock, 2005). Features associated with a good prog nosis include the following (Andreasen & Black, 2006):

- Onset of the illness occurs in the late 20s to 30s.
- The illness comes on acutely.
- Mood symptoms are present.
- Psychotic or negative symptoms are mild to moderate.
- There was good premorbid functioning.
- The individual is married.
- The individual has a high intelligence level.
- There is no family history of schizophrenia.

With medications, the majority of schizophrenics can become symptom free in a few months, but over half of these individuals will have one or more relapses sometime during their lifetime (National Institute of Mental Health, 1999). Those who remain on medication and visit a psychiatrist regularly have a much greater chance of remaining symptom free than those patients who fail to take their medication and irregularly visit their physicians.

At the conclusion of the film *A Beautiful Mind*, the screenwriter wrote the following lines for Dr. Nash (Russell Crowe) to speak at his Nobel Prize acceptance speech:

What truly is logic? Who decides reason? My quest has taken me to the physical, the metaphysical, the delusional, and back. I have made the most important discovery of my career—the most important discovery of my life. It is only in the mysterious equations of love that any logic or reason can be found.

Are You Confidant and Personable?

Make Check Mark (✓) in Appropriate Column	Little of the Time 1 point each ✓	Some of the Time 2 points each ✓	A Lot of the Time 3 points each ✓	Most of the Time 4 points each ✓
I feel others control my thoughts and emotions.				
I hear and see things that others say they do not hear and see.				
I have a difficult time expressing myself in ways that others can understand.				
I feel I have nothing in common with others.				
I don't know whether what I'm thinking is real or not.				
I have magical powers that I can't explain.				
I feel others are plotting against me.				
I talk to other people inside my head that no one can hear.				
I feel that my thoughts are broadcast to others on a loudspeaker.				
I get special messages from the radio or TV.				
Multiply ✓ by the value given in each column.				

Add the total for each column to get the **Grand total** = _____

SCORING

10–14 points = You get along well with others

15–24 points = Some people may think you are a little different

25–34 points = You may have problems in social situations

35–40 points = You have a great deal of difficulty relating to others

Complete Mental Health

A Clinician's Quiz

1. Define and describe the positive symptoms of schizophrenia.
2. Define and describe the negative symptoms of schizophrenia.
3. Name five factors that contribute to the development of schizophrenia.
4. Name the five types of schizophrenia and give the predominant symptoms of each.
5. Name four illnesses that can be confused with schizophrenia and give the differentiating symptoms of each.
6. Give four types of delusional disorders.
7. What was the first antipsychotic discovered, and when was it discovered?
8. Treatment with Clozaril, a breakthrough medication, allowed thousands of patients to be released from hospitals. Give three side effects that limited its use.
9. When choosing an antipsychotic medication the _____ and the _____ must be considered.
10. Research into psychotherapy shows that medications in combination with five therapeutic approaches provide the best outcome for schizophrenia. Name those five treatment approaches.

CHAPTER 6

Anxiety and Related Disorders

Freeze-Frame

D r. Leonard Coleman began shaping my life when I was just a teenager. One of the last of a dying breed of true rural Texas doctors, Dr. Coleman had medicine flowing through his veins: Doctors rested on every branch of his family tree. He passed on his love of medicine by mentoring dozens of young physicians. When I was only 17, my uncle, one of Dr. Coleman's best friends, told him I dreamed of being a doctor myself someday. A few weeks later, just after midnight, my uncle awakened me. "Dr. Coleman called. There has been a terrible accident, and a man is badly hurt. Do you want to help in surgery?"

Contemplate a time unburdened by paperwork; a time free of medical malpractice suits; a time when physicians, not the government or insurance companies, determined what was best for the patient; a time when a good medical history and physical examination preempted diagnostic tests. The era you have just imagined had no pagers, no cell phones, no fax machines, no computers, no copiers—and no highway patrol with radar guns. The roads were narrow and poorly marked. The cars had no seat belts. Under this veil of simplicity, a middle-aged man, taking a curve in a country road too fast, was thrown from his car. A telephone pole turned him into a wishbone. He entered the operating room with a ripped pelvis, two fractured hips, a ruptured spleen, and assorted other injuries considered major on an ordinary Saturday night.

That man's misadventure introduced me to the mystery, majesty, and magic of surgery. Adrenaline flowing, the urgency of the moment took over and blinded me to the blood and gore. Dr. Coleman's unwarranted but complete trust in my ability to serve him gave me the confidence to plunge right in, literally, bloodying my protective gloves as I held the retractors and snipped sutures during the surgery. After that experience, I worked as Dr. Coleman's surgical assistant for four summers. In addition to the routine appendectomy, gall bladder, and bowel surgeries, we also repaired abdominal aneurisms and patched those gored by bulls, thrown from horses, flipped by tractors, bit by mules, and hit over the head with beer bottles. By the time I enrolled in medical school, I had seen and done more than a first-year surgical resident.

That is why my panic attack seemed so odd. I was interviewing at Baylor College of Medicine (BCM) for a position in the upcoming first-year class. When I arrived at the initial group screening, held in a huge auditorium on the Houston campus of BCM, all the other candidates looked smarter and more sophisticated. On the first evening of the interview process, Baylor, quite proud of their cardiac surgery department, showed a film of their star pioneers, Dr. Denton Cooley and Dr. Michael DeBakey, performing some of their innovative procedures. Although I had taken an active part in numerous bloody and traumatic procedures in both the emergency department and the surgical suite, I became concerned. "What if I faint or vomit?" I asked myself. As the film continued, my fear about becoming nauseated grew. I looked to my right and to my left. Fate had positioned me in the exact middle of a row, surrounded by seven or eight rows crowded with candidates. If I got up to leave, everyone would notice and think that I couldn't tolerate seeing blood, I thought. Nausea began to build. I began to sweat. I put my head down and tried not to think about where I was. My pulse began to race, faster and faster, as I had a difficult time getting air, and my heart pounded so loudly I thought the people sitting next to me could hear it. I thought I was going to pass out . . . or worse, die. A cold, unremitting fear came over me. When the film ended, I was saturated with sweat but happy to be alive. I didn't get into Baylor Medical School. I was right; they were all smarter than me . . . and calmer. I was, however, accepted at the University of Texas Medical Branch in Galveston; thankfully, they showed no film. I never had a panic attack again, but to this day, I always sit on the outside seat whenever I attend movies, meetings, or conferences. Anxiety is a peculiar symptom. It can come on anytime, and the horror of the experience can last a lifetime.

The Physiology of Anxiety

When we become anxious, from either an actual physical threat or a perceived threat, the nerve cells in the brain's hypothalamus send hormonal signals to the pituitary gland, causing the release of ACTH (adrenocorticotropic hormone) into the bloodstream, stimulating the adrenal glands to release the hormone adrenaline. Adrenaline increases alertness, speeds reaction time, improves perception, and increases the pulse rate and blood pressure. This "fight-or-flight" (Cannon, 1929) mechanism is beneficial when we become threatened by impending danger, but it is disabling when caused by psychological problems.

While fear is the unpleasant response to a valid external threat, anxiety is a painful reaction to an internal conflict. Fear persists only as long as the danger lasts; anxiety lingers to produce physical and emotional symptoms. Emotional stress produces the same physiological effects as fear, but with disastrous results. Tremors, nervous tics, choking sensations, and breathlessness become evident. Chronic anxiety causes a disruption in the skeletal, gastrointestinal, and cardiovascular systems. Fatigue, generalized weakness, and loss of energy develop (Selye, 1956).

Causes of Anxiety

Anxiety develops from a combination of factors—stress, childhood conflicts, genetics, and faulty learning. Our response to environmental conditions varies widely depending on cultural, family, and personal experiences. An unanticipated traumatic event such as a near accident can elicit physiologic effects of anxiety. The anticipation of a stressful event often provokes more anxiety than the event itself; for example, stomach cramps and nausea before school exams or rapid pulse and sweating before a job interview. Even the absence of stress is a cause of anxiety: Experimental volunteers subjected to extreme environmental deprivation developed anxious symptoms (Lilly, 1977). Because of our enormous adaptive capacity, most of us adjust to the everyday stress of living, but once problems escalate faster than they can be solved, clinical anxiety results.

Emotional conflicts that cause anxiety may be out of our awareness, leaving us with a vague uncomfortable feeling of dread. A variety of emotional conflicts may produce anxiety (Seligman, Walker, & Rosenhan, 2001). The fear of losing love, affection, and support can produce anxiety. For example, a grown woman may be getting adequate love and attention, but because she was deprived of love in childhood, she may fear that adult affection will similarly be withdrawn. This fear of abandonment becomes severe when she is unable to recognize and deal with the cause. Some people harbor resentment and anger based on past conflicts. A fear of losing control of these aggressive impulses produces the symptoms of chronic anxiety. The fear of losing control of sexual impulses can also contribute to anxiety. Others associate success with aggression and may develop the fear of succeeding. The fear of retaliation for perceived aggression generates an unwanted success anxiety.

On the other hand, some patients fear failure, especially those who put undue pressure on themselves that may have generated from harsh parental expectations. Fear of transgressing moral and ethical values can produce anxiety. An inappropriate, unrealistic anxiety response is often a manifestation of learned habits. An individual who has lived through a hotel fire may never want to sleep in a hotel again; a child who has a particularly harsh and critical teacher may learn to fear all authority figures. Soldiers returning from a war may fall to the ground whenever they hear a loud noise that reminds them of combat sounds.

Types of Anxiety Disorders

Anxiety often coexists with other medical conditions, especially depression, and plays a large part in the development of psychosomatic illnesses, conversion disorders, and somatoform disorders. There exists a high comorbidity with substance abuse. With 16% of the population suffering from generalized anxiety disorder (GAD), panic disorder, social anxiety, phobias, obsessive-compulsive disorder (OCD), post-traumatic stress syndrome, and dissociative disorders, anxiety ranks as the most common psychiatric disorder (U.S. Department of Health and Human Services, 1999) **(Table 6-1)**.

TABLE 6-1	
One-Year Prevalence of Anxiety Disorders, Ages 18–54	
Any anxiety disorder	16.4%
Simple phobia	8.3%
Social phobia	8.3%
Agoraphobia	4.9%
Generalized anxiety disorder	3.4%
Panic disorder	1.6%
Obsessive-compulsive disorder	2.4%
Post-traumatic stress disorder	3.6%

From "Mental Health: A Report of the Surgeon General—Anxiety Disorders," by the U.S. Department of Health and Human Services, 1999, U.S. Department of Health and Human Services, Substance Abuse and Mental Health Services Administration, Center for Mental Health Services, National Institutes of Health, National Institute of Mental Health, Rockville, MD, retrieved July 24, 2009, from http://www.surgeongeneral.gov/library/mentalhealth/home.html.

Generalized Anxiety Disorder

A 36-year old female presented to the walk-in clinic complaining of fatigue, headaches, muscle tension and aches, difficulty swallowing, trembling, twitching, sweating, and hot flashes. She said she knew something bad was going to happen; her husband might lose his job, she said, or the kids might flunk out of school, or a tornado might come blowing through like it did yesterday in Tulsa. The worry list went on and on. "Am I having a nervous breakdown?" she asked.

People with GAD misperceive events, magnify difficulties, and make pessimistic assumptions on little evidence (National Institute of Mental Health, 2007). Overly attentive to anything that seems threatening, they have an energy-sapping feeling of unease. Insomniacs keep themselves awake worrying about whether they are getting enough sleep. Senior citizens worry so much about losing their memory that they do not have time to keep their minds productively active. An astrophysicist with GAD could think of a lot to worry about: What if the universe is shrinking instead of expanding? What's going to happen 10,000 billion years from now when the sun stops giving heat? This is not to mention the threat of being sucked into a black hole where molasses is faster than light.

Substance abuse, a frequent complication of GAD, develops when patients use alcohol or drugs to restrain their symptoms (Andreasen & Black, 2006). Many patients with GAD have other anxiety disorders.

Due to the chronic nature of the illness, GAD may overlap with major depression. In these cases, sanguine psychiatrists make the diagnosis of "mixed anxiety-depression disorder" (American Psychiatric Association, 2000). (Anxious psychiatrists simply worry that they have made the wrong diagnosis.) Whether a mixed anxiety-depression or generalized anxiety, antidepressants are some of the most effective treatments for anxiety syndromes, generalized anxiety in particular **(Table 6-2)**.

Panic Disorder

Mildred, at home reading a book, began to feel tightness in her chest; she began to sweat and hyperventilate. With every heartbeat, she felt increasingly ill. She was convinced she was going to die. Feeling faint and terrified, she somehow made it to her phone to call 911. A thorough physical examination and reassurance by the emergency room physician failed to prevent subsequent attacks. These panic attacks were predictably irregular. Sometimes, they would occur when she was cooking. At other times, she was playing bridge or working in the garden. She estimated that she had three or four, maybe five, attacks a week.

TABLE 6-2

Medications for Generalized Anxiety Disorder

MEDICATION	COMMENTS	SIDE EFFECTS
Benzodiazepines— Xanax (alprazolam, Klonopin (clonazepam) Ativan (lorazepam) Librium (chlordiazepoxide), Valium (diazepam)	Use for the short term while a non-dependence-inducing therapeutic program is implemented	Sedation, dizziness, weakness, ataxia, anterograde amnesia; deaths due to benzodiazepine ingestion are relatively rare
Tofranil (imipramine)— a tricyclic antidepressant	4–6 weeks after initiating treatment, this is as effective as Librium Dose = 25–300 mg	Sedation, blurred vision, dry mouth, constipation, urinary hesitancy, orthostatic hypotension, tachycardia, arrhythmias, delirium
Effexor R (venlafaxine)— a SNRI	FDA approved; most patients obtain some benefit within 2 weeks Dose = 75–300mg	Headaches, nervousness, insomnia, sedation, nausea, diarrhea, sexual dysfunction, hyponatremia, dose dependent increase in blood pressure
Paxil (paroxetine)—a SSRI	FDA approved; dose may need to be higher (50 mg) than antidepressant dose	Sexual dysfunction, nausea, diarrhea, constipation, dry mouth, tremors, headache
Celexa (citalopram)	FDA approved; dose 20–60 mg	Sexual dysfunction, nausea, diarrhea, insomnia, sedation, tremor
Remeron (mirtazapine)	Because it is sedating and increases appetite— excellent choice for underweight insomniacs	Sedation, weight gain, dry mouth, dizziness, abnormal dreams, confusion, change in urinary function, hypotension

Adapted (in part) from text in Schatzberg et al., 2007.

Anxiety and Related Disorders

A panic condition is an acute, terrifying apprehension accompanied by rapid heartbeat, nausea, tremulousness, dizziness, weakness, shortness of breath, and occasionally chest pain. These attacks begin and remit spontaneously, usually occurring at least once a week. Although the individual commonly is unable to determine what precipitated the attack, panic symptoms are usually connected to some sort of psychological problem.

Because most of the symptoms of a panic attack are physical, many sufferers think they are having a heart attack. While it is important to rule out medical causes of panic symptoms—shortness of breath, chest pain, palpitations, sweating—frequent visits to the emergency room become unnecessary once physical causes for the symptoms have been eliminated by a thorough medical workup. It is often panic that is overlooked as a potential cause for the physical symptoms—not the other way around.

Medical Causes of Panic
- Hyperthyroidism
- Hyperparathyroidism
- Vestibular disease
- Seizure disorders
- Mitral valve prolapse
- Cardiac arrhythmias
- Coronary insufficiency
- Pheochromocytoma
- Substance-induced anxiety from use of amphetamines, cocaine, PCP (phencyclidine), marijuana, caffeine, energy drinks

A comprehensive physiologic explanation of panic postulates that multiple systems contribute to a nervous system network that is centered on the amygdala—an almond-shaped structure within the medial temporal lobes of the brain that is involved in emotional processing and memory. The amygdala plays a central role in panic, sending out efferents to the hypothalamus, which increases adrenocorticoid release; the locus coeruleus, which increases norepinephrine release; and the parabrachial nucleus, which increases respiratory rate (Hollander & Simeon, 2003).

Although panic disorder is a serious illness, once the proper diagnosis is made, the condition is highly treatable. Almost everyone responds well to a combination of SSRIs (selective serotonin reuptake inhibitors)—Zoloft, Lexapro, Paxil, Celexa, Prozac, or Luvox—and the benzodiazepines.

Benzodiazepines present a risk of physical dependence, can produce oversedation, drowsiness, and breakthrough anxiety, but patients who take them have a reduction of panic attacks within a few days while antidepressants take weeks to work (Vasudeva & Kilgus, 2009). When patients attempt to stop benzodiazepines, panic symptoms may return and anxiety, agitation, tremor, and confusion may result from rebound withdrawal symptoms unless the medication is withdrawn slowly (1–6 months) depending on the dose and the length of action of the medication. Klonopin, the preferred benzodiazepine, has long-lasting effects causing less breakthrough anxiety and dependency than Xanax, the most popular anxiolytic.

The SSRI and Klonopin are administered concurrently. After a few months when the SSRI has developed full effect, Klonopin can be gradually discontinued. If necessary the SSRIs, generally well tolerated, can be continued indefinitely unless side effects—nausea, diarrhea, insomnia, jitteriness, sedation, and sexual dysfunction, preclude their use.

Cognitive and relaxation therapies can be helpful. Patients who have panic disorder think they are going to die—they unwittingly turn their symptoms into a catastrophe. When people become fearful, more blood goes to the muscles, preparing them to fight or flee. Blood flow to the brain decreases slightly. The lower oxygen level in the brain causes a faint feeling. The fear of fainting produces more symptoms, starting a vicious cycle that leads to a full-blown panic attack. Training patients to reinterpret these symptoms as fleeting anxiety, instead of a sign of a heart attack or some other catastrophic event, stops panic progression in the majority of patients (Seligman, 1993).

Panic Disorder With Agoraphobia

A 36-year-old married woman with three young children developed panic disorder that went undiagnosed for several years. Because the panic attacks were severe, frequent, and unpredictable, she became fearful of having these attacks while in the grocery store. Soon, this anticipatory dread began to cover all aspects of her life, and eventually she became completely homebound. Throughout this progressive deterioration, the patient had several physical workups for heart disease, cardiopulmonary illness, and endocrine disorders. After each physician visit, she was given new medications and then, later, medications to treat the side effects. The side effects and interaction of these medications added to her dysphoria. Soon, she began to drink while she watched daytime soap operas, reality shows, and television reruns. Her husband became exhausted grocery shopping and hauling the children from soccer, Girl Scouts, and all the other places active kids go without any help. Finally, the patient received a psychiatric referral. Her husband attempted to lead her by the hand into the psychiatrist's office, but she resisted. Eventually, a wheelchair was used to bring her into the psychiatrist's office, where she was found to be slightly intoxicated. The husband handed the psychiatrist a bagful of her medications. Treatment consisted of education about the illness, proper medication, and encouragement.

Agoraphobia (fear of public or open spaces) often develops as a response to panic attacks. Patients fear leaving home, being alone, or being in situations where they feel trapped or may become embarrassed. The patient may become afraid of traveling in trains, planes, or automobiles. Some people will not go into grocery stores or restaurants. They avoid theaters and crowds. Standing in line causes extreme anxiety. Occasionally, the patient becomes housebound or entirely dependent on others to take them shopping or traveling. In some cases, dependent character traits are recognized before agoraphobic symptoms appear. At other times, the agoraphobic symptoms cause dependent character traits.

Phobias

When he was a young child, Jim's stepmother locked him in a small closet for hours while she supplemented the family income by entertaining male visitors. Following college graduation, Jim's first job took him far away from his Appalachian childhood and into the big city, where he worked in a high-rise building. Jim developed a phobia of riding in elevators, but he functioned quite well in all other aspects of his life. The phobia became severe enough for Jim to seek counseling. His therapist induced a relaxed state in the businessman and rode in an elevator with him. Within 45 minutes, Jim began to feel comfortable even when the stop button was pushed, causing the elevator to jerk to a stop between floors. Following a repeat session a few days later, the patient's phobia completely disappeared.

Phobia, an excessive and irrational fear of something posing little or no actual danger, becomes an illness when symptoms become so intense that they interfere with day-to-day activities. Often, the phobic realizes that the dread is unreasonable yet will go to great lengths to avoid the feared object.

Phobias are the most common type of anxiety disorder—almost 8% of American adults suffer from a phobia (American Psychiatric Association, 2000). While it is normal to experience fear in dangerous scenarios, those with phobias have an intensely exaggerated fear in the midst of commonplace situations **(Table 6-3)**. Just about everyone fears a snarling, unchained rottweiler, but fleeing in terror from a friendly, leashed golden retriever indicates a strong possibility of having a dog phobia. Treatment becomes necessary when persistent phobias interrupt daily activities. Purposeful exposure to the feared object while in a relaxed condition is often the most effective treatment (Seligman, 1993).

Social Phobia

Although Donny Osmond made his television debut on the Andy Williams

TABLE 6-3	
Fantastic Phobias	
Ailurophobia	Fear of cats
Astraphobia	Fear of storms
Baccilophobia	Fear of bacteria
Ballistophobia	Fear of bullets
Decidophobia	Fear of making decisions
Ergophobia	Fear of work
Gynophobia	Fear of women
Hematophobia	Fear of blood
Hydrophobia	Fear of water
Latrophobia	Fear of doctors
Nosophobia	Fear of disease
Nyctophobia	Fear of night
Peccatophobia	Fear of sinning
Pyrophobia	Fear of fire
Sophophobia	Fear of learning
Thanatophobia	Fear of death
Xenophobia	Fear of strangers

Show at the tender age of 6, he began to have symptoms of anxiety when he was 11 years old. "There are times I remember before I walked on stage, where if I had the choice of walking on stage or dying, I would have chosen death." After forgetting the words to several songs during a concert in the 1960s, Barbra Streisand developed a phobia of performing before a live audience. She didn't sing again in public for nearly 30 years.

Anxiety and Related Disorders

Both of these celebrities suffered from social phobia—the fear of embarrassing themselves in front of others. Patients respond to a gradual step-by-step exposure to those situations they dread (Seligman, 1993). For some, training in social skills is helpful. The Food and Drug Administration (FDA) has approved Effexor, Zoloft, and Paxil for the treatment of social phobia (Mayoclinic.com, n.d.). Beta-blockers are useful for performance anxiety but ineffective for social phobia (Hollander & Simeon, 2003). Clinicians need to remember that the beta-blockers produce bronchospasm in asthmatic patients and peripheral constriction in Raynaud's disease. Side effects that are more common include bradycardia, hypotension, weakness, and fatigue (Schatzberg et al., 2007).

Post-Traumatic Stress Disorder

A 19-year-old woman flipped the car in which she was driving when the brakes failed on a slippery curve. Several days following the accident, the patient began to complain of painful flashbacks, traumatic dreams, and intrusive thoughts of the event. Following discharge, the patient was encouraged to return to driving as soon as possible. With help from her boyfriend, the patient developed the courage to drive again. One year following the patient's accident, her symptoms of post-traumatic stress disorder (PTSD) had completely remitted, and she was driving her car without fear.

Post-traumatic stress disorder consists of chronic anxiety that occurs following car accidents or other traumatic events, such as fires, airplane crashes, floods, earthquakes, rape, assault, or combat. Generally, the symptoms remit within 6 months after the onset of the trauma, although occasionally symptoms may last for decades. Acute stress disorder consisting of dissociative symptoms—depersonalization, emotional numbing or detachment, and amnesia for important aspects of the trauma—predicts the development of chronic PTSD (Andreasen & Black, 2006).

Symptoms of PTSD can occur following any life-threatening altercation. In those exposed to an acute, intense stress, the dangerous situation can be reexperienced through intrusive recollections of the confrontation, flashbacks of the original adversity, anxiety, nightmares, anger, fragmented sleep, and social withdrawal. Chronic PTSD commonly occurs following childhood sexual abuse or combat. In addition to recurrent distressing recollections, dreams, and dissociative flashbacks of the traumatic event, the patient attempts to avoid conversations, activities, places, and people that arouse recollections of the trauma. The patient may experience the inability to recall important aspects of the event. In addition, diminished interest in activities,

	TABLE 6-4	
	Fabulous Phobias of the Famous	
CELEBRITY	**OCCUPATION**	**PHOBIA**
Anne Rice	Bestselling author of vampire novels	Fear of dark
Steven Spielberg	Movie director and producer	Fear of insects
Kim Bassinger	Actress	Fear of open spaces
John Madden	Football coach and television personality	Fear of flying
Billy Bob Thorton	Actor, singer	Panophobia (fear of antique furniture)
Nicole Kidman	Actress	Lepidopterophobia (fear of butterflies)
Orlando Bloom	Actor	Fear of pigs
Madonna	Singer, performer, actress	Fear of thunder
Carmen Electra	Actress	Fear of water
Woody Allen	Writer, actor, and director	Fear of insects, sunshine, dogs, bright colors
Sarah Michelle Gellar	Actress	Fear of graveyards

a feeling of detachment, and the inability to experience loving feelings can follow a devastating trauma. Sleep disturbance, irritability, poor concentration, and an exaggerated startle response are common symptoms of PTSD.

Pharmacological treatments for PTSD have focused on treating a variety of symptoms (Alderman, McCarthy, & Marwood, 2009). The SSRIs and the serotonin-norepinephrine reuptake inhibitors (SNRIs) are helpful for anxiety and depression associated with PTSD. Beta-blockers (Inderal 10–40 mg three to four times daily) diminish the physiologic symptoms of anxiety (rapid heartbeat, tremors, sweating). Mood stabilizers can be useful in controlling irritability. Atypical antipsychotics can help alleviate flashbacks. Because of

Anxiety and Related Disorders

an increase of drug and alcohol abuse in patients with PTSD, benzodi-azepines are best avoided.

Nightmares can be reduced by the generic drug Prazosin (or Minipress), an antihypertensive (Raskind et al., 2003). Prazosin, an alpha 1 antagonist, normalizes rapid eye movement (REM) sleep by blocking the brain's response to norepinephrine. Dosage begins with 1 mg at bedtime for the first 3 days and gradually increases over a 4-week period until the traumatic dreams remit. The maximum dose is 15 mg. Prazosin also seems to help the other symptoms of PTSD. The most frequent side effects associated with Minipress are dizziness, headache, drowsiness, weakness, palpitations, and nausea. With continued therapy, most side effects attenuate.

Therapeutic treatment of acute PTSD consists of getting the person involved in the activity that resulted in the fear. Those traumatized by an automobile accident should be encouraged to drive as soon as possible; a swimming accident, to return to the pool; or a skiing accident, to go down the slopes with the next snowfall.

Psychotherapy is considered the first-line approach for PTSD (Alderman et al., 2009). The U.S. Department of Veterans Affairs has summarized the treatment approaches that have demonstrated promising results, including cognitive-behavior therapy, psychodynamic therapy, group therapy, marital and family therapy, social rehabilitative therapies, and eye-movement desen-sitization and reprocessing (EMDR). EMDR consists of visualizing images of the trauma while engaging in back-and-forth eye movements (National Cen-ter for Posttraumatic Stress Disorder, 2007).

Obsessive-Compulsive Disorder

A woman washes her hands repeatedly; she checks and rechecks the gas burners on the stove and opens and closes the refrigerator door to satisfy herself that the light did go out. She also irons her shoelaces. A bench-warmer on the high school basketball team fears making a mistake if he is put into a game. Repeatedly turning his head to the right in a tic-like fash-ion takes away the anxiety briefly, but the negative thoughts soon return. A writer fears having his manuscript criticized by his editor. He spends hours trying to get a sentence "just right" and misses his deadline. A cinematog-rapher shoots 163 hours of film for a 16-minute sales DVD because he wants to justify his enormous fee. He then spends months editing the 163 hours. He knows that this is foolish overkill, but when the DVD wins an award, his compulsive behavior is reinforced. A woman is obsessed with the thought that she has bad breath. Brushing her teeth and gargling relieves the fear briefly. In a minute or two, the fear of halitosis returns, and the ritual is repeated. This pattern continues throughout the evening, and the suffering girl never gets a chance to kiss her date.

Compulsive behavior is characterized by driven, repetitive behavior—hand washing, checking, cleaning, arranging, counting, or repeating words. These time-consuming compulsions significantly interfere with the person's occupational, academic, and social activities. The tormented individual recognizes that the compulsions are excessive and unreasonable but feels that the distressing behavior cannot be stopped. Obsessions, consisting of unwanted ideas, images, and impulses, repeatedly run through the person's mind. A person with OCD does not want to have these thoughts and finds them disturbing, but he or she cannot control them. Sometimes, these thoughts just come on occasionally and are only mildly annoying. Other times, a person who has OCD will have obsessive thoughts all day long. Studies showed that a little over 2% of the general population may have OCD at any time (Hollander & Simeon, 2003).

Obsessive thoughts generally drive the compulsive behavior. These thoughts can range from incapacitating to somewhat useful. No single, proven cause for OCD has been found. A deficiency in brain serotonin seems to be connected with OCD. The SSRIs Prozac, Zoloft, Paxil, and Luvox often help reduce obsessions and compulsions. The tricyclic Anafranil may be the drug of choice.

A special form of cognitive-behavior therapy, called exposure-response prevention, exposes the patient to the obsession and prevents actions that relieve the fear (Hollander & Simeon, 2003). For example, a person with a hand-washing ritual is forced to touch a dirty floor and is then prevented from washing his or her hands. Over time, the person learns to become less and less afraid of germs and surrenders the compulsion to repeatedly wash the hands **(Table 6-5)**.

Dissociative Disorders

A 26-year-old graduate student in the School of Fine Arts came to the student health center complaining of overwhelming anxiety and feelings of unreality. Often when sketching, she would feel as if her mind floated upward and could view her body from above. This feeling was so disturbing that she was forced to quit her work.

The American Psychiatric Association (2000) listed four categories under the rubric of dissociative disorders: dissociative amnesia, dissociative fugue, dissociative identity disorder (also called multiple personality disorder, MPD), and depersonalization disorder, all of which result from overwhelming anxiety.

Dissociative amnesia, a sudden onset of the inability to recall important personal information, can occur after accidents or other acutely distressful events, while dissociative fugue, the assumption of a new identity with the

TABLE 6-5	
Common Obsessions and Compulsions	
COMMON OBSESSIONS	**COMMON COMPULSIONS**
Fear of harming a family member or friend	Seeking constant reassurance and approval
Thinking about certain sounds, images, words, or numbers all the time	Saving newspapers, mail, or containers when they are no longer needed
Fear of thinking evil or sinful thoughts	Counting over and over to a certain number
Worry that a task has been done poorly, even when the person knows this concern is unfounded	Ordering and arranging items in certain ways
Fear of dirt or germs	Cleaning and grooming, such as washing hands, showering, or brushing teeth over and over again

inability to recall one's prior identity, can be precipitated by overwhelming life events, as in the classical example of the runaway bride.

Dissociative identity disorder, the occurrence of several distinct integrated personalities in the same individual, is, in my opinion, a bogus diagnosis. I tell my students that multiple personality disorder (MPD) occurs only in patients with severe personality disorders who consciously use the claim of MPD to get attention and to avoid the anxiety precipitated by society's expectation that the patient follow the regular rules and regulations of a responsible individual. When I interview a patient claiming to have a multiple personality, I simply reply that there is no such diagnosis. I never hear from Crystal/Bridgette/Tiffany/Brittany/Eve or Sybil again, and the patient begins taking responsibility for individual behavior. (Of course, in doing so I have missed the opportunity to write a bestselling book.)

Approximately half of adults encounter a brief episode of depersonalization characterized by feeling detached from one's body or experiences. Nearly one third of individuals exposed to a life-threatening event will face a transient dream-like condition (American Psychiatric Association, 2000). Generally, this event comes up in the course of a diagnostic interview as in, "Hey doc, I once had this experience of floating away from my body." Reassurance is all that is called for in these cases. In episodes of persistent depersonalization, management consists of treating the underlying anxiety that precipitated the event.

Complete Mental Health

Treatment of Anxiety Disorders

Selective serotonin reuptake inhibitors have been effective in a number of different anxiety disorders. In addition, they do not have the dependence, withdrawal, alcohol interaction, or abuse liability of the benzodiazepines. Despite these drawbacks, benzodiazepines are often used as an adjunctive treatment with SSRIs or as the primary treatment of anxiety because benzodiazepines have a faster onset of action than the SSRIs. The net result is only a small decline in the use of benzodiazepines over the past decade.

Benzodiazepines work quickly to relieve generalized anxiety. Usually, just one pill will bring a sense of calm. But, they cause problems. They make the brain fuzzy and sleepy and the body somewhat uncoordinated. After a while, they may lose their calming effects, requiring a higher dose to get the same benefits.

If anxiety is not paralyzing or so intense that it interferes with activities of daily living, medications run a distant second in preference to relaxation techniques **(Table 6-6)**. Meditation and relaxation techniques are safer than drugs. Their lifetime benefits make them more effective than the benzodiazepines. They may not offer the almost instantaneous relief that the benzodiazepines provide, but if practiced regularly, they ameliorate anxiety and worry for a lifetime.

Activities such as yoga, meditation, and progressive muscle relaxation strengthen the body's relaxation response—the opposite of the stress response involved in anxiety and panic. Not only do these relaxation practices dispel anxiety, but also they increase feelings of joy and equanimity. So, patients should be encouraged to make time for them in their daily routines.

In counseling, therapists can help patients become aware of automatic thoughts and underlying schemas so that the patients can objectively evaluate them. One way to do this is by making vague worries more specific. Patients can then be taught how to set goals and rehearse a life without worry. Having a nonworrying therapist is essential because patients, like children, learn by imitation.

Attending Dr. Leonard Coleman's funeral last year, I reflected on the unique personality of the man. Although I saw him confront numerous traumatic situations, he never appeared anxious. I remembered a particular case of a man struck by a train rushed to the emergency room with a dilated pupil and left extremity paralysis indicating that he had a subdural hematoma (a blood clot on the brain). Just as Leonard was set to cut a section out of the skull to relieve the life-threatening pressure on the brain, a tornado struck our hospital, rendering the hospital lightless. We were in total darkness, the wind roaring all around, when the hospital generator failed. I fumbled for a flashlight, and while I held it aloft, Leonard finished the operation. Not then, or at any other time, did I ever see Leonard anxious, flustered, or irritated. I

TABLE 6-6	
Self-Help Tips for Anxiety Disorders	
ADVICE	**DESCRIPTION**
Learn about your illness	Read; visit informative Web sites.
Avoid caffeine-containing drinks	Coffee, caffeinated beverages, energy drinks, diet pills, over-the-counter medications containing stimulants.
Focus on full, cleansing breaths, a simple technique that can be practiced anywhere	Hyperventilation—shallow, fast breathing—can precipitate panic.
Practice the relaxation response (RR)	*The Relaxation Response,* by Herbert Benson (HarperCollins, 2000) tells you how.
Practice progressive relaxation	Tense the muscles in your right foot, hold for a count of 10, focus on the tension flowing away as you breathe deeply; do the same for your left foot, and your right calf . . . all the way up the body. Alternate contracting and relaxing all the muscle groups.
Practice meditation	Very similar to the RR; choose a quiet environment, get comfortable with your spine straight, repeat a phrase throughout the 20-minute session. Don't fight intrusive thoughts; just return to repeating your phrase.
Use guided imagery	Imagine a peaceful scene: hear, see, smell, and feel those things that surround your imagined place.
Practice yoga	Slow, steady movements combined with gentle stretching and deep measured breathing brings stress relief.
Use tai chi	Tai chi, a series of slowly flowing body movements, is best learned from an instructor.

Adapted from "Relaxation Techniques for Stress Relief," by Helpguide.org, n.d., retrieved July 24, 2009, from http://helpguide.org/mental/stress_relief_meditation_yoga_relaxation.htm.

have witnessed the same equanimity in war-time pilots performing feats of bravery, medics going down helicopter hoists to perform miraculous rescues during the most harrowing of conditions, firefighters rushing into burning homes, policemen facing notorious killers. None allowed anxiety to interfere with their work. Yet, there are those of us who at a job interview nearly pass out with fright. Why is this? It is a mystery. That is what makes the study of people and their nuances of behavior the most fascinating of all occupations.

Do You Have an Anxiety Disorder?				
Make Check Mark (✓) in Appropriate Column	Little of the Time 1 point each ✓	Some of the Time 2 points each ✓	A Lot of the Time 3 points each ✓	Most of the Time 4 points each ✓
I worry about something.				
I feel like something terrible is going to happen.				
I feel restless.				
My palms are sweaty or moist.				
I have muscle tension.				
I have difficulty falling asleep.				
I get tired easily and feel run down.				
I have difficulty concentrating because of worry.				
I am so anxious that my mind goes blank.				
My hands are shaky and tremulous.				
Multiply ✓ by the value given in each column.				

Add the total for each column to get the **Grand total** = _____

SCORING

10–14 points = Cool as a cucumber

15–24 points = Just about all of us worry every once in awhile

25–34 points = Anxiety interferes with your happiness, work, and social life

35–40 points = Incapacitating anxiety

Do You Have Panic Disorder?				
Make Check Mark (✓) in Appropriate Column	Little of the Time 1 point each ✓	Some of the Time 2 points each ✓	A Lot of the Time 3 points each ✓	Most of the Time 4 points each ✓
I have periods of intense fear.				
This fear causes shortness of breath.				
When I am afraid I have a fast heart rate.				
During these episodes of fear, I sweat profusely.				
During these periods of intense fear, I experience trembling, nausea, dizziness, or tingling.				
I worry about having additional attacks.				
I sometimes think I am having a heart attack or am going to die when I have these attacks.				
I feel embarrassed about these attacks.				
These fearful episodes begin without warning.				
These episodes go away spontaneously.				
Multiply ✓ by the value given in each column.				

Add the total for each column to get the **Grand total** = _____

SCORING

10–14 points = Rock solid

15–24 points = Not much bothers you

25–34 points = Panic attacks are part of your life

35–40 points = Severe panic attacks

Do You Have Obsessive-Compulsive Disorder?				
Make Check Mark (✓) in Appropriate Column	Little of the Time 1 point each ✓	Some of the Time 2 points each ✓	A Lot of the Time 3 points each ✓	Most of the Time 4 points each ✓
I have anxious thoughts that interfere with my daily life.				
I can't ignore these distressing thoughts.				
I can't get rid of these thoughts by thinking about something else.				
These thoughts come from my own mind.				
I know these thoughts are inappropriate.				
I repeatedly wash my hands or clean things.				
I repeatedly count or repeat words silently.				
I repeatedly check the locks on doors or check other things to make certain they are safe.				
These repetitive behaviors are aimed at preventing distress.				
I can't stop these behaviors.				
Multiply ✓ by the value given in each column.				

Add the total for each column to get the **Grand total** = _____

SCORING

10–14 points = No significant obsessions

15–24 points = Most successful people are a little obsessive

25–34 points = Treatment will help

35–40 points = Totally preoccupied with obsessions and rituals

Do You Have Post-Traumatic Stress Disorder?

Make Check Mark (✓) in Appropriate Column	Little of the Time 1 point each ✓	Some of the Time 2 points each ✓	A Lot of the Time 3 points each ✓	Most of the Time 4 points each ✓
I have recurrent thoughts of a traumatic event.				
I have recurrent nightmares about a traumatic event.				
I have recurrent flashbacks of a traumatic event.				
Exposure to noises or sights that remind me of the traumatic event causes anxiety and startle reactions.				
I avoid activities that remind me of the trauma.				
I don't like to talk about the stressful event.				
I have trouble sleeping and concentrating.				
I tend to isolate myself from others.				
I feel numb and detached from people and things around me.				
I am irritable.				
Multiply ✓ by the value given in each column.				

Add the total for each column to get the **Grand total** = _____

SCORING

10–14 points = A pristine and protected life

15–24 points = Stressful situations don't seem to bother you

25–34 points = Significant distress

35–40 points = Severe distress

Complete Mental Health

A Clinician's Quiz

1. List 5 factors that contribute to anxiety.
2. Discuss the symptoms and causes of generalized anxiety.
3. What are the physical symptoms of anxiety?
4. What combination of medications are used to treat panic disorder?
5. Agoraphobia often results as a response to _____.
6. What is the most common type of anxiety disorder?
7. What medication is best avoided in treating PTSD?
8. List four categories under the rubric of dissociative disorder.
9. What are the problems of using benzodiazepines in the treatment of anxiety?
10. List 5 nonpharmacological ways to limit anxiety.

CHAPTER 7

Psychosomatic Illness
Worry Wounds

O. Henry's poignant short story *The Last Leaf* tells the tale of Johnsy, a young artist stricken with pneumonia. The doctor gives her a 10% chance of surviving, explaining to Johnsy's roommate that the true odds depended on her will to live: "Whenever my patient begins to count the carriages in her funeral procession I subtract 50 per cent from the curative power of medicines. If you will get her to ask one question about the new winter styles in cloak sleeve I will promise you a one-in-five chance for her, instead of one in ten." Unmotivated by fashion, instead Johnsy decides that her time to die will come at the moment the last leaf falls from an ivy vine seen outside of her bedroom window. Day after day, despite winter's savage breath, the last ivy leaf refuses to let go of its grip on the vine. Interpreting this miracle as a second chance, Johnsy thoroughly recovers. The story ends with the revelation that the last ivy leaf would indeed never perish—a compassionate fellow artist had masterfully painted it onto the wall.

As O. Henry's story poetically illustrates, our thoughts and emotions play a substantial role in our physical health. Countless anecdotes circulate among medical professionals about patients who "miraculously" recover from terminal cancer or other normally fatal diseases. Just as common are the case studies that demonstrate a rapid decline in health without physical explanations. It is truly difficult to underestimate the link between the mind and the body. No formula exists for improving health through positive thinking alone, yet the desire to get well does often influence recovery. The converse is also true: Significant psychological components can be found in two thirds of patients with physical complaints. Most of these are psychosomatic illnesses, in which emotional factors contribute to the existence of an actual physical disease. At other times, though, patients complain of physical ailments without demonstrable organic findings. Understanding the complex web of connections between physical symptoms and emotional dysfunction can be an overwhelming, yet exciting, pursuit.

In the decades after World War II, prolific author and researcher Hans Selye changed the ways we viewed the connection between body and mind. (Gabriel, 2009). In 1926, Selye, then a 19-year-old medical student, began investigating what it meant to be ill—the nonspecific effects of illness and the links between diseases. Selye had noticed that individuals show characteristic fatigue and general discomfort following either a physical or emotional event. Exploring these similarities, Selye subjected rats to traumatic injury, extreme changes in temperature, bacterial infection, and prolonged immobilization. Following persistent stress, autopsy of the dead animals revealed enlarged adrenal glands, bleeding ulcers, and atrophied lymph and thymus glands (Gabriel, 2009).

From these studies, Selye proposed the general adaptation syndrome, which involves three stages: the alarm reaction, the resistance stage, and the exhaustion stage. The alarm reaction involves the fight-or-flight reaction of the autonomic nervous system. In the resistance stage, the hypothalamus continues to stimulate the pituitary to produce hormonal and neural changes throughout the body until the stressful situation has passed. Continued stress leads to the exhaustion stage; individuals unable to receive sufficient rest to restore the body's equilibrium will deteriorate and eventually die. With these experiments, Selye demonstrated the negative effects caused by emotional tension, such as frustration or suppressed rage (Gabriel, 2009).

Building on Selye's work, Robert Ader and his partner Nicholas Cohen (1975) at the University of Rochester gave rats a combination of saccharine-laced water and the cancer drug Cytoxan, which induces nausea and suppresses the immune system. Later, they fed the same rats saccharine-laced water minus the Cytoxan. They discovered that the saccharine-laced water alone suppressed the immune system of the rats. In other words, a signal from the taste buds had been conditioned to affect the immune system. This breakthrough gave birth to an exciting new science—psychoneuroimmunology (PNI).

Whenever we have a thought or a feeling, our brains make chemicals known as neuropeptides. These protein-like molecules attach to the receptor sites of other brain cells, allowing brain cells to "talk" to each other chemically. Immune cells that heal wounds and protect us from diseases also have receptors for these neuropeptide chemical messengers from the brain. Chemical messengers released from the limbic area (the feeling part of the brain) "plug in" to neuroreceptor "sockets" into blood cells. Likewise, chemical messengers from the blood cells attach to "sockets" in the brain, resulting in a back-and-forth conversation between the body's immune system and the brain.

Messages that flow between the brain and neuroreceptor sites on the lymphocytes are transported instantaneously, so that when we experience joy or feel enthusiastic, the white blood cells receive that message immediately. Conversely, when we are unhappy, a negative message is transmitted directly to the white blood cells. Thus, our emotional reaction influences physical health.

What is even more exciting is the finding that certain cells in the stomach, intestines, kidneys, and other organs can make the same chemicals that the brain makes when it thinks (Levenson, 2003). When we say, "A cheerful heart is good medicine, but a downcast spirit dries up the bones" (Proverbs 17:22), we are speaking both metaphorically and literally—our body cells are actually producing the harmful or beneficial chemicals.

In 1979, Norman Cousins penned the bestseller *Anatomy of an Illness*, chronicling his personal journey through disease and recovery. Frustrated by inept hospital care, Cousins took a radically proactive approach to his battle against a serious collagen disorder. Cousins self-prescribed a regimen of daily belly laughter induced by Marx Brothers' films. His doctors, initially skeptical, partially attributed Cousins's remarkable recovery to his own mental powers—courage, humor, tenacity, and a positive attitude.

The idea that the mind and body interact with each other leads to a better understanding of how psychological factors can, directly or indirectly, affect physical disorders and, in turn, how physical disorders can influence the emotions. The term *psychosomatic* emphasizes that emotional disturbances directly influence physical disease. Illnesses influenced by psychological factors, including heart disease, gastrointestinal problems, some cancers, and most skin diseases, are interconnected with and difficult to disentangle from psychological factors.

Thoughtful reflection makes it clear that both healthiness and infirmity are influenced by emotional factors, so psychosomatic illness, in the broadest sense, encompasses all ailments. There are, however, certain illnesses that have been studied more closely for the psychosomatic component in their etiology. These illnesses include diabetes mellitus, Cushing's disease, coronary artery disease, hypertension, asthma, chronic obstructive pulmonary disease, rheumatoid disease, peptic ulcer disease, irritable bowel syndrome, psoriasis, acne, and urticaria (Levenson, 2003) **(Table 7-1)**.

TABLE 7-1
Psychological Factors in Selected Diseases

DISEASE	PSYCHOLOGICAL FACTORS
Cancer	Significant losses and stress are risk factors; there is better outcome in breast cancer patients with a "fighting spirit"; data are mixed on the so-called cancer-prone type C patient who is cooperative, nonassertive, and suppresses negative emotions.
Diabetes mellitus	Stressful life events and depression adversely affect outcome.
Heart disease	Associated with type A behavior; hostility component in type A behavior is especially important as a contributing factor; anxiety/depression adversely affect outcome.
Hypertension	High anxiety levels may precipitate a hypertensive crisis; psychosocial stressors—overcrowding, disruptive social conditions, job stress, and poverty—may contribute to the etiology of hypertension.
Asthma	Anxiety and emotional events can precipitate asthmatic attacks.
Chronic obstructive pulmonary disease	Depression and anxiety lower exercise tolerance, cause less adherence to treatment, and increase disability.
Rheumatoid disease	Depression, very common in rheumatoid arthritis, is associated with more pain and greater disability independent of the severity of the rheumatoid symptoms.
Peptic ulcer disease	While only a fraction of patients exposed to the reputed causes of peptic ulcer disease—*Hellcobacter pylori* or nonsteroidal anti-inflammatory drugs—have the disease, a substantial amount of research shows that environmental disasters, occupational or family conflict, anxiety, or depression contribute to 30–65% of ulcers.
Irritable bowel syndrome	Associated with panic attacks, depression, and somatization disorder.
Psoriasis	Feeling stigmatized because others avoid touching them because of their skin disease results in despair and isolation in patients with psoriasis; those who seek support and express feelings have improved physical and emotional health.
Acne	Associated with anxiety, depression, and low self-esteem.

Psychosomatic Illness

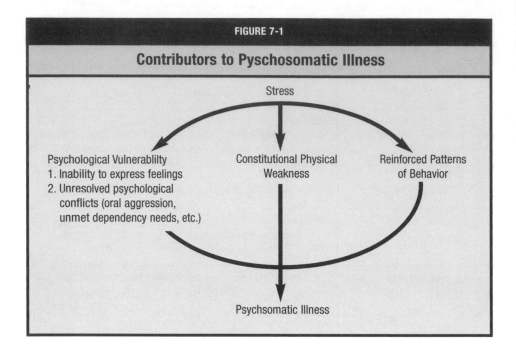

FIGURE 7-1

Contributors to Pyschosomatic Illness

Stress

Psychological Vulnerablilty
1. Inability to express feelings
2. Unresolved psychological
   conflicts (oral aggression,
   unmet dependency needs, etc.)

Constitutional Physical
Weakness

Reinforced Patterns
of Behavior

Psychsomatic Illness

Causes of Psychosomatic Illness

Like all illnesses, causes of psychosomatic maladies are multifaceted **(Figure 7-1)**. Unresolved psychological conflicts, an inability to appropriately express emotions, constitutional predisposing factors, personality, and lifestyle risk factors all interact and contribute to the development of psychosomatic illness.

Stress

Holmes and Rahe (1967) found an almost linear relationship between stressful changes in life events and frequency of illness. They developed the Social Readjustment Rating Scale, which ranks 43 common environmental stresses according to severity. The more life change units (LCU) an individual experiences within a 6-month period, the greater the chance that he or she will develop an illness. Although the LCU score cannot predict the type of disease, life changes can help distinguish individuals who are vulnerable to illness.

The stress of daily living, which cannot be easily quantified—traffic jams, disparaging remarks from an employer, family arguments—can also produce biochemical reactions reminiscent of the flight-or-fight reaction, including increased pulse rate, elevated blood pressure, decreased immune response, and increased respiration. Failure to manage these ongoing emotional changes usually results in chronic illness.

Unresolved Psychological Conflicts

The link between stress and illness fails to explain why some individuals develop psychosomatic disorders rather than physical sickness, or why other individuals develop no illness at all. Some investigators believe that patients prone to psychosomatic illness are incapable of expressing feelings appropriately.

Unmet dependency needs, sexual and aggressive conflicts, grief and bereavement, guilt, worry, and negative thinking, combined with other factors discussed in this chapter, can surface in the form of psychosomatic illness (J. I. Walker, 1981).

Personality Style

Many attempts have been made to connect particular personality profiles with specific organic illnesses. For example, Dunbar (1947) proposed that hypertensive patients exhibited lifelong patterns of anxiety, perfectionism, and difficulty with authority figures. Recent research has refuted most of her proposals as oversimplifications.

Alexander (1950) designated seven psychosomatic disorders: asthma, peptic ulcer, ulcerative colitis, hypertension, thyrotoxicosis, neurodermatitis, and rheumatoid arthritis. He proposed that these illnesses, called the "holy seven," result from a particular personality style. For example, dependent individuals develop ulcers when their dependency needs are frustrated; those individuals with chronic anger develop hypertension. Subsequent research has failed to confirm a relationship between a particular personality pattern and a specific illness.

Two cardiologists, Meyer Friedman and R. H. Rosenman (1974), contended that the primary risk factors of heart disease—hypertension, obesity, smoking, and elevated lipids—failed to fully explain the high rate of heart disease. Subsequent studies offered evidence that a highly competitive, aggressive and, impulsive personality style—designated type A behavior—was associated with an increased risk of heart disease three times more often than in those with an easygoing attitude—type B behavior. Type A personalities show significantly higher levels of serum triglycerides, cholesterol, and stress hormones (adrenalin and steroids) than do type B individuals.

> He was an inch, perhaps two, over 6 feet, slimly built, and he advanced directly at you, head forward, with an intense stare that made you think of a sprinter straining for the tape. His voice was deep and loud, and his manner displayed a kind of resolute aggressiveness that was directed, it seemed, at the ticking clock as he rushed from examining room to examining room, taking pleasure in the number of patients he saw daily. During

the lunch hour, Dr. Rath hurriedly engulfed a sandwich, returning calls, signing charts, dictating reports, and ignoring the comfort of his expansive office. Arriving home, he dove into jogging clothes and, with stopwatch in hand, charged around the neighborhood oblivious to children playing or women strolling, toddlers in tow, toward the park, as he focused on besting his running time from the day before. Competitively devoted to tennis during the summer months, he would go into a rage when he lost, yet felt vaguely dissatisfied when he won. He spent the winter months in the weight room trying to lift more than those half his age. Preoccupation with money and power milked the joy from his family life, as it always does with men of his type.

According to Friedman and Rosenman (1974), type B patients, as represented by Dr. Comfort, have fewer heart attacks.

A well-loved doctor need not be top in his class, but he must have a warm bedside manner, as Dr. Comfort, a 61-year-old family physician, had demonstrated throughout his career. Immensely popular with the patients who he had started caring for almost 30 years before, and now, also, with their children and grandchildren, his calendar remained constantly full. He never seemed to hurry, but to the contrary always had time to chat with his patients, whom he considered to be his friends. Most satisfied in doing a thorough job, he never hesitated to consult with other physicians, who were always eager to help when he found a case that was particularly puzzling. At lunchtime, Dr. Comfort would stroll across the street to a well-established restaurant, where, sitting outside on warm days and by the fireside during the winter months, he had lunch with lifelong friends, with whom he shared an enthusiasm for Shakespeare and 19th century American architecture. Following a busy afternoon, he would spend a few minutes alone in the relaxed warmth of his office, mulling over the day's events. Returning home, Dr. Comfort invariably took a pleasant walk around the neighborhood with his wife, stopping to chat with neighbors and friends. On Wednesday afternoons, he played golf for fun and relaxation, slicing notoriously, putting poorly, and laughing loudly about his always-pathetic score. Unconcerned by the petty annoyances of life and little bothered by the quest for possessions, he remained invigoratingly cheerful, destined to live a long and happy life.

Those with type B behavior patterns know that the pursuit of temporal material things interferes with a contented life, while virtuous choices—choices that leave us with no regrets—allow us to pursue values that strengthen the romance, mystery, and beauty of a life fully lived.

TABLE 7-2	
Type A and Type B Behavior	
TYPE A BEHAVIOR	**TYPE B BEHAVIOR**
Is impatient	Is patient
Is aggressive	Has a casual lifestyle
Has a sense of urgency	Enjoys the moment
Is highly competitive	Is useful, helpful
Interrupts others' speech	Is a good listener
Craves recognition	Appreciates leisure and beauty
Frequently checks time	Rarely looks at watch
Obsessed with multitasking	Does things one at a time
Seeks fame, wealth, and power	Enjoys work
Is quick tempered	Is a peaceful, deliberate thinker
Is angry	Expresses affection openly
Has rapid speech	Has slow, deliberate speech
Is unable to relax	Is calm
Has facial tension	Smiles and laughs easily
Always seeks more	Enjoys the present
Is a complainer	Is content
Has tongue and teeth clicking	Has tranquil expressions
Has audible forced inspiration of air	Has relaxed breathing
Is a perfectionist	Accepts own imperfections

TABLE 7-3

Behavior Risk Factors for Medical Illness

- Obesity, anorexia, and other dietary problems
- Smoking
- Alcohol or drug abuse
- Reckless behavior—sexual indiscretion, irresponsible friends, careless driving
- Participation in extreme sports such as hang gliding, mountain climbing, bungee jumping, and the like
- Noncompliance with medications and medical treatment
- Unsettling or stressful lifestyle
- Intermittent violence or suicidal gestures
- Personality disorder or troublesome personality traits
- Failure to heed warning signs of overwork

Despite what commonsense wisdom would lead us to believe, research has produced inconsistent findings regarding the association between type A behavior and coronary disease. Most individuals with a type A personality style escape heart attacks, while some type B personalities suffer coronaries. Researchers found that a tendency to react to unpleasant situations with anger, frustration, irritation, and disgust is a more reliable indicator of coronary disease than the other characteristics of type A behavior. Smoldering anger seems to be the most significant personality predictor of heart disease (Lachar, 1993).

Drills Against Hostility
- Strive to diminish sensitivity to affronts of others.
- Increase awareness of the needs of others.
- Avoid inflicting personal ideals on others.
- Become less critical of self (self-criticism generates smoldering anger).
- Remember that not everything that makes us feel better is good for us, and not everything that hurts is bad for us. Control hostility when things don't go exactly as planned.
- Eliminate the idea that life must always be fair, easy, and stress free.

Conditioned Response
Psychosomatic illness, to a certain degree, can be a learned response. Respiratory patterns that approximate asthmatic breathing can be induced by experimentally reinforcing certain breathing behavior. Children may learn

the visceral responses of chronic asthma by being allowed to stay home from school when they have a cough. Thus, psychosomatic illness may develop through accidental conditions and the individual's susceptibility to a disease of a certain type. Wolff (1950) suggested that individuals can be classified as heart reactors, stomach reactors, and so on, depending on the particular types of physical condition that stress characteristically produces in them.

Lifestyle Risk Factors
Harmful lifestyle choices such as smoking, alcohol abuse, and obesity contribute greatly to the development of psychosomatic illnesses. Many of these can be counteracted by exercise **(Table 7-4)**.

Cigarette Smoking
Cigarette smoking, the greatest cause of preventable premature death, contributes to myocardial infarction, peripheral vascular disease, cancer, and chronic obstructive pulmonary disease (Peto, Lopez, Boreham, Thunham, &

TABLE 7-4	
Secondary Benefits of Exercise	
SECONDARY BENEFIT	**HOW THE BENEFIT WORKS**
Improves brain function	• Boosts neurotropic factor—"Miracle-Gro" for the brain. • Builds better connections between brain cells. • Increases function in the hippocampus— the memory factory of the brain.
Reduces stress response	• A fast-paced workout relaxes the muscles. • Reduces worry. • Diminishes agitation.
Diminishes anxiety	• Boosts brain serotonin.
Improves mood	• Increases brain norepinephrine.
Fights addictions	• Redirects thought away from the substance of abuse. • Reduces stress. • Replaces addiction to substances with addiction to exercise.
Improves concentration	• Sharpens alertness.
Revitalizes the aging brain	• Improves blood flow to the brain. • Increases several brain neurotransmitters responsible for clear thinking.

Heath, 1992). Bupropion (Wellbutrin) plus cessation counseling provides the most effective intervention (Levenson, 2003). Results from the highly touted medication Chantix, which blocks nicotine receptor sites, have been disappointing because of the tendency of this medication to cause agitation, psychotic episodes, and suicidal behavior (RxList, 2009a).

Alcohol Abuse

Whereas over 65% of American adults occasionally drink alcohol, those who drink almost daily, becoming intoxicated several times monthly, comprise 12% of the population. At least 25% of medical-surgical beds in general hospitals are occupied by alcoholics, and 50–60% of psychiatric inpatients have the diagnosis of alcohol abuse/addiction as one of their psychiatric disorders (Andreasen & Black, 2006). Alcohol is implicated in 50% of fatal traffic accidents, 34% of homicides, 50% of rapes, 60% of violent crimes, 36% of suicides, and more than half of child abuse cases (Alcholics Victorious, 1994). Alcohol leads to an increased incidence of cirrhosis, cardiovascular disease, gastrointestinal bleeding, oral cancers, pancreatitis, and many other illnesses, making alcoholism the third leading cause of death in the United States (Andreasen & Black, 2006).

Obesity

Obesity, the most critical health crisis in America, the fastest-growing cause of disease and death, and the only disease that is completely preventable through regular exercise and healthy eating habits, has produced an array of alarming statistics (Department of Health and Human Services, 2007 a & b):

- Nearly two of every three Americans are overweight or obese.
- Obesity contributes to the number one cause of death in our nation: heart disease.
- Excess weight has also led to an increase in the number of people suffering from type 2 diabetes—now affecting over 17 million Americans—an illness that can lead to eye diseases, cardiovascular problems, kidney failure, and premature death.
- One of every eight deaths in America is caused by an illness directly related to overweightness and obesity.
- Since the 1960s, when just over 4% of 6- to 17-year-olds were overweight, the obesity rate has more than tripled, to over 15%.
- Nearly three of every four overweight teenagers may become overweight adults.

Speaker and author Marilyn vos Savant has, since 1986, written a column for *Parade Magazine,* which has a readership of 79 million. She is listed in the *Guinness Book of Work Records* as possessing the world's highest IQ. Who better to get advice on proper eating than from the smartest person in the world (Marilynvossavant.com, 2004)?

- Have a light breakfast (low-fat yogurt or fruit or cereal) and a small lunch (a bit of cheese and crackers).
- For dinner, have just about anything you want, including bread and a little butter, plus a dessert, except no burgers, fries, fatty meats, gravies, and soups with cream.
- Be tough on yourself with unbreakable rules:
    - No snack food. Keep the cupboard bare.
    - No eating between meals, including fruit or juice.
    - No milk or sugar added to beverages.
    - No effort to eat everything on the plate.
- Take a long time to eat dinner.
- Enjoy each bite.
- Don't change your dining routine on the weekends.
- Don't underestimate the calories you consume—fruits and "healthy" foods have a lot of calories.

Treatment and Prevention of Psychosomatic Illness

If hate, fear, doubt, depression, and despair can contribute to physical illness, then love, hope, faith, laughter, and confidence must have therapeutic value. Often engaging the natural resources of body and mind becomes the best one can do to oppose psychosomatic and other serious illnesses.

Emotional Health

Love and joy have proven to be effective in reducing contributing factors to illness. Scientists studying cholesterol metabolism in rabbits found that a group of rabbits that were petted, cuddled, and caressed failed to get high cholesterol levels despite being fed the same high-cholesterol diet as another group of rabbits that were not petted and cuddled. Rabbits that received the loving energy metabolized cholesterol differently, resulting in normal serum cholesterol levels (Dossey, 1982).

In another study, two groups of premature infants were observed. Those premature infants who were loved, stroked, and cuddled gained almost 50% more weight per day than the premature infants who received no physical demonstration of love. The researchers proposed that loving energy increased the level of growth hormone in the cuddled infants (Palmer, 2004).

The Power of Humor

A joyful heart is healing, while a dreary spirit leads to sickness. Joyless opportunities deplete vigor and dull the senses. Sports and games that bring more frowns than laughter are an absurd use of time. Instead, learn to view leisure time as a valuable opportunity to enjoy life, love, and laughter.

Avoid sarcasm and self-deprecating humor. The unconscious mind cannot tell the difference between positive and negative tone. Self-deprecating humor, no matter how much others may laugh, impacts your unconscious mind to accomplish those things you joke about. Likewise, sarcasm reflects passive hostility toward the other person.

Healthy humor, on the other hand, comes in the form of cosmic humor and belly laughs. Hearty, energetic laughter invigorates those around you. Watching funny movies or listening to classic comedy recordings are good warm-up exercises for developing a daily habit of laughter.

Above all, avoid taking life too seriously. Finding the absurdity in human foibles allows you to brush off the "dust and soot" of life.

Dealing With Stress

In this life, experiences and situations that cause stress and anxiety are inevitable. Dealing with life's stresses in a productive way is an important key to emotional health, which in turn leads to better overall physical health. Techniques for dealing with stress include exercise, yoga, meditation, prayer, and relaxation techniques.

The Power of the Mind

Mentally making a decision to rise above our chromosomes and circumstances can decrease the negative effects of stress while elevating our "set point" for joy. This is good news: Those who cultivate certain habits can learn to live a joyful, contented life no matter what circumstances occur. Joy transcends happiness (Table 7-5). While happiness depends on happenings, joy depends on the conviction that adversity brings about strength of character. To drive home that point, consider Holocaust survivors, who learned that being unhappy about trivial things insults human dignity. After living through any tragic event, survivors appreciate those values that make life worth living—love, friendship, and an abiding appreciation for finding pleasure in the common hour (Frankl, 1964).

The trained mind knows that thoughts about events are more powerful than the events themselves. When we learn to shape our thinking, we use our minds to overcome a series of unfortunate events. Replacing negative emotions with optimistic thoughts cultivates contentment. Teach the following techniques to your patients to enable them to suppress negative thinking:

TABLE 7-5

Happiness Versus Joy

HAPPINESS	UNHAPPINESS	JOY
Red Lamborghini	Totaled Lamborghini	A walk in the park
Corner office	Windowless basement office	Contentment in all things
One-night stand	Sexually transmitted disease	A wife of noble character
Executive power	Servitude	A willing and obedient heart
Fully funded 401-K	Bear market at retirement	Generosity
Fame and fortune	Feeling harassed and helpless	Feeling humble and grateful
Tequila sunrise	Hangover	A fruitful vine
Intelligent and knowledgeable	Ignorant and apathetic	Wise and discerning
Superiority	Inferiority	Selflessness
Possessing worldly things	Craving, lusting, boasting	Living a virtuous life
Pride in accomplishments	Arrogance and hubris	Warm-hearted appreciation

- **Teach your body to work for you.** Because motion creates emotion or, to put the axiom in another way, because physiology creates feelings, teach your body to give you the positive results you want. Smile (even if you don't feel like it), stand erect, walk briskly, speak rapidly, and alter the pitch and tone of your voice. When you change the way you talk, speak, and move, you become more confident, more helpful to others, and yes, happier.
- **Act "as if" you have already achieved the results you want.** If you want to quit smoking, throw away the ashtrays and air fresheners. If you want to lose weight, tell yourself, "I weigh 145 slim, trim pounds."
- **Cultivate an environment that makes you feel better about yourself.** Replace squalor with uncluttered neatness. Hang paintings and photographs that convey peace of mind. Tape encouraging words to your mirror.

- **Think and talk positively.** The mind is like a computer. Speak positively, and the mind is programmed for success. Negative speech programs the mind for failure. When life becomes disappointing, speak more positively, and you will begin to feel and act better. Scientists estimate that we create approximately 60,000 thoughts a day. Most of these thoughts—about 95%—are repetitive. These thoughts make up our philosophy of life, our personality. One way to change our personality is to change our thought patterns through a concentrated effort to think more positively.

Excellent health goes beyond positive thinking to include a positive philosophy of life. Positive thinking is better than negative thinking, but a benevolent view of life is better still. Those individuals who view life with love, joy, peace, patience, kindness, goodness, faithfulness, softness, and self-control are much more likely to have excellent physical health. Feeling, really feeling, loved changes the biochemistry of our bodies in a beneficial way.

Are You Type A?				
Make Check Mark (✓) in Appropriate Column	Little of the Time 1 point each ✓	Some of the Time 2 points each ✓	A Lot of the Time 3 points each ✓	Most of the Time 4 points each ✓
I get upset with slow highway drivers.				
I am angry.				
I interrupt people when I talk.				
I enjoy reading a list of my accomplishments.				
I want to win at all costs.				
I have difficulty resting and relaxing.				
I like doing things quickly.				
Long conversations bore me.				
I enjoy accomplishing things more than I enjoy being around people.				
I feel that a person's self-worth depends on accomplishments.				
Multiply ✓ by the value given in each column.				

Add the total for each column to get the **Grand total** = _____

SCORING

10–14 points = Type B

15–24 points = Calm and relaxed almost all the time

25–34 points = Heart attack waiting to happen

35–40 points = 5-star type A

Do You Know How to Have Fun?				
Make Check Mark (✓) in Appropriate Column	Little of the Time 1 point each ✓	Some of the Time 2 points each ✓	A Lot of the Time 3 points each ✓	Most of the Time 4 points each ✓
I enjoy hobbies without feeling guilty about not working.				
I am optimistic and cheerful.				
I surround myself with happy, positive, and fun-loving people.				
I correct my mistakes and blunders but don't continue to worry about them.				
I take a long weekend away from work when I begin to feel burned out and tired.				
Leisure activity helps me feel rested.				
Sports and games bring me more laughs than frowns because I play to have fun not necessarily to win.				
I enjoy creative play—dancing, painting, party games, playing a musical instrument, and so on.				
I laugh at least once a day.				
I take vacations without worrying about the job.				
Multiply ✓ by the value given in each column.				

Add the total for each column to get the **Grand total** = _____

SCORING

10–14 points = Find it difficult to have fun

15–24 points = Party pooper

25–34 points = Fun to be around

35–40 points = Life of the party

A Clinician's Quiz

1. Who is the "father" of stress research and what breakthroughs did he make?
2. Describe the relationship between stress and frequency of illness.
3. Who were Holmes and Rahe?
4. Describe the differences between type A and type B Behavior.
5. What 3 personality characteristics have linked heart disease with behavior?
6. Name 5 behavior risk factors associated with medical illnesses.
7. Give 7 benefits of exercise.
8. Discuss the protective factors against psychosomatic illness.
9. In treating psychosomatic illness what is the most effective way to reduce emotional factors that contribute to illness—medication, traditional psychotherapy, or the patient's motivation to change?
10. What can the therapist do to help motivate a patient to change?

CHAPTER 8

Understanding and Managing Somatoform and Factitious Disorders

Those Low-Down, Mind-Messin', Waitin'-in-the-Doctor's Office Blues

She slinks—no, oozes—into the room, her face wrinkled with worry, worry that suggests no one will ever love her, appreciate her, or even like her. Hers is a face worried by selfishness, reflecting no love and thus receiving none. She represents those unlikable patients with repeated admissions, sour with disappointment, whining with complaints, a person who seems less sick than bitter, one who makes others want to disappear. That's why no one mentions her name.

Every hospital has an unwritten law: the law of unmentionable names. Speaking aloud the name of one of these unmentionables guarantees their readmission within 24 hours. It's true. When the inevitable happens, and the unmentionable is again caught slinking through the hospital door, admissions staff and on-call physicians sprint for the break room. Those patients who create a cacophony of chaos and confusion usually have a diagnosis that falls under the category somatoform disorder; say their names, and they are back.

Patients who repeatedly seek treatment for physical symptoms for which there is no medical explanation may be seen as a nuisance, but the pain and suffering they experience is almost always real. Symptoms of somatoform disorders are linked to psychological factors. Whereas Chapter 7 explored the mind–body connection in the sense that emotional factors can contribute to actual disease, in these cases, the mind fabricates or exaggerates physical symptoms with little or no medical evidence to support the claims.

The intriguing psychodynamics displayed by this rather diverse group of somatoform disorders, which includes hypochondriasis, somatization disorder, conversion disorder, body dysmorphic disorder, and some pain disorders, make them fascinating challenges **(Table 8-1)**. If we understand their frenetic maneuvers as an attempt to compensate for a lost childhood; if we recognize that they will never "get well" in the sense of what is normally considered healthy living; if we appreciate that their odd behavior acts, in part, as a defense against emotional closeness lest they get hurt again as they did in childhood; if we realize that they will invariably leave therapy when they discover that no matter how great a therapist we are we will never be capable of satisfying their ravenous appetite for emotional nourishment; and if we develop a warm sense of humor to enable us to deal with the nuances of their behavior, we will find these patients an interesting group with whom to work, patients that we will be able to help far more than we initially realized when we refused to say their names.

Somatization Disorders

Patients with somatization disorders present to clinicians with a litany of complaints: headache, cough, back pain, stomachaches, chest pain, and abdominal pain. They often dramatize their symptoms: "I'm vomiting like a volcano"; "I almost fainted and fell down three flights of stairs"; "my headaches are the worst in the world" (Zebro & Kilgus, 2009). They generally go from doctor to doctor looking for a surgical cure or a medication that will relieve their suffering. Although no identifiable medical explanation exists, these patients are not fabricating their symptoms; unconscious psychological conflicts contribute to their illness.

> A 41-year-old woman reported frequent episodes of nausea and vomiting. Headaches, musculoskeletal problems, and painful menstruation had dominated her life. When asked about her current medications, she produced a brown sack containing no fewer than 22 prescriptions from five different clinicians. Most of the medications were narcotics, analgesics, minor tranquilizers, sedative-hypnotics, and laxatives. A physical examination revealed a road map of abdominal scars.

Differential Diagnosis

Exaggerated physical complaints are indicative of a somatization disorder, but multiple somatic complaints can also be found in other medical and

	TABLE 8-1	
	Somatoform Disorders	
DISORDER	**DEFINITION**	**EXAMPLES/DESCRIPTION OF SYMPTOMS**
Conversion Disorder	Anxiety/anger converted into one symptom that cannot be explained by a medical condition	• Paralysis of an extremity with normal reflexes • Pseudoseizures (false seizures) • Vomiting with no physical causes • Pain without physical findings • Blindness with pupils that dilate when exposed to light • Difficulty swallowing ("globus hystericus")
Somatization disorder	Multiple physical complaints	• No physical findings
Undifferentiated somatoform disorder	One or two physical complaints that cannot be fully explained by a medical condition	• Fatigue • Loss of appetite • Gastrointestinal complaints • Urinary complaints
Hypochondriasis	Persistent preoccupation with the idea of having a disease secondary to the misinterpretation of physical symptoms	• Impairment in social and work performance • Symptoms not based on delusions
Body dysmorphic disorder	Persistent preoccupation with an imagined defect in appearance	• Not due to other illnesses such as anorexia nervosa or bulimia
Pain disorder	Pain is the predominant focus	• Psychological factors play a predominant role in the severity of the pain

physical conditions. Depressed patients may complain of fatigue, anorexia, constipation, and diminished sexual interest, but unlike the patient with a somatization disorder, the onset of the illness is acute, with a disturbance in mood predominating. Schizophrenic patients often have bizarre somatic delusions compared to the nondelusional complaints of the somaticizer. Physical illnesses with unusual presentations may cause the unalert clinician to erroneously assume that the patient has a somatization disorder. The physician must be careful not to confuse somatization disorder with multiple sclerosis and other illnesses that may present with multiple organ involvement **(Table 8-2)**.

A diagnosis of somatization disorder should only be made after all other causes of illness have been ruled out. If the patient exhibits all the stigmata of somatization disorder and there is no other explanation for the complaints, then the diagnosis is confirmed.

An illness similar to somatization disorder is undifferentiated somatoform disorder. The dynamics and treatment of undifferentiated somatoform disorder are identical to somatization disorder. The only differences between the two are in the characteristics of the illnesses. While somatization disorder involves multiple organ systems, undifferentiated somatoform disorder is characterized by one or two somatic complaints.

Etiology

A lifetime risk for the illness is estimated at around 1–2%. The disorder is more common in women with a limited, rural education who had been sexually abused as children (Andreasen & Black, 2006). Neuropsychological testing revealed that those with somatization disorder had problems with attention and memory, with bilateral anterior frontal lobe dysfunction (Yutzy, 2003). Women who were adopted before age 3 were five times more likely to have somatization disorder if their biological parents were either alcoholics or antisocial (Yutzy, 2003).

The illness tends to run in families. Approximately 20% of female first-degree relatives of somatization patients met the criteria for the illness (Yutzy, 2003). A familial association could result from environmental influences, genetic factors, or a combination of the two.

Altman (1975) postulated that patients with somatization disorders failed to establish satisfying relationships with others during their childhood years, generating loneliness and anxiety that is defended against by learning to gain affection and care through illness. Patients with clinging-dependent somatization establish a pattern of illness and suffering when they learn that illness

TABLE 8-2	
Selected Illnesses That Could Be Confused With Somatoform Disorders	
PHYSICAL ILLNESS	**DIAGNOSTIC MARKERS**
Endocrine disorders	Abnormal endocrine tests
Porphyria	Urine positive for porphobilinogen
Multiple sclerosis	Magnetic resonance imaging shows disseminated central nervous system lesions
Systemic lupus erythematosus	Positive antinuclear antibody
Pernicious anemia	Low vitamin B_{12} levels

supplies them with the attention that they crave. These patients, emotionally neglected as children, feel compelled to prove repeatedly that others are concerned about them. The clinician is sought as a surrogate parent by these patients, but their escalating demands often provoke the clinician to reject them, thus reproducing the neglect that they suffered in childhood.

Treatment

A good therapeutic outcome with somatization disorder, an illness difficult to treat, depends on the establishment of a solid relationship between the patient and clinician. Because these patients always have multiple physical complaints, the primary care physician might be the best clinician to work with them, answering questions about symptoms and offering information by sharing the patient's vital signs and laboratory studies.

Education is a crucial part of therapy. The patient can be encouraged to peruse several excellent Internet blogs that give information on somatoform illness (e.g., MedlinePlus, 2008). A warm and understanding clinician who enables the patient to talk about his or her illness while redirecting the patient toward positive change can eventually help the patient have a better outlook on life (Blazer, 1977). One role of the clinician is to encourage activity, and one of the best motivators is to have the patient recognize the opportunities missed because of the illness. If the patient learns to be more active—e.g., going to a party, visiting a friend, or playing with the grandchildren—despite the physical symptoms, the physical complaints will eventually diminish.

When treating the somaticizer, the clinician aims to provide the patient with a stable and long-standing relationship. From the first interview, the clinician allows the patient to talk about symptoms without interruption. Empathetic listening establishes a good clinician–patient relationship and actually saves time and frustration in the end by helping to prevent unnecessary telephone calls and visits in the middle of the night. After 15 minutes, the clinician can say, "Mrs. Johnson, we are going to have to stop now, but I want to hear more about your case. How about next Wednesday at 3:15?"

Nonessential tests and treatments should be avoided after an initial diagnostic workup satisfies the clinician that there are no organic causes for the patient's complaints. The clinician can offer support in the following manner:

> Mrs. Johnson, I have performed all of the necessary examinations but can find nothing life threatening. Just because I could find no source for your symptoms does not mean that your symptoms are not real. I can tell that you are experiencing a great deal of discomfort. I can't relieve all of your symptoms, but I would like to work with you to help you deal with them the best we can.

The physician, by establishing regular appointment times with the patient and encouraging the patient to keep the appointment no matter how well the patient is feeling, implies that the clinician cares for the patient, which establishes a relationship based on trust rather than illness. After the initial workup and evaluation are completed, the clinician can establish a regular 15- to 30-minute appointment once weekly, during which the patient's current activity level is discussed and new activities are encouraged.

> Mrs. Johnson, despite your terrible abdominal discomfort and headache, wasn't it great that you went to the church picnic? I am proud of you for learning to live with your disease and not letting it control you. You are getting out of the house much more. You will find over time that when you stay active despite your symptoms, you will be able to do more and more and enjoy being with people more. (Note the almost hypnotic use of the word more.)

An increase in the patient's physical complaints generally indicates environmental stresses. Unnecessary diagnostic workups, medication, and physician shopping can be prevented if the physician encourages both more frequent appointments and more social activities until the complaints have diminished. Here are some hints for working with patients with somatization disorder:

- Use terms that paint a picture of success.
- Offer hope without promising a cure.
- Praise good behavior and increased activity.
- Turn negatives into positives.
- Don't don't be afraid to just sit there (doing as little as possible in the form of surgeries and procedures is best).
- Have a cosmic sense of humor—realize that life is filled with absurdities, and you might as well enjoy them.
- Don't get discouraged that after working with these patients for years, most of them will eventually leave to look for someone who will give them a pill that will cure their every ill.

Patients often seek reassurance by requesting medication that should be avoided. If it is necessary to use medications, the lowest dose of the least-harmful medication should be used. Because many of these patients have low-grade depression and high anxiety, a selective serotonin reuptake inhibitor (SSRI) like 10–20 mg Celexa can help relieve some of the dysphoria these patients experience. Low doses of long-acting benzodiazepines (e.g., 5 mg Valium once or twice daily) can help relieve generalized anxiety. Opioids and other narcotics should be avoided because of the tendency of these patients to want to increase the dose rather rapidly.

What to Do If You Have Somatization Disorder
- Have a thorough physical exam annually.
- Find a physician who will:
  - Listen to you.
  - Encourage you to lead a full life despite your symptoms.
  - Avoid prescribing needless medications.
  - Avoid useless diagnostic procedures and surgeries.
- Find a therapist who will help you deal with childhood emotional deprivation.

Conversion Disorder

Conversion disorder derives its name from the "conversion" of anxiety into a physical symptom that results in two benefits for the patient. The conversion symptom prevents awareness of the internal psychological conflict (primary gain) and simultaneously allows the patient to avoid a particular activity or receive a benefit that would otherwise be unattainable (secondary gain). It is important to remember that conversion symptoms are out of the patient's conscious awareness. The patient is not malingering, although to the uninitiated it would certainly seem so.

> After becoming enraged with his employer regarding excessive paperwork requirements, a man developed a sudden "paralysis" of his arm (primary gain). The paralysis prevented him from striking his boss and allowed him a graceful way to avoid paperwork (secondary gain).

The most common conversion symptoms are those that suggest a neurological deficit, such as paralysis, blindness, or seizures. Conversion symptoms occasionally involve the autonomic nervous system. In one case, for example, a patient vomited after sexual intercourse, symbolically indicating the patient's disgust with the act. The most common endocrine involvement occurs with pseudocyesis—a false pregnancy representing the wish to become pregnant **(Table 8-3)**.

Conversion disorder is more common than most therapists and clinicians realize. More than one fourth of medically ill women reported having had conversion symptoms at some time during their life. Depending on which epidemiological survey one reads, more than 5% of psychiatric outpatients have conversion disorder symptoms, and 5–14% of general hospital patients have a history of conversion symptoms (Yutzy, 2003). Factors associated with conversion disorder include:

TABLE 8-3	
Gaining From Conversion Disorder	
GAIN	**SYMPTOMS**
Primary gain	Rids the self of anxiety.
Secondary gain	Enables the individual to avoid situations that produced the anxiety or gives the patient attention and support that otherwise would have been unavailable.

- Lower socioeconomic status
- Lower education
- Lack of psychological sophistication
- Living in a rural setting

Treatment of conversion disorder consists of giving the individual reassurance and relaxation. Hypnosis may be effective. In 1995, Ford suggested "three Ps"—predisposing factors, precipitating stressors, and perpetuating factors—which are worth examining and addressing in psychotherapy.

- Predisposing factors—Patients with histrionic personality are more prone to the development of conversion symptoms. These patients demonstrate dramatic behavior, over-talkativeness, excitability, and emotional liability. They tend to be shallow in emotional responsiveness and frequently ignore, deny, or repress unpleasant situations. The dependent personality, characterized by a lack of self-confidence and feelings of helplessness, also predisposes the individual to the possibility of a conversion experience.
- Precipitating stressors—Conversion symptoms often develop during a period of extreme stress. Unsuccessful love affairs, an unhappy marriage, fear of pregnancy, sexual difficulties, are frequent precipitants of conversion symptoms; threats to self-esteem, or problems at work may also result in conversion reactions. Sometimes, the precipitating event appears trivial to others, but to the patient the situation has special meaning. Therapy involves helping the person understand how the current stressors, combined with the patient's personality style, precipitate a conversion disorder.
- Perpetuating factors—Systems resist change, or as they explain in east Texas, if one crab in a bucket tries to climb out, the other crabs will pull the ambitious critter back down. To resolve almost all psychological conflicts, the patient's family must be educated to help them

consciously understand how their behavior might contribute to the perpetuation of the illness. A conversion disorder example is the case of a young woman who craved attention from her mother and developed a pseudoseizure. Because the girl's dramatic flopping around on the floor made the mother excited and worried (thus fulfilling the patient's desire for attention), the episodes increased. Family therapy with an emphasis on education brought an end to the cycle of seizures.

Most symptoms of conversion disorder last a relatively short time. The more severe the symptoms, the more quickly they tend to disappear. However, the disorder may indicate that the person has persistent trouble coping with stress and conflict and would benefit from ongoing support.

Hypochondriasis

The cardinal feature of hypochondriasis is an unrealistic interpretation of physical signs and sensations as abnormal, resulting in a preoccupation with the fear or belief of having a disease (American Psychiatric Association, 2000).

> A 42-year-old woman presented to the medical clinic with a 6-year history of abdominal pain that indicated, to her, that she had abdominal cancer similar to the carcinoma of the colon that had killed her tyrannical father 6 years earlier. Although her examination was normal, she visited physician after physician trying to find someone who would remove her "cancerous colon."

Patients with hypochondriasis lack the multiplicity of symptoms or the early onset of illness characterized by a somatization disorder. Treatment goals are similar to those of somatization disorder.

Body Dysmorphic Disorder

Those with body dysmorphic disorder, the so-called imagined ugliness disease, cannot stop thinking about a flaw in their appearance—a flaw that to others is so minor that it is almost unnoticeable, but to the patient is so distressing that it interferes with social interaction and job performance.

Those with body dysmorphic disorder intensely obsess over their appearance and body image, seeking cosmetic procedures to "fix" a perceived flaw. In many cases, body dysmorphic disorder overlaps with obsessive-compulsive disorder, delusional disorder, and depression.

> An attractive 25-year old woman, convinced that her nose was too big, avoided mirrors and refused to be photographed. When a plastic sur-

geon told her there was no defect, she refused to believe him. Insecurity about the size of her nose limited her contact with others. A perfectionist in her work as a computer programmer, a job that provided little social interaction, she showed no other signs of obsessions or compulsions, but began having suicidal thoughts. Increasingly isolating himself, she was given a course of electroconvulsive therapy when she failed to respond to antidepressant medications. Later, she responded well enough to Luvox, an SSRI useful in treating obsessive-compulsive disorder, to become socially active, although her nose size continued to bother her.

The cause of body dysmorphic disorder is unknown. From 6% to 15% of patients seeking cosmetic surgery have this disorder, and it is found equally in men and women (American Psychiatric Association, 2000). Treatment is difficult and involves psychoeducation, medications (SSRIs and other antidepressants and antipsychotics if the condition is severe enough to be considered delusional), and supportive psychotherapy. Sometimes, helping the patient understand that the illness is psychiatric rather than physical is helpful. A wide range of therapeutic techniques have been tried, none of which seems to have a better outcome than the other (Yutzy, 2003).

Chronic Pain

A survey found that 43% of American families have at least one family member with chronic pain (King, 2003). The *Diagnostic and Statistical Manual of Mental Disorders, Fourth Edition, Text Revision (DSM-IV-TR)* divides chronic pain into two types (American Psychiatric Association, 2000). The first type consists of pain in which psychological factors are judged to have the major role in the onset, intensity, and maintenance of the pain; general medical conditions play either no role or a minimal role. The second type of chronic pain is one in which both a medical condition and psychological factors play an equitable part in the disorder. The majority of pain syndromes—knee and joint pain, neck and shoulder pain, whiplash, muscle pain, jaw pain, trigeminal neuralgia, shingles and postherpetic pain, low back pain, fibromyalgia, and migraine headache—meet the second category. (A third category of pain disorder, in which a viable medical condition is the sole cause of pain, is not considered a mental disorder and is listed under axis III in the *DSM-IV-TR*.)

Medications for Chronic Pain

The following medications can be helpful in treating chronic pain:

- Cymbalta, a dual-mechanism antidepressant, inhibits pain by elevating serotonin (5-HT) and norepinephrine (NE) between the first neurons in the pain pathway and the spinal cord neurons that project up to higher centers (Stahl, 2008). Relief of chronic pain is independent of antidepressant effects. The dose is 60 mg. Because Cymbalta has a flat dose curve, doses above 60 mg generally fail to increase efficacy (Schatzberg, Cole, & DeBattista, 2007).

- Tricyclic antidepressants (Elavil and Pamelor) also elevate 5-HT and NE. Tricyclics are a first-line treatment option for peripheral pain. They have an added advantage because they are sedating and anxiolytic. Anticholinergic side effects, heart block, and suicide risk limit use in some patients. The Elavil dose is 75–300 mg. The Pamelor dose is 50–150 mg. Monitoring plasma levels in patients unresponsive to Pamelor helps with dosing decisions because Pamelor has a therapeutic window with a decrease in response at plasma levels greater than 150 ng/mL (Schatzberg et al., 2007).
- Remeron boosts 5-HT and blocks alpha 2 adrenergic presynaptic receptors, thereby increasing NE. Histamine 1 receptor antagonism explains sedation and weight gain effects. Remeron augments the effects of Effexor XR (Stahl, 2008).
- Lyrica, the first treatment for diabetic peripheral neuropathy, crosses the blood–brain barrier to bind to the 2-delta subunit to close presynaptic calcium channels, diminishing excessive neuronal activity. Lyrica, also effective for postherpetic neuralgia and fibromyalgia, can reduce neuropathic pain and anxiety in 1 week. Lyrica is excreted renally and can be removed by hemodialysis. Hepatic impairment mandates no dose adjustment, with a 75-mg initial dose twice daily increased to 150 mg twice daily after 3 days; dosage can increase to 300 mg twice daily after 1 week. Maximum dose is 600 mg daily (Stahl, 2008).
- Neurontin binds to the alpha 2-delta subunit, closing calcium channels, thereby diminishing neuronal activity. The dose can work up to 300 mg three times daily on day 3. Pain relief may require 600 mg or more three times daily (Stahl, 2008).
- Ibuprofen, aspirin, naproxen, and other nonsteroidal anti-inflammatory drugs (NSAIDs) inhibit cyclooxygenase (COX) enzymes, thereby reducing the generation of inflammatory and pain-causing mediators like the prostaglandins. Ibuprofen, aspirin, and naproxen are nonselective between COX-1 and COX-2 inhibition, resulting in a risk of gastric ulcers (King, 2003).
- Celebrex and Vioxx are selective for COX-2, giving fewer gastrointestinal side effects. Because COX-2 inhibition increases the risk of cardiovascular side effects, the COX-2 agents Bextra and Vioxx were withdrawn from the market. Celebrex remains a viable option (King, 2003).

- Opioids mimic the endogenous painkillers—the endorphins and enkephalins. Descending opioid pathways run from pain-processing centers in the brain down the spinal cord. Opioid drugs activate the mu (m) opioid receptor on presynaptic terminals of pain-sensing fibers, called nociceptive C fibers (Stahl, 2008).

Before prescribing opioids, a risk assessment should be done. The more positive answers to the following questions, the greater the risk for opioid and other substance abuse (King, 2003):

- Is there a personal history of alcohol, illegal drug, or prescription drug abuse?
- Is there a family history of alcohol, illegal drug, or prescription drug abuse?
- Is there a history of preadolescent sexual abuse?
- Is the patient between 16 and 45 years of age?

After screening for risk of abuse and addiction, the following additional guidelines should be considered when using opioids for the treatment of chronic pain (King, 2003):

- Opioid medications should only be used if other nonopioid medications or therapies will not provide adequate relief.
- When opioids are used for the treatment of chronic pain, a written treatment plan should be established that includes measurable goals for reduction of pain and improvement in function.
- The patient should sign a written agreement regarding treatment with opioids that includes the risks and benefits of the treatment.
- Regular monitoring should be conducted with face-to-face visits.
- Opioid treatment should be discontinued if treatment goals are not met or if adverse events occur.

Behavior Therapy for Chronic Pain

Chronic pain management focuses on improving function rather than on alleviating pain. Even when a general medical condition plays a major role in the cause of the pain, psychologically-based therapies are helpful. A supportive clinician understands that individuals with chronic pain feel angry and frustrated about many issues.

Because anyone who has chronic pain will have psychological problems secondary to the pain, those clinicians dealing with chronic pain must use a multimodal treatment approach when helping their patients. Psychologically based treatment modalities include operant conditioning, cognitive-behavior therapy, biofeedback, relaxation training, and hypnosis.

On a hot summer's day in Sea World in San Antonio, you will find most of the crowd watching Shamu the whale jump out of the water. (Those who are smart sit in the splash zone so that when Shamu jumps, they get a heavy dousing of water that cools them off.) Now, how did those Sea World people get Shamu the whale to jump out of the water at their command? Did they row out in the middle of the Pacific Ocean and with bullhorn to mouth shout, "Hey whale! Come join us. We've got a good job for you in San Antonio. Good retirement program. Good insurance. Plenty of things to do. Good sights to see. We'll give you all of this—all you have to do is jump way out of the water when there are a lot of people around." No, Sea World does not do it that way. Instead, they get a little bitty baby whale. Whenever the little bitty whale swims over a rope, they feed him a fish. The whale swims over the rope, feed him a fish. Raise the rope a little; when the whale swims over the rope, feed him a fish. Soon, the rope is way out of the water, and the whale is jumping over it because every time he does he gets a fish, a bucket of fish, or several buckets depending on his size and his jump. He also gets attention and hugs from his trainers and the audience. Lo and behold, you've got a high-jumping whale.

That is operant conditioning. Doctors and clinicians can use the same type of techniques to help patients deal with chronic pain more effectively. The patient keeps a diary of things he or she does during the day. The patient rates pain on a scale of 0 to 10, with a 10 indicating the most severe pain. The patient learns those things that make the pain worse and those things that help relieve the pain. The patient learns to avoid those things that aggravate pain or, better still, learns how to cope with those things that cause pain. The patient also increases activities that help relieve the pain **(Table 8-4)**.

Factitious Disorders

According to the *DSM-IV-TR*, the essential feature of factitious disorder is the intentional production of physical or psychological symptoms (American Psychiatric Association, 2000). Variations in the disorder are infinite: One patient may complain of acute chest pain in the absence of any such pain; another may manipulate a rectal thermometer by relaxing and contracting the anal sphincter thus creating the illusion of fever; a third may swallow blood then vomit; another may prick their finger and squeeze blood into their urine sample, mimicking hematuria; some inject insulin to produce hypoglycemia or put a small amout of feces in the urine to suggest a urinary tract infection; others swallow glass, coins, nails, or fish hooks; and some burn themselves using a hot iron (Kilgus, 2009). In some cases, psychological symptoms predominate (e.g., presenting with signs of major depression).

The clinician must differentiate malingering from factitious disorder. This

TABLE 8-4

Psychological Treatment Modalities for Chronic Pain

TYPE OF TREATMENT	TECHNIQUE	BENEFITS
Operant conditioning	Reinforces positive behavior with rewards; decreases negative behavior through withholding rewards or withdrawal of approval.	Helps improve healthy activity.
Cognitive therapy	Corrects distorted attitudes and beliefs.	Reduces pain complaints and improves patient's ability to cope with pain.
Progressive muscle relaxation	Patient learns to relax muscle groups by contracting and then relaxing each one.	Reduces muscle tension and pain in those patients with muscle contractions and "trigger" points.
Biofeedback	Feedback devices convert information such as heart rate, blood pressure, muscle tone, and brain waves into light and sound waves that can be monitored and manipulated by the patient through breathing and muscle relaxation techniques.	Reduction of body tension helps relieve pain.
Hypnosis	While in a relaxed state of mind and body, the individual imagines being injected with pain medication or floating in ice water.	A combination of relaxation, suggestion, imagery, and dissociation helps relieve pain.
Interpersonal psychotherapy	Teaches patients how to get along with others by helping others meet their needs, thereby getting their own needs met.	Improved social skills and social interaction reduce pain by focusing the mind away from noxious stimuli.

is a difficult task. In a pure factitious disorder, the individual is unaware of the underlying reasons driving the behavior, and external motivators are absent. By contrast, the malingering patient is motivated by tangible gain (American Psychiatric Association, 2000). Some reasons for malingering might include insurance fraud, monetary gain, avoidance of prosecution, or simply to secure a place to sleep for the night.

A patient reported that he took 600 mg of Seroquel in a "suicide attempt" so that he could be admitted to the hospital in hopes of enrolling in a methadone program. Differentiating between malingering and factitious disorder is almost impossible unless one is lucky enough to have a patient admit: "I took some Seroquel because I was craving and needed a fix."

Munchausen Syndrome

An interesting form of factitious disorder is Munchausen syndrome, named after an 18th century German baron who told many fantastical adventures about himself, which Rudolf Raspe published as *The Surprising Adventures, Great And Imminent Dangers, Miraculous Escapes, And Wonderful Travels Of The Renowned Baron Munchausen* (1802). In 1951, Asher described patients who fabricated signs and symptoms of illness and named this condition after the baron (Leamon, Feldman, & Scott, 2003).

The essential feature of the disorder is the patient's credible presentation of self-induced physical symptoms to gain hospital admission. Limited only by the patient's medical knowledge, sophistication, and imagination, the symptoms often mimic actual physical conditions, including abdominal discomfort, vomiting, rashes, burns, kidney and back pain, hemoptysis, and abscesses.

Munchausen patients enjoy talking dramatically and at length about their illness, creating chaos on the hospital units by their demands for analgesics and sedatives or in their attempts to pursue surgery until, exposed, they leave the hospital against medical advice to seek admission to another hospital on another day. Although their intriguing pathologic lying, dramatic clinical presentation, disruptive behavior, noncompliance with hospital rules and regulations, continued demands for pain medication, multiple surgical scars, and extensive medical knowledge give clues to the diagnosis, the patient has usually left the building before treatment can be initiated or legal charges submitted.

Several theories regarding the cause of this fascinating illness have been posited. Perhaps the patient seeks a relationship with the physician as a mother substitute (Kolb, 1977), or maybe these patients are acting out a grudge against the medical profession; perhaps they harm themselves to assuage unconscious guilt, but most likely, they seek treatment because they enjoy the medications they receive, the warmth of a hospital bed, the reassurance of a regular meal, and the appreciation gained from a well-told story.

Munchausen's by Proxy

There have been a number of cases cited, articles penned, and books written about Munchausen's by proxy, in which a caregiver intentionally

FIGURE 8-1

From a Hospital's Record Room List of "Professional Patients"

NAME: Roger Cleverdale

ADDRESS: P.O. Box 5100, Lynn Grove, TX

DESCRIPTION: Male, Caucasian, 6 feet 2 inches, 185 pounds, 45 years old

MEDICAL COMPLAINT: Kidney stones

MODUS OPERANDI: Enters emergency room complaining of kidney pain. Has been known to prick finger to put blood in the urine sample. Describes symptoms in detail. Generates believable story of great wealth from Internet company. Requests private room.

induces illnesses in a child, leading to needless, often invasive, diagnostic tests and procedures. One study estimated that this unfortunate event occurs in two or three children under 1 year of age per 100,000 and in less than one case per 100,000 children between ages 1 and 16 (Leamon et al., 2003). Treatment, made difficult due to to the caregiver's denial, begins with involving child protective services and progresses best when directed through the legal system.

Classic Comparisions: Don Quixote

A discussion of the fantastic tale of Baron Munchausen and the patients who suffer from the eponymous syndrome causes the discerning reader immediately to reflect on Don Quixote, who instead of turning fake symptoms into a hospital bed, turned a commonplace village inn into a castle; instead of turning sympathetic statements into a concerned nurse, turned a rough farm girl into a beautiful maiden; and instead of turning a list of symptoms into concerned physicians, turned herds of sheep into gallant armies. Don Quixote, an idealist with a dream to right unspeakable wrongs, began as a man crazed to the pitiless point of absurdity by too much reading of chivalric romances and became one of the most beloved figures in all of literature. By contrast, those with Munchausen by proxy or any other factitious disorder began—and remain—pathetic creatures trying to beat the system.

In treating patients with somatoform disorder, to carry the analogy one step further, the physician would do well, like Don Quixote's devoted niece, to sit at the patient's bedside doing little more than listening and empathizing. With proper encouragement from astute caregivers, patients can perhaps develop the insight to surrender their absurdities and deceptions while pursuing a life not consumed with physical symptoms and madness, but filled with purpose and dreams.

Do You Have Somatization Disorder?

I've had physical complaints beginning before age 30 that have interfered with my work and social life; these physical symptoms include the following:	
Headaches	
Backaches	
Joint or extremity pain	
Chest pain	
Diarrhea from food intolerance	
Nausea, bloating, or vomiting	
Menstruation or urinary pain	
Sexual indifference or erectile dysfunction, orgasmic dysfunction, irregular menses or excessive menstrual bleeding	
Impaired coordination or balance, paralysis, deafness, seizures, or loss of consciousness	
After a careful examination doctors cannot explain these symptoms, or the symptoms are in excess of what would otherwise be expected.	
Add ✓ marks (1 point for each ✓)	

Add the total for each column to get the **Grand total** = _____

SCORING

0 points = Take the test again, you missed one or two

1–4 points = Everybody gets sick once in a while

5–8 points = Do think these symptoms are part of a specific illness?

9–10 points = How do you explain this high score?

A Clinician's Quiz

1. List five disorders that are part of the rather diverse group listed under the somtoform disorders division.
2. Discuss the differential diagnosis of somatization disorder.
3. What is the difference between somatization disorder and undifferentiated somatoform disorder?
4. Discuss the psychodynamics of somatization disorder.
5. Discuss the treatment of somatization disorder.
6. Give a one sentence definition of conversion disorder and discuss primary and secondary gain.
7. What is the difference between hypochondriasis and somatization disorder?
8. List the three types of chronic pain.
9. Discuss Munchausen syndrome.
10. What is Munchausen syndrome by proxy? Discuss.

CHAPTER 9

Personality Patterns, Conflicts, and Disorders

Excuses Extraordinaire

She listens more than she talks, her green eyes intense and sparkling. She makes everyone feel special because she believes they are. Her cheerful telephone greetings brighten the common hour.

A master of directness, she tells you what she thinks in a way that makes you feel good about yourself. Her pleasing counsel, sweet to the soul and healing to the bones, comes from a discerning heart. She avoids nagging and guards against quarrelsome words. She speaks the truth from her heart, respects everyone, and casts no slur on anyone. She looks for the good in everything. She understands and forgives.

She's as steady as an incoming tide. Once she makes up her mind, she almost never changes it. Because our strengths are, in excess, our greatest weaknesses, she's hard-headed and prone to perfectionism.

She's intolerant of overabundant exuberance and excessive enthusiasm. I must curb my unembarrassed tendency to improve a story by expanding the truth. Her upturned eyes tell me that my free use of gesticulation and theatrics have overextended her tolerance for my unfettered excitement.

She covers her eyes during crucial parts of an exciting basketball game and at the scary parts of a movie. She doesn't like mice or getting her finger pricked, but other than that she can withstand just about anything.

When malice attacks her grandchild, she comes to the rescue firm chinned and determined.

She's centered on each day, treasures time, and wastes no hour. She abhors regret and believes the future will work out the way it's been planned. She's as radiant as the sweet-seasoned sun on a spring day and soothing as a downy pillow.

From the description of this woman, we recognize enduring patterns of relating to the environment, others, and self that make her unique from anyone else. Her personality traits reflect a flexible and appropriate adjustment to the world that enables her to cope with normal stresses and allows her to develop enduring relationships with family, friends, and coworkers.

Only when personality traits engender rigid adaptations to daily challenges that cause significant impairment in relationships, work, and personal satisfaction do they constitute personality disorders. Blaming, excuse making, and refusing responsibility for personal behavior mark a person with a personality disorder. Those with personality disorders have poor frustration tolerance, impulse control problems, the inability to delay gratification, and poor self-esteem that may be masked by grandiose thinking or a masochistic effort to please others. These character flaws reflect lifetime behavior patterns that began in late adolescence or early adulthood **(Figure 9-1, Table 9-1)**.

Causes of Personality Disorder

Just as both genes and environment contribute to healthy personalities, the same is true for those who develop personality disorders. Research using distinctive designs with a wide range of groups from different countries indicated that roughly 40–60% of behavior variance seems to be under genetic control (Carey & DiLalla, 1994). Studies suggest that the choices we make through life are akin to those made by genetically similar individuals (Selig-

---

FIGURE 9-1

Definition of Personality Disorder

A pervasive pattern of behavior that remarkably deviates from cultural expectations and leads to impairment in work, love, and friendships. Characterized by constant blaming, excuse-making, and refusal to take responsibility for personal behavior. This unusual behavior begins in adolescence or early adulthood and is unrelated to drug abuse, a medical condition, or another mental disorder.

TABLE 9-1	
Adaptive Personality Traits Versus Maladaptive Personality Disorder Traits	
ADAPTIVE TRAITS	**MALADAPTIVE TRAITS**
Has a flexible outlook	Rigid, inflexible, truculent
Appropriately evaluates mistakes	Makes excuses
Works on improving personal flaws	Blaming
Is accountable for personal obligations	Refuses responsibility for behavior
Considers options and consequences	Impulsive
Works to achieve worthwhile goals	Unable to delay gratification
Overcomes challenges	Poor frustration tolerance
Finds the good in others	Wants others to find the good in them
Enjoys both solitude and society	Has relationship problems

man, 1993). Events occurring in early childhood exert a powerful influence on behavior later in life. Most likely, environmental factors contribute to the development of personality disorders in genetically susceptible individuals (Paris, 1993).

Several factors increase the risk of developing a personality disorder, including (Rosenhan, Seligman, & Walker, 2001; Vaillant, 1994):

- A family history of personality disorders or other mental illness.
- Emotional, verbal, physical, or sexual abuse during childhood.
- An unstable family life during childhood.
- Environmental stress or deprivation.

Frequency and Comorbidity of Personality Disorders

Although the frequency of personality disorders in the general population may be higher than most people believe, the diagnosis of these disorders depends on the strictness of the diagnostic criteria. Some studies showed that as many as 20% of the general population have a personality disorder (Andreasen & Black, 2006). Other studies put the range between 10% and 15% (Phillips, Yen, & Gunderson, 2003). In mental health clinics, these rates are much higher—30–50% (Koenigsberg, Kaplan, Gilmore, & Cooper, 1985).

Epidemiological studies gave the community rates for the various personality disorder categories.

Those individuals with personality disorders are more vulnerable to depression, anxiety, drug and alcohol abuse, and psychosomatic or somatoform disorders than the general population. Patients with a primary psychiatric disorder in combination with a personality disorder are less likely to respond to pharmacology and other treatment modalities; they also comply poorly to medication treatment, and they have higher relapse rates than those without a personality disorder (Phillips et al., 2003).

Classification of Personality Disorders

The *Diagnostic and Statistical Manual of Mental Disorders, Fourth Edition, Text Revision* (*DSM-IV-TR*; American Psychiatric Association, 2000), divides personality disorders into three groups:

- Cluster A—individuals with this pattern of behavior appear odd or eccentric. This group includes the paranoid, schizoid, and schizotypal personality disorders.
- Cluster B—these individuals are dramatic, emotional, and erratic. This group includes antisocial, borderline, histrionic, and narcissistic personality disorders.
- Cluster C— includes those people who are anxious or fearful. Avoidant, dependent, and obsessive-compulsive personality disorders are included in this cluster.

Cluster A

Individuals with paranoid, schizoid, and schizotypal disorders belong to the first cluster of personality disorders, which is marked by odd or eccentric behavior. These individuals do not recognize that their behavior is abnormal, and their personality traits reflect this detachment from reality.

Paranoid Personality Disorder

The paranoid personality interprets the actions of others as deliberately threatening or demeaning. Untrusting and unforgiving, the paranoid is prone to angry or aggressive outbursts without justification. Because they perceive others as unfaithful, disloyal, condescending, or deceitful, they are jealous, guarded, secretive, and scheming. They are excessively serious and emotionally "cold." Paranoid personalities are found in 0.5–2.5% of community populations (American Psychiatric Association, 2000).

President Richard Nixon was probably a paranoid personality. He was slated to win the presidential election by a huge margin, and he did. But, his henchmen broke into the Democratic headquarters just to see if they had anything on him he didn't know about. He thought the people of the press were against him. When he lost the nomination for governor of California, he told the press, "You won't have Richard Nixon to kick around anymore." He made a miraculous comeback, becoming president of the United States, and yet he still felt everybody was against him. Sure enough, the press did have him to kick around again and kick they did (Jennings & Brewster, 1998).

Almost all dictators are paranoid. Hitler was the prototypical paranoid. His book, *Mein Kampf* ("my struggle") was a paranoid rail against other European powers and the Jewish people, who he thought, through their banking and business contacts, would take over the world. Rising to power, he formed the Secret Service (SS) to investigate and eliminate his perceived enemies. He went into paranoid rages. On at least one occasion, he fell to the floor and started biting the carpet because of his anger toward his generals, whom he thought had betrayed him. He stayed out of sight as much as possible, hiding in remote fortresses. He wore a bulletproof vest and had 3.5 pounds of steel-plate lining under his military cap. He probably never consummated his relationship with his mistress, Eva Braun. In the end, he was even suspicious that the cyanide capsules he would take to commit suicide were filled with harmless powder (Shirer, 1960).

A person with pervasive distrust of others and the suspicion that their motives are malevolent can also be marked by the following traits (APA, 2000):

- Has a belief that others exploit him or her.
- Is preoccupied with doubts about the loyalty and trustworthiness of associates.
- Has a reluctance to confide in others out of fear that the information would be maliciously used against him or her.
- Twists benign remarks into threats or malicious comments.
- Bears unforgiving grudges.
- Without justification reacts angrily to perceived attacks.
- Without validation suspects spouse or lover of infidelity.

Schizoid Personality Disorder

Introverted, withdrawn, solitary, emotionally cold, and distant, those with schizoid personality disorder fear closeness and intimacy with others. They are rarely seen in clinical settings. Czech writer Franz Kafka wrote grotesque descriptions of fantasies that appear to have no purpose or meaning. His characters, deprived of security and tortured by anxiety, depicted loneliness and alienation (Hornek, 2005).

A pervasive pattern of detachment can be marked by the following (APA, 2000):

- Has no desire for close relationships.
- Enjoys and chooses solitary activities.
- Has little interest in sex.
- Enjoys neither close relationships nor activities.
- Has no friends.
- Is indifferent to praise or criticism.
- Is emotionally detached and cold.

Schizotypal Personality Disorder

Schizotypal individuals, marked by a pattern of peculiarities, often display odd or eccentric manners of speaking and dressing. They have difficulties forming relationships and experience extreme anxiety in social situations. Some claim a "sixth sense" that makes them believe they can see into the future or read other people's minds. Schizotypal personality disorder is found in 3% of the general population.

The artist with the iconic, flamboyant mustache, whose most famous work, *The Persistence of Memory,* depicted the surrealistic image of a melting pocket watch, could be the poster boy for the schizotypal personality (Etherington-Smith, 1995). Salvador Dali would walk down the street ringing a bell to draw attention to himself, and he once delivered a lecture in a diving suit to show he was "plunging deeply into the human mind." He often referred to himself in the third person and insisted he was immortal.

This pervasive pattern of distortions and eccentricities can include (APA, 2000):

- Thoughts that others are talking about him/her.
- Odd beliefs or magical thinking—belief in clairvoyance, telepathy, or a "sixth sense."
- Bodily illusions.
- Overelaborate, vague, metaphorical, or odd speech.
- Suspiciousness.
- Inappropriate or detached way of relating to others.
- Peculiar behavior.
- No close friends.
- Excessive social anxiety and paranoid fears.

Cluster B

Four related personality disorders—antisocial, borderline, histrionic, and narcissistic—are associated with dramatic-erratic behavior, poor impulse control, and emotional instability. While almost 75% of individuals with borderline disorders are female, the vast majority of sociopaths (with antisocial personality disorder) are male.

Antisocial Personality Disorder

Those with antisocial personalities ignore normal rules of social behavior. Impulsive, irresponsible, and callous, they often have a history of legal difficulties caused by belligerent, aggressive, and violent behavior. They have no remorse about the effects of their behavior on others. The disorder is found in 3% of men and 1% of women.

The list of famous antisocial personalities could fill the pages of this book—Charles Manson, Richard Speck, son of Sam Berkowitz, most of Hitler's confidants. Movies and television programs glorify them—*Bonnie and Clyde, The Untouchables, Desperados, The Departed, Unforgiven, Dallas, The Sopranos.*

One of the most notorious, Al Capone, traded a fourth-grade education for a lawless empire of gambling, bootlegging, and prostitution. He served 8 years for tax evasion. By the time of his release from prison, syphilis had rendered him demented (Luciano, 2003).

Antisocial personality disorder is characterized by pervasive disregard for the rights of others as demonstrated by these symptoms (APA, 2000):

- Repeated acts that are grounds for arrest.
- Deceitfulness—lying or conning others.
- Impulsivity.
- Repeated assaults.
- Reckless disregard for the safety of others.
- Financial or work irresponsibility.
- Lack of remorse for hurtful behavior.

Borderline Personality Disorder

Borderline personality disorder (BPD) is found in 2% of the general population. However, it can be found in 10% of patients seen in outpatient mental health clinics, 30% of psychiatric inpatients, and from 30% to 60% of all clinical populations (American Psychiatric Association, 2000). BPD is the most widely studied personality disorder (Phillips et al., 2003). This syndrome merits more attention than other personality disorders because patients with BPD are more likely to respond and commit to therapy. Also, the study of this multifaceted disorder is intriguing to therapists across the board. Let's face it: Alex Forrest as played by Glenn Close in *Fatal Attraction* is more exciting than the wilting wallflower of a dependent personality.

Borderline is a misnomer. The term originated in the 1930s when psychiatrists thought that emotionally unstable patients dwelt on the border between neurosis and psychosis. The classification "emotional instability disorder" better describes these individuals, but the term BPD is used here for the purpose of continuity.

People with BPD often have highly unstable patterns of social relationships. While they can develop intense but stormy attachments, their attitudes toward family, friends, and loved ones may suddenly shift from idealization (great admiration and love) to devaluation (intense anger and dislike). They may form an immediate attachment marked by lavish praise and affection, but when a slight separation or conflict occurs, they switch unexpectedly to the other extreme and angrily accuse the other person of not caring for them at all. Individuals with BPD are highly sensitive to rejection, reacting with anger and distress to such mild separations as a vacation, a business trip, or a sudden change in plans. Suicide threats and attempts can occur as a maladaptive attempt to prevent abandonment. Intense anger can develop when the individual with BPD feels rejected. Self-mutilation can result from an attempt to reduce emotional stress. For the individual with BPD, physical pain is preferred over emotional distress. People with BPD often exhibit other impulsive behaviors, such as excessive spending and risky sexual activity.

Origin of Borderline Behavior

Anyone who has a child knows that around 18 months of age, the youngster toddles out of the room, plays alone for a few minutes, and then toddles back in the room looking for mother. With a wide-eyed smile, mama picks up her toddler, gives a warm hug, and coos encouragement. Consistent maternal and paternal affection enables the child to develop a stable sense of self, and with dependable parental behavior, the child develops the ability to soothe the self—the ability to tolerate the vicissitudes of life.

Unfortunately, sometimes a child toddles back into the room, only to find that mama has disappeared, is drunk, or is verbally, emotionally, physically, or sexually abusive. Inconsistent, negligent, and abusive parental behavior generates a fear of abandonment and retards the toddler's emotional development. The toddler feels alone, lost, and worthless.

As the years pass, feelings of worthlessness and a poor sense of self can cause frequent changes in careers, jobs, friendships, and values. Individuals with BPD view themselves as fundamentally bad or unworthy. They feel unfairly misunderstood or mistreated, bored, and empty. These feelings result in frantic efforts to avoid being alone. The emotionally clinging behavior exhibited by these individuals repulses others. The fear of abandonment felt by those with BPD generates hostile behavior that results in the very rejection that they fear.

Nature Versus Nurture

Although no gene has been identified as a precursor to BPD, neuroimaging studies are intriguing. Positron emission tomographic (PET) scanning and functional magnetic resonance imaging (fMRI) studies demonstrated enhanced amygdala and prefrontal activation in subjects with BPD. Excess activity in the cingulate gyrus is associated with BPD. These findings are non-specific indicators of intense emotional activity (Schmahl & Bremner, 2006).

Common sense indicates that some children are more sensitive than others. Just as some geneticists believe they have isolated a gene for shyness, a gene that serves as a biological marker for BPD may someday be identified. Remember—a gene must be activated before an illness occurs. That is, many of us may have a genetic marker for schizophrenia, but a stable emotional life prevents the gene from becoming activated.

A Quintet Causative Theory of Borderline Behavior
- A genetic predisposition to emotional instability and impulsive aggression.
- Intense emotional activity as reflected in enhanced amygdala, cingulate gyrus, and prefrontal activation in PET scanning and fMRI studies.
- A traumatic childhood—abandonment, sexual or physical abuse.
- Inattention to the child's emotions and attitudes.
- Exaggerated maternal frustration that aggravates the child's anger and fears.

Differential Diagnosis
BPD often occurs together with other psychiatric problems, particularly bipolar disorder and depression. While a person with depression or bipolar disorder typically endures the same mood for weeks, a person with BPD may experience shorter, intense bouts of anger and depression that may last only hours or at most a day.

Bulimia and other eating disorders, dissociative states, and anxiety syndromes are commonly associated with BPD. Substance abuse is a common problem in BPD; 50% to 70% of psychiatric inpatients with BPD are drug or alcohol dependent.

The pervasive instability of BPD can be marked by these characteristics (APA, 2000):

- Ambivalence (e.g., "I hate you, don't leave me").
- Chronic feelings of emptiness.
- An unstable self-image.
- Rejection hypersensitivity—considering the slightest inattention of an individual as a totally rejecting attitude.
- Frantic efforts to avoid abandonment.
- Rapid onset of intense and profound depression.
- Bouts of inappropriate, intense anger.
- Self-damaging impulsivity.

- Self-mutilating behavior.
- Emotional instability that disrupts family and work life.
- World experienced in extremes, viewing others as either "all good" or "all bad."

Histrionic Personality Disorder

Emotionally shallow, overdramatic, and provocative describes those with histrionic personality disorder, which is found in 2–3% of the population. Heroines of the histrionic type populate our literature. My favorite, Scarlett O'Hara of *Gone With the Wind* (Mitchell, 1968), used her physical appearance to draw attention to herself, and considered her relationship with Ashley more intimate than it actually was. Inappropriately sexually seductive, she combined an exaggerated expression of emotion with merciless aspiration. She married for money and retribution on the hero Rhett Butler, but her shifting, shallow deceptions drove him away.

This pervasive pattern of emotional outbursts and attention seeking is marked by (APA, 2000):

- Desire to be the center of attention.
- Seductive or provocative behavior.
- Rapid shifting and shallow expression of emotions.
- Using physical appearance to draw attention.
- Impressionistic speech that lacks detail.
- Theatrical expression of motion.
- Is easily influenced by others.
- Considers relationships to be more intimate that they actually are.

Narcissistic Personality Disorder

Absorbed by an exaggerated sense of self-importance and fantasies of unlimited success, narcissists seek constant attention. Oversensitive to failure, they swing between self-admiration and insecurity. They exploit interpersonal relationships. In epidemiological studies, narcissistic personality disorder has made up less than 1% of the community population, but this figure may be low because those with narcissistic personality disorder are adept at hiding symptoms (American Psychiatric Association, 2000).

One suspects that Donald Trump would not mind being called a narcissist as long as he is known as the greatest, richest, most handsome narcissist of all time. "The Trumpster," a real estate developer who operates numerous casinos and hotels across the world, talks in superlatives—"the greatest baby," "the best baby," "the biggest baby." He uses his favorite pronoun, "I," only slightly more than "me," "my," and "mine." Trump's over-the-top lifestyle has been amplified by his reality show, *The Apprentice*, on which he makes evident that he values wealth, power, money, and beauty over all else, and he doesn't care who he manipulates to achieve his goals of being the biggest and the best.

This pattern of grandiosity, need for admiration, and lack of empathy can be indicated by these characteristics (APA, 2000):

- Expectsing to be recognized as superior without commensurate achievements.
- Preoccupation with fantasies of unlimited success, power, brilliance, beauty, or ideal love.
- A belief that one is special.
- Demanding excessive admiration.
- A sense of entitlement.
- Taking advantage of others to achieve desirable results.
- Lacking empathy.
- Being envious of others.
- Being arrogant and haughty.

Cluster C

Three disorders—avoidant, dependent, and obsessive-compulsive—comprise cluster C personality disorders. Although the symptomatic expressions differ between these three disorders, they can all be recognized by manifestations of anxious, fearful behavior.

Avoidant Personality Disorder

Hypersensitive to rejection, those with avoidant personality disorder are excessively timid and uncomfortable in social situations. They fear criticism or saying something considered foolish by others. They have no close relationships outside their family circle. They compose about 0.5–1% of the population.

Emily Dickinson, considered one of the most gifted poets in American literature, was a recluse who never married and, after turning 30, seldom saw anyone other than her immediate family. Sequestered on the second story of her parents' home, she wrote about every aspect of nature, life, and death. Only 11 poems were published during her lifetime, all against her permission. Almost all of her 1,700 poems were discovered after her death.

Criteria for Avoidant Personality Disorder

Pervasive pattern of inhibition, feelings of inadequacy, and hypersensitivity to negative evaluation as indicated by these traits (APA, 2000):

- Avoids activities out of fear of criticism, disapproval, or rejection.
- Avoids people unless certain of being liked.
- Fears shame and ridicule.
- Is preoccupied with being criticized or rejected in social situations.

- Is inhibited in new interpersonal situations out of fear of inadequacy.
- Feels socially inept, unattractive, or inferior.
- Is reluctant to take risks.

Dependent Personality Disorder

Those with dependent personality disorders rely on others to make decisions for them. Requiring excessive reassurance and advice, they are easily hurt by criticism or disapproval and feel uncomfortable and helpless when alone. Dependent personality disorder is among the most frequently reported personality disorders encountered in mental health clinics.

In 1879, Henrik Ibsen wrote *A Doll's House* about women's rights before women's rights became a household phrase. In the play, Torvald regards his wife Nora as an entertaining doll—an amusing toy. Nora charmed, cajoled, and chattered because Torvald would not love his doll without her dependency on him. When Nora sees her husband for what he is—a domineering hypocrite, she announces her equality and with unassailable finality, slams the door, leaving the doll's house behind her, proving that, at least in literature, those with a dependent personality can change.

Criteria for Dependent Personality Disorder

An excessive need for care as marked by these traits (APA, 2000):

- Is unable to make decisions without advice and reassurance.
- Expects others to assume responsibility for day-to-day choices.
- Has difficulty disagreeing with others due to fear of rejection.
- Lacks self-confidence to initiate projects.
- Volunteers for unpleasant tasks to obtain approval.
- Feels helpless when left alone.
- Urgently seeks a supportive relationship when a close relationship ends.
- Is preoccupied with fears of inadequacy to care for self.

Obsessive-Compulsive Personality Disorder

Overly conscientious, those with obsessive-compulsive personality disorder (OCPD) strive for perfection but are never satisfied with their achievements. Marked by rigid reliability and methodical inflexibility, they are often incapable of adapting to changing circumstances. They are highly cautious. OCPD is found in 1% of the community population and 3–10% in mental health clinics. Fastidious Felix Ungar from the *Odd Couple* perfectly exemplified OCPD.

Many people confuse OCPD with obsessive-compulsive disorder (OCD), which is an anxiety disorder. Those with OCD have persistent obsessions marked by repetitive thoughts and compulsive behaviors, such as hand-washing rituals. Rarely are such physical rituals present in patients with OCPD.

Most successful people have some obsessive traits—their willingness to try and try again contributes to their achievements. Almost no doctor, attorney, certified public accountant—you name it—can graduate from their professional school without an obsession to succeed. Writers are famously obsessive for revising their books and submitting them to publishers again and again. Jack Canfield and Mark Victor Hansen received 140 rejections before their initial *Chicken Soup for the Soul* (1993) anthology was finally published. Now, you can find a different *Chicken Soup* book for just about every niche market out there. One might make the case that Canfield and Hansen's branding efforts border on the obsessive.

Criteria for Obsessive-Compulsive Personality Disorder
A preoccupation with perfectionism as marked by these traits:

- Gives more importance to details, rules, lists, and organization than the activity to be achieved.
- Perfectionism interferes with completion of a task.
- Is excessively devoted to work to the exclusion of family, friends, and fun.
- Is inflexible regarding morality, ethics, or values.
- Hoards worthless objects with no sentimental value.
- Is reluctant to delegate.
- Is miserly—hoards money for some imagined future catastrophe.
- Is rigid and stubborn.

A Summary of Diagnostic Points
There's an old joke that says people with personality disorders don't get sick, they make other people sick, indicating that people with a personality disorder don't understand the effect they have on others. They lack empathy. Blaming, excuse making, and failure to assume responsibility are other general hallmarks of a personality disorder. Although specific signs and symptoms differ in each personality disorder subtype, almost all of the subtypes will demonstate blaming, excuse making, failure to assume responsibility, and lack of empathy for others.

Here are some signs and symptoms that indicate different personality subtypes:

Cluster A—the eccentric disorders
Paranoid personality disorder
Distrust
Suspiciousness
Others' motives interpreted as malevolent
Schizoid personality disorder
Alienation from others
Restricted range of emotional expression

Emotional coldness
Constricted or flat affect
Schizotypal personality disorder
Cognitive or perceptual distortions
Eccentric behavior
Cluster B—the dramatic disorders
Antisocial Personality disorder
Violation of the rights of others
Lack of guilt for malfeasances
Borderline personality disorder
Instability in personal relationships
Severe impulsivity
Hypersensitive to rejection
Fragmented self-esteem
Intense anger at slight provocations
Profound depression engendered by minor conflicts
Histrionic personality disorder
Excessive emotional reactions
Seductive attention seeking
Narcissistic personality disorder
Grandiosity
Need for admiration
Quest for power and prestige
Cluster C—the anxious disorders
Avoidant personality disorder
Social inhibition
Views self as inferior to others
Feelings of inadequacy
Fears being shamed, ridiculed, rejected
Dependent personality disorder
Submissive behavior
Clinging behavior
Excessive need to be taken care of
Obsessive-compulsive personality disorder
Preoccupation with orderliness
Perfectionism
Need for control of emotions
Personality disorder not otherwise specified
Meets general criteria for personality disorder
Mixed symptoms of other personality types

Treatment of Personality Disorders

The symptoms of personality disorder make these illnesses difficult to treat.

Paranoid individuals are almost impossible to treat because they lack trust for the therapist. Those with schizoid, schizotypal, and avoidance personalities cannot tolerate intimacy. Antisocial individuals must embrace long-term imprisonment if they have any hope of change. Therapy, even prison therapy, invariably fails. The best hope for an antisocial individual is an epiphany experience—a sudden intuitive leap of understanding, especially through an ordinary but striking occurrence. Those with OCPD often respond to cognitive-behavior therapy or other conventional treatments.

Those with borderline personalities, because of their intense suffering, may respond to treatment—although only especially talented, experienced, and patient therapists can tolerate the neediness, emptiness, anger, and ambiguity that these patients display. Histrionic, narcissistic, dependent, and (very rarely) antisocial patients respond to treatment if their suffering is great enough to motivate an attempt to change their lifelong patterns of behavior.

Those with personality disorders usually have close relatives or friends who inadvertently support their outrageous behavior by repeatedly rescuing them from the consequences of their actions. These loved ones use lectures and admonitions in an attempt to change these unfortunate individuals. Talking never works. Those with personality disorders respond only to firm, consistent action as in the following scenario (although the boy mentioned had not reached the age to be classified as having a personality disorder, the principles of firmness hold true whether the individual is 15 or 55):

A 14-year-old boy was arrested for playing mailbox baseball with some older friends. In this game, several boys jump into a vehicle and take turns knocking over roadside mailboxes with a baseball bat. When the boy's father arrived at the jailhouse where his son clung to the bars, shaking, he gave the boy a stern glace and turned to the jailer, motioned toward his son and commanded in a firm voice, "Keep him." Because the boy was underage, he instead was released to his father. The next day at the father's firm instruction, the boy repaired the mailboxes using his allowance and earned money. After a stellar job assured by his father's watchful eye, the boy apologized to each smashed mailbox victim. The task over, the father never mentioned the infraction again. He never said, "Remember when you busted those mailboxes? I knew you would turn out useless" (or some other negative statement). Instead, he expected the boy to follow the rules and regulations of society. If the youngster broke the rules, he was punished in a manner that fit the crime (for a speeding ticket, pay the fine and no driving for a week; for missing a homework assignment, no weekend date; etc.). The boy responded to this "tough love" and now is a successful—and honest—businessman.

Therapy That Works (Sometimes)

When I encounter a person with a personality disorder, the first thing I do is call a family meeting with all significant members present—mother, father, grandparents, wife, significant other, and adult children. I don't want anyone spoiling the treatment approach by rescuing our patient. I then say something like this:

> Your son has a personality disorder—he refuses to accept responsibility for his behavior and is always blaming others or situations for his difficulty. He will not respond to talk. He will only get better with rules and regulations followed by action that backs up those rules. He is 28 years old. The first thing you must do is insist he leave the home today—not tomorrow, today. Even if he has to live in the street, he should be out of your home by sundown tonight. The next thing—no paying the monthly car bill, no buying him gasoline; refuse to pay his car insurance. In other words, after today, he is his own man with all the responsibilities and obligations expected of young men his age.

You can imagine the "Yes, buts" I get. The loved ones begin to list all the real good reasons for refusing to follow my advice. I counter with something like this:

> What you have been doing for the past 28 years hasn't worked. If you keep doing what you have been doing, you will get the same results. I have had 48-year-old "boys" in this office. Just yesterday, I was dealing with a 55-year-old "girl." Keep doing what you are doing, and that 28-year-old will turn into a 48-year-old "boy." If you don't change the way you manage your son, I can guarantee that he will never grow to emotional manhood. If you stand firm on the rules and regulations we outline, he has a small chance of changing. Which would you rather have, a small chance or no chance? Of course, there is a chance that the techniques I outline won't work. Your son may end up in jail, or he may starve to death or die from an overdose of drugs if you do what I suggest. But, if you don't start changing the way you manage your son, there is absolutely no hope for him.

Many families fail to heed my advice and walk out the door, shaking their heads. Others half-heartedly try my approach. Those few who agree with me spend many agonizing hours in therapy changing their behavior. When they change, their boy begins to change. (For many of these families, I recommend a 12-step approach discussed in the section on alcohol and drug abuse found in Chapter 10.) The crux of family therapy involves educating family members regarding personality disorders. Improving communication will help resolve the two poles of inappropriate family response: overinvolvement (rescuing) and neglect.

Traditional Therapies

During psychotherapy, patients learn about their maladaptive behavior patterns and how their behavior contributes to depression, anxiety, dysphoria, guilt, shame, romantic disappointments, conflicts with friends, and failure at work. Using the insights and knowledge gained in psychotherapy, the patients learn responsible ways to manage their actions. All psychotherapy teaches, directly or indirectly, that certain rules of society must be learned and followed to get along in the world, and that to break the social, ethical, and moral rules leads ultimately to self-destruction. Through therapy, the patients learn how their irresponsible behavior is self-defeating, producing myriad conflicts. Therapy teaches patients how to meet their needs more effectively while allowing others to fulfill their needs.

Traditional psychotherapy for the personality disorders includes psychodynamic therapy, cognitive-behavior therapy, and interpersonal therapy. These techniques are discussed in Chapter 16.

Group Therapy

Group psychotherapy allows maladaptive behavior patterns to display themselves among peer patients, whose feedback is used by the therapist to identify and correct unsuitable patterns of behavior. Sessions are usually once a week, and duration of treatment may last from several months to years.

Dialectic Behavior Therapy

Dialectic behavior therapy is an option for all personality disorders but has been studied primarily with borderline patients because they are more amenable to treatment (Linehan, 1993). This technique is based on the Socratic method of discovering the truth. The therapist asks a series of questions exploring the what, where, when, why, and how of conflict and stress. When the therapists asks questions the patient learns appropriate responses for managing stress and conflict, just as Socrates helped those he debated to broaden their views by asking questions. There are three elements of dialectic behavior therapy:

- The therapist communicates verbally and nonverbally to the patient that the therapist cares enough to be involved in helping the patient learn self-discipline. The therapist sets limits. He or she does not give in to the excessive demands of the patient. At the same time, the therapist is reliable and steady. The therapist avoids rescuing the patient when the patient gets into difficulties in his or her daily activities of living, remaining kind and understanding.

- The patient keeps a daily journal that records events as well as feelings and thoughts generated by daily events. The therapist asks a series of questions to enable the patient to learn better ways of handling conflict.
- Therapy allows the patient to learn specific skills in dealing with stress and interpersonal conflict:

> 1. Evaluation of distorted thinking—the patient is helped to see different viewpoints in a conflict and to focus on present issues instead of feelings from the past.
>
> 2. Dealing with stress—the patient learns to manage emotions that are triggered by distressing events, including those that cannot be immediately resolved.
>
> 3. Dealing with conflict with others—the patient is assisted in maintaining good relationships with others. Through a series of questions, the therapist helps the patient learn that certain rules of society must be followed to get along in the world, and that to break social, ethical, and moral rules leads to self-destruction. Using the Socratic method, the therapist helps the patient find ways to fulfill personal needs in a way that allows others to fulfill their needs.
>
> 4. Developing emotional stability—the patient learns self-soothing behavior by changing distorted beliefs and inappropriate actions. For example, a series of questions can help improve the patient's response to perceived rejection:
>
> > a. What are you thinking (or doing) right now?
> > b. Is what you are thinking (or doing) helping you?
> > c. What thoughts (or actions) can help you feel better about yourself? (Several options may be formulated until the best solution is discovered.)
> > d. Will you commit to changing your thoughts (or actions)?
> > e. How will you demonstrate that you have committed to change?

Medication Therapy

Medications can be used for coexisting disorders such as depression and anxiety. Mood stabilizers may help in impulse control. Antipsychotics would help paranoids, but they rarely can be convinced to take medications. Schizotypal and schizoid personality disorders will respond to antipsychotics to some extent, but individuals with these disorders generally are not motivated to take medications. Those with OCPD and avoidant personality disorder may benefit from selective serotonin reuptake inhibitors (SSRIs). (When these medications are used to help with symptoms in those with personality disorders, the side effects of these mediations are no different from the side effects mentioned in other chapters.)

Those with BPD respond to a variety of medications depending on the symptom cluster. The chemical messenger serotonin helps regulate emotions, including sadness, anger, anxiety, and irritability. Drugs that enhance brain serotonin function may improve emotional symptoms in BPD. Likewise, mood-stabilizing drugs that are known to enhance the activity of gamma-aminobutyric acid (GABA), the major inhibitory neurotransmitter of the brain, may help people who experience BPD-like mood swings. An imbalance of dopamine, the so-called pleasure neurotransmitter, may contribute to impulsivity and anger. Antipsychotic medications can help regulate dopamine balance. Benzodiazepines, because their disinhibition properties may add to mood instability, should be avoided (Schatzberg, Cole, & DeBattista, 2007).

None of these treatment approaches has been studied systematically in placebo-controlled studies involving a high enough number of patients to make the results clinically significant.

For Patients Who Have Been Diagnosed As Having a Personality Disorder

If your therapist or physician has told you that you have a personality disorder, here are a few things you can do to make your life better:

- Set reasonable goals and expectations of yourself.
- Keep a daily journal to express your emotions and your reactions to others.
- Read books that will help you get along with others. *How to Win Friends and Influence People* by Dale Carnegie is a good start.
- Get out of the house and participate in activities.
- Cultivate friends by paying attention to their needs rather than yours.
- Join a health club and exercise regularly. You not only will get in better shape, but also will get to know people. Sweat, don't fret.
- Try to find the good in all situations and try to recognize the pleasant qualities in your family members.
- When you get upset, walk away, count to 10, and think of something pleasant—anything will do as long as you don't lose your temper and put a hole in the wall or a cut on your arm.

Complete Mental Health

- When upset, remind yourself, "This too shall pass."
- Learn to love yourself for who you are, not who people think you are.
- Eat healthy food at regular intervals and get plenty of rest. Hungry, tired people say and do outrageous things.
- Practice relaxation techniques.
- Organize your time. Do the most important things first but save some time each day for fun.
- Laugh. Remember, he who laughs, lasts.
- Decide to be hopeful and fun-loving.
- Every day ask yourself, "Am I having fun yet?"
- Surround yourself with people who fill you with joy and laughter.
- Be an inverse paranoid—think the world is out to do you good.
- When a situation becomes stressful, pretend it's all a *Punk'd* episode.
- Listen to humor regularly.
- Don't take yourself so seriously.
- Plan an occasional long weekend away from work.
- Take up a hobby. Hobbies prevent boredom.
- Read. Reading provides a life of constant renewal.

A Clinician's Quiz

1. The personality disorders are divided into three clusters—A, B, and C—based on descriptive similarities. Give a description of each of the three clusters.
2. Name the personality disorders under each of the three clusters.
3. Give the diagnostic criteria for antisocial personality disorder.
4. Give the diagnostic criteria for for avoidant personality disorder
5. Give the diagnostic criteria for schizoid personality disorder.
6. Give the diagnostic criteria for dependent personality disorder.
7. Dialectic behavior therapy helps a patient with personality disorder learn specific skills in dealing with stress and interpersonal conflict. Name and discuss four of those skills.
8. Discuss the psychodynamics of borderline personality disorder.
9. Give four factors that increase the risk of developing a personality disorder.
10. Medications are used for target symptoms in the treatment of personality disorders. Name those target symptoms and give a medication used for each.

Complete Mental Health

CHAPTER 10

Addictions and Abuse
Traitors of Denial

nformed that General Ulysses S. Grant drank whiskey while serving in the field during the Civil War, Abraham Lincoln quipped: "Find out, to oblige me, what brand of whiskey Grant drinks, because I want to send a barrel of it to each one of my generals" (McClure, 1901). Ten years after his graduation from West Point, and after distinguished service in the Mexican War, Grant was relieved from duty for excessive drinking, returning to uniform in 1861 when Lincoln called for Union volunteers, and despite his inclination for intemperance, he served with such distinction that in 1864 he became commander of the Union armies. Most historians agree that Grant, a binge drinker, drank to excess when bored or lonely, but his drinking never jeopardized his ability to command. As historian James McPherson explained:

> His predisposition to alcoholism may have made him a better general. His struggle for self-discipline enabled him to understand and discipline others; the humiliation of prewar failures gave him a quiet humility that was conspicuously absent from so many generals with a reputation to protect; because Grant had nowhere to go but up, he could act with more boldness and decision than commanders who dared not risk failure. (1988, p. 588)

Grant's ability to successfully command an army despite his addiction is not the norm, however. In most cases, addiction to alcohol and other drugs

TABLE 10-1

Alcoholics Who Probably Drank Themselves to Death

Dylan Thomas: The shy, insecure poet escaped from self-doubt through drinking: Preoccupied with death, his prediction of death before 40 came true—he died at age 39.

F. Scott Fitzgerald: Fitzgerald worked hard, played hard, and drank hard in an effort to find happiness, which he believed was just around the corner. When he died at age 44, he thought he had been a literary failure. His notebooks and letters published in 1945 were entitled *The Crack-up*.

Jack London: London claimed to have begun drinking at age 5. The author of *The Call of the Wild* and 49 other volumes, novels, short stories, and essays drank heavily throughout his life until his death of drug and alcohol overdose at age 40.

Edgar Allen Poe: Poe died of delirium tremens at age 40.

W. C. Fields: Legendary comedian and alcoholic, Fields drank 2–4 martinis for breakfast each morning and continued drinking throughout the day. Boozing finally caught up with him: He spent his last years in a sanitarium.

leads to disastrous consequences. Substance abuse, resulting in physiological addiction, is one of the leading health problems in the United States. Like obesity (another major health issue), it is also completely preventable by abstaining from the behaviors that precipitate the disease. Despite massive amounts of money spent on drug prevention education, the problem persists **(Table 10-1)**.

Alcohol Use and Abuse

Only about 10% of Americans report being lifetime abstainers of alcohol (American Psychiatric Association, 2000), meaning that alcohol is by far the most commonly used drug in our society. In a 2006 survey, slightly more than half of Americans aged 12 or older reported being current drinkers of alcohol (Centers for Disease Control and Prevention, n.d.). More than one fifth (23.3%) participated in binge drinking at least once in the 30 days prior to the survey (Centers for Disease Control and Prevention, n.d.). More than 7% of the population aged 18 years and older have problems with drinking; 500,000 children between the ages of 9 and 12 are dependent on alcohol (retrieved January 8, 2010 from alcoholism-information.com/Alcoholism-Statistics.html). Alcohol plays a role in almost 25% of all hospital care expenses, 50% of violent deaths, and just fewer than 40% of traffic fatalities (Mack, Franklin, & Frances, 2003). In view of the number of alcoholics and the incapacitating, and sometimes fatal, outcome of the disease, alcoholism is second only to obesity as the major health problem in America.

Social Drinking, Alcohol Abuse, and Alcoholism

Not everyone who drinks ends up having a problem with alcohol. Most social drinkers are able to consume one to two alcoholic beverages without adverse consequences such as drunkenness, loss of control, and negative changes in behavior. These consumers stay within their limits and rarely have second thoughts about their alcohol use (Addiction Recovery Basics, 2008).

Abusers of alcohol constitute a second tier of drinkers. These individuals have periodic episodes of dangerous or potentially dangerous drinking. Examples of alcohol abuse include driving under the influence or interference with work or home life (Addiction Recovery Basics, 2008).

An addiction to alcohol is marked by an inability to set and keep limits on drinking. Alcoholics spend increasing amounts of time thinking about drinking. As their alcohol consumption increases, tolerance to alcohol also rises, resulting in a spiraling cycle of needing more and more alcohol. Denial and an inability to stop drinking characterize the disease. This involuntary disability is progressive and often fatal (Addiction Recovery Basics, 2008) **(Table 10-2)**.

TABLE 10-2
Difference Between Abuse and Addiction

ABUSE Involves One of the Following Four Items Related to Substance Use	**ADDICTION** Involves Three of the Following Seven Items Related to Substance Use
1. Failure to fulfill obligations at work, school, or home	1. Tolerance—have to use more substance to get the same effect
2. Driving or some other dangerous activity while using	2. Withdrawal symptoms
3. Recurrent legal problems	3. Can't stop using
4. Continued substance use despite persistent social or interpersonal problems caused by the substance	4. Unsuccessful at cutting down on the substance
	5. Spend a great deal of time obtaining the substance
	6. Give up important social, occupational, or recreational activities to use the substance
	7. Continued substance use despite physical or social problems

Causes of Alcoholism

Alcoholism, a chronic medical condition, is defined as a brain disorder that results in a compulsion to drink; several factors play prominent roles in its development (Vaillant, 1978):

- **Genetic background.** In response to the overwhelming evidence from twin, family, and adoption studies noting a major genetic influence on the development of alcoholism, numerous studies are under way to identify the specific genes underlying this vulnerability. More than one gene is likely to be responsible for alcoholism, but whether these genes are specific for alcohol or define something more general, such as differences in temperament, is yet to be determined (Goodwin, 1990).
- **Physiology.** Longitudinal studies and physiological findings have identified several biological markers that may predispose individuals to the development of alcoholism (Mack et al., 2003).
- **Biological mutations.** Evidence indicates that alcohol affects hormone and neurotransmitter-activated signal transduction, leading to short-term changes in regulation of cellular functions and long-term changes in gene expression (Stahl, 2008). This shows that people who consume alcohol are partially responsible for manifesting the disease by their behavior. In other words, if alcohol is not consumed, no cellular and gene changes occur; therefore, no alcoholism results. This seems self-explanatory but demonstrates how the behavior itself (drinking alcohol) constitutes one of the causes of the medical disorder (alcoholism).
- **Availability.** When alcohol is cheap and readily available, consumption goes up.
- **Onset of action.** High-proof drinks such as vodka and whiskey lead to alcohol dependency more quickly than less-potent drinks such as beer and wine.
- **Culture.** Higher rates of alcoholism are found in countries that are more alcohol friendly (e.g., Ireland, Russia, France, Scandinavia) than cultures that frown on drunkenness (e.g., Islamic, Chinese, and Mediterranean cultures).
- **Environment.** Some studies indicated that childhood unhappiness may lead to an increased rate of alcoholism during adulthood. Another example of how environment plays a role is the individual who wants to "escape" from an unpleasant situation, using alcohol as a method of masking pain.
- **Physical dependence.** The discomfort of withdrawal symptoms reinforces continued drinking.

Diagnosis of Alcohol Abuse

Alcohol abuse may go undetected because the vast majority of alcoholics continue to work, and can even have a normal family life. Asking the five questions remembered by the non-standardized acronym ABUSE would help in the diagnostic process:

1. Have you ever felt   **A**nnoyed by criticism of your drinking?
2. Have you had   **B**lackouts when drinking?
3. Do you drink everybody else **U**nder the table?
4. Do you ever drink   **S**ecretly?
5. Do you ever feel   **E**xcessively eager to have a drink?

An affirmative response to any of the five questions is incomplete but suggestive evidence of alcoholism. Those individuals who respond positively to more than one of the ABUSE questions should be confronted with the existence of a drinking problem, but even when challenged with clear evidence demonstrating a pattern of abuse, many alcoholics refuse help.

Warren began to drink in college. He noticed that drinking loosened him up and allowed him to talk and joke with others without his usual anxiety. Later, when serving a turn of duty in the military, Warren became bored with the regimented military life. He detested his job as a communications officer, did not delegate responsibilities well, and feared criticism from his superiors. He began to drink daily. His drinking gradually increased to five or six drinks nightly with even heavier drinking over the weekends. On discharge from the military, Warren joined his cousin's insurance business. As the years passed, Warren assumed more and more responsibility in the business, and as his workload increased so did his drinking. During an intervention involving his wife, children, cousin, pastor, friends, and coworkers, Warren became angry and refused inpatient therapy for his alcoholism, promising to stop drinking on his own willpower. After an 8-month period of sobriety, he began drinking again, and after he had lost his job, he continued to drink. He was arrested on two occasions for driving under the influence of alcohol. Although his driver's license was suspended, Warren died when the car he was driving ran off a bridge. His blood alcohol level was three times the legal limit.

Alcohol-Induced Medical Disorders

Advances in neuroscience have made it possible to investigate the pathophysiology of alcoholism at a cellular and molecular level. Such changes in the brain probably underlie many of the acute and chronic neurological events in alcoholism (Stahl, 2008).

The repercussions of alcoholism can be manifested in several different ways, ultimately resulting in one or more related medical disorders. Clinicians should be alert to the warning signs of these complications, which are illustrated in the next few case studies. Usually, individuals with these disorders require specialized treatment in rehabilitation facilities.

Alcohol Intoxication

Arriving at the emergency room to evaluate an alcoholic patient with a blood alcohol level of 0.448, I found a young man as steady as a trapeze performer carrying on a conversation with the staff in a radio announcer voice. After I told him he should be dead, he replied, "I've been drinking for a long time, doc."

As the living alcoholic with a blood level of .448 confirmed, the onset of alcohol intoxication, time limited and reversible, depends on tolerance, speed of ingestion, and the amount of food in the stomach, medical condition, and weight. **Table 10-3**, derived from several sources, gives a rough estimate of the alcohol level and symptoms based on the amount of alcohol ingested on an empty stomach in a 150-pound nontolerant man.

Alcohol Withdrawal

Another man had a coarse tremor of the hands, rapid pulse, sweating, fluctuating blood pressure, irritability, weakness, and nausea, symptoms that could be caused by a viral infection or numerous other medical conditions

TABLE 10-3			
Alcohol Blood Levels and Effects			
AMOUNT OF BEVERAGE	**EFFECTS**	**BLOOD ALCOHOL LEVEL (SERUM %)**	**TIME (HOURS) TO LEAVE BODY**
1 cocktail, 1 bottle of beer, or one 5-ounce glass of wine	Mild euphoria	0.03	2
2 drinks	Feeling of warmth and mental relaxation	0.06	4
3 drinks	Exaggerated behavior; talkative or morose	0.09	6
4 drinks	Unsteadiness in standing or walking	0.12	8
5 drinks	Gross intoxication	0.15	10
10 drinks	Coma or death	> 0.4	—

until I discovered that he had been drinking for several days. After I told him he had alcohol withdrawal symptoms, he replied, "Impossible, I'm still drinking," drawing from his back pocket a pint flask of cheap whisky, liberally sampled. He admitted, on further questioning, that he had cut down on his drinking in the last 24 hours because he was running out of money. Just as I told him I was sticking with my original diagnosis because I suspected the relative drop in blood alcohol was enough to produce withdrawal symptoms, he fell to the floor and began to seize, not to protest my diagnosis, but because he was having a "rum fit." As is typical in 10% of all chronic drinkers, he had a second grand mal seizure, but happily, he failed to develop delirium tremens as one third of heavy drinkers do, and his seizures did not progress to status epilepticus as in 2% of alcoholics. I admitted him to the hospital and began him on the benzodiazepine Librium to prevent more rum fits and to treat the other withdrawal symptoms. I gradually tapered him off Librium and found no medical reason to treat him long term for alcohol-induced seizures, but on discharge, he continued to drink, showing up at my office from time to time when his urge to drink lasted longer than his monthly paycheck.

Patients with mild alcohol withdrawal symptoms can be managed at home under the care of a physician or a paraprofessional. It is best, however, for an alcoholic suffering from withdrawl to be treated at a detoxification center or hospital. In addition to benzodiazepines, the alcoholic needs to eat well and to have the proper fluid intake. During withdrawal, the patient will be given vitamin preparations including vitamin B_1 to prevent brain damage from Wernicke's encephalopathy, a serious neurological disorder associated with malnutrition. Antiseizure medications can be added following an alcohol withdrawal seizure, but continuation of this medication following detoxification is unnecessary.

Alcohol Withdrawal Delirium (Delirium Tremens)

Tiring of academic medicine associated with the demands for research, teaching, administration, and low pay (I was slow; it took me over 20 years to learn that I was paying academic centers to let me work there), I settled down in a rural, one-psychiatrist town where they had a 10-bed unit but very few patients and where I was given the mandate to "fill 'er up" (Texas talk for "increase the census"). I decided to prove my worth (they doubled my academic salary) by admitting all comers, but I wasn't counting on Barney to be my first admission. His tremor, slurred speech, sweating, and unsteady gait told me he had already gone into withdrawal, while an alcohol level of 0.332 forewarned an impending alcohol withdrawal delirium when the level dropped lower. 24 hours later, I didn't know who was sweating more, Barney or me. Agitated, terror stricken, hallucinating, thrashing, and delusional, with an elevated pulse and blood pressure, he kept trying to get out of bed despite high doses of intramuscular benzodiazepines, oral clonidine, and antipsychotic injections. Although the fatality rate for alcohol withdrawal delirium is low at around 1%, I worried that Barney might die, especially because he was the first patient I had admitted to the unit. I stayed up with him all night, occasionally wishing I were back in academia where the residents took care of patients with middle-of-the-night delirium tremens. Within 36 hours, except for a fine tremor and the pink rabbits that he kept seeing hopping around in his room, he was much better. The tremor persisted, but the pink rabbits were gone in 3 days.

Alcohol-Induced Persisting Dementia

After 33 years of heavy alcohol use, a patient entered his fifth alcohol rehab unit. Three weeks after detoxification from alcohol, he continued to have problems with his memory. His dementia, for which no other cause could be found, continued to progress so that he became unable to manage day-to-day activities. Eventually, he required total care.

Alcohol-Induced Persisting Amnestic Disorder (Korsakoff's Syndrome)

After withdrawing from alcohol at home, a patient was admitted to the hospital with classic signs of Wernicke's encephalopathy resulting from inadequate intake of thiamine (vitamin B1) with continued carbohydrate ingestion. He had ataxia, nystagmus, ophthalmoplegia (paralysis of eye muscles), hypothermia, syncope, and confusion. Later, as occurs in about 80% of patients following an attack of Wernicke's encephalopathy, he developed the telltale sign of Korsakoff's syndrome: severe impairment of short-term memory coupled with a spotty memory of distant events. The bewildered patient began to fabricate stories in an attempt to cover his memory defects. Medical students visiting the unit became fascinated by his jocular confabulations, told with dramatic flair and panache. In the meantime, the attending physician continued the patient on 100 mg of thiamine daily. In contrast with most patients with Korsakoff's syndrome, who experience a progression to prolonged institutional care, this very fortunate patient improved 14 months after onset of Wernicke's encephalopathy.

Alcohol-Induced Psychotic Disorder With Delusions and Hallucinations

A heavy drinker, 48 hours after reduction in alcohol, began hearing humming, ringing bells, and chanting. Occasionally, he heard threatening, derogatory voices. Luckily, his hallucinations receded within a few days.

Rarely, this type of patient may develop a paranoid delusion state indistinguishable from schizophrenia (Mack et al., 2003).

Treatment of Alcohol Abuse and Dependence

Treating alcoholism requires a lifelong, multifaceted approach. Most experts agree that once an individual reaches the point of alcohol addiction, permanent abstinence is the only solution. Getting the patient to willingly abandon alcohol for the rest of his or her life is a difficult task. Physical and psychological dependence on alcohol squeezes the patient in a vise-like grip. The first step in the process is confronting the alcoholic with the severity of the problem.

Interventions

Most alcoholics postpone a decision to abstain from alcohol until a major crisis forces the issue. If the family chips away at the individual's denial, he or she will be better prepared to seek treatment when a crisis develops. Family members, friends, and coworkers often must intervene to help the patient realize his or her drinking is serious enough to require intensive treatment. Emphasizing to the individual the concept that alcohol is a disease helps facilitate acceptance of treatment. The family member might say, "Alcoholism is an illness that can happen to anyone, and just as with other illnesses, you can be helped."

If the individual continues to deny that a drinking problem exists, the family member can ask the loved one to keep a drinking diary and then allow the facts to prove the point. At times, the individual may admit to having a drinking problem but blame the drinking on his or her stress level. For example, the individual might say that the conditions at work are so exasperating that drinking offers the only escape. The family member can empathize with this position while insisting that the alcoholic seek treatment.

Psychopharmacological Treatment

Because alcohol enhances GABA (gamma-aminobutyric acid, a calming neurotransmitter), decreases glutamate (an excitatory neurotransmitter), and stimulates, either directly or indirectly, opiate and cannabinoid receptors in the central nervous system, pharmacological treatment of alcohol abuse and dependence centers on affecting these receptor sites or neurotransmitters (Stahl, 2008). The following medications have been used or proposed for this purpose:

- Naltrexone—blocks opiate receptors that theoretically contribute to the euphoria of heavy drinking (dose is 50 mg daily).
- Acamprosate—mitigates GABA deficiency and glutamate hyperactivity (dose is two 333-mg tablets three times daily).

- Depakote—enhances GABA, can be used to treat rum fits, may prevent a return to drinking, and is especially useful in alcoholics with bipolar disorder (dose is 10 mg times body weight to maintain level of 50–100 mg/L).
- Benzodiazepines—work through the GABA receptor and are the drugs of choice for alcohol withdrawal prevention. The protocol for alcohol withdrawal is as follows:

  - Librium: 25–100 mg every 4–8 hours and gradually taper as tolerated.
  - Thiamine: 100 mg intramuscularly for 3 days, then orally (thiamine is a cofactor involved in two pathways of carbohydrate metabolism).
  - Folic acid: 1 mg daily (to prevent megaloblastic anemia).
  - Multiple vitamins (to restore nutrition).
  - Potassium and magnesium replacement as needed.
  - Fluid replacement as needed.
  - Optional: Depakote at 10–30 mg times body weight as loading dose, then 10 times the body weight daily to make severe withdrawal more tolerable, prevent rum fits, and possibly decrease kindling. (Kindling causes the severity of withdrawal symptoms to increase after repeated withdrawal episodes. Kindling may also contribute to a patient's relapse risk and to alcohol-related brain damage.)

Antabuse blocks an intermediary step in alcohol metabolism, leading to the accumulation of acetaldehyde in the body, resulting in nausea, vomiting, headache, and extreme discomfort when an individual drinks only a small amount of alcohol within a few days or weeks of taking the drug. This aversive technique is useful only when the alcoholic takes the medication regularly. The dose is 500 mg daily for 1 week, then 250 mg daily.

Alcoholics Anonymous

Alcoholics Anonymous (AA) began in 1935 in Akron, Ohio, as the outcome of a meeting between a surgeon and a New York broker, both of whom were considered end-stage alcoholics. Using the basic principles of healthy well-being borrowed from religion and medicine, these two men, known as Dr. Bob and Bill W., eventually designed a 12-step program that destined them to become cofounders of the AA fellowship (Alcoholics Anonymous World Services, 2007).

After 3 years of discovery and failure, Dr. Bob and Bill W. formulated basic tenets that would help the alcoholic begin the process of recovering. By 1938, three successful AA groups emerged—the first in Akron, the second in New

York, and the third in Cleveland. Even then, no more than 40 certain recoveries could be found in the combined groups.

Nevertheless, Dr. Bob, with the help of members in the three groups, wrote about a method to deal with the problems of overdrinking in a book that was released in April 1939. The book, *Alcoholics Anonymous,* described from the alcoholic's point of view the struggles of achieving and maintaining sobriety. The core of the book—the 12 steps—codified personal responsibility and the spiritual ideas of AA: Step 1—we admitted that we were powerless over alcohol and that our lives had become unmanageable; Step 2—We came to believe that a Power greater than ourselves could restore us to sanity (**Figure 10-1**). The importance of a higher power in the recovery from alcoholism was emphasized. The remaining three fourths of the book consisted of 30 stories devoted to inspirational experiences and recoveries.

In 1939 with the publication of the first edition of *Alcoholics Anonymous*— soon to be called *The Big Book*—a prodigious growth in the organization occurred. A respected theologian of the 1940s, Dr. Harry Emerson Fosdick, reviewed *Alcoholics Anonymous (The Big Book)* favorably. Clergymen and doctors alike gave the AA movement generous support and endorsement.

FIGURE 10-1

The 12 Steps of AA

1. We admitted that we were powerless over alcohol—that our lives had become unmanageable.
2. Came to believe that a Power greater than ourselves could restore us to sanity.
3. Made a decision to turn our will and our lives over to the care of God, *as we understood Him.*
4. Made a searching and fearless moral inventory of us.
5. Admitted to God, to us, and to another human being the exact nature of our wrongs.
6. Were entirely ready to have God remove all these defects of character.
7. Humbly asked Him to remove our shortcomings.
8. Made a list of all persons we had harmed, and became willing to make amends to them all.
9. Made direct amends to such people wherever possible, except when to do so would injure them or others.
10. Continued to take personal inventory and when we were wrong promptly admitted it.
11. Sought through prayer and meditation to improve our conscious contact with God, *as we understood Him,* praying only for knowledge of His will for us and the power to carry that out.
12. Having had a spiritual awakening as the result of these steps, we tried to carry this message to alcoholics, and to practice these principles in all our affairs.

Alcoholics Anonymous World Services (aa.org). The 12 Steps of Alcoholics Anonymous Service material for the general service office AA World Service New York: Alcoholics Anonymous. Retrieved October 25 from http://www.aa.org/en_pdfs/smf-121_en.pdf

---

In the spring of 1940, John D. Rockefeller, Jr. invited AA members to tell their stories at a dinner for many of his friends. A feature article by Jack Alexander (1941) in the *Saturday Evening Post*, the most popular American magazine in the 1940s, gave a powerful endorsement of AA. Largely because of continuous publicity given by newspapers and magazines around the world, thousands on thousands of alcoholics flocked to AA meetings. The canon of *Alcoholics Anonymous (The Big Book)* has remained the same through four editions. Even the page numbers continue unchanged. Page 64 in the first edition, for example, contained the same material as page 64 in the fourth edition. Some of the personal stories have changed, however, to reflect changes in society.

Due in large part to *The Big Book* and the publicity surrounding it, there are currently over 100,000 AA groups with more than 2 million members in 150 countries. Spin-offs from AA—Overeaters Anonymous, Narcotics Anonymous (NA), and Smokers Anonymous—abound.

Alcoholics Anonymous emphasizes both group and individual treatment approaches. Meetings are devoted to testimonials and discussions of the problems of alcoholism. Through mutual help and reassurance, the alcoholic gains a new sense of confidence and more successful coping abilities.

Alcoholics Anonymous is an effective treatment if the individual continues to attend meetings regularly. An extensive survey conducted by the General Service Office of Alcoholics Anonymous (1990) found what anyone would intuitively guess—the longer one continues to attend AA meetings, the better the chances of successful sobriety **(Table 10-4)**.

Illicit Drug Use

Although many still consider drug addiction a moral disease, 20 years of research tells us that about 50% of addiction is genetically generated, and the other half comes from social and cultural factors such as poverty or stressful events (Volkow & David, 2009). Furthermore, damage caused to the brain circuits by the abused drugs impairs self-control, making the user vulnerable to relapse. Investment in research and clinical services represents a fraction of the costs associated with drug-related incarceration, lost productivity, and the treatment of medical consequences—car accidents, cancer, HIV, overdoses, and mental illnesses. Knowing that addiction is a brain disease will enable us to treat it as we do other medical illnesses.

Those who use illicit drugs are made more miserable by the drugs they use, compelling repeated use of that which renders them wretched. Put another way: Our brain has a reward circuit known as the mesolimbic dopamine pathway that some call the "pleasure center," which with proper stimulation releases the "pleasure neurotransmitter" dopamine (Stahl, 2008). Delightedly delightful people—the fulfilled, the contented, the blissful—trig-

TABLE 10-4

Attendance and Sobriety

YEARS IN AA	% OF ATTENDEES	CHANCE OF ONE ADDITIONAL YEAR OF SOBRIETY
1 year or less	40% of attendees have been sober for less than 1 year	40%
1 to 5 years	An additional 40% have been sober for 1 to 5 years	80%
More than 5 years	20% have been sober for more than 5 years	90%

From "World Services Comments on AA's Triennial Surveys," by General Service Office of Alcoholics Anonymous, December 1990, retrieved July 24, 2009, from http://www.aa.org/lang/en/subpage.cfm?page=222

ger the release of dopamine naturally through achievement, athletic accomplishments, and artful endeavors; through the satisfaction of friendships and family; through falling in love and fulfilling altruistic purposes; through experiencing an orgasm, running a marathon, or enjoying music; through the pleasure of hard work or the joy of creativity. All of these healthy behaviors produce "natural highs" by releasing our intrinsic transmitters—the brain's morphine/heroin (endorphins), the brain's marijuana (anandamide), the brain's nicotine (acetylcholine), and the brain's big one, the pleasure transmitter dopamine (Stahl, 2008).

Miserable people, those who fail to use healthy release mechanisms, stimulate the brain's same pleasure chemicals by taking illicit drugs, drinking, gambling, overeating, perusing pornography, or overspending money. Because illicit drug use releases natural transmitters quickly and in high doses, "diabolical learning" reinforces use of those drugs that are most harmful to lasting pleasure (Stahl, 2008) **(Table 10-5)**.

Epidemiology

Periodically, the Department of Health and Human Services releases *The National Survey on Drug Use and Health* (2007), which gives an intricately detailed public domain report on drug use in the United States. According to the results from the 2007 survey, an estimated 19.9 million Americans aged 12 or older were current illicit drug users. Marijuana was the most commonly used illicit drug, at 14.4 million users. In 2007, there were 2.1 million current cocaine users aged 12 or older, comprising 0.8% of the population.

TABLE 10-5	
Definitions Revolving Around Abuse and Addictions	
TERM	**DEFINITION**
Drug abuse	Culturally disapproved excessive drug use unrelated to acceptable medical practice that causes adverse consequences.
Reinforcement	The tendency of the pleasure-inducing action or drug to lead to repeated use.
Drug tolerance	Diminished effect of the drug with regular use of the same dose.
Addiction	Compulsive use of a drug and the tendency to relapse after discontinuation of the drug.
Psychic dependence	Compulsion to use a drug either continuously or episodically.
Physical dependence	Withdrawal of the drug produces physiological symptoms.
Therapeutic dependence	Use of the drug mitigates physical symptoms (e.g., the use of insulin to treat diabetes mellitus).
Withdrawal	The psychological or physical reactions secondary to discontinuation of a drug or action.
Relapse	The return to the original situation, condition, or drug following effective treatment.

Hallucinogens were used by 1.0 million persons (0.4%) aged 12 or older in 2007, including 503,000 (0.2%) who had used Ecstasy (3,4-methylene-dioxymethamphetamine, MDMA). There were 6.9 million (2.8%) persons aged 12 or older who used prescription-type psychotherapeutic drugs non-medically. Of these, 5.2 million used pain relievers, and 2.1 million used tranquilizers. In 2007, there were an estimated 529,000 current users of methamphetamines who were aged 12 or older (0.2% of the population). Inhalants were used by 600,000, and 200,000 used heroin. Between 2002 and 2007, youth rates declined significantly for illicit drugs in general (from 11.6% to 9.5%).

Types and Descriptions of Various Drugs

The U.S. Drug Enforcement Administration (n.d.) has created a schedule of various types of drugs, detailing their potential for abuse. The range of these drugs goes from schedule I (illegal drugs) to schedule V (over-the-counter drugs). Schedule II through schedule IV drugs have a variety of medical uses, but the abuse potential varies according to the scale. The next several sections of text are devoted to explanations of some of these drugs. Clinicians must continually update their knowledge of drug abuse because different types of drugs go in and out of vogue over time. **(Table 10-6)**.

Marijuana

The short-term effects of a joint, bong hits, blunts (or, in the concentrated resin, hashish) are tachycardia, red eyes, and euphoria in which colors and sounds seem more intense and time seems to pass slowly. Chronic daily use of marijuana can produce lethargy, decreased ambition, social deterioration, and mental and physical sloppiness. Heavy use can produce paranoid psychosis. Marijuana is more carcinogenic than tobacco. Damage to the hippocampus can cause short-term memory loss.

TABLE 10-6		
Scheduled Drugs		
SCHEDULE	**DEFINITION**	**EXAMPLES**
Schedule I	Illegal	LSD, heroin, marijuana
Schedule II	Strong addiction potential but medically useful	morphine, phencyclidine (PCP), cocaine, methadone, and methamphetamine
Schedule III	Moderate abuse potential	Anabolic steroids, codeine and hydrocodone with aspirin or Tylenol®
Schedule IV	Mild abuse potential	Darvon®, Talwin®, Valium®, and Xanax®
Schedule V	Minimal abuse potential	Cough preparations, antidiarrheals

Administration, US Department of Justice, 2005 Retrieved October 25, 2009, from http://www.usdoj.gov/dea/pubs/abuse/1-csa.htm#Formal

Hallucinogens

LSD—acid, mellow yellow—produces visual hallucinations and disorientation. This twilight state can be pleasant or upsetting depending on the amount of drug taken combined with the user's personality, mood, surroundings, and expectations. The effects, which include dilated pupils, sweating, increased pulse and elevated blood pressure, and "crossover" sensations of hearing colors and seeing sounds, generally last for 12 hours. Long-term effects include flashbacks and, for some, long-lasting psychosis. The cause of flashbacks remains unknown, but those with schizotypal and borderline personalities are considered high-risk patients, as are those with a family history of psychosis. Psychedelics can easily rekindle a preexisting psychosis (Rea & Kilgus, 2009).

MDMA (Ecstasy)

Similar to methamphetamine and mescaline, 3.4 methylenedioxymethamphetamine MDMA (Ecstasy), similar chemically to methamphetamine and mescaline, is a schedule I "party drug." In the short term, Ecstasy acts as a stimulant and psychedelic, producing a feeling of closeness, empathy, and sexuality. The stimulant effects are similar to the amphetamines. In primate animal studies, damage to serotonin nerve terminals may last for 6–7 years.

Amphetamines and Methamphetamines

Methamphetamines are the third most commonly abused drug in the Midwest behind alcohol and marijuana. Known as speed, ice, crystal, or crank, it can be manufactured rather easily using over-the-counter preparations containing pseudoephedrine, phenylpropanolamine, and ephedrine.

Amphetamines release dopamine in the brain, increasing wakefulness, euphoria, and energy. Orally ingesting the drug gives a relatively long-lasting high. Injecting 1 gram every 2 or 3 hours intravenously is known as a "run." Long-term effects include anxiety, confusion, paranoia, hallucinations, and aggression. High doses of amphetamines can produce symptoms indistinguishable from schizophrenia. Fifty percent of central nervous system dopamine and serotonin cells are destroyed with long-term use. Withdrawal results in depression, fatigue, paranoia, and craving.

Cocaine

Cocaine, used in tonics, toothache cures, and as chocolate cocaine tabs and espoused by the pharmaceutical company Parke-Davis as a preparation that would make "the silent eloquent, coward brave, and render the sufferer insensitive pain" was sold over the counter until 1914. From 1886 until the early 1900s, Coca-Cola contained cocaine, and its formula still includes coca leaves with the cocaine extracted (Spillane, 1990). Cocaine remains a schedule II drug and is still used as a topical anesthetic for nose and throat pain.

Otherwise known as coke, C, snow, toot, blow, flake, happy dust, and nose candy, cocaine is a vegetable alkaloid derived from the leaves of the coca plant found on eastern slopes of the Andes Mountains in Peru. A snort of cocaine in each nostril can produce an exhilarating half hour of drive, sparkle, and energy but has a dark and destructive side when euphoria is followed by depression and irritability. Chronic use can produce hallucinations, paranoia, physical collapse, nasal septum perforation, and cardiac arrest.

Phencyclidine

Phencyclidine (PCP), commonly known as angel dust, rocket fuel, or embalming fluid, is an extremely dangerous hallucinogen. The drug was originally introduced as a surgical anesthetic, but researchers soon found that many of the individuals given the medication became psychotic, agitated, and incredibly strong. PCP soon became prominent on the black market, primarily because it could be misrepresented and sold on the street as THC (tetrahydrocannabinol, the chief intoxicant in marijuana), LSD, cocaine, or amphetamine. PCP can cause a highly varied picture; occasionally, the individual may be sleepy and calm, and at other times, the individual is paranoid, disoriented, and agitated. PCP also produces numerous medical complications, including vomiting, seizures, and extremely high blood pressure. Management of PCP abuse requires the most expert care.

Barbiturates

Barbiturates, first introduced for medical use in the early 1900s, quickly became a popular sedative, leading to the synthesis of over 2,500 compounds; now, secondary to the safer benzodiazepines, about a dozen barbiturates remain on the market. Those who abuse drugs prefer the shorter-acting schedule II barbiturates—Amytal, Nembutal, or Seconal. These drugs produce mild sedation to coma. Tolerance to the drug develops, so the therapeutic dose comes close to the toxic dose quickly.

Narcotics

Opium, derived from poppy seeds, has been used as a euphorogenic for over 6,000 years and is described in Homer's works the *Iliad* and the *Odyssey* (850 BC). In 1805, the German pharmacist F. W. Serturner isolated the active ingredient in opium, naming it morphium after Morpheus, the Greek god of dreams. Heroin and codeine are synthetically or naturally derived from opium. During the Civil War, physicians dispensed opium pills and injected morphine sulfate for war wounds.

Heroin; morphine; the morphine derivative MS-Contin; oxycodone marketed alone or as time-released OxyContin (hillbilly heroin, kicker) or in combination with aspirin (Percodan) or acetaminophen (Percocet); or other narcotics can quickly produce physical dependence and addiction. With these drugs, tolerance quickly develops, so increasing amounts of the drug are required to produce the same effect. As an individual takes increasing amounts of the drug, the potential for acute overdose occurs. Respiratory depression can be treated with Narcan (0.4–2 mg IV).

Withdrawal from higher doses produces dilated pupils, tremor, goose bumps (from which "cold turkey" gets its name), muscle cramps, vomiting, and diarrhea. The withdrawal state reaches its height in 2 to 3 days but gradually subsides without treatment in 5 to 10 days.

Benzodiazepines
Although estimates indicated that from 11% to 15% of the adult population take a benzodiazepine one or more times a year, data extrapolations indicated that only 1–2% take these medications daily for 12 months or longer. Still, Xanax, Klonopin, Valium, and Ativan are listed among the top 100 most commonly prescribed medications, and their pharmacology indicates that these drugs possess an abuse potential (Longo & Johnson, 2000).

While benzodiazepines carry a low risk of acute toxicity, fatal overdoses of benzodiazepines in combination with alcohol have occurred. The benzodiazepines produce intoxication symptoms similar to alcohol and, in high doses for a long period, produce physical dependence, leading to withdrawal symptoms that are also similar to alcohol withdrawal. They also can cause drowsiness, poor concentration, incoordination, emotional blunting, and memory impairment.

Predatory Drugs
Sexual assaults facilitated by Rohypnol (a benzodiazepine marketed as a powerful soporific known as "roofie") and ketamine (an animal anesthetic) are difficult to prosecute because these amnesia-inducing, quickly metabolized drugs are odorless and invisible when dissolved in water or other liquids.

Inhalants
Inhalants are a diverse group of substances that include volatile solvents, gases, and nitrites that are sniffed, huffed, snorted, or bagged and produce intoxicating effects similar to alcohol. Because common household products contain these mind-altering vapors, young people often experiment with inhalants before moving on to harder drugs. Inhalants can deprive the body of oxygen causing hypoxia. Brain cells are especially sensitive to hypoxia. Repeated use of inhalants damages the hippocampus, which helps control

memory, so that the user has difficulty learning new things and eventually may be unable to carry on simple conversations. Long-term inhalant abuse can also break down myelin, a fatty tissue that protects nerve fibers. Damage to myelin can produce muscle spasms, tremors, impair ambulation, and damage speech. Inhalants can also produce liver and kidney damage. Sniffing solvents or aerosol sprays can induce heart failure and death with repeated inhalation. Deliberately inhaling from a plastic bag can increase the chance of death. (National Institute on Drug Abuse, 2009).

Identification and Management of Prescription Drug Abuse

In the April 15, 2000, issue of *American Family Physician*, Longo, Parran, Johnson, and Kinsey published a classic article on the management of drug-seeking patients, a summary of which is paraphrased here. The prescription drugs most commonly abused are the narcotic analgesics, sedative-hypnotics, and stimulants. Physicians' concerns about possible sanctions related to controlled substances may contribute to increased pain and anxiety, which in turn leads to needless suffering and lost productivity. On the other hand, the clinician must recognize and manage drug-seeking patients. Although addiction disorders affect 15–30% percent of patients seen in primary care settings, 20–50% of hospitalized patients, and up to 50% of patients with psy-

TABLE 10-7		
Selected Intoxication and Withdrawal Symptoms of Illicit Drug Use		
DRUG	**INTOXICATION SYMPTOMS**	**WITHDRAWAL SYMPTOMS**
Amphetamines	Psychomotor agitaton, weight loss, paranoia	Depression, "crash" symptoms similar to cocaine
Cocaine	Euphoria, cardiac toxicity	Fatigue, lassitude, irritability
Opioid	Lethargy, coma, shock, pinpoint pupils	Flu-like symptoms, diarrhea, diaphoresis, cramping
PCP	Bizarre aggression, vertical nystagmus	Impaired judgment, conduct disorders
Hallucinogens	Depersonalization, derealization, illusions	Flashbacks
Cannabis/marijuana	Sense of slowed time, social withdrawal	Apathy
Inhalants	Slurred speech, ataxia	Slowed mentation

chiatric illnesses, most patients with addiction disorders remain undiagnosed and untreated. Characteristics of patients who abuse prescription drugs include the following:

- Escalating use—"overuse" of a prescribed medication can be the result of clinicians underestimating the magnitude of the symptoms, mandating careful consideration of the clinical need to increase the dose of medication. Nonetheless, if a pattern of increasing escalation of use develops, an addiction assessment is necessary.
- Drug-seeking behavior is manifested by the following:
  - The patient may describe symptoms that markedly deviate from objective findings.
  - The patient may insist on receiving a controlled drug prescription, claiming that nonaddictive medications don't work.
  - The patient gives reports of "losing" prescriptions. (When patients tell me that they have lost a prescription for a drug of abuse, I tell them they must wait until the regular time for a refill to get another prescription.)
  - Doctor shopping—seeing multiple physicians to obtain an increasing supply of controlled prescriptions. Monitoring by pharmacies and insurance companies can aid the physician in identifying these patients.
  - Continuing to "push" the physician to prescribe a controlled substance in the hopes that the physician will gradually give in to demands.

Characteristics of overprescribing clinicians can be remembering by the four "Ds":

- Dated—refers to clinicians who have failed to keep up with changes in pharmacology and the management of chronic pain, sleep, and anxiety disorders.
- Duped—clinicians who cultivate a caring and trusting relationship based on mutual respect while honestly attempting to help patients may be drawn into the patients' own system of denial. A codependent clinician may fear abandonment by the patient if the clinician fails to meet the patient's demands. A fine line exists between empathy and codependence. The clinician's heightened awareness of these issues can improve clinical outcomes. A clinician who feels the a need to rescue a patient, or feels inappropriate anger, guilt, pity, revulsion, or any other emotion outside their usual experiences of compassion and concern, may look inward to consider the possibility that they have a codependent relationship with the patient.

- Dishonest—some clinicians may write prescriptions in exchange for personal or financial gain.
- Disabled—chemically dependent physicians may be less likely to con front patients who are abusing substances.

Clinicians who prescribe controlled substances for legitimate medical purposes can optimize risk management by implementing the following safeguards:

- Maintain a current knowledge base regarding pharmacology and signs of intoxication and withdrawal.
- Carefully document and chart in progress notes the diagnosis, clinical indications, expected outcome, and expected symptom endpoint. There is a certain subset of patients, for example, who may benefit from treatment with benzodiazepines for extended periods. As long as the physician records the reasons for continued treatment, avoids extensive use of refills without regular visits, and watches for escalating doses, the patient can receive the benefits of long-term medication while the physician avoids fear of disciplinary action from state regulatory agencies.
- Avoid prescribing controlled substances without involving the patient in other treatment modalities such as psychotherapy or physical therapy.
- Failure to inform a patient of the risk of driving while taking a sedating medication may lead to a claim of negligence.
- Warning: it is unlawful to provide maintenance prescriptions for a narcotic to a patient who is addicted to controlled substances unless that patient is registered with the Drug Enforcement Agency in a treatment program.

General Principles of Treatment

Treatment should always begin with an appropriate assessment (Mack et al., 2003). The essential substance use history includes:

- Review of all the substances used and drug of choice.
- Assessment of present and past withdrawal symptoms.
- History of abuse, including dates of first and last use.
- Amount, frequency, and route of administration.
- History of past treatment and response.
- Longest period of sobriety.
- History of psychiatric illness.

- Medical history including medications, allergies, HIV, tuberculosis, and hepatitis status.
- Family history of psychiatric disorders and substance use.
- History of sexual or physical abuse.
- Psychosocial history, including legal history and accident history.
- Answering questions such as: Does the family need psychotherapy? Are there any positive role models in the family?

Building a positive therapeutic alliance, important in any psychiatric illness, deserves special attention with abusers because of the patient's lack of trust for the caregiver and because of the high rate of personality disorder conflict. Respect for the individual user with attention to the specific style of relating to others helps build trust. Optimism, flexibility, persistence, patience, and frustration tolerance are virtues possessed by the ideal therapist working with substance abusers. Boundaries must be established for the therapist (e.g., no rescuing, no overinvolvement) and for the patient—willingness to involve the family when appropriate, participation in AA/NA when recommended, agreement for medications when necessary, and prompt attendance and payment for services.

Therapy begins with a direct but empathetic approach aimed at dealing with the patient's denial of substance abuse problems and the tendency to minimize the consequences of the abuse. Education, books, DVDs, creation of support groups, attention to the family system, and homework assignments keep the patient engaged in therapy. Group therapy, psychodynamically oriented therapy, cognitive-behavior therapy (CBT), and dialectical behavior therapy, all of which have been used in treating substance abusers, lack evidence-based documentation of effectiveness. AA/NA and Al-Anon for family members should anchor all treatment approaches and techniques. Because of the importance of AA in treating substance abusers, perhaps a good way to end this chapter is to leave with a few paragraphs from the *Big Book* as an example of the book's flavor. This from the *Big Book*, step 10:

> When we retire at night, we constructively review our day. Were we resentful, selfish, dishonest, or afraid? Were we kind and loving toward all? What could we have done better?
>
> On awakening, let us think about the twenty-four hours ahead. We consider our plans for the day. Before we begin, we ask God to direct our thinking, especially asking that it be divorced from self-pity, dishonest or self-seeking motives. . . . In thinking about our day, we may face indecision. We may not be able to determine which course to take. Here we ask God for inspiration, an intuitive thought, or a decision. We relax and take it easy. We don't struggle. We are often surprised

how the right answers come after we have tried this for a while. What used to be a hunch or the occasional inspiration gradually becomes a working part of the mind. ... We usually conclude the period of meditation with a prayer that we be shown all through the day what our next step is to be, that we be given whatever we need to take care of such problems. We ask especially for freedom from self-will, and are careful to make no request for ourselves only. We may ask for ourselves, however, if others will be helped. We are careful never to pray for our own selfish ends. Many of us have wasted a lot of time doing that and it doesn't work. You can easily see why.

Are You an Alcoholic?				
Make Check Mark (✓) in Appropriate Column	Little of the Time 1 point each ✓	Some of the Time 2 points each ✓	A Lot of the Time 3 points each ✓	Most of the Time 4 points each ✓
I have had something to drink every day for a month.				
I get angry when someone says I have a drinking problem.				
I have to have an morning "eye-opener" to get going.				
I feel guilty about my drinking.				
I tried to stop drinking, but I eventually return to drinking.				
Once I start drinking, I can't stop.				
I have drinking binges that last 2–3 days.				
I have been arrested for driving while intoxicated or public intoxication.				
I have missed work because of drinking.				
Drinking has interfered with my family life.				
Multiply ✓ by the value given in each column.				

Add the total for each column to get the **Grand total** = _____

SCORING

10–14 points = Clean and sober

15–24 points = Social drinker

25–34 points = Listen to your family and friends and get to an AA meeting as soon as possible

35–40 points = You are drinking too much

Are You a Substance Abuser?

Make Check Mark (✓) in Appropriate Column	Little of the Time 1 point each ✓	Some of the Time 2 points each ✓	A Lot of the Time 3 points each ✓	Most of the Time 4 points each ✓
I need to take more and more drugs to get the same effects.				
I don't get the same effects from drugs as I did in the past.				
I get the "shakes" or start feeling down when I don't take drugs.				
I crave drugs.				
I try to stop using drugs, but I eventually return to using them.				
I take more drugs than I intend to.				
I spend a great deal of time and money obtaining drugs.				
I visit multiple doctors to get the drugs I need for pain or anxiety.				
I keep using drugs even though drugs have caused physical or emotional problems.				
Drugs have caused problems with my family/friends/employers.				
Multiply ✓ by the value given in each column.				

Add the total for each column to get the **Grand total** = _____

SCORING

10–14 points = Drug free

15–24 points = Getting dangerously close to abusing drugs

25–34 points = Listen to your family and friends and get help as soon as possible

35–40 points = Using too many drugs, too often

Addictions and Abuse   *193*

A Clinician's Quiz

1. Discuss genetic background, physiology, and biological mutations as factors in the development of alcoholism.
2. How does alcohol abuse differ from alcohol addiction?
3. List the factors that influence alcohol intoxication.
4. List the signs and symptoms of alcohol withdrawal delirium.
5. Discuss the Alcohol Anonymous concept of "cure."
6. Discuss the "pleasure center."
7. What is a Schedule III drug? Give some examples.
8. What are the symptoms of amphetamine withdrawal?
9. What signs and symptoms can cocaine induce?
10. What are the symptoms of opiate withdrawal?

Complete Mental Health

CHAPTER 11

Emotional Problems in Children and Adolescents

Childhood Interrupted

Famous author and playwright J. M. Barrie was the 9th of 10 children in the Lowland village of Kirriemuir born to David Barrie, a handloom weaver, and Margaret Ogilvy, the daughter of a stonemason. When James was 6, his older brother, David—his mother's favorite—died in a skating accident. The diminutive James claimed that when he reached age 13, the age of his brother's death, he himself stopped growing (Read Print Publishing, 2009). Barrie's most famous work, *Peter Pan*, is a children's story that is also a great work of literature (Barrie, 1991):

> All children, except one, grow up. They soon know that they will grow up, and the way Wendy knew was this. One day when she was two years old, she was playing in a garden, and she plucked another flower and ran with it to her mother. I suppose she must have looked rather delightful, for Mrs. Darling put her hand to her heart and cried, "Oh, why can't you remain like this for ever!" This was all that passed between them on the subject, but henceforth Wendy knew that she must grow up. You always know after you are two. Two is the end.
>
> (Barrie, 1991, p. 1)

Yes, Wendy did grow and move far beyond the age of 2 "until her hair became white, and her figure little again," experiencing some of the same pleasures and pains that all of us who grow old do accumulate. Children, though, are not little adults. They progress through different developmental stages that expose them day by day to new and different challenges, puzzles, insights, and sadly, mental illnesses.

Why do some children experience emotional disorders while others sail through adolescence unscathed? The answer isn't easy to ascertain. A combination of nature and nurture—genetic predisposition and environmental factors—may ultimately be responsible. For some diagnoses, such as attention deficit/hyperactivity disorder (ADHD), biology plays a bigger role. Other disorders show up as physical manifestations of an inner conflict. Immature coping mechanisms might lead to unwanted or unhealthy behavior. For example, while adults may abuse alcohol as an escape, young children may "act out" their stress with inappropriate or passive-aggressive behavior.

Because so-called adult psychiatric disorders can begin in childhood and, furthermore, because childhood psychiatric disorders can lead to significant adult pathology, the *Diagnostic and Statistical Manual of Mental Disorders, Fourth Edition, Text Revision* (*DSM-IV-TR*; American Psychiatric Association, 2000) has established a category—disorders usually first diagnosed in infancy, childhood, or adolescence. This chapter serves as a brief overview of the most important and most interesting of these disorders.

Attention Deficit/Hyperactivity Disorders

In 1910, O. Henry wrote "Ransom of Red Chief," about a boy so hyperactive that the kidnappers paid the parents to take him back (Henry, 2002). This humorous story reveals that hyperactivity in children is nothing new. In 1902, Sir George Frederick Still, England's first professor in child medicine, presented a series of three lectures to the Royal College of Physicians in London, at which time he described the characteristics of attention deficit disorder (Mayes & Rafalovich, 2007). Over time, the diagnosis has undergone a series of refinements, ultimately culminating in several developmental variations collectively known as attention deficit/hyperactivity disorders (ADHDs). The *DSM-IV-TR* (American Psychiatric Association, 2000) listed three variations: attention deficit/hyperactivity disorder, predominantly hyperactive-impulsive type; attention deficit/hyperactivity disorder, predominantly inattentive type; and attention deficit/hyperactivity disorder, combined type.

Parents, especially parents of toddlers, often wonder what constitutes normal energy levels versus what may be indicative of problem behavior. Although there is no approved test for ADHD, the teacher rating scales like the the SNAP-IV Rating Scale (Swanson, Nolan, and Pelham, 1983) provide the best indication (Kilgus & Adams, 2009). **Table 11-1**, plus the informal and nonstardized quiz at the end of this chapter, will help.

TABLE 11-1

Core Symptoms of ADHD in Children

For at least 6 months, the child demonstrates six of nine hyperactivity/impulsive symptoms or at least six of nine inattention symptoms

HYPERACTIVITY	IMPULSIVITY	INATTENTION
Fidgets or squirms	Blurts out answers before questions are completed	Makes careless mistakes
Unable to remain seated		Poor attention span
Inappropriate and excessive running and climbing	Difficulty awaiting turn	Poor listener
	Interrupts conversations or games	Leaves tasks unfinished
Difficulty playing quietly		Poor organizational skills
"On the go" as if "driven by a motor"		Avoids sustained mental effort
		Frequently loses things
Talks excessively		Distracted by extraneous stimuli
		Forgetful

Clinical Course

Approximately 3–7% of school-aged children have ADHD marked by the triad of impulsivity, hyperactivity, and inattention. Just under half of ADHD children experience a good outcome, completing school on time with acceptable grades whereas 60% of children with severe ADHD have symptoms into adulthood. Adult ADHD symptoms include disorganization, inability to finish projects, inattention, accidents, and frequent job changes and partner changes (Kilgus & Adams, 2009).

ADHD commonly occurs with substance use disorders, conduct disorders, oppositional defiant disorders, and learning disorders. Untreated ADHD can lead to substance abuse as patients seek to relieve symptoms by self-medicating. If ADHD is consistently treated, the risk of substance abuse is the same as in the general population. Psychostimulant treatment of ADHD appears to protect against the development of substance abuse (Kilgus & Adams, 2009).

Those with combined ADHD and conduct disorder have a poor prognosis with about a fourth of these children developing an antisocial personality disorder associated with failure to complete school, substance abuse, legal difficulties, accidents, and suicide attempts. Biological vulnerability and low childhood self-esteem may contribue to a propensity for mood disorders in adulthood (Kilgus & Adams, 2009). Considerable symptom overlap be-tween bipolar disorder (BPD) and ADHD may lead to diagnostic confusion, especially because BPD and ADHD can coexist. As previously stated, key distinguishing features of ADHD include inattention, hyperactivity, and impulsivity, while diagnostic features of BPD include elation, grandiosity, racing thoughts, decreased need for sleep, pressured speech and mood instability.

Theoretical Cause of ADHD

A prominent theory for the cause of ADHD—inattention, hyperactivity, and impulsivity—rests on arousal abnormalities in the prefrontal cortex of the brain. Scientifically speaking, the neurodevelopmentally compromised prefrontal cortex modulates the prefrontal motor cortex, which regulates hyperactivity; impairs the dorsal anterior cingulate cortex, having an impact on selective attention; and negatively influences the orbital frontal cortex, which regulates impulsivity. Genetic factors combined with environmental factors—difficulties during pregnancy, prenatal exposure to alcohol and tobacco, premature delivery, significantly low birth weight, excessively high body lead levels, and closed head injuries—contribute to the problems in the prefrontal cortex (Stahl, 2008).

Treatment

Although the diagnosis of ADHD can be made by 3 years of age, identification is often delayed until school age, when demands for stability become more pronounced. Controversy has developed over what some thought was overdiagnosis of ADHD, with a special concern about the amount of drugs used in treatment. There is little doubt, however, that medications have improved the lives of thousands of children and prevented associated morbidity such as substance abuse, oppositional defiance disorder, conduct disorders, and learning disorders (Kilgus & Adams, 2009).

In 1937, Dr. Charles Bradley, introduced the use of stimulants for treating hyperactive children, and in 1956 Ritalin (methylphenidate) was used as the treatment of choice. In 1996, Adderall, approved by the Food and Drug Administration (FDA) for the treatment of ADHD, soon became the standard to which all other medications were compared. Since then, several long-acting preparations have been added to the pharmacopoeia. Currently, approximately 4% of U.S. children take medications for ADHD (Mays, Bagwell, & Erkulwater, 2009).

Persistent target symptoms sufficiently severe to cause functional impairment at school, home, and with peers call for the initiation of a psychostimulant if the child has failed to improve with psychoeducation and school consultation and if the parents are willing to monitor the medicines and regularly attend meetings. Based on 200 double-blind studies demonstrating efficacy in both boys and girls, psychostimulant medication has been shown to improve cognitive and inattention symptoms (Kilgus & Adams, 2009).

Because hyperactive individuals appear overstimulated, it seems counterintuitive that stimulants would be used to treat ADHD. As the theory goes, the compromised prefrontal cortex results from deficiencies in arousal networks. Ritalin and Adderall increase dopamine and norepinephrine in the prefrontal cortex, enhancing attention, concentration, and the efficiency of information processing. Enhanced dopamine actions in the basal ganglia may improve hyperactivity (Stahl, 2008). Because the use of psychostimulants may cause insomnia, decreased appetite, and worsened irritable mood and may induce clinically insignificant growth retardation, drug-free trials during holidays and the summer months may be indicated.

Other drugs used to treat ADHD include the tricyclic antidepressants, the dopamine-enhancing antidepressant Wellbutrin, the norepinephrine drug Strattera, and the norepinephrine-serotonin reuptake blocker Effexor. The antidepressant medications, including Strattera, take 4–6 weeks to act, whereas the psychostimulants show almost immediate benefits (Stahl, 2008).

The alpha-2 noradrenergic agonist clonidine, beginning at 0.05 mg at bedtime, has been helpful with ADHD patients who are impulsive, defiant, highly aroused, and labile. The dose can be gradually titrated upward, given three or four times daily. Sedation, hypotension, and dizziness are limiting side effects (Cozza, Cozza, Crawford, & Dulcan, 2003) **(Table 11-2, Table 11-3)**.

Psychotherapy

Multimodal treatment for ADHD in addition to medication therapy includes parent and child education, behavior management techniques, and family support. Although most experts would agree that medication alone is more effective in treating ADHD than behavioral treatment alone, combining the two approaches is synergistic.

Behavior modification helps the child develop new skills for interacting with others. Guidelines for behavior modification include

- Start slow—initially, goals should be easy to accomplish, setting the child up for success.
- Aim for consistency—the child should be expected and encouraged to maintain the desired behavior in different places, with different people around, and at different times of the day.

TABLE 11-2		
The NIMH List of ADHD Medications and the Approved Age for Use		
TRADE NAME	**GENERIC NAME**	**APPROVED AGE (Years)**
Adderall	Amphetamine/dextroamphetamine	3 and older
Adderall XR	Amphetamine/dextroamphetamine (extended release)	6 and older
Concerta	Methylphenidate (long acting)	6 and older
Daytrana	Methylphenidate patch	6 and older
Desoxyn	Methamphetamine hydrochloride	6 and older
Dexedrine	Dextroamphetamine	3 and older
Dextrostrat	Dextroamphetamine	3 and older
Focalin	Dexmethylphenidate	6 and older
Focalin XR	Dexmethylphenidate (extended release)	6 and older
Metadate ER	Methylphenidate (extended release)	6 and older
Metadate ER	Methylphenidate (extended release)	6 and older
Methylin	Methylphenidate (oral solution and chewable tablets)	6 and older
Ritalin	Methylphenidate	6 and older
Ritalin SR	Methylphenidate (extended release)	6 and older
Ritalin LA	Methylphenidate (long acting)	6 and older
Strattera	Atomoxetine	6 and older
Vyvanse	Lisdexamfetamine dimesylate	6 and older

• Take baby steps. Remember, the development of new skills takes time.

Concerned parents of children with ADHD founded Children and Adults With Attention Deficit Hyperactivity Disorder (CHADD) in 1987 as a place where families could turn for education and support regarding the illness. Their Web site, http://www.chadd.org, offers information about local chapters and a wide range of publications.

According to CHADD (2008), health professionals and parents should

TABLE 11-3			
Commonly Used Medications for Attention Deficit Disorder			
	RITALIN	**ADDERAL**	**CONCERTA**
How supplied (mg)	5, 10, 20	5, 10, 20, 30	18, 36
Usual daily dose (mg)	10–60	5–40	18–54
Usual starting dose (mg)	5–10 daily or twice daily	2.5–5 daily	18
Maintenance dose/ day (mg)	Two or three times daily	One or two times daily	Once daily

work together to come up with a list of target behaviors—either behaviors that need to stop or new skills that need to be learned—for treatment goals. These goals may be improved play, obedience, or attention.

Therapy Goals for Children With ADHD
- Teaching how to get along with others.
- Helping solve social problems.
- Teaching sport and game-board skills.
- Decreasing bossiness and selfishness.
- Helping the child cultivate close friendships.
- Helping learn cause and effect (certain actions result in certain results).
- Taking responsibility for actions.

Parent training may include helping parents to learn and to implement the following techniques:

- Establishing routines.
- Praising wanted behaviors.
- Ignoring mild unwanted behaviors.
- Using "when-then" techniques (unwanted behavior results in fewer privileges).
- Making plans on how to manage children in public places.
- Using "time-outs" during unwanted behavior.
- Using daily charts and point systems for rewards.
- Using school notes to reward school behavior and to track homework.

Although these methods of behavior modification used by parents are commonsense approaches, they are more difficult to accomplish if a child has ADHD and require encouragement and support to keep after the simple techniques day after day and week after week.

Conduct Disorders

A persistent pattern of aggression, destruction of property, deceitfulness, theft, and serious violations of rules characterizes conduct disorder. Of children with ADHD, 20–30% eventually meet the criteria for conduct disorders (Andreasen & Black, 2006). Conduct disorders also often coexist with learning disorders and mood disorders. The earlier the onset of symptoms and the more severe the psychopathology, the worse the prognosis for developing adult sociopathy. A combination of substance abuse disorders, mood disorders, and antisocial personality disorder may be the endpoint for intractable cases. Those with milder symptoms may accomplish acceptable occupational and social adjustment as adults (Kilgus & Adams, 2009).

Conduct disorders may develop from physical and sexual trauma; untenable socioeconomic factors; negligent conditions; absent, alcoholic, antisocial, or emotionally disturbed parents; parental abandonment or rejection; shifting caregivers—the list is extensive (Kilgus & Adams, 2009).

Former football coach Lou Holtz once said that 80% of success is showing up. Likewise, 80% of being a successful parent is showing up. The other 20% is showing up with love, compassion, and concern. Parents of the conduct-disordered patient often do not show up, and when they do, they frequently show up frustrated and irritable.

There are thousands of words written on treatment suggestions, all of which seem to point, after all is said and done, to increased parental involvement (Kilgus & Adams, 2009). Multi-systemic therapy involves direct training of parents and careful assessment and intervention of maladaptive family interactions. The key to mitigating conduct disorders is to cultivate, through parenting classes and individual parental tutoring, the gradual development of reliable, caring, and concerned parents who show up day after day with love in their hearts. Placement away from home may be necessary in recalcitrant cases, cases for which the parent is absent, or if the parent refuses to work in therapy.

Along with parent involvement, treatment with medication may be indicated in certain cases. Antipsychotics such as Risperdal may help control violent behavior; lithium may help with aggression in children with and without comorbid BPD. Stimulants are useful in patients with comorbid ADHD (Sadock & Sadock, 2005).

Even children who come from unfortunate psychosocial environments can benefit from an approach that offers encouragement, optimism, and hope.

Children are resilient. The most challenging symptoms can be swept away by future experiences and opportunities. Early treatment intervention is essential in establishing a foundation that allows the child to take advantage of later developmental milestones. Looking for the divine spark in every child and the ray of goodness in the most neglectful parent will offer the opportunity for change and growth.

Oppositional Defiant Disorders

Oppositional defiant disorder, marked by temper tantrums, arguing, blaming, and spiteful behavior without violating societal norms and the rights of others has a better prognosis than conduct disorder (Kilgus & Adams, 2009).

Disobedient, negativistic, and provocative opposition to authority figures is often the only way a child feels capable of exerting control over a situation governed by adults. Most of the time, a child's aggressive behavior signifies the struggle to develop a separate identity and a sense of control over one's environment. For example, the little girl who throws down a toy from her high chair is just testing out her new power over her surroundings—flexing her muscles. She is experimenting with control over objects.

Intractable stubbornness that most children exhibit around the age of 2 years—the so-called terrible twos— reflects a time when children learn to assert themselves without fear of abandonment. Toddlers, conflicted about growing up, show opposite behavior patterns—they want to explore and learn; at the same time, their occasional tendency to exhibit clinging behavior indicates their wish to remain dependent on their parents. Negative behavior reflects this natural ambivalence, which will eventually be resolved with repeated environmental testing.

Extended provocative behavior often indicates a need or desire for structure. Children actually want instruction on how to behave. Problem behavior begins when parents are unable or unwilling to set consistent limits. If a parent punishes undesired behavior one time and the next time lets it go, the child becomes confused about the real rules of the house. The mere word "No" means nothing to a child; action and follow-up provide effectiveness for behavior change.

The appropriate management for disobedient behavior involves refraining from struggle with the child while reinforcing responsible behavior through a flexible approach:

- Recognize the child's need for self-assertion.
- Set appropriate limits.
- Allow the child to express acceptable angry feelings. Squelching a child's angry feelings can cause inappropriate guilt regarding anger

while thwarting natural aggression, necessary for curiosity and exploration.
- Learn to combine love and logic.

Psychiatrist Foster Cline and educator Jim Fay advocate raising responsible children by helping them practice logical decision making. "Drill sergeant" parents who give orders to their children may cause rebellion while "helicopter parents" who hover around their children restrict their autonomy. "Love and Logic" parents teach their children responsibility and logic by allowing them to solve their own problems, providing skills for dealing with the challenges of life. Cline and Fay's book, *Love and Logic* (2006) discusses the principles of teaching children responsibility and provides strategies for applying the method to actual situations such as doing homework and learning the benefit of work.

> One frustrated mother, at her wit's end over her 8-year-old daughter's disobedient behavior, sought advice in counseling. The mother had a teachable spirit and readily took the advice I gave. She sat down with her husband first, agreeing on and writing down specific behaviors that would no longer be tolerated and the appropriate punishments for breaking the rules. The list of new rules (which was purposefully short at first) was communicated to the child and posted as an "if . . . then" chart on the refrigerator. For example, no longer would the little girl be allowed to scream and yell when she didn't get her way. Instead, she was allowed to express her anger by going to her room and punching a pillow to vent frustration. The program took several weeks to produce consistent behavior change, but it worked because husband and wife were on the same page, and the rules were clearly communicated.

Pervasive Developmental Disorders
Pervasive developmental disorders refer to neurobiologically impaired children and adolescents with persistent social, communication, motor, and behavioral problems.

Autism
Autism, with a prevalence rate somewhere between 2 and 20 cases per 10,000 children and a median rate of 5 cases per 10,000, is a relatively rare disorder (American Psychiatric Association, 2000). With concordance in identical twins much higher than fraternal twins, recognizable chromosome abnormalities in some autistic children, and a 50 times greater chance of an autistic sibling having the disorder than the expected prevalence, the etiology of

autism demonstrates striking genetic factors (Kilgus & Adams, 2009). Magnetic resonance imaging (MRI) studies show reductions in the volume of the hippocampus and amygdala and enlargments of the temporal and frontal lobes that may explain, partially, why some individuals with autistic disorder show subnormal intelligence (Kilgus & Adams, 2009).

Parents usually are the first to pick up on warning signs of autism, and although they may not know anything about the disorder, parents often suspect that something is "wrong" with their child at an early age. Autistic babies usually don't like to be held, and they avoid eye contact. Games of "peek-a-boo" don't interest them. Speech is usually delayed or may appear as robotic-like mimicry instead of actual attempts to communicate (American Psychiatric Association, 2000).

Characteristics of Autistic Children
- Failure to develop peer relationships.
- A lack of sharing interests, achievements, or enjoyments.
- Impairment in nonverbal behaviors necessary to establish rapport with others.
- Impaired development in spoken language.
- The inability to establish and sustain conversations.
- Stereotyped or idiosyncratic language.
- Lack of imaginative play.
- Stereotyped behavior—head banging, rocking, twisting.
- Inflexibility in routines.
- Preoccupation with restricted patterns of interest.
- Persistent preoccupation with parts of objects.

This neurodevelopmental disorder presents treatment challenges. Psychoeducation training provides parents with behavior management guidelines to reduce the autistic's stereotypical behaviors. Specialized day care can help parents improve the child's language and social skills (Andreasen & Black, 2006). Low doses of haloperidol (0.5–4 mg daily) or low doses of risperidone (0.5 mg) have been shown to decrease aggressiveness and temper tantrums (Cozza et al., 2003). Mood stabilizers may help with impulsivity; Luvox with obsessive-compulsive disorder (OCD) symptoms; and selective serotonin reuptake inhibitors (SSRIs) with anxiety and depression (Popper et al., 2003).

Autistic disorder, generally a lifelong condition, has a poor prognosis. Those with a higher IQ and better language development can show gradual improvement. Depending on the severity of the disorder, perhaps 2–15% progress through school and live independent lives as adults (Popper et al., 2003).

Asperger's Disorder

Asperger's disorder, with language, cognition, learning skills, and adaptive behaviors largely preserved, is more common than autism. The child with Asperger's disorder lacks appropriate boundaries (such as personal space) and social skills. The child may talk at length about a favorite subject or be able to repeat almost verbatim a story that was read aloud. The child may have delayed motor skills and fine motor impairment.

In 1944, an Austrian pediatrician, Hans Asperger, identified four children with normal IQ who had difficulty with social interactions, had poor nonverbal communication skills, were clumsy, and lacked empathy; he called their condition "autistic psychopathy" because the condition was marked, primarily, by social isolation. It was not until 1981, almost 40 years after World War II, that an English physician named Loma Wing published a series of case studies with similar symptoms that she called Asperger's syndrome. In 1994, the disorder was added to the fourth edition of the *DSM* (*DSM-IV*; American Psychiatric Association, 1994).

> He discussed his favorite subject, geology, almost continuously, speaking in an overly formal manner; his intense gaze, clumsy gesturing, and enthusiastic recitation of hundreds of arcane facts interfered with his ability to recognize boredom in his listener. He admitted to having no deep friendships, preferring solitude that allowed him the freedom to learn more about geology, sometimes becoming so fascinated with a new finding that he would repeat the facts hour after hour, losing awareness of everything else around him. He had no idea that others considered him odd.

The course of Asperger's disorder tends to be stable with, perhaps, some gradual gains. In adulthood, social deficits may be partially hidden by verbal strengths. Many adults formerly diagnosed with schizoid personalities are now known to have pervasive developmental disorder which has as its cardinal feature a lack of social reciprocity (Kilgus & Adams, 2009).

Depression

Instead of showing the biological signs typically found in adults with depression (weight loss, decreased appetite, decreased sleep, and decreased sex drive), children often act out their depressed state with destructive anger, withdrawal, running away, psychosomatic complaints (headaches, stomachaches, earaches), or poor academic performance. Therefore, it may be difficult to tell if a child is depressed or oppositional. A precipitation event, such as trauma, parental separation or divorce, or a move to another city, can often trigger depression.

Some Warning Signs of Depression in Children and Teens
- Sudden changes in behavior, speech, dress, sleep, or appetite.
- Risky behavior.
- May be aggressive and angry or withdrawn and isolated.
- Low self-esteem.
- Self-mutilation.

Suicide, a lethal complication of depression, is the third leading cause of death among 15- to 24-year-olds, accounting for over 12% of all deaths in that age group each year. Among 15- to 24-year-olds, one suicide resulted for every 100–200 attempts. In 2005, over 16% of U.S. high school students acknowledged a grim consideration of suicide during the 12 months preceding the survey. More than 8% of students admitted attempting suicide during that same period (Centers for Disease Control and Prevention, National Center for Injury Prevention and Control, 2007).

Concern that the use of antidepressant medications may provoke suicidal thoughts has created a clinical firestorm. Following a review of all available clinical trials of children and adolescents taking antidepressants, the FDA in 2004 warned about an increased risk (2–3%) of suicidal thoughts or behavior in children and adolescents treated with SSRI antidepressant medications. In 2006, an FDA advisory committee recommended that the warning include young adults up to age 25 (National Institute of Mental Health [NIMH], 2008).

The warning also noted that those children and adolescents taking SSRI medications should be closely monitored for uncharacteristic behavior or emergence of suicidal thinking, especially during the first 4 weeks of treatment, when SSRI medications may, for unknown reasons, trigger agitation and atypical behavior in certain individuals.

Although the FDA found no completed suicides among nearly 2,200 children taking SSRI medications, about 4% percent of those treated with SSRIs experienced suicidal thinking or behavior, including actual suicide attempts—twice the rate of those taking placebo or sugar pills (NIMH, 2009).

Results of a comprehensive review of antidepressant trials in children and adolescents conducted between 1988 and 2006 suggested that the benefits of antidepressant medications likely outweigh their risks to children and adolescents with major depression and anxiety disorders (Bridge et al., 2007). An increase in completed suicides in adolescents since the FDA warning in 2004 corresponds to the reduction in prescribed antidepressants (Kilgus & Adams, 2009). As with all medical decisions, doctors and families should weigh the risks and benefits of treatment for each individual patient.

The SSRI medications and a closely related antidepressant, Effexor (venlafaxine), have fewer side effects and are safer if taken in overdose than the older tricyclic antidepressants. Although Prozac (fluoxetine) is the only medication approved by the FDA for use in treating depression in children aged 8 and older, physicians often prescribe the other SSRI medications and Effexor for treatment of depression on an "off-label" basis. In June 2003, however, the FDA declared Paxil (paroxetine) contraindicated in treating childhood depression because it was found ineffective and unsafe (NIMH, 2009).

Initially, psychotherapy can be tried in treating mild-to-moderate depression before beginning an antidepressant medication (NIMH, 2009). Two types of psychotherapy are often used in children and adolescents—cognitive-behavior therapy (CBT), which teaches new ways of thinking about conflicts, and interpersonal therapy (IPT), which helps patients work through troubled personal relationships. (These therapies are discussed at length in Chapter 16.)

A study funded by the NIMH (Treatment for Adolescents With Depression Study [TADS] Team, 2004) has shown that a combination of medication and CBT constitute the most effective treatment for adolescents with depression. The clinical trial divided 439 patients aged 12–17 into four treatment groups. After 12 weeks, the results were tabulated **(Table 11-4)**.

Those prescribed an SSRI medication require close medical monitoring for treatment response and side effects. If the child experiences suicidal thinking or behavior, nervousness, anxiety, mood instability, agitation, or any other unusual symptoms, parents should promptly seek medical advice. Although the SSRIs are not addictive or habit forming, once started, SSRIs should be tapered off slowly to prevent withdrawal symptoms related to serotonin depletion.

TABLE 11-4	
Research Study Showing the Effects of Cognitive Behavior Therapy and Prozac	
TREATMENT GROUPS	**RESULTS**
Prozac + CBT	71% response
Prozac only	61% response
CBT only	43% response
Placebo treatment	35% response

From "Fluoxetine, Cognitive-Behavioral Therapy, and Their Combination for Adolescents With Depression: Treatment for Adolescents with Depression Study (TADS) Randomized Controlled Trial," by Treatment for Adolescents With Depression Study (TADS) Team, 2004, *Journal of the American Medical Association, 292*(7), 807–813.

Eating Disorders

The eating disorders anorexia nervosa and bulimia nervosa are discussed next.

Anorexia Nervosa

Characterized by a compulsive drive toward thinness, anorexia nervosa generally begins between the ages of 10 and 30 years and occurs predominantly in females (Sadock & Sadock, 2005). In attempt to lose weight, food intake is drastically reduced, vomiting is sometimes induced, and exercise is often prolonged and excessive. Episodes of gorging followed by induced vomiting can be found. Laxative and diuretic use may be excessive. Anorexics maintain an abnormally low, unhealthy body weight, which can lead to an interruption in the menstrual cycle. Anorexia has a mortality range from 5% to 18% (Sadock & Sadock, 2005).

Anorexia nervosa has two dynamic factors: The need for control and an impairment of psychosexual development by which the adolescent fears developing sexual attractiveness.

Treatment consists of behavior modification—with rewards for eating and consequences for excessive exercise and undereating—in a hospital setting. Family therapy can relieve the power struggle between parent and child. Individual therapy can build self-esteem, reframe thinking, and help with interpersonal conflicts. Medications can help alleviate secondary symptoms—mood disorders, anxiety, delusions.

Bulimia Nervosa

Frequent episodes of out-of-control binge eating, followed by purging, characterize bulimia. Less incapacitating than anorexia, bulimia (age at onset between 16 and 18 years) reflects society's focus on thinness (Sadock & Sadock, 2005). Patients, who tend to be perfectionists with difficulties adjusting to adolescent demands, incline toward impulsivity. Although often friendly and sociable, they possess difficulties separating from caregivers, experiencing anxiety and depression over family strife and perceived or actual neglect.

Behavior modification, psychodynamic therapy, CBT, and SSRIs have shown some promise for treatment. Long-term follow-up studies are unavailable (Halmi, 2003). Personal experience with fewer than a dozen older adolescents indicated that about 60% of patients respond to multimodal therapy, but relapse rates can be as high as 50% during stressful life events such as leaving home for college or work.

Other Behavioral Disorders and Concerns

There are several other behavioral disorders and concerns: separation anxiety, timidness, nightmares and excessive fears, tic disorders, stuttering, bed wetting (enuresis), thumb sucking, and nail biting.

Separation Anxiety

More common in 7- and 8-year-olds and with an estimated prevalence of 4% of school-aged children (Sadock & Sadock, 2005), separation anxiety, a morbid fear that something will happen to the mother (or major attachment figure), often appears as a school phobia. Separation anxiety may be converted into physical symptoms—stomachaches, nausea, vomiting, sore throat, breathing difficulties, cough—to prevent separation from the caregiver. Separation anxiety must be differentiated from the following:

- Generalized anxiety, which is not focused on separation.
- Panic disorder with agoraphobia, which generally begins beyond 18 years of age.
- Truancy in the conduct-disordered patient, which has little to do with anxiety.

Fearful parents make children fearful. Children, sensitive to parental apprehension, may react by avoiding separation to protect the parent's feelings. Secure parents give children confidence. Parents who discuss their fears with a therapist or other mature adult—without the child present, of course—can be given support that will mitigate their fears. When the parents relax, the children relax. Almost all authorities agree that the best treatment of school phobia involves returning the child to school immediately. Children respect and honor firm and consistent behavior from their parents. In more severe cases, antidepressants can attenuate the child's anxiety to the point of tolerating separations and attending school. The terribly anxious parent may also benefit from treatment (Kilgus & Adams, 2009). Persistent separation anxiety and school phobia may require family psychotherapy.

Timidness

Toddlers initially fear strangers. Timid and shy behavior that continues after the child is 3 years old, however, may slow the child's educational and social development, and lower self-esteem. Genetic sensitivity, early illnesses, early losses, overprotective parents, and poor parental modeling may contribute to the cause of separation anxiety. A firm expectation for interaction with others and attempting new activities and tasks usually gives the child enough encouragement to engage. Excessive reassurance should be avoided, as it tends to heighten anxiety. In general, anxiety is treated with exposure and response prevention.

Nightmares and Excessive Fears

Persistent anxiety, excessive fears, nightmares, restless sleep, and physical symptoms such as headaches and stomachaches mark the overanxious child.

A family who provides love and attention contingent on good school, athletic, and social performance can exacerbate fear of failure. Unconditional love usually corrects the problem. A verbal and nonverbal message that indicates appreciation for the child rather than the child's behavior gives the child security. Paradoxically, a message of acceptance actually enhances performance.

Fear can be an expected response to certain conditions. In young children, survival fear, fear of fire, or fear of deep water can signal a normal protective response to serious threats. Many fears occur naturally in the growing process and vanish as the child develops. The following responses can abate unusual or persistent fears:

- Avoid forcing children into unnecessary fearful situations in the misguided belief that it will "toughen" them.
- On the other hand, avoid overprotecting the child from persistent, immature fears.
- Concentrate on helping the child develop self-confidence through trying new things bolstered by the support of consistent love, encouragement, praise, and unconditional acceptance.

Tic Disorders

The *DSM-IV-TR* (American Psychiatric Association, 2000) lists a variety of tic disorders—Tourette's disorder, chronic motor or vocal tic disorder, transient tic disorder, and tic disorder not otherwise specified—most of which wax and wane over time. Rapid, repetitive involuntary motor tics are 100–1,000 times more frequent than Tourette's. The symptoms usually last 4–6 years and stop in early adolescence (Sadock & Sadock, 2005). Tics in Tourette's disorder can be simple motor tics that include eye blinking, head jerking, or facial grimacing and can progress to hitting oneself or jumping. Coughing and grunting can transform into coprolalia (use of vulgar words). Obsessive-compulsive symptoms, learning problems, and ADHD are associated with the disorder. Haldol or Risperdal can lead to improvement in 85% of cases (Sadock & Sadock, 2005).

Stuttering

Almost all cases of stuttering occur before the age of 12. In some children, stuttering may represent a conflict over aggression. The child attempts to control others through hesitant speech patterns. Over 50% and perhaps as many as 80% of children who stutter recover spontaneously. The best treatment, in the majority of cases, is for the parents to ignore the condition because calling attention to the speech deficiency only increases the problem. For those children who fail to remit spontaneously, speech therapy can help solve mechanical problems, whereas psychotherapy resolves emotional conflicts that contribute to the disorder.

Nocturnal Enuresis (Bed Wetting)

One of the most common childhood problems, nocturnal enuresis occurs in roughly 10% of children aged 5 years, 5% of 10-year-olds, and fewer than 1% of adults. Enuresis may result from a variety of organic causes, including urinary tract infection, diabetes, and structural abnormality of the urinary tract, especially if it occurs during the day as well. However, behavioral problems such as faulty learning, regression, anxiety, and hostility, as well as variations in brain maturation, are commonly thought to be the most frequent causes.

For many children bed wetting is not deliberate, and the best treatment method may be for the parents to take a noncritical attitude toward helping the child overcome the problem. Too often, parents take a desperate stance, such as saying, "You've got to stop wetting the bed," or "Only babies wet their beds." Parents often feel embarrassed about the child's problem, quickly become frustrated, and then become angry. Parental frustration and anger only increase the child's bed wetting, and a vicious cycle is established.

Parents can end the cycle by giving the child more responsibility for washing sheets. Parents can complement this strategy by using a variety of treatments, such as rewards for dry nights, encouraging daytime retention of urine for as long as possible, and the use of an enuresis alarm.

Although behavior methods seem to be the better alternative, medications may help somewhat. An analog of antidiuretic hormone, DDAVP (desmopressin) (20–40 mg intranasally or 200–400 mg orally at bedtime) has been used for nocturnal enuresis, but once the medication is stopped, the problem returns (Cozza et al., 2003). Occasionally, the antidepressant imipramine, given an hour or two before bedtime, may help.

Thumb Sucking

A natural sucking instinct leads some babies to suck their thumbs during the first six months of life, but thumb sucking can continue in toddlers as a way to sooth themselves. Gradually most children stop sucking their thumbs between ages 3 and 5. After the age of 5 thumb sucking may indicate anxiety, some other emotional problem, or a sign of continued dependency on the parents that often involves the parent and child in a massive struggle over control. Splints, mitts, and scolding generally prolong the habit. The best treatment, just as for bed wetting, is to pay as little attention as possible to the behavior. A token economy with rewards may be helpful, for example, an ice cream cone if the child does not suck his or her thumb for a day, or a trip to the zoo if the child avoids thumb sucking for a week. If the problem persists, dental or speech problems can occur. If it continues after age 6, the child may benefit from professional help (WebMD.com, 2008).

Nail Biting

Beginning at about 5 years of age and increasing up to the 12th year, nail biting is a symptom of anxiety and environmental stress. Treatment consists of understanding and relieving the underlying source of anxiety. The nail biting should gradually disappear as the child talks about fears and concerns but can become habitual, lasting into adulthood.

General Principles of Psychotherapy

Psychotherapy, the cardinal treatment for childhood emotional disorders, consists of a variety of modalities.

TABLE 11-5		
Behavior Concerns: What's Normal/What's Over the Top		
BEHAVIOR	**NORMAL**	**OVER THE TOP**
Separation anxiety	Mild apprehension about going to a new school lasting 2–3 days	Stomachaches, nausea, vomiting, breathing difficulties for weeks on end
Timidness	Hiding behind mother's skirt at age 3	Hiding behind mother's skirt during college graduation ceremony
Nightmares/fears	Fear of the dark in young children; "healthy" fear of fire and deep water	Scared of his or her own shadow
Tic disorders	Occasional involuntary muscle spasms	Head jerking and facial grimacing, progressing to violence and outbursts of vulgarity
Stuttering	Unable to finish a "tongue twister"	Unable to finish a single sentence in normal, everyday conversation
Bed wetting	Occasional accidents	Soaked with urine every morning
Thumb sucking	A naural sucking instinct causes some babies to suck their thumbs and many toddlers use thumb sucking to sooth themselves	Thumb sucking after age 6
Nail biting	Picking or biting at an occasional hangnail	Biting down to the quick, causing bleeding cuticles and nail beds

Individual Psychotherapy

Psychodynamically oriented psychotherapy, useful for stress-related or neurotic symptoms, aims to provide a corrective emotional experience for the child. The therapist and child meet once or twice weekly with the goal of symptom resolution, behavior change, and a return to the normal developmental process. Supportive therapy serves best to help resolve a particular crisis faced by parent and child. The therapist listens empathetically and gives judicious advice on managing the particular stressful life event. Time-limited therapy focuses on one particular problem or related sets of problems in an attempt to resolve the conflict within a relatively short period, say 6 months or so. Cognitive-behavior techniques have proven useful for depression, OCD, post-traumatic stress disorder (PTSD), and social phobia in adolescents and mature late-latency-age children.

Behavior Therapy

Based on the concept that maladaptive behavior stems from faulty learning, poor habits, or detrimental situations, behavior therapy focuses on modifying positive and negative environmental factors that influence behavior. The token economy, using stars or checkmarks exchanged for privileges, can be used to reinforce positive behavior. Systematic desensitization techniques similar to those used in adults can be effective in treating anxiety disorders. Hypnosis can be used for treatment of physical symptoms with a psychological component or for nausea and pain associated with medical illnesses.

Family Therapy

Family therapy, an adjunct in almost all childhood emotional disorders, is especially useful in treating impaired communication and dysfunctional interactions. Educating all family members regarding the patient's illness improves treatment response, assists in alleviating concerns regarding the disorder, and helps siblings understand how to interact with the emotionally disturbed child.

Parental Guidelines and Counseling

Being a parent is a perplexing privilege. Parents must be relaxed and forgiving while being immovable when the situation calls for firmness. This dichotomy of purpose is what makes parenting so difficult. It's an uneasy balance between rules and freedom, passion and prudence.

Parenthood requires flexibility. Observant parents realize that every child has a different personality, a distinct set of coping mechanisms. Parents who learn nuances of behavior can maximize each child's potential. And, most importantly, parents who cultivate patience and a sense of humor can enjoy their children.

Successful parenting is like handling an eaglet—you've got to hold on tightly to keep it from flying away prematurely, yet hold gently enough so it won't be squeezed to death. This section discusses ways that parents can walk that thin and narrow tightrope of parenthood—how they can maintain a balance of nurture and discipline that allows them to treasure moments with their children.

Responsibility

Treatment for most childhood emotional problems begins at home by teaching responsibility. Responsible behavior promotes successful living, while irresponsible behavior is self-defeating. Teaching responsible behavior requires time and persistence but can be used effectively for almost any disciplinary or behavioral problem. Responsible behavior begins with a home that promotes good manners, justice, and cooperation. Before they can assume responsibility for their own lives, children must learn to be contributing members of a family. Chores teach basic living skills, enhance a child's feeling of worth, and provide a sense of accomplishment.

To bring up responsible children, parents must set definite rules of behavior, communicate these rules (and consequences for breaking the rules) to their children, and expect them to follow through. When the rules are inevitably broken, the parents must administer the appropriate consequences with consistency. This is the most difficult step. Most parents either think up a punishment in the heat of the moment or ignore the transgression, hoping it will just go away on its own. These extremes can be avoided by being proactive. Parents should agree on a set of rules and consequences in advance and post them in a visible place. An *if . . . then* type of chart takes the emotion out of the moment and makes the disciplinary process go more smoothly.

Discipline begins with good communication. Family meetings, held at least once weekly, improve communication by covering achievements, expectations, and responsibilities. Fun and a spirit of acceptance enhance productive meetings.

Guidelines for Cultivating Responsible Behavior
- Communicate verbally and nonverbally to the child that appropriate self-discipline, the framework for success, can be learned.
- Question inappropriate behavior.
- Help the child understand that inappropriate behavior is self-defeating and prevents achieving long-range plans.
- Help the child make a plan that will more effectively allow needs to be met.
- Request a commitment to new and better alternatives.
- A handshake or written agreement helps seal the contract.

- Give praise for good behavior to solidify progress toward responsible living.
- Withhold privileges as punishment for breaking rules.
- Expect increased maladaptive behavior the first few months after a plan for responsible behavior is initiated.
- Stick with the plan. Real changes will take several months to occur.

Love and Respect

Love and respect go hand in hand. The foundation of a healthy home rests on the two pillars of unconditional love and mutual respect.

Love, real love, means accepting our children exactly as they are while encouraging them to grow emotionally, intellectually, and spiritually. Love means we demand less and encourage more. A loving parent is also not hesitant to show tenderness—to give hugs, kisses, and pats on the back.

Love, of course, is more than affection. Love requires setting aside time for our children. When children are small, we can hold them on our laps and read to them. Reading with children when they're very young is a wonderful way to spend rich time with them and combines learning, imagination, and touch. As children mature, we can go on walks with them, camp, and fish together. Attending a child's school functions, music concerts, tennis matches, and award ceremonies builds the child's self-esteem and gives the entire family memories to treasure.

If we want children to act maturely, we must treat them with respect. As parents, we learn to master the difficult task of allowing our children freedom to make mistakes while providing guidance to prevent the mistakes from being big ones.

Respect is a two-way street. As parents, we are the authority figures and the buck ultimately stops with us. Children are to be respectful and submissive to their parents' authority, even if they don't always like the rules. If love is the foundation of the home and rules are made with the child's best interests in mind, respect should naturally follow.

Avoid Overgratification

In the first 3 years of life, children need attention, comfort, and protection. But, constant attention can be just as damaging as unlimited candy and sweets. Overgratification produces an infantile, self-centered adult. Don't be a slave to your children. If you are making three or four trips a day hauling them from place to place, you are traveling too much. Decide on the important functions and set limits.

To cure children from attention addiction, put your marriage first. A healthy marriage provides a secure foundation on which children can build self-esteem, autonomy, and independence.

Many of us have conditioned our children to a material standard beyond what we expect for ourselves. Giving children everything they ask for destroys the will to persist.

Every family will experience crisis and conflict. The sooner children learn that life is difficult, the better they will learn to overcome frustration. Studies have shown that resolved crises bring families closer together. A good parent models the attitude, "We will overcome this challenge and learn from it."

Take Charge

Parents must have the courage of their convictions. Don't bargain. Don't plead. Don't bribe. Don't threaten. Don't give second chances. You cannot win when you try to reason with children.

Eloquent explanations mean nothing. When a parent makes a decision and the child screams "Why?" the response can be, "Because I said so. I'm in charge here until you become an adult." Parents must make the final decisions.

Turn Off the Television

Television watching inhibits sequential thinking, motivation, curiosity, initiative, reasoning, and imagination. Watching television also shortens a child's attention span. Numerous studies have shown a direct causal link between media violence and increased aggressiveness. Children who watch violent television programs demonstrate increased kicking and punching behavior when compared to children who watch nonviolent television programs.

Other than those things, television isn't bad. Educational programs, especially those that teach reading and social skills, can be encouraged—in moderation. The maturing child can watch sports and entertainment programs if content and time are monitored.

Reducing the use of television and other media (video games, Internet surfing, MP3 players) might leave many families perplexed about what to do for entertainment. Encourage your children to use clay, finger paints, building blocks, and other toys that will cultivate their creativity. Play games as a family. Go on walks together. Take turns reading good books aloud (*Cheaper by the Dozen* is a family favorite). Have pillow fights, "wrestling" matches, and tickle tournaments. The possibilities are endless.

The Happy Home

No home is perfect—each teaches both vice and virtue. Our early home experiences, good or bad, become the moral compass that guides us for the rest of life's journey. As parents, we will make mistakes. Our children will make mistakes. However, we must strive for a home that creates an overall ambiance of love, respect, good manners, and simple justice. Such a home is a treasure indeed.

A Code for Enlightened Parents

- Catch your child doing something right and reward that behavior.
- Walk what you talk. Behave the way you want your children to behave.
- Be consistent when making rules and bestowing punishment.
- When your child misbehaves let the child know that you expect better.
- Keep the lid on your temper when things go wrong. Anger is okay. Losing your temper is not.
- Punish the behavior, love the child.
- Verbalize the positive.
- Give praise for effort and persistence.
- Avoid living your life through your children. Have your own life.
- Keep your word. When you give a warning or make a promise, follow through.
- Tell the truth.
- Admit your mistakes.
- Be flexible. Go with the flow. Laugh a lot. Remember: "This too shall pass."
- Spend time with your children. Look at them. Listen to them.
- Read to them.
- Turn off the television.
- Eat meals together.
- Wherever you are, be there. Give full attention.
- Hug them. Hold them. Cuddle them. You can never snuggle enough.
- Remember how quickly time passes. One day, they will be gone.
- Enjoy each fleeting moment.

Are You an Adequate or Good Enough Parent?
(Every Parent Makes Mistakes)

Make Check Mark (✓) in Appropriate Column	Little of the Time 1 point each ✓	Some of the Time 2 points each ✓	A Lot of the Time 3 points each ✓	Most of the Time 4 points each ✓
I avoid nagging and negative comments.				
I take time to listen to my children.				
I set aside time for one-on-one communication with each child.				
I read to my children.				
I hug my children.				
I have specific rules and regulations for my children.				
I follow through with punishment.				
Punishments are based on withholding privileges.				
I speak positively to my children and model positive living.				
I praise my child's efforts and persistence.				
Multiply ✓ by the value given in each column.				

Add the total for each column to get the **Grand total** = _____

SCORING

10–14 points = You would benefit from a parenting skills class

15–24 points = Parenting is the most difficult and most important activity in life

25–34 points = Parent of the year

35–40 points = Parent of the decade

Are You an Encouraging Parent?

Make Check Mark (✓) in Appropriate Column	Little of the Time 1 point each ✓	Some of the Time 2 points each ✓	A Lot of the Time 3 points each ✓	Most of the Time 4 points each ✓
I praise accomplishments that require considerable effort.				
I praise persistence.				
I praise personal progress on tasks.				
I teach the value of failure.				
I praise hard work and diligence.				
I am specific with praise.				
I encourage trying new things.				
I avoid comparisons with other children.				
I encourage the development of unique gifts and talents.				
I focus on the pleasure of learning.				
Multiply ✓ by the value given in each column.				

Add the total for each column to get the **Grand total** = _____

SCORING

10–14 points = You are frustrating and irritating

15–24 points = Reset your values

25–34 points = Children are attracted to you

35–40 points = A creative genius

Do You Teach Life Skills?				
Make Check Mark (✓) in Appropriate Column	Little of the Time 1 point each ✓	Some of the Time 2 points each ✓	A Lot of the Time 3 points each ✓	Most of the Time 4 points each ✓
I teach ethical behavior.				
I teach my children to love learning and reading.				
I teach my children to think critically.				
I teach my children communication skills.				
I involve my children in serving others.				
I teach my children to enjoy life.				
I teach my children to be creative independent thinkers.				
I teach my children how to establish a budget, how to save money, and how to stay out of debt.				
I teach the value of spiritual growth.				
I teach leadership skills.				
Multiply ✓ by the value given in each column.				

Add the total for each column to get the **Grand total** = ___ _____

SCORING

10–14 points = You would do well to find a life training teacher

15–24 points = You would benefit from becoming a student of living well

25–34 points = Your children are learning to become independent

35–40 points = Your children are learning to set life skill standards for others

Is Your Child Hyperactive?

Make Check Mark (✓) in Appropriate Column	Little of the Time 1 point each ✓	Some of the Time 2 points each ✓	A Lot of the Time 3 points each ✓	Most of the Time 4 points each ✓
He or she shifts from one activity to another.				
He or she is easily distracted.				
He or she has the inability to concentrate on schoolwork.				
He or she has difficulty sticking to play activity.				
He or she has difficulty staying seated.				
He or she is always on the go.				
He or she doesn't listen.				
He or she demonstrates excessive fidgeting.				
He or she is unable to complete tasks.				
He or she is tiresome to just about everyone around.				
Multiply ✓ by the value given in each column.				

Add the total for each column to get the **Grand total** = _____

SCORING

10–14 points = Shy

15–24 points = Most children are active

25–34 points = Extremely active

35–40 points = Talk with your child's teachers about getting a formal evaluation

Is Your Child Depressed?				
Make Check Mark (✓) in Appropriate Column	Little of the Time 1 point each ✓	Some of the Time 2 points each ✓	A Lot of the Time 3 points each ✓	Most of the Time 4 points each ✓
He or she has had a sudden drop in school grades.				
He or she has developed a circle of new friends.				
He or she has begun dressing differently.				
He or she has withdrawn from social activities.				
He or she has developed behavior problems at school.				
He or she is no longer interested in family activities.				
He or she has trouble sleeping.				
He or she fights excessively.				
He or she has lost interest in usual activities.				
He or she tends to isolate from others.				
Multiply ✓ by the value given in each column.				

Add the total for each column to get the **Grand total** = ___ ___ ___ ___

SCORING

10–14 points = Happy and content

15–24 points = Average kid

25–34 points = Would benefit from a thorough evaluation by a clinician

35–40 points = Consider consultation with a clinician as soon as possible

A Clinician's Quiz

1. Give at least 6 inattention symptoms of ADHD (there are 9).
2. ADHD commonly occurs with other childhood disorders. Name four of them.
3. Discuss the theoretical neurobiological cause of ADHD.
4. What three disorders may be the endpoint for intractable cases of conduct disorder?
5. Give four symptoms that are characteristic of oppositional defiant disorder.
6. Discuss the differences and similarities between ADHD, conduct disorder, and oppositional defiant disorder.
7. Describe the differences and similarities between autism and Asperger's disorder.
8. Discuss the controversy over the concern that the use of antidepressant medications may provoke suicidal thoughts.
9. Give the symptoms of separation anxiety. What three disorders might be confused with separation anxiety?
10. Discuss the three most commonly used psychotherapies for childhood emotional disorders.

CHAPTER 12

Alzheimer's Disease and Other Age-Old Concerns

Dulled Wit

Last summer, my wife gave me a dozen handkerchiefs. Now they are gone, disappeared: not in the handkerchief drawer or the sock drawer, not in the clothes hamper. I began to wonder: "Do I have Alzheimer's disease?" Probably not. The better explanation for the disappearance of my handkerchiefs—the hiders. The hiders are sneaky. They put pencils behind my ear. They hide my car keys in the refrigerator. They have the audacity to slip my eyeglasses on my face at the very time I'm looking for them. The hiders are ubiquitous. In every household, they do their dastardly deeds. They are responsible for everything from lost airplane tickets to the Bermuda triangle disappearances.

Rather than resulting from senility, our tendency to lose things is more likely due to mindless behavior. Forgetting why we entered a room, saying hello to mannequins, misplacing items—these activities reflect a brain on automatic pilot, a brain that acts without thinking. Almost all of us have seen this mindless behavior in others. A department store clerk will ask you to sign the back of your credit card. After you have signed the card and then the receipt, the clerk holds the receipt next to your credit card to see if the signatures match. Mindless behavior? Did the hiders climb into the clerk's skull and conceal her brains? Or, does she have Alzheimer's disease (AD)? It is doubtful, but these little memory gaps and mindless actions make us wonder, especially as we reach the "senior moments" stage.

Dementia

Alzheimer's disease is 1 of 50 or so medical illnesses that can cause memory impairment and cognitive decline. The all-inclusive term for memory impairment is *dementia*. The causes of dementia are so numerous that a mnemonic is useful in remembering the broad group of medical illnesses responsible for cognitive decline. The causes of dementia can be recalled using the acrostic A COGNITIVE, in which each letter represents a disease group **(Figure 12-1)**. (It is an imperfect list that calls for a vivid imagination, but what do you expect from someone who contends with the hiders on a daily basis?).

About 10% of people with dementia have excessive alcohol intake as the cause of their cognitive decline. Another 10% of people with dementia have vascular causes—small strokes of the brain (called multi-infarct strokes), cerebral vascular accidents, or malignant hypertension. Of the dementias, 20% are caused by dozens of illnesses, many of which are rare. Of all the causes of dementia, AD is the most common. Approximately 60% of people with dementia have AD as the cause of their memory disturbance (Trinkle, Downs & Kilgus, 2009).

An ancient legend told of Damocles, a courtier in the service of Dionysius II, who coveted the pleasures of royalty. Saracen magic placed him at the king's table eating sumptuous food, drinking the finest wine, and enjoying more pleasures than his imagination could conceive. Reclining at the table in satisfaction, Damocles glanced upward. His eye became transfixed on a sword dangling by single horsehair just above his head. Damocles turned

---

FIGURE 12-1

A Cognitive Acrostic: Common Causes of Dementia

A = **A**lzheimer's disease.
C = **C**losed head injuries and other traumatic blows to the head.
O = **O**piates and **O**ther drugs.
G = **G**in and other alcoholic beverages.
N = **N**eurological illnesses such as multiple sclerosis, Parkinson's disease, Huntington's disease.
 I = **I**nhibitions lacking—patients with frontotemporal dementia exhibit childlike behavior characterized by disinhibition, distractibility, and decreased social awareness.
T = **T**umors of the brain.
 I = **I**nfections of the brain and spinal cord—meningitis, HIV, Jakob-Creutzfeldt disease.
V = **V**itamin deficiencies and **V**ascular defects—strokes, poor circulation of the brain.
E = **E**ndocrine abnormalities such as thyroid disease, diabetes, and adrenal illnesses and **E**lectrolyte disturbances—potassium depletion, low levels of sodium.

---

pale. His hands trembled. His joy vanished as he realized that much pleasure brings much danger.

Perhaps the myth of Damocles overdramatizes the risk of AD. After all, more than half of 90-year-olds never experience the illness (Mace & Rabins, 2006). Nonetheless, as we grow older, we sometimes contemplate the threat of ⋯⋯ ⋯ above our eyes.

⋯ed what he considered a rare pro-⋯ed by microscopic neurofibrillary ⋯at AD would be the most common sixth leading cause of death in the ⋯port, 2002). Scientists still search ⋯e horsehair to support that sword.

⋯y eliminating every other cause of ⋯uire a complete neurological evalu-⋯he memory impairment. A series of ⋯omplete blood count; metabolic and ⋯ey, thyroid, and adrenal function-⋯mentia. In some cases, a computed ⋯onance imaging (MRI) of the brain

⋯th

⋯ disease of the brain. Several factors combine with a cascade of events ⋯ cause brain cell death in AD. At autopsy, microscopic sections of brain tissue reveal plaques and tangles of proteins in the neurons. The plaques are deposits of amyloid proteins. The tangles are made of filaments of a protein called tau. Current research implicates amyloid-beta as a key factor in disease progress. Through a series of complex interactions, aggregates of amyloid-beta eventually twist and turn the tau proteins into neuron killers. The accumulation of amyloid-beta protein, twisted tau proteins, and other factors destroys the electrical wiring of the brain, progressively killing 100 billion neurons, give or take several billion or so. Investigators are looking for drugs that could inhibit the production of amyloid-beta and therapies that could stop the tau proteins from twisting (Wolfe, 2006).

Symptoms of Alzheimer's Disease

An initial sign of AD may be depressive symptoms—waking in the middle of the night with an inability to return to sleep, appetite disturbance, decreased libido, poor concentration, lack of interest in usual activities, and apathy.

TABLE 12-1			
Radiological Techniques in the Diagnosis of Dementia			
RADIOLOGICAL METHOD	**THEORETICAL FRAMEWORK**	**PROCEDURE**	**HELPFUL IN DETECTING**
The CT scan	Founded on the diverse capacity of various tissues for absorption of photons.	Narrow X-ray beams scan the head, producing thin slices of the brain that a computer organizes and records photographically.	• Brain tumors • Other intracranial masses • Hydrocephalous • Nonspecific cortical atrophy
Magnetic resonance imaging (MRI)	Produces microscopic images of the brain.	Scanning the head with tremendously high-powered magnets produces three-dimensional images of the brain.	• Early strokes • Brain swelling • Cerebral bruises • Bleeding in the brain • Small tumors
fMRI (functional MRI)	Produces images of the brain while the brain is performing a mental activity.	Superconducting magnets show activity in the nucleus of the hydrogen atom.	• Areas of brain inactivity • Alzheimer's disease and other dementias
PET (positive emission tomography)	Produces colorful images of the brain performing mental tasks.	Injected radioactive material shows brain sections activated by mental activity.	• Reduced metabolic activity • Alzheimer's disease and other dementias

These depressive symptoms may indicate that neurons are dying. Depression resulting from an awareness of cognitive decline exacerbates the senile condition. A major reason for being on the alert for depressive symptoms comes from the discovery that early treatment of depression may prevent or slow the progression of AD. Of course, older people can have depression without ever developing AD.

Alzheimer's disease begins insidiously. Short-term memory begins to fade. The patient with AD fails to recall events of the past few days—a phone call from the grandchildren, conversations with a friend—while recollections from long ago remain intact. Names and telephone numbers are forgotten. Attempts to cover up intellectual deficits result in social withdrawal, confabulation, and exaggeration of personality traits. Some individuals begin to keep more lists; other individuals become more extreme in dress and mannerisms. Attempting to complete tasks requiring logical reasoning produces anxiety and irritability. Inhibitions vanish. Planning deteriorates.

Patients with AD who function fairly well during the day may have a difficult time at night—the so-called sundown syndrome. During the golden hour, shadows begin to lengthen. The fading light diminishes environmental cues. As darkness increases, patients with AD become disoriented. Confusion often precipitates anger and agitation.

As the illness progresses, daytime confusion rivals nocturnal agitation. Remote memory begins to fade. Details regarding occupation, family life, and childhood grow fainter. Eventually, even loved ones go unrecognized. Vulgar language, neglect of personal hygiene, and disregard for conventional rules of conduct mark the progressive downhill course. As the mental functions gradually deteriorate, imprecise vocabulary degenerates to vague, incomprehensible speech. The names of body parts are forgotten. The insidious decline can lead to anorexia, malnutrition, infection, loss of respiratory drive, and death.

Visiting a nursing home facility that specializes in the care of patients with AD and dementia gives one a sobering glimpse of the wide variety of symptoms found in patients with AD. Marge, a smiling, spry octogenarian, constantly asks visitors if they play bridge. When they answer in the negative, she's disappointed but cheerfully explains that she used to be in four weekly bridge clubs: "One on Tuesday, one on Thursday morning, one on Thursday afternoon, and one on Friday." She repeats the entire sequence with each person she comes in contact, sometimes multiple times with the same person. Bill, a wheelchair-bound World War II veteran, remembers little about what happened 5 minutes ago but talks in great detail about his war experiences as an accountant for the Army. Gertie is a relatively young patient, able to walk well, but her nose constantly runs. She doesn't notice. She approaches visitors with a wild, intense stare, grips their arm tightly, and babbles nonsensical phrases with great urgency. A fellow patient yells at Gertie angrily when she comes near, "You get out of here, you crazy witch!" Another wheelchair-bound patient, Nelda, battles confusion, paranoia, and fear. Panic stricken, she often shouts that she needs to get to the airport: Her plane to New York City is about to leave, and she needs to go see her son. She bends down, reaching for some unknown object on the floor, trying desperately to grasp it with her fingers. Some patients dance to absent music. Others exhibit childlike, playful behavior. Still others rarely get out of bed, staring vacantly into space for hours on end (**Table 12-2**).

Risk for Developing Alzheimer's Disease

Estimates indicated that more than 5.3 million Americans have AD; a new

TABLE 12-2

Guide to Alzheimer's Stages
(Stages May Vary; Symptoms May Develop)

DISEASE STAGE	AVERAGE DURATION	COMMON SYMPTOMS
Mild	2–4 years or longer	Has memory loss for recent events Has depressed mood Has loss of interest in usual activities Has trouble remembering names for common items Repeats statements and questions Gets lost Loses personal items Has personality changes Is more dependent on others
Moderate	2–10 years or longer	Memory loss for past events Difficulty with simple household chores Neglected personal hygiene Irritable Argumentative Temper outbursts Night-time confusion Wandering at night Delusions and paranoid thinking Close supervision required
Severe	1–3 years	Difficulty naming parts of body Inability to recognize family members Loss of social skills Loss of impulse control No frustration tolerance Constant supervision required Loss of bowel and bladder control Anorexia Severe weight loss Malnutrition Total care from others required

case is diagnosed every 70 seconds (Alzheimer's Disease Facts and Figures, 2009). AD is the sixth leading cause of all deaths in the United States, but the annual death rate fails to keep up with the diagnosis of new cases. In 2050, the incidence of AD is expected to approach nearly a million people per year, with a total estimated prevalence of 11 to 16 million people.

Genetic mutations on chromosomes 1, 14, and 21 predict AD before age 60. The ApoE (apolioprotein E) gene on chromosome 19 has been associated with late-onset AD. ApoE comes in three forms—ApoE2, ApoE3, and ApoE4. One of these forms is inherited from each parent. Those who inherit the ApoE4 gene have a greater risk for developing late-onset AD. Two copies of ApoE4 increase the risk of AD 10-fold. The majority of patients who inherit the ApoE4 gene fail to develop AD (Shankle & Amen, 2004) **(Table 12-3)**.

Treating Alzheimer's Disease

Although no cure for AD exists, several medications have proven helpful in combating its symptoms. Unfortunately, most patients receive insufficient

TABLE 12-3	
Alzheimer's Coconspiritors	
CONTRIBUTING FACTORS FOR AD	**DISCUSSION**
Free radicals cause cell destruction	• Beta-amyloid plaque damages mitochondria that produce energy for the cells. • Mitochondria malfunction produces an overabundance of free radicals, causing cell destruction.
Advanced age	• After age 65, the risk for AD doubles every 5 years. • Between the ages of 65 and 74, 3% will have AD. • Between the ages of 75 and 84, 19% will develop AD. • For those beyond 85, 47% will have AD. • More than 95% of those less than 70 years old have no memory loss. • Over 50% of those over 90 years old show no serious mental deterioration.
Alzheimer's disease before age 60 is strongly hereditary	• 200,000 Americans have AD before age 60. • Mutations on chromosomes 1, 14, and 21 predict early-onset AD. • A genetic mutation gives a 50% chance of inheriting AD.
When compared to men, twice as many women have AD.	• Because women live longer than men, they have a greater chance of developing AD. • A dramatic decline in estrogen levels at menopause may increase the chance for AD.
Obesity	• Excess weight promotes AD.
Emotional stress	• Stress contributes to the death of neurons in the hippocampus, the memory-switching station of the brain.
Physical inactivity	• Physical inactivity contributes to AD.

treatment. Approximately 50% of AD patients are diagnosed and only half of those diagnosed with AD receive treatment (Stahl, 2005).

Repairing Neurotransmitter Malfunction

Alzheimer's disease impairs the function of several neurotransmitters. Treatment of AD aims at repairing neurotransmitter damage. Depletion of the chemical messenger acetylcholine seems particularly significant in AD. The medication Aricept blocks acetylcholinesterase, an enzyme responsible for the normal decomposition of acetylcholine. Exelon inhibits two enzymes, acetylcholinesterase and butyrylcholinesterase, that cause normal depletion of acetylcholine. These medications therefore increase the levels of acetylcholine, resulting in improved neuron transmission. Unfortunately, these medications fail to repair past damage. Instead, they merely slow the development of the disease. Side effects of both these medications are similar and include nausea, diarrhea, vomiting, anorexia, weight losss, insomnia, dizziness, muscle cramps, and increased gastric acid secretion. Exelon, if not titrated slowly, causes more gastrointestinal side effects than Aricept (Stahl, 2005).

In contrast to cholinesterase inhibitors, Namenda slows cognitive decline in patients with severe AD by blocking excessive activity of the excitatory neurotransmitter glutamate. Although Namenda has been approved for the treatment of severe dementia, the medication can improve cognitive impairment in mild cases as well. Notable side effects are dizziness, headache, and constipation (Stahl, 2008) (**Table 12-4**).

Multimodal Treatment for Secondary Symptoms

Most physicians believe that a variety of medications can be used to slow the progress of AD. Along with a medication to increase the level of the neurotransmitter acetylcholine in the brain, another medication is necessary to prevent brain cell death, a third improves the health of the neuron, and a fourth acts as an antidepressant. In addition, medications may be needed to fight mood swings, irritability, paranoia, agitation, sleep disturbance, and anxiety (Stahl, 2008). Atypical antipsychotics reduce agitation; antidepressants treat concomitant depression, lack of interest, and apathy. Depakote can be used to treat aggression, agitation, and impulsivity (Stahl, 2005) (**Table 12-5**).

Complementary Therapies

A variety of vitamins, hormones, and herbs are thought to be helpful in treating symptoms of AD, and most can safely be combined with the typical medications used for AD. However, no product is risk free. The use of herbal supplements should be disclosed to doctors and pharmacists to prevent drug

TABLE 12-4

Medications Frequently Used to Treat Alzheimer's

MEDICATION	DOSE	BENEFITS	SIDE EFFECTS
Aricept (donepezil)	5 mg once daily for 4–6 weeks, then 10 mg daily.	Can increase focus and productivity; reduces delusions; decreases agitation; useless for severe AD.	Mild; infrequently can cause nausea, diarrhea, anorexia, sleep disturbance, fatigue, and muscle aches.
Exelon (rivastigmine)	Titrate slowly and take with a full meal to retard gastrointestinal side effects; if tolerated, dose can gradually be increased to the maximum dose of 6 mg twice daily.	70% of patients who respond poorly to Aricept respond to Exelon. Exelon, like Aricept, slows the progression of AD. Useless for severe AD.	During the first few weeks of treatment, 40% of patients may develop nausea, vomiting, or diarrhea. Taking Exelon with a full meal may prevent side effects.
Namenda (memantine)	Gradually increase to 10 mg twice daily.	Approved to treat moderate-to-severe AD.	Impressively benign; very few side effects.

TABLE 12-5

Medications for Secondary Symptoms of Alzheimer's Disease

NEUROTRANSMITTER	SYMPTOMS	MEDICATION
Dopamine	Imbalance causes paranoia, agitation, and psychosis.	Antipsychotics—Risperdal, Seroquel, Geodon, Zyprexa, Abilify, Haldol, Trilafon
Glutamate	Excess destroys neurons.	Namenda decreases overactivity of N-methyl-d-aspartate (NMDA) subtype of glutamate receptor antagonist, decreasing calcium entering neurons
Norepinephrine	Deficiency causes lethargic depression, fatigue, chronic pain.	Dual-mechanism antidepressants: Effexor XR, Cymbalta
Serotonin	Deficiency causes compulsions, anxious depression, panic.	Selective serotonin reuptake inhibitors: Prozac, Zoloft, Paxil, Lexapro, Celexa
GABA (gamma-aminobutyric acid)	Deficiency causes aggression, agitation, and impulsivity.	Depakote

TABLE 12-6

Complementary Herbs, Nutrients, and Hormones

PRODUCTS	DOSE	BENEFITS	CAUTIONS
Premarin (conjugated equine estrogen)	0.3–1.25 mg	Improves verbal memory, vigilance, and reasoning.	Contraindicated with blood clotting abnormalities, liver disease, and estrogen-dependent cancer; 10–20 years of estrogen use may cause a modest chance of breast cancer.
Estrace or Cenestin (estradiol)	0.05–2 mg daily	Natural soy-based estrogen reported to be "more easily accepted and used by the body."	Has the same warnings as Premarin, but the tablet is half as expensive.
Vitamin E	1,000–2,000 IU daily	Reduces free-radical damage to brain cells.	High dose may cause bleeding and gastrointestinal problems.
Ginkgo biloba	120–200 mg daily	Contains flavonoids that act as antioxidants; may increase oxygen flow and improve neurotransmission.	German brands have better quality control.

interaction problems. The prudent consumer balances skepticism with hope (Mace & Rabins, 2006) **(Table 12-6)**.

Preventing Alzheimer's Disease

A Princeton train conductor coming down the aisle punching the tickets of every passenger noticed the brilliant physicist Dr. Albert Einstein frantically looking for his ticket. The conductor said, "Dr. Einstein, I know who you are. I'm sure you purchased a ticket. Don't worry about it." Einstein replied, "Young man, I, too, know who I am. What I don't know is where I'm going."

As senior citizens age, they think they do know where they are going—they are certain they're going to get AD. This is not necessarily so. Diet, supplements, and other preventive measures can slow the progression of AD **(Table 12-7)**.

Although we have yet to find a cure for AD and we don't know exactly what causes it, we do have some good ways of preventing or at least slowing the aging process (Mace & Rabins, 2006):

TABLE 12-7

Diet and Supplements to Prevent Alzheimer's Disease

RECOMMENDATION	SOURCE/COMMENT
Reduce saturated fats, which play the single greatest role in raising blood cholesterol	Limit intake of whole milk, butter, ice cream, cheese, and animal fat.
Avoid trans fats (also called hydrogenated fats), which raise low-density lipoprotein (LDL or bad cholesterol) while lowering HDL (or good cholesterol)	Avoid margarine, chips, deep-fried foods, and commercially baked goods, including cookies, crackers, white bread, doughnuts, and pastries.
Eat foods with HDL	Olive oil, avocados, olives, nuts, corn, sunflower seeds, and fish.
Eat at least two servings of foods high in omega-3 fatty acids twice weekly	Soy, canola oils, walnuts, pumpkin seeds, tofu, lake trout, salmon, mackerel, tuna, halibut, herring, and sardines.
Eat five to seven servings of antioxidant-rich foods each day	Tomatoes, tomato paste, ketchup, prunes, raisins, blueberries, other berries, spinach, brussels sprouts, plums, broccoli, oranges, red grapes, cherries, onions, corn, and eggplant.
Consume antioxidant-rich drinks	3 cups of green tea or 3½ to 5 ounces of red wine daily.
Supplement vitamin, mineral, and omega-3 fatty acids	• 500–1,000 mg of vitamin C • 50–100 mg of selenium • 400–800 IU of vitamin E for prevention of AD • 1,000–2,000 IU of vitamin E for treatment of AD • 1,000–3,000 mg of omega-3 fatty acids daily
Maintain hydration	• Drink 64 ounces of water daily (eight 8-ounce glasses). • Avoid excessive caffeine and alcohol, which dehydrate the body.
Reduce inflammation	Take one aspirin daily—either 81 mg or 325 mg—depending on your doctors instructions.
Estrogen for postmenopausal women	0.05–2 mg of estradiol daily.

- **Stay physically fit.** In a study involving 4,600 men and women aged 65 years or older, those who exercised regularly reduced the chance of developing AD by 30%. A study involving 6,000 women showed that those women who walked at least 10 miles weekly (or 2 miles on 5 days a week) reduced their risk of dementia by 30–40% (Mace & Rabins, 2006). Exercise stimulates the brain to make new neurons (Shankle & Amen, 2004). Regular workouts reduce the risk factors that can lead to AD, including high blood pressure, obesity, diabetes, and stroke. Studies also indicated that regular exercise builds brain cell synapses and improves brain blood flow. In addition, exercise causes a boost in endorphins, the "feel good" hormones that enhance mood and memory.

- **Train your brain.** Watching television more than 2 hours daily increases the risk for AD (Shankle & Amen, 2004). Read. Write. Play a musical instrument. Learn a foreign language. Memorize songs, poems, or Bible verses. Play Scrabble, Trivial Pursuit, Scattergories, Chess, and Rummikub. Do crossword or jigsaw puzzles. Any activity that makes us think stimu-lates the brain and reduces the chance of AD.

- **Reduce stress.** Stress reduction prevents cell death in the hippocampus, the memory switch of the brain. Contemplative prayer, meditation, and yoga are stress reducers that can be incorporated into a daily schedule. Cultivating friendships also reduces stress.

- **Reduce brain shrinkage with a "good-fat" diet.** The risk of developing AD goes up with the number of calories in the diet. Those individuals who consume the most calories double the risk of AD when compared with those who consumed a low-calorie, good-fat diet. The high-density lipoprotein (HDL) (or good) cholesterol foods include mono-unsaturated and polyunsaturated fats. The omega-3 fatty acids, in addition to being antiarrhythmic, antithrombotic, and anti-inflammatory, reduce the risk for coronary artery disease, hypertension, and rheumatoid arthritis (Shankle & Amen, 2004). They also guard against depression, bipolar illness, and AD (Stahl, 2008). Because most "oily" fish are loaded with omega-3 fatty acids, the American Heart Association recommends two servings of fish each week. Taking, in pill form, 2,400 to 4,800 mg of omega-3 fatty acids daily builds cell membrane phospholipids crucial for neurotransmission.

- **Drink 3½ to 5 ounces of red wine each night.** (Those who do not drink alcohol or wine can eat red grapes.) Resveratrol, abundant in grape seed and in red wine, is a powerful antioxidant that also dilates arteries by enhancing nitric oxide (Mace & Rabins, 2006). You can get antioxidants from other foods and vitamins, but the drug Viagra and alcohol are the most common sources for enhancing nitric oxide (Stahl, 2008).

- **Supplement the diet with antioxidants.** Research has shown that adding vitamins C and E to resveratrol provides a greater degree of brain protection than any of the antioxidants alone because each of these antioxidants scavenges a different group of free radicals (Mace & Rabins, 2006).

- **Take aspirin.** Epidemiological studies suggested that nonsteroidal anti-inflammatory drugs (NSAIDs) such as aspirin, ibuprofen, and naproxen prevent the brain inflammation that plays an important role in the development of AD. Several studies have shown that long-term NSAID use may reduce the risk of AD by as much as 50% (Mace & Rabins, 2006).

- **Consider estradiol for postmenopausal women.** Estrogen docking sites—places where estrogen attaches itself to brain tissue, including the hippocampus—have been identified, indicating that estrogen plays a role in memory and cognitive functioning in the brain. Declining levels of estrogen have a negative impact on language skills, mood, concentration, and attention. Parenthetically, estrogen has a major role in preventing the development of osteoporosis in women. Because estrogen replacement therapy may increase the risk for heart disease and certain cancers, each woman's personal and family history must be evaluated before estrogen is prescribed. Most experts recommend the use of natural, soy-based estrogens—estradiol—for replacement therapy because estradiol is the main type of estrogen made by the ovaries (Mace & Rabins, 2006).

- **Enhance antioxidant intake with supplements.** Multi-B vitamins, vitamin C, vitamin E, and selenium can help prevent AD.

- **Hydrate.** As a country doctor who practiced in the Big Thicket of east Texas once said, "Most people don't drink enough water, and their brains shrivel up." Elderly people are more prone to dehydration because they have a lower thirst response, their kidneys concentrate urine less well, and they have 60% water content in their bodies compared with younger adults who have about 70% water content. Many of the elderly take diuretics and laxatives that increase fluid loss. Dehydration can cause orthostatic hypotension resulting in dizziness, fainting, and an increased risk of falling. Those with dementia may become more confused and lethargic with dehydration (Kim-Miller, 2000).

Brain-Boosting Workouts for Memory Power

Just as keeping a healthy heart requires regular physical exercise, a healthy brain requires regular neuron "workouts." When brain cells are consistently stimulated, especially in areas involved with language, motor skills, and memory, brain cell death can be slowed.

Playing games that stimulate visual, auditory, and motor skills can keep the brain conditioned in life skills such as dressing, buttoning clothes, and taking care of personal hygienic needs. Because memory can be stored in so many places in the brain, particular types of memory require regular workouts. Try spending 30 minutes on "brain boosting" daily. Alternate activities.

Aging is a process that we all inevitably will face. Most look on it with dread and apprehension, but the prospect of growing old doesn't have to frighten us. By using the prevention techniques described (along with good luck and good genes), growing older can be a joy, not a hardship. As we age, we can look back and celebrate the gift of a life well lived. It's attitude that counts. As Mark Twain quipped, "Age is an issue of mind over matter. If you don't mind, it doesn't matter."

CHAPTER 13

Sexual Dysfunction and Romantic Resolution

The Viagra Monologues

Despite Masters and Johnson (1970); despite Alex Comfort and the *Joy of Sex (2004)*; despite *Deep Throat* and *The Devil and Miss Jones*; despite *Playboy*, *Cosmopolitan*, *Sex and the City*, *Desperate Housewives*, dildos, vibrators, Internet porn, Viagra, and Cialis, or perhaps because of these things, sexual dysfunction is rampant, and often leads to broken marriages. In a survey reported by Andreasen and Black (2006), 31% of men and 43% of women acknowledged having one or more types of sexual dysfunction. Divorce, settling around the 50% mark, has spawned a new subculture: separation, single-parent families, blended families, visitation, custody, and support battles. Fragmenting of the traditional family structure and family life cycle has altered parenting and a child's right of passage (Fields, Morrison, & Beets, 2003).

Sexual Dysfunction

The *Diagnostic and Statistical Manual of Mental Disorders, Fourth Edition, Text Revision* (*DSM-IV-TR*; American Psychiatric Association, 2000) divides sexual disorders into three categories: sexual dysfunction, which is disruption of sexual arousal or performance; paraphilias, which are culturally unsuitable patterns of sexual arousal; and gender identity, which is a discomfort with one's own gender along with a persistent desire to be of the opposite sex. The diagnosis and treatment of sexual dysfunction are the focus of this chapter.

Sexual dysfunction occurs when there are disruptions in any of the four stages of sexual response: appetitive stage (desire to have sexual activity), excitement stage (erotic feelings causing vaginal lubrication or penile erection), orgasmic stage, or resolution stage. Studies have shown a wide range in prevalence estimates for sexual dysfunctions (Becker & Johnson, 2003). A survey involving a representative sample of the U.S. population between the ages of 18 and 59 reported by the American Psychiatric Association (2000) suggested the following prevalence estimates:

- Hypoactive sexual desire, 33%
- Male erectile difficulties, 10%
- Female sexual arousal problems, 20%
- Female orgasm problems, 25%
- Male orgasm problems (anorgasmia), 10%
- Premature ejaculation, 27%
- Female dyspareunia, 15%

Sexual dysfunction is multidetermined. Becker and Johnson (2003) discussed the factors that could contribute to sexual dysfunction, including the following:

- Misinformation regarding sexual interactions.
- Guilt concerning sexual activity.
- Performance anxiety.
- Poor communication between partners.
- Unacknowledged homosexual orientation.
- Lack of sexual desire secondary to repeated episodes of sexual dis–satisfaction.
- Anger or hostility.
- Judging sexual performance rather than enjoying the sexual experience.
- Medical illnesses (sexually transmitted diseases [STDs], prostate disease, thyroid dysfunction, diabetes mellitus, spinal cord disease, high blood pressure, atherosclerosis, liver disease).
- Alcohol (increases the desire, decreases the performance).
- Illegal drugs.
- Side effects of prescription and over-the-counter medications, including sedative-hypnotics, morphine, codeine, estrogens, cortisone, antihistamines, most "cold" preparations, and many antihypertensive medications. In a study involving 152 men and 192 women who were taking

selective serotonin uptake inhibitors (SSRIs), 58% of subjects reported sexual dysfunctions, including delayed orgasm or ejaculation, loss of libido, anorgasmia, and erectile dysfunction (Becker & Johnson, 2003).

Hypoactive Sexual Desire Disorder

Characterized by a persistent lack of desire for sexual activity that causes marked distress or interpersonal difficulty, hypoactive sexual desire disorder is associated with lack of sexual fantasies and failure to initiate sexual activity. The individual with inhibited desire only engages in sexual activity when, with vigorous determination, the partner demands engagement. Physical pain, body image problems, and low self-esteem may have deleterious effects on sexual desire. The most difficult sexual dysfunction to treat, hypoactive sexual desire disorder, responds best to a combination of cognitive therapy to deal with false beliefs regarding the sexual act; marital therapy to manage emotional conflicts —anxiety, anger, guilt, fear—associated with the dysfunction; and behavior therapy consisting of exercises to enhance sexual behavior. No clinical evidence suggests that testosterone improves sexual arousal (Becker & Johnson, 2003).

Male Erectile Disorder

Although sensate focus exercises—beginning with nongenital, nondemand caressing that gradually progresses to direct sexual activity—has been effective in treating male erectile disorder, the medications Viagra or Cialis, both of which increase blood flow to the penis, work faster and more efficiently. Psychotherapy can help alleviate emotional conflicts secondary to performance anxiety.

Female Sexual Arousal Disorder

Characterized by the persistent inability to maintain sexual excitement (vasocongestion in the pelvis, vaginal lubrication and expansion, and swelling of the external genitalia) until completion of the sexual activity, female sexual arousal disorder may result in painful intercourse, sexual avoidance, and marital or sexual relationship disturbance. Anxiety secondary to impairment in female sexual arousal can be treated with systematic desensitization in which the patient is progressively exposed in fantasy and then in vivo to the authentic sexual circumstance that creates anxiety. In one study, 71% of women with female sexual arousal disorder reported improved sexual experience when treated with Viagra (Berman et al., 2001).

Female Orgasmic Disorder

Psychological factors associated with female orgasmic disorder, a recurrent delay in or absence of orgasm following a normal sexual excitement phase, include hostility toward men, anger at partner, fear of impregnation, guilt feelings about sexual impulses, and marital conflicts (Sadock & Sadock, 2005). Therapy is directed toward the cause. Education on the various sexual positions that allow stimulation of the clitoris during intercourse can be helpful, as can systematic desensitization for women who have a difficult time enjoying themselves during sexual intercourse (Becker & Johnson, 2003). Viagra helped 67% of women have an orgasm in a study done by Salerian and associates (2000).

Male Anorgasmia
Male anorgasmia can be treated with behavior techniques, including sensate focus exercises. Orgasmic functioning was improved in 77% of males treated with Viagra (Salerian et al., 2000).

Premature Ejaculation
Premature ejaculation, the most common of all male sexual problems, can be caused by a variety of medical conditions, including arteriosclerosis, benign prostate hyperplasia, and diabetes mellitus. Anxiety regarding the sex act and other psychological conflicts can contribute. Individual therapy aimed at discovering and resolving the psychological conflicts can be helpful. Behavior modification using the start-stop technique and the "squeeze" technique introduced by Masters and Johnson in 1970 has proved helpful in repressing ejaculation. Because the SSRIs delay orgasm, these medications can be used to treat premature ejaculation.

Painful Intercourse (Dyspareunia)
After organic pathology has been ruled out, dyspareunia (painful intercourse) can be treated with relaxation techniques, systematic desensitization, psychosexual education, or individual psychotherapy. Vaginismus (involuntary spasm by the musculature of the outer third of the vagina) caused by a history of rape, childhood sexual abuse, or psychosexual conflicts can be treated with individual psychotherapy aimed at resolving the underlying cause. The systematic insertion of dilators of graduated sizes has proven helpful (Becker & Johnson, 2003). Extreme aversion to genital sexual contact (sexual aversion disorder) can be treated by systematic desensitization (Kaplan, 1974).

Premenstrual Dysphoric Disorder
Although premenstrual dysphoric disorder is not included in the sexual dysfunction category of *DSM-IV-TR* (American Psychiatric Association, 2000), the condition is included here because symptoms occurring 1 week before menses (late luteal phase), remitting within the first day or two following the

onset of menstruation, and characterized by bloating, breast tenderness, cramping, depressed mood, anxiety, irritability, lethargy, and sleep disruption can cause disturbances in sexual functioning. SSRIs given throughout the month have been effective in treating premenstrual dysphoric disorder. Calcium carbonate at a dose of 1,200 mg daily has provided improvement by the second or third menstrual cycle. Vitamin B_6 at doses no greater than 100 mg daily, magnesium, and vitamin E are less effective but are worth a try in recalcitrant cases. Diuretics are useful for premenstrual bloating and edema, while anti-inflammatories can alleviate pelvic pain and cramping (Burt & Hendrick, 2003).

Sexual Abuse

Sexual abuse has many devastating consequences, and contributes enormously to sexual dysfunction as well as other mental and emotional disorders. An estimated 10–20 million Americans have suffered from sexual abuse, although the exact number is difficult to pinpoint because abuse often goes unreported. Incest by close family members, the most common form of child abuse, comprises 43% of sexual abuse cases. Another third of victims are abused by someone they know, while 24% are molested by strangers. In my own clinical private practice, over half of my female patients (and many males) report having been sexually abused as children. Sexual abuse remains a huge problem because only a small percentage of victims ever seek help and during a clinical interview, those who have been sexually abused will often fail to reveal they have been traumatized unless directly asked.

Incest, a particularly damaging form of sexual abuse, is defined as inappropriate sexual behavior between close family members. Usually, incest takes the form of an older adult (e.g., mother, father, stepparent, uncle) abusing a child. Because the perpetrator is in a position of authority, pressure for the victim to keep silent is overwhelming. Sadly, whereas children molested by a stranger can run home for help, victims of incest cannot. These children suffer in silence because they fear being punished, blamed, or ridiculed. Sometimes, the victims deny that anything wrong is happening. They may falsely believe the abuser's explanation that the sexual activity is a normal learning experience that happens in every family. Incest is not limited to intercourse but can also include other inappropriate sexual actions such as touching, verbal suggestions to engage in sexual conduct, pornographic photography, or seductive kissing and caressing.

Victims of any form of sexual abuse suffer from many mental, emotional, and physical consequences. Initially, they typically register shock, numbness, and denial. Self-esteem plummets. Nightmares and flashbacks are common. Sexual abuse also contributes greatly to mental disorders such as anxiety, depression, borderline personality disorder, substance abuse, eating disorders, and post-traumatic stress disorder. Sometimes, patients involuntarily repress memories of the abuse events. This biochemically induced amnesia, due to endocrine and neurological changes, acts as an emotional coping mechanism.

People who have been abused suffer in their interpersonal relationships long after the episodes of sexual abuse have stopped. Sexual dysfunction and aversion to sex occur much more frequently in those with a history of abuse than in the general population. In one study of abuse victims, 80% of women and all of the men reported sexual problems.

Recovery from sexual abuse is a difficult, painful, and life-long process. Healing only begins when the victim admits that he or she needs help. In my private practice, I open the door for honest communication by asking patients if they have ever been sexually abused. Although many answer "yes," most patients don't like to talk about it, and those who do often blame themselves, making it very difficult to move forward. The best I can do in these circumstances is to reassure them that it's not their fault. When patients are receptive to therapy, many resources are available to help them begin the recovery process. Books, support groups, and organizations such as RAINN (Rape, Abuse, and Incest National Network, http://www.rainn.org) are good places to start. Group therapy, in which patients discuss their victimization with other empathetic survivors of abuse, helps alleviate feelings of guilt and shame and paves a pathway to healing.

Time for Romance

In healthy relationships, such as within the confines of marriage, sex is a blessing to be enjoyed by both partners. However, when sexual function is impeded, marriages deteriorate, and in turn, when a marriage goes through inevitable rocky times, the sexual relationship suffers. All marriages fluctuate between good times and bad, challenges and rewards, happiness and sadness, perplexity and indifference. If, through the years, partners can rely on a solid foundation that can withstand the difficult times, the marriage will blossom. Here, then, are some ideas on the fundamentals of a stable marriage.

Commitment and Praise

In a time when half of marriages end in divorce, long-term commitment seems an oxymoron. However, unwavering faithfulness to marriage is the most important trait in laying the foundation for a healthy relationship. A stable home gives reassurance to both partners and to children. Those who want a solid marriage don't even let the word "divorce" become a part of their vocabulary.

When both partners emotionally commit to a marriage, they can coexist with a sense of security. Those who have the courage to commit themselves to marriage reflect quiet confidence and self-assurance—an inner power devoid of the desire to control. Because there is no need to dominate, those with self-assurance have a magnetic quality.

The bottom line is, be engaged. Be committed. Offer emotional security. Be someone your spouse can trust.

One of the best pieces of advice for those who want a stable marriage is this: Catch your spouse doing something right and praise him or her for it. Everyone loves praise, and some of us will do just about anything to get a compliment from those we love. We are just little kids grown older, after all.

When your spouse fails to live up to your expectations, don't nag. Nagging often reinforces bad behavior. Ignore bad behavior and it may well diminish. Praise good behavior and it will increase. Instead of nagging, bite your tongue. Wait until your spouse is doing something right and then say to him or her, "I'm proud of you." Watch your spouse beam with pleasure and enjoy the improvement in your relationship.

Communication

Neuroscientists have recently discovered that the corpus callosum—the fibers that connect the right and left hemispheres of the brain—are more prominent in women than in men, giving women more artistic and verbal skills, while men have more white matter in the brain—material that facilitates sensory and motor coordination. This suggests that women may be more romantic and more verbal because of brain physiology.

Of course this is a generalization, and not true in every case. For example, most men are taller than most women, but any one woman may be taller than any one man. Similarly, some men talk more than their wives, and some women are more task-oriented than their husbands. Some people talk more, while others are better listeners.

Some of the most frequent complaints that people have about their spouses are, "He/she doesn't talk to me," and "He/she doesn't listen to me." Talk to your spouse. And listen . . . really listen. Don't listen while the TV is on. Don't listen while you are reading the paper. Don't give advice. Don't try to fix things. Give your spouse your full and complete attention. A little goes a long way and soon, he or she will notice.

If you want your spouse to be more interested in your life, show more of an interest in his or her life. This means that you may have to do some unappealing things. If your spouse is a sports fan, try watching a game—or even attending one—together. If he or she enjoys dining out, suggest a night out at a new restaurant. As with listening, a little goes a long way, and before long, your spouse will reciprocate.

Romance

Genuine love is an extension of the self. When we love, we focus on helping those we love grow emotionally, intellectually, and spiritually. We can forget our own egos by creating happiness for our loved ones. Paradoxically, the more we give of ourselves, the more we extend ourselves—the more we receive, the more we are replenished. Enduring love, then, is an act of will. Genuine love transcends emotion.

The key to keeping romance alive is regular dating and courting. It's important to set aside at least one night a week to go out together. Dining at a gourmet restaurant (or even a fast food restaurant as long as you take time to be together without the children), a night of dancing, or an evening at the movies can help keep the romance alive.

To maintain the sparkle in a marriage, schedule a weekend away from home from time to time. A monthly excursion adds an anticipatory excitement to the marriage. Scheduling this engagement on the calendar and sticking with the plan to get away, no matter what, will reinforce commitment to the relationship.

Learn to appreciate each other's company. Enjoy a walk on the beach holding hands, or even just a walk around the block together after dinner. Sit out on the patio together when the moon is full. Never forget birthdays, anniversaries, or Valentine's Day. Give spontaneous gifts. Remember: A rose in time is more valuable than a $1,000 gift too late. It's also less expensive.

While it's essential that couples spend time together, it's also good for each person to spend some time alone. When you come home from work, give each other a few minutes alone before trying to engage in conversation or complain about your day. With a few minutes to decompress, you will both be more responsive.

Make sure to thank your spouse when he or she does something to help around the house, even if it's small. Something as small as, "thank you for changing the light bulb," or "I really appreciate it when you do the dishes," will show your partner that his or her efforts are not going unnoticed. As I said before, a little praise goes a long way.

Once a week or so, spend some time apart with your respective friends. This compromise works especially well if you suggest it: "I appreciate the work you've done around the house this week. It's made my life a lot easier. Why don't you go do something fun on Saturday?"

Sexual Intimacy

When you and your partner have an open line of communication about your desires, sex will become fun, adventurous, and stimulating. Talk with your partner about his or her sexual preferences. Some people prefer visual stimuli; others would rather hug and kiss prior to sex. Some value intimate conversation; others would rather not talk at all. Being honest about your feelings in this way will build trust and closeness in other areas of your life together. Ideally, both partners will receptive, understanding, forgiving, and engaged in the present moment. Intimacy, the replenishing gift of romance, renders requited love.

Are You Too Dependent on Your Lover?

Make Check Mark (✓) in Appropriate Column	Little of the Time 1 point each ✓	Some of the Time 2 points each ✓	A Lot of the Time 3 points each ✓	Most of the Time 4 points each ✓
I am devastated when a romantic partner disapproves of me.				
I feel bad when my partner does not want to be with me.				
I worry about being left by my partner.				
I worry that I love my partner more than I am loved.				
I become anxious when I have no romantic partner.				
I need to be reassured that I am loved.				
I get frustrated when my romantic partner is unavailable.				
I feel like my romantic partner does not want as much intimacy as I do.				
I worry about doing something that will cause me to lose my partner.				
I worry about not looking or acting good enough for my partner.				
Multiply ✓ by the value given in each column.				

Add the total for each column to get the **Grand total** = _____

SCORING

10–14 points = Independent and confident

15–24 points = Just about everyone has a few concerns regarding romance

25–34 points = Dependency interferes with intimacy

35–40 points = You may want to consider reading *Co-dependent No More*

Are You More Lusty Than Loving?

Make Check Mark (✓) in Appropriate Column	Little of the Time 1 point each ✓	Some of the Time 2 points each ✓	A Lot of the Time 3 points each ✓	Most of the Time 4 points each ✓
At the movies, making out keeps us from recalling the movie plot.				
Looking at my partner makes me think of wild, passionate sex.				
My partner's body excites me more than anything else.				
My partner and I had sex on our first date with each other.				
My feeling for my partner is like a raging fire.				
Anger makes my partner look sexy.				
I would rather talk about sex than talk about anything else.				
For our 6-month anniversary, we stayed in bed for the weekend.				
Hugs make me want to have sex.				
I can't keep my hands off my partner.				
Multiply ✓ by the value given in each column.				

Add the total for each column to get the **Grand total** = _____

SCORING

10–14 points = Get your testosterone checked (yes, women have testosterone, too)

15–24 points = A dull romance

25–34 points = Hot and heavy

35–40 points = Spend the weekend in a cold shower

How Romantic is Your Relationship?

Make Check Mark (✓) in Appropriate Column	Little of the Time 1 point each ✓	Some of the Time 2 points each ✓	A Lot of the Time 3 points each ✓	Most of the Time 4 points each ✓
My partner and I are compatible physically.				
I feel loved by my partner.				
My partner and I enjoy talking with each other.				
Our friends say that our relationship is romantic.				
We both enjoy romantic surprises.				
We enjoy being with each other.				
We both feel comfortable holding hands and hugging.				
I feel secure when I am with my partner.				
I am confident of my partner's faithfulness.				
Looking in my partner's eyes warms my heart.				
Multiply ✓ by the value given in each column.				

Add the total for each column to get the **Grand total** = _____

SCORING

10–14 points = Ice

15–24 points = Not much there

25–34 points = Warm, cozy, and fun

35–40 points = Very romantic

Complete Mental Health

A Clinician's Quiz

1. Give and define the three categories of sexual disorders.
2. About _____% of men and _____% of women acknowledged having one or more types of sexual disfunction.
3. Name the four stages of sexual response.
4. Describe and discuss the symptoms of sexual abuse.
5. What is the most difficult sexual dysfunction to treat?
6. What is the most common male sexual disorder?
7. In a study of sexually abused men and women, what percent of women and what percent of men reported sexual problems?
8. How can praise strengthen a relationship?
9. What is one way to increase romance in a relationship?
10. How can partners express their sexual intimacy?

CHAPTER 14

Sleep Disorders
Nature's Soft Nurse

For 6 consecutive weeks, while working as a correspondent during World War II, Ernest Hemingway slept only 2 hours a night. Known for his inexhaustible tenacity, Thomas Edison reportedly slept no more than a few minutes a night, although he often took catnaps during the day to make up for the deficit. Leonardo da Vinci had perhaps the most bizarre sleep pattern, each day napping for 15 minutes every 4 hours.

With our increasingly busy lifestyles, we may wonder if, perhaps, following the examples of these "short sleepers" might be the answer. After all, aren't we wasting time sleeping 8 hours a night? Why snooze one third of our lives away when we could be using that precious time to accomplish more tasks?

Until the early 1950s, little was known about sleep. Then, Aserinsky and Kleitman (1953) discovered that rapid eye movements of the sleeping person were associated with both dreaming and brain wave changes. This discovery launched a surge of remarkable research. Since that time, dozens of sleep research centers have documented the basic pattern of sleep and have uncovered the tremendous benefits of getting a good night's sleep.

Normal Sleep

Getting adequate sleep plays an extremely important role in physical, mental, and emotional health. While we are awake and active, our bodies and brains progressively deteriorate at a cellular level. During sleep, cells are restored, synaptic nerve connections are strengthened, muscle tissue is repaired, and growth hormones are excreted (Biology Online, 2000). Several studies have shown that sleep deprivation negatively affects personality, temper, sense of humor, cognition, creativity, and accuracy. Drivers who do not get adequate sleep have been shown to have impairment similar to or worse than drunk drivers (Cable News Network, 2000). Individuals who are extremely sleep deprived become prediabetic in as little as 1 week (Knutson, Ryden, Mander, & Van Cauter, 2006). Withholding sleep for extended periods of time causes death in laboratory rats (Rechtschaffen, Gilliland, Bergmann, & Winter, 1983).

Sleep studies have shown that the vast majority of people need at least 6 hours of sleep a night or performance is affected. One study indicated that the optimum amount of sleep time for adults is 7 consecutive hours (Rutledge, 2009).

During a typical night, the individual progresses into deeper and deeper sleep. Periods of restful sleep cause the heart rate, blood pressure, and respiratory rate to diminish, and the brain wave patterns slow rhythmically (Rutledge, 2009). About every 90 minutes throughout the night, this peaceful rest is interrupted by increased brain wave frequency, heart rate, and respiratory rate; by elevated blood pressure; and by increased body movement. It is during this time that dreaming occurs (Wagner, 2009). While dreaming, the eyes of the sleeping individual dart about rapidly behind closed lids, hence the term rapid eye movement (REM) sleep. In an average 7- to 8-hour night of sleep, a person will cycle through the sleep stages four times (Neylan, Reynolds, & Kupfer, 2003).

Dreams

Everyone dreams. Some people just don't remember their dreams. Research laboratories have documented that approximately one fourth of sleeping time is spent in dream sleep, but because most of this time is preceded and followed by cycles of deeper sleep, most dreams are forgotten. Waking in the middle of a dream allows an individual to remember dreams more clearly.

Despite much research into the area of dreams, the exact purpose of this fascinating phenomenon remains a mystery. Many experts theorize that dreams allow the brain to process and organize the day's events (Wagner, 2009). Others suppose that dreams serve a psychotherapeutic function, enabling the dreamer to subconsciously connect thoughts and feelings.

Dreams can be thought of as a story with a beginning, middle, and end. If we accept the premise that dreams offer an intuitive solution to a current real-life problem, then the sleeper's job is to understand the dream's problem and the solution offered by the dream.

A surgeon dreamed he was a robot. As the dream progressed, he became increasingly mechanical; finally, his partner threw him on a junk heap. The surgeon had been having problems with elbow pain. He was concerned that the pain would cause him to be unable to work and would take away his freedom (hence the dream of becoming a robot and eventually being discarded). The next morning, the surgeon sought treatment for his elbow pain.

Stories of recurring dreams, two people having similar dreams on the same night, and dreams that seem to predict the future are mysterious, but little evidence currently exists that would attribute these to anything more than coincidence.

ABRAHAM LINCOLN'S CATAFALQUE DREAM

A few days prior to his assassination, Lincoln recounted the following dream: "About ten days ago I retired very late. I had been up waiting for important dispatches from the front. I could not have been long in bed when I fell into a slumber, for I was weary. I soon began to dream. There seemed to be a deathlike stillness about me. Then I heard subdued sobs, as if a number of people were weeping. I thought I left my bed and wandered downstairs. There the same pitiful sobbing broke the silence, but the mourners were invisible. I went from room to room; no living person was in sight, but the sounds of distress met me as I passed along. It was light in all the rooms; every object was familiar to me; but where were all the people who were grieving as if their hearts would break? I was puzzled and alarmed. What could be the meaning of all this? Determined to find the cause of a state of things so mysterious and so shocking, I kept on until I arrived at the East Room, which I entered. There I met with a sickening surprise. Before me was a catafalque, on which rested a corpse wrapped in funeral vestments. Around it were stationed soldiers who were acting as guards; and there was a throng of others weeping pitifully. 'Who is dead in the White House?' I demanded of one of the soldiers. 'The President,' was his answer; 'he was killed by an assassin!' Then came a loud burst of grief from the crowd."

From *With Malice Toward None: The Life of Abraham Lincoln*, by S. B. Oates, 1977, Harper and Row, New York, pp. 425-426. Reprinted with permission.

Abnormal Sleep

Approximately 15% of the estimated 30% of adults who experience a sleep disturbance seek treatment (Sadock & Sadock, 2005). Disturbed sleep can result from psychiatric disorders or result from a primary sleep disorder. The *Diagnostic and Statistical Manual of Mental Disorders, Fourth Edition, Text Revision* (*DSM-IV-TR*; American Psychiatric Association, 2000) divided the primary sleep disorders into two groups: the dyssomnias (disturbances in quality, timing, or amount of sleep) and the parasomnias (unfortunate events occurring during sleep or on the verge of wakefulness) **(Table 14-2)**.

Dyssomnias

The following dyssomnias are discussed next: primary insomnia, primary hypersomnia, narcolepsy, breathing-related sleep disorders, circadian rhythm sleep disorder (sleep-wake schedule disorder), and restless leg syndrome.

Primary Insomnia

Primary insomnia is marked by difficulty falling asleep, awaking several times during the night, or nonrestful sleep. For insomnia to be correctly diagnosed as a primary sleep disorder, it must last more than a month, be unrelated to a psychiatric or medical disorder, and not be due to substance abuse or medication. Often, a primary sleep disorder follows an acutely traumatic event or a change in lifestyle. Usually, something sets a pattern for poor sleep, and once the initial condition has cleared, the sleep disturbance continues; it has become a conditioned response. An individual may develop difficulty falling asleep because of a transient stressful situation and may quickly learn to associate the simple process of going to bed and turning off the light with frustration and sleeplessness. Proof of this hypothesis comes from reports that patients sleep better when they travel away from home and sleep in a different bed; or they may have no difficulty falling asleep in an easy chair, but when they crawl into their own bed they become wide-eyed awake.

Some with primary sleep disorder have an anxious overconcern about life in general— these are the constant worriers who sleep fitfully because they cogitate on a series of unfortunate events that could strike at any time. As we age, our sleep patterns are more easily interrupted, and our need for sleep shortens, making some of us complain of poor sleep when we are transitioning to another phase of life (Andreasen & Black, 2006).

No matter the precipitating event, once the poor sleep Ferris wheel gets started, it becomes difficult to get off. Worrying about not getting enough sleep leads to a vicious cycle of tossing and turning through even more sleepless nights. Daytime naps, drinking coffee during the day to fight drowsiness, drinking alcohol to induce sleep, rebound insomnia caused by sedative-hypnotics, and spending excessive time in bed make matters worse.

TABLE 14-2

Sleep Disturbances Related to Mental Disorders

MENTAL DISORDER	TYPE OF SLEEP DISTURBANCE
Schizophrenia	Psychotic episodes cause severe disruption of sleep with a reduction in stage 4 sleep
Depression	Early-morning awakening; diminished deep sleep; REM sleep earlier in the night
Dysthymia	Increased sleep
Mania or hypomania	Reduced need for sleep
Anxiety disorders	Delayed sleep onset
Post-traumatic stress disorder	Disturbing dreams
Panic disorder	Sudden awakening from sleep associated with fear of impending doom
Acute alcohol use	Reduced wakefulness the first 3–4 hours of sleep with subsequent increased wakefulness
Chronic alcohol use	Fragmented sleep
Abstinence following alcohol abuse	Insomnia and nightmares initially with gradual improvement over weeks or months
Delerium	Wandering, agitation during early evening and nighttime hours; frequent awakenings

A thorough medical and psychiatric history often reveals secondary causes of insomnia, including:

- Chronic pain.
- Central nervous system (CNS) lesions or metabolic, endocrine, or other diseases.
- Overuse of caffeinated products.
- Alcohol or other substance use.

Many believe that insomnia can be easily treated with sedatives. Sedatives may work for 1 or 2 weeks, but chronic use will cause serious sleep difficulties. Higher and higher doses will be required to induce sleep. To complicate matters, sedatives can decrease dream sleep producing irritability, anxiety, and depression. Unpleasant physical side effects can also accompany sedative use or the sudden termination of sedatives.

A 28-year-old housewife was seen in consultation because of a sudden onset of seizures that could not be explained. The initial fear that Mrs. Davis had a brain tumor had been ruled out. Now, her physicians considered she might have a conversion disorder with psychological factors causing her symptoms. A detailed history revealed that the patient had been taking increasing doses of the sedative Xanax for several months to combat insomnia. When she had stopped the medication abruptly, she had begun to have withdrawal seizures.

Some use alcohol as a sedative because after a couple of drinks it produces relaxation, peaceful feelings, and sleepiness. Unfortunately, the effects of alcohol wear off in 3 or 4 hours, and a rebound hyperalertness is produced. This explains why after drinking alcohol you can sleep soundly for a few hours and then wake up in the middle of the night and can't go back to sleep. Alcohol withdrawal causes difficulty going to sleep, an increase of dream sleep (usually nightmares), and frequent awakenings during the night. Insomnia and sleep disturbance may persist as long as 6 months after withdrawal from heavy alcohol use.

Paul, a 42-year-old textile sales representative, complained that when he went on sales trips he could only get a few hours of sleep. He reported that he drifted off to sleep without any difficulty, but a few hours later, he would awaken with anxiety and agitation and be unable to return to sleep. While at home, he slept soundly. A detailed interview revealed that Paul drank heavily when on the road; at home, he had no more than two drinks nightly and often did not drink at all. Cutting back on his drinking while traveling alleviated Paul's sleep disturbance.

Caffeine is probably the most overlooked cause of insomnia. Caffeine causes a decline in total sleep time, decreased deep sleep, and a decrease in dream sleep. The poor sleep at night results in daytime grogginess and a tendency to consume more and more caffeine during the day, increasing the vicious cycle. Caffeine is found in a variety of preparations (Reid, 2005):

Hershey's milk chocolate with almonds bar, 6 ounces	25 mg
Espresso, 1-ounce shot	40 mg
Brewed tea, 8-ounce cup	50 mg
Coca-Cola, 20-ounce bottle	57 mg

Sleep Disorders

Red Bull energy drink, 8.3-ounce can	80 mg
Excedrin pain reliever, 2 tablets	130 mg
Brewed coffee, 12-ounce cup	200 mg
Mountain Dew, 64-ounce Double Gulp	294 mg

Rose, a 26-year-old secretary, complained of daytime grogginess and poor sleep at night. She reported that she could hardly keep her eyes open while typing during the day; she attributed this sluggishness to the boring reports that she typed. While the reports were indeed boring, her main sleep problem was high coffee intake. She drank three cups of coffee with breakfast, a couple of cups of coffee during the morning and afternoon breaks, and one or two cups of coffee with lunch. In addition, she was constantly sipping from a cup of coffee next to her typing stand, and she would supplement her caffeine intake with several cola drinks during the day. The stimulus she received from the caffeine during the day prevented her from sleeping well at night, while the boring reports that she typed during the day induced her to drink more and more coffee. After Rose realized the cause of her grogginess, she began to reduce her consumption, methodically using a chart to help her. For 1 week, she documented the cups of coffee she drank. She then reduced this amount by eliminating one cup of coffee every third day until she was down to one cup of coffee in the morning and one cup for each break period during the day. Her grogginess abated, and her sleep at night improved. The reports, however, remained boring.

Patients with chronic insomnia respond to "sleep hygiene" measures, which include the following:

- Divert attention from business activity an hour before going to bed by reading a novel, preferably a dull one.
- Go to bed only when sleepy.
- When failing to go to sleep in 15 to 20 minutes, get out of bed and return only when sleepiness recurs.
- Establish a routine bedtime and a routine time for waking every day, even on weekends.
- Avoid daytime naps.
- Avoid using the bed as a place to watch television, read, or work.
- Exercise regularly to induce a slight amount of physical fatigue but avoid exercise at night.
- Reduce or discontinue the consumption of caffeinated beverages, alcohol, cigarettes, and sedative-hypnotic drugs.

- Avoid a heavy nighttime meal.
- Avoid late evening stimulation; substitute relaxed reading for television.
- Try body temperature-raising bath soaks near bedtime.
- Practice progressive muscle relaxation or meditation at bedtime.
- On being unable to return to sleep within 15–20 minutes of awakening in the middle of the night, get out of bed, read a book, practice relaxation techniques, or do work around the home. Avoid returning to bed until sleepy.

Primary Hypersomnia

Primary hypersomnia is the diagnosis for 5–10% of individuals presenting to sleep disorder clinics complaining of daytime sleepiness. This disorder is evidenced by frequent daytime sleep episodes or prolonged sleep not resulting from other causes (American Psychiatric Association, 2000). Despite sleeping longer at night than is usually expected, patients awaken groggy and take prolonged naps once or twice daily.

Treatment involves sleep hygiene techniques and stimulant drugs (Ritalin or Adderall), both of which are Schedule Class II drugs that can be prescribed no more than a month at a time and require a written prescription for each refill (Trinkle & Kilgus, 2009). Ritalin and Adderall enhance wakefulness by activating the dopamine and norepinephrine system in the medial frontal cortex and hypothalamus. An increase of dopamine and norepinephrine in the dorsolateral prefrontal cortex improves attention, concentration, and wakefulness. Side effects include headache, nervousness, irritability, tremor, and anorexia. Dangerous side effects include psychosis, seizures, hypertension, arrhythmias, and dependence (Stahl, 2005).The usual dosage range for Adderall is 5–40 mg daily in divided doses; for Ritalin, 10–20 mg a day in divided doses, but the doses can be increased to 60 mg for both Adderall and Ritalin if necessary.

Provigil (modafinil) increases neuronal activity in the hypothalamus that enhances cognitive performance and reduces daytime sleepiness within 2 hours of first dosing without preventing falling to sleep when needed (Stahl, 2005). The usual dose is 200 mg each morning but the dose may require increasing to 800 mg in narcolepsy. Provigil presents a viable option for primary hypersomnia because of a better side-effect profile and less chance of abuse. Because Provigil is a Schedule Class IV medication, refills are allowed without writing another prescription. A long acting well-absorbed medication, Provigil has few side effects, the most common one being an initial headache, which subsides within a few days or weeks. If the headache is severe, the dose can be lowered. Provigil may also reduce the potency of oral contraceptives, mandating an increase in birth control dosage (Trinkle and Kilgus, 2009).

Narcolepsy

Affecting about 1 in 2,000 persons, narcolepsy, marked by irresistible sleep attacks, can be associated with secondary symptoms of cataplexy, hypnagogic hallucinations, and sleep paralysis. Those with narcolepsy tend to almost immediately enter REM sleep during daytime naps and at night enter into REM sleep within a few minutes after sleep onset instead of the typical 90-minute lag period for entering REM sleep (Andreasen & Black, 2006).

About 70% of narcoleptics develop cataplexy, characterized by a sudden, brief loss of muscle tone usually preceded by a strong emotional stimulus such as laughter, anger, or surprise (American Psychiatric Association, 2000). Dream-like perceptual phenomenon of REM sleep called hypnagogic hallucinations (if they occur just before falling asleep) and hypnopompic hallucinations (when occurring on awakening) can be found in 20–40% of narcoleptics as opposed to 15–20% in the normal population. Almost 50% of narcoleptics experience sleep paralysis, the inability to speak or move for a few seconds up to a few minutes. Sleep paralysis that occurs just before falling asleep or on awakening can be terrifying when combined with hallucinations. About half of normal sleepers also report sleep paralysis occurring at least once in a lifetime, but these are briefer in duration (American Psychiatric Association, 2000). The dream-like hallucinations, sleep paralysis, and cataplexy found in narcoleptics, though poorly understood, seem to be related to REM activity (Neylan et al., 2003).

Several drugs have been found effective in the treatment of narcolepsy. The psychostimulants Ritalin or Adderall can be used to treat sleep attacks. The usual dosage range for Adderall is 5–60 mg daily in divided doses; for Ritalin 20–60 mg/day in 2–3 divided doses (Stahl, 2005). The dose of both drugs can be started at 5 mg and gradually worked up to a total daily dose of 60 mg or higher.

Provigil has been approved by the Federal Drug Administration for promoting wakefulness in patients with excessive daytime sleepiness associated with narcolepsy. Human narcolepsy is associated with a loss of hypocretin cells in the lateral hypothalamus, and Provigil increases c-fos activity of hypocretin cells. In addition, Provigil appears to increase glutamate (a stimulating neurotransmitter) in the posterior hypothalamus, hippocampus, and ventral thalamus and to suppress GABA (gamma-aminobutyric acid, a sedating neurotransmitter) in the posterior hypothalamus (Stahl, 2008). These findings are consistent with the promotion of wakefulness. The highly selective CNS activity of Provigil that results in no blood pressure or heart rate change distinguishes Provigil from the psychostimulants that can cause an increase in autonomic activity. In addition, Provigil, a schedule IV drug, has a lower abuse potential than schedule II or III drugs, and Provigil fails to increase irritability and agitation as can occur with the psychostimulants.

The recommended dose of Provigil is 200–800 mg taken once daily in the morning. Studies showed that Provigil in the morning can increase wakefulness throughout the day without interfering with nighttime sleep. Although some patients in clinical trials did report anxiety or nervousness, these reports were, in general, similar for patients taking placebo.

Provigil is generally well tolerated. When side effects do occur, they are generally mild and manageable. Headache is the most frequently reported side effect. Other side effects include nausea, infection, nervousness, anxiety, and insomnia. Discontinuing Provigil is not associated with withdrawal symptoms, although daytime sleepiness may return.

In relatively low doses (e.g., 10–75 mg imipramine at bedtime), REM-suppressing tricyclic antidepressants can be used to treat cataplexy, sleep paralysis, and dream-like illusions. Side effects of tricyclics include blurred vision, constipation, urinary retention, dry mouth, weight gain, dizziness, and sedation. Life threatening side effects include paralytic ileus, lowered seizure threshold, orthostatic hypotension, arrhythmias, hepatic failure, and sudden death (Stahl, 2005).

Breathing-Related Sleep Disorders

Breathing-related sleep disorder, also known as sleep apnea, can, rarely, result from a failure in central respiratory drive. The much more common obstructive sleep apnea is characterized by frequent respiratory pauses during sleep. These apneic events can last for a half minute or more and occur 10–15 times each hour, resulting in significant oxygen deficiency (Neylan et al., 2003). Terminated by loud gasping and brief arousals, the apneic events can lead to excessive daytime sleepiness. The diagnosis is often made by the bed partner, who complains that the patient snores, gasps, and snorts so loudly and frequently that no rest can be experienced by either sleeper.

Impaired nighttime sleep and excessive daytime sleepiness can engender memory disturbance, irritability, and personality changes. Sleep deficiency can also cause injuries and lead to social and occupational impairment. Cardiac abnormalities, hypertension, arrhythmias, and elevated pulmonary arterial pressure can be life threatening (Neylan et al., 2003).

The majority of individuals with obstructive sleep apnea syndrome are overweight. Because upper airway narrowing can occur due to excessive bulk of soft tissue, individuals with a neck circumference greater than 17 inches in men and 16 inches in women are at greater risk. Individuals of normal weight with sleep apnea most likely have a localized structural abnormality such as a maxillomandibular malformation or adenotonsillar enlargement that can be corrected by surgery (American Psychiatric Association, 2000).

Weight loss, avoidance of sedative-hypnotics, and training the patient to avoid the supine position when sleeping can ease symptoms. Other treatment approaches include tongue-retaining devices and orthodontic appliances, but continuous positive airway pressure (CPAP), by which air blown into the nose through a nasal mask maintains the patency of the oropharynx during respiration, remains the treatment of choice (Andreasen & Black, 2006). Compliance is an issue for some patients who abhor the constriction of the CPAP mask and discard it. Regular follow-up and encouragement enhance compliance.

Mr. Mullins, an obese 67-year-old former hardware store owner, made an appointment for a sleep evaluation at the insistence of his wife. Recently retired, Mr. Mullins had looked forward to going on cross-country trips in his recreational vehicle with his wife and grandchildren, but after their first trip, the grandchildren refused to go again. They said their grandfather snored too loudly. His wife said that Mr. Mullins did snore loudly, but she had learned to sleep through it. Associated with this snoring were long pauses in his breathing during the night and violent thrashing in the bed. Mr. Mullins said he felt groggy during the day, and he had no pep or energy but felt that this was due to "old age." Physical examination revealed an irregular heart rhythm and high blood pressure. A detailed study in the sleep laboratory documented that Mr. Mullins had sleep apnea. Following CPAP initiation and a 50-pound weight loss, his hypertension and irregular heartbeat returned to normal. At last, Mr. Mullins happily reported that he was going on a trip to Red River, New Mexico, with his wife and grandchildren.

Circadian Rhythm Sleep Disorder (Sleep-Wake Schedule Disorder)

Disrupted sleep results when the sleep-wake cycle becomes interrupted by the irregularity of a person's daily schedule. There exist four types of circadian rhythm disturbance. The first type, delayed sleep phase, occurs when an individual is unable to go to sleep until late at night and sleeps until late the next day. This pattern may develop during college years, when students typically stay up late at night and sleep through the morning classes, or when people get into the habit of staying up for late-night TV and then sleeping through the mornings. After awhile, this pattern gets "locked in." Diligent application of sleep hygiene techniques can correct the problem over time.

Blake, a 21-year-old college student, complained that he slept through his early morning classes. Often, he would not hear the alarm clock; when he did, he would groggily turn it off, roll over, and go back to sleep. Blake's sleep patterns were reinforced by his weekend activities. Over the weekends, he would frequently party until 3 or 4 A.M., falling into bed exhausted and not awakening until around noon. After a detailed history and physical examination revealed no emotional or physical abnormalities, Blake was diagnosed as having delayed sleep phase syndrome. He was instructed to get out of bed, no matter what, every morning at 7 A.M. For the first few weeks, his fraternity brothers literally dragged him out of bed and pushed him into the shower. He began using sleep hygiene techniques. With great difficulty, his sleep patterns normalized.

World travelers who cross time zones develop a mismatch between the desired time of sleep and expected wakefulness, known as *jet lag*. Symptom severity is proportional to the number of time zones traveled in less than 24 hours. Eastward travel that advances the sleep-wake hours makes for more difficult adjustment than westward travel that delays sleep-wake hours. Judicious use of hypnotic agents helps minimize symptoms.

Workers rotating on different shifts force sleep and wakefulness misalignments known as *shift work sleep disorder*. Shift workers have higher rates of drug abuse, divorce, and gastrointestinal, cardiac, and reproductive disorders; physicians and air traffic controllers make more errors while working night shifts (Neylan et al., 2003). Provigil taken just prior to the start of the work shift promotes alertness during working hours and improves sleep during the off hours.

Although not mentioned in *DSM-IV-TR*, clinical experience has shown that the elderly often experience *advanced sleep phase syndrome*, manifested by excessive sleepiness in the early evening hours followed by midnight arousal. Replacing the before-dinner glass of wine with a hot cup of tea helps, as does the practice of other sleep hygiene measures.

Restless Leg Syndrome

Some scientists estimated that restless leg syndrome (RLS) affects as many as 12 million Americans; others believed that underdiagnosis or even misdiagnosis renders the rate much higher (National Institute of Neurological Disorders and Stroke [NINDS], 2009). Just prior to sleep, a tingling, burning, itching, or crawling sensation in the muscles of the extremities prompts an irresistible, distressing desire to move the legs, and in some cases the arms, making sleep almost impossible.

More than 80% of people with RLS also experience a more common condition known as periodic limb movement disorder (PLMD). PLMD is characterized by involuntary leg twitching or jerking movements during sleep that typically occur every 10 to 60 seconds, sometimes throughout the night. The symptoms cause repeated awakening and severely disrupted sleep. Unlike RLS, the movements caused by PLMD are involuntary—people have no control over them. Although many patients with RLS also develop PLMD, most people with PLMD do not experience RLS. Like RLS, the cause of PLMD is unknown (NINDS, 2009).

Restless leg syndrome, and to a certain extent **PLMD**, respond to Requip (ropinirole), a dopamine agonist first approved for the treatment of Parkinson's disease (RxList, 2009b). Dosing begins with 0.25 mg at night for two nights, then is increased to 0.5 mg nightly; this is titrated upward as needed to control symptoms. Side effects are rare and include dizziness, nausea and headaches.

Parasomnias

The following parasomnias are discussed next: nightmares, sleep terror, and sleepwalking.

Nightmares

Nightmares usually occur in the middle or the later third of the night when REM cycles are increased. These frightening episodes often cause the victim to wake in the middle of the dream, rather than sleeping right through the REM cycle as normal, so it may seem that nightmares occur more frequently than they actually do. However, the incidence rate increases in patients with existing psychiatric disorders. Withdrawal from alcohol, barbiturates, benzodiazepines, and the use of selective serotonin reuptake inhibitors (SSRIs) increases vivid dreams and nightmares. Withdrawal from SSRIs also causes vivid dreams (Andreasen & Black, 2006).

Sleep Terror

Sleep terror is a sudden arousal from the deepest sleep, associated with extreme panic. Typically, such people sit up in bed, looking frightened. Their pupils may be dilated; generally, they are sweating profusely, and their hearts thump rapidly. Although they have their eyes open, they are confused and dazed. Usually, there is amnesia for the entire episode the next morning. This condition is thought to be due to a disturbance of deep sleep and is not associated with psychiatric illness. Sleep terror occurs mostly in children, and usually the condition gradually resolves by late adolescence (American Psychiatric Association, 2000).

Sleepwalking

Sleepwalking commonly occurs between the ages of 6 and 12, and most children grow out of it. The best thing that you can do for a sleepwalker is to make certain the walker does not hurt himself or herself. Sleepwalkers generally do not have full consciousness. Their coordination is poor, and they are likely to stumble or lose their balance despite open eyes. Adults who have problems with sleepwalking generally have some personality disturbances or emotional conflict (American Psychiatric Association, 2000).

Improving Sleep

Several medications have proven helpful in combating certain sleep disorders (Schatzberg et al., 2007), as indicated by **Table 14-3** and **Table 14-4**.

However, as stated, medications actually contribute to poorer sleep in the long run. The better solution is to implement techniques that improve conditions for a good night's sleep. The sleep hygiene methods listed in the section on insomnia are a good starting point. In my practice, I often teach patients a hypnotic relaxation technique. The following "script" works best when a willing partner (i.e., spouse, roommate, friend) reads it aloud in a very slow, monotonic, sonorous voice. Once learned, patients can use the technique at home by meditating on the words before falling asleep to induce beta-wave rhythm.

TABLE 14-3		
Selected Medications for Sleep Disturbance		
MEDICATION	**DOSE**	**NOTES**
Restoril	15–30 mg	Slow absorption (45–60 minutes or longer) suggests that the medication be taken an hour or two before bedtime; short half-life (8 hours) with no active metabolites results in little hangover effect.
Lunesta	1–3 mg	Approved for both acute and maintenance treatment of insomnia.
Rozerem	8 mg	A specific melatonin receptor agonist, reduces the time to go to sleep but probably has little advantage when compared to over-the-counter melatonin supplements.
Sonata	5–10 mg	1- to 2-hour half-life; could take in the middle of the night and not feel too groggy the next morning
Ambien	5–10 mg	2- to 4-hour half-life; currently the most popular sedative, but patient may not sleep through the night because of the short half-life.
Trazodone	50–200 mg	Initially approved as an antidepressant; has no abuse liability and no withdrawal symptoms.
Neurontin	100–900 mg	Released for use in seizures, can be safely used because no more than 900 mg can be absorbed from the gastrointestinal tract at one time; also has analgesic effects.

TABLE 14-4

Selected Medications for Sleep Disturbance

MEDICATION	HOW IT WORKS	SIDE EFFECTS
Restoril	Enhances inhibitory effects of GABA.	Daytime sedation, fatigue, depression, dizziness, ataxia, slurred speech, confusion, hyper-excitability, nervousness.
Lunesta	Enhances the inhibitory effects of GABA.	Unpleasant taste in the mouth, daytime sedation, dizziness, headache.
Rozerem	A melatonin type 1 and type 2 receptor agonist, Rozerem targets two receptors in the brain's suprachiasmatic nucleus that regulate sleep and wakefulness: the homeostatic system—a sleep inducing process and the circadian system— an arousal promoting process, Rozerem induces sleep by turning off the alerting signal generated by the circadian system and turning on the sleep inducing process of the homeostatic system.	Associated with decreased testosterone in some men; avoid using in patients with severe hepatic involvement.
Sonata	Binds selectively to the alpha 1 isoform of the benzodiazepine receptor; may enhance GABA inhibitory actions.	Daytime sedation, dizziness, ataxia, dose dependent amnesia, hyper-excitability, nervousness.
Ambien	Binds selectively to the alpha 1 isoform of the benzodiazepine receptor; may enhance GABA inhibitory actions.	Daytime sedation, dizziness, ataxia, dose dependent amnesia, hyper-excitability, nervousness.
Trazodone	Robustly blocks serotonin 2A receptors, antihistamine properties, blocks alpha adrenergic 1 receptors.	Daytime sedation and "hangover." Nausea, edema, constipation, dry mouth, dizziness, hypotension. Rare priapism.
Neurontin	Binds to the alpha 2 delta subunit of voltage-sensitive calcium channels.	Daytime sedation, dizziness, ataxia, fatigue, vomiting, dry mouth, peripheral edema

Complete Mental Health

First I get into a relaxed position... and... I take a deep breath in... as I breathe in relaxation... and breathe out tension... with each breath I go deeper and deeper into a relaxed state of mind and body... deeper and deeper relaxed... breathing in relaxation and breathing out tension ... relaxing first my right foot ... deeper and deeper relaxed... now my left foot is relaxing... as I breathe in relaxation and breathe out tension... until my left ankle... and left leg become relaxed ... and now my right leg and right ankle are relaxed... breathing in relaxation and breathing out tension ... relaxing the front of the thigh muscle... the left thigh muscle and the right thigh muscle... now the back of the thigh... the right and the left... deeper and deeper relaxed... breathing deeper and deeper... breathing in relaxation and breathing out tension... relaxing now the hips... and the pelvic girdle... as I feel more and more relaxed... relaxing the buttocks and the back muscles... the muscles running up and down the spine ... relaxing deeper and deeper... breathing in relaxation... breathing out tension... relaxing the chest muscles... the front of the chest ... around the ribs... the left side of the ribs and the right side of the ribs ... all the way to the back of the ribs where they meet the muscles running up and down the spine... the left back of the ribs and the right back of the ribs... breathing deeper and deeper relaxed... as I relax my neck muscles... the back of the neck and the front of the neck... and the shoulder muscles ... relaxing down the arms ... relaxing the right shoulder... and the left shoulder... and the right arm... and the left arm ... deeper and deeper relaxed... feeling relaxed all over ... deeper and deeper... relaxing the muscles, ligaments, and joints around the elbow ... the right elbow ... and the left elbow... and the right lower arm ... and the left lower arm ... and the muscles, ligaments, and tendons around the right wrist ... and the left wrist... and the hands... and the fingers ... and the thumbs... feeling more and more relaxed... breathing in relaxation and breathing out tension... deeper and deeper relaxed... now up the neck to the face muscles... the muscles around the mouth... and around the nose ... and around the eyes... relaxing all the muscles of the face... the forehead... and the scalp ... as I relax all the muscles of the body... I imagine myself about to get on an elevator and go down, down, down into a deeper state of relaxed mind and body... deeper and deeper relaxed ... deeper and deeper relaxed ... getting on the elevator... and as I close the door I feel deeper and deeper relaxed ... and now I push the down button on the elevator... and go down ... down ... down ... I see the number 10 on the elevator panel ... and I look at the panel and I see the number 9... 8... 7 ... 6 ... 5... 4... 3... 2... 1 and I push number one because I am getting more and more relaxed as I go down, down, down the elevator... I am now going down to the ninth floor ... and the eighth floor ... going deeper and deeper relaxed... and now the seventh floor ... and the sixth ... and the fifth ... sinking down... down... down into a relaxed state of mind and body... the fourth floor... more and more relaxed ... the third floor... the second floor... deeper and deeper relaxed ... and now the first floor... and now I step off the elevator... and see many soft, fluffy clouds ... and because I am so sleepy... so sleepy and relaxed ... I just want to lie on one of those fluffy white clouds and go into a deep, deep sleep... and so I do... I lie on one of those fluffy white clouds ... and I sink down, down, down into a soft cloud that seems like a soft ... soft pillow... that engulfs me... as I sink down into a soft... soft... soft... deep... deep... deep... sleep.

CHAPTER 15

The Uses and Abuses of Pyschiatric Medications

Pills, Poisons, and Placebos

"**N**o thanks. . . . I don't want to be a zombie!" yelled my manic patient, almost knocking over a nearby lamp as he leapt to his feet, bug-eyed and frantically wringing his hands. He was my last patient of the day, and I had just spent the last 20 minutes explaining with precise detail the reasons he needed to continue his medication for bipolar disorder.

Medication is a tricky business. On the one hand, you have patients who want to pop a pill for whatever ails them: from hangnails to hangovers, from gas pains to growing pains, from boils to bellyaches. On the other hand, you find those patients who will do anything to avoid taking medication, even drugs that will literally save their lives. Drug abuse, including misuse of prescription drugs, was thoroughly covered in Chapter 10. The example of my manic patient represents the other extreme, those who are noncompliant to medical treatment. Studies for noncompliance in all illnesses have shown interesting findings. A national survey found that during the previous 12 months (Kripalani, Henderson, & Chiu, 2006):

- 30% of patients took prescription medications less often than prescribed.
- 26% delayed filling a prescription.
- 21% stopped taking a prescription sooner than prescribed.
- 18% never filled a prescription.
- 14% took smaller doses than prescribed.

Improving Treatment Compliance

Several methods can increase patient compliance. When adequately informed about medications, patients become more aware of the importance of taking their medications. All pharmaceutical companies have wonderful patient information material. They supply checklists, reminders, and personal testimonies. Sometimes, they even provide informative DVDs for patients. When patients know about their illness and the proper medications to treat it, compliance increases. I tell patients I want them to know more about their medications than I do. This statement enhances the doctor–patient alliance by indicating that the patient can take part in learning, knowing about, and even helping with the choice of medication.

When a patient brings in information about the medication, let them watch you read the material, indicating that you care about their opinion. Encourage patients to use the Internet. Even chat rooms that debunk medicines increase compliance as long as the patient feels free to discuss negatives with the physician. Debating pros and cons empowers patients to feel part of the medication process.

Asking questions increases compliance. Ask the patients if they take their medications. When? How often? In what situation do they forget to take their medication? Where do they keep their medication? Why do they take their medication? Can they tell how the medication works? Can they remember what they were told about the medication? Did they have a chance to read the material they were given? Do they notice any side effects? Does the medication cause them any other problems? Has another doctor prescribed medications? Which over-the-counter drugs do they take? Is it okay if family members help them remember to take the medication? The more questions you ask, the more compliance improves.

Humor helps. If you can use humor effectively, say something to the patient like the following: "Please don't take your medication—then you will have to return to the hospital, and I can make more money to buy that bass boat I've wanted."

How Medications Work

Teaching patients how their medication works—at a level that the patient can comprehend—is fundamental to patient compliance. Here is an oversimplified analogy that may help patients better understand the need for medication.

Anatomically, the brain consists of an estimated 100 billion neurons with over 100 trillion axons and 100 trillion synapses (gaps between nerve cells). To visualize this, imagine all the houses in the world jam-packed together into a single, crowded subdivision. Now, imagine that in each house, the light switches are turned on, waking up the children. The children run to the kitchen and get Mom to make some pancakes. The children also wake up

Dad, who gets busy on his Saturday morning project of rearranging the living room furniture.

The brain's neurons are the individual houses dotting the streets of the subdivision. The axons are analogous to high-voltage power cables that bring electricity to the houses. Electrical impulses travel down the cables to the gaps between the neurons, where the electrical impulses stimulate the manufacture of biochemical signals that attach to receptor sites (plugs) embedded in the cell membrane (wall of the house). These "plugs" penetrate into the "house," where tiny protein molecules called G-proteins are activated (the light switches are turned on), stimulating second messengers (the children) and having an impact on neurotransmitter function (Mom making the pancakes). Second messengers also are involved in gene expression: Dad rearranging the furniture represents the production of new genes.

Loss of function in any of these steps can lead to the manifestation of mental and emotional disorders. Medication improves function in one or more of these areas. For example, certain drugs stimulate improvement in neurotransmission; you could say that the medication makes Mom's pancakes tastier and more nutritious.

Psychopharmacology and Neurotransmission

Chemical neurotransmission alters the function of target neurons, creating cellular action and biological effects. Neurotransmission also regulates genetic expression. Experiences, education, physiological adaptations, disease, drugs, psychotherapy, and medications enhance or alter our genetic traits or tendencies through neurotransmission. Thus, genes and neurotransmission modify one another (Stahl, 2008).

The neuron and its synapses are changeable and malleable. Synaptic connections, formed at a furious rate between birth and age 6, are eliminated and restructured during pubescence and adolescence, allowing two thirds of the synapses present in childhood to survive into adulthood. Neurodevelopment experiences and genetic programming determine which connections are kept and which are destroyed. Thinking and learning provoke the release of neurotropic factors, which promote synaptic connections (Stahl, 2008).

Some neurotransmitter impulses travel from one neuron to another in milliseconds; some signals cause biochemical cascades that last for days. Chemical messages sent by one neuron to another can also transmit to sites distant from the initial synapse by diffusion (similar to transmission with cellular telephones). Thus, the brain consists of a collection of wires and cables simmering in a sophisticated "neurotransmitter soup" (Stahl, 2008).

Speed of transmission depends on the neurotransmitter. Scientists have now recognized several dozen neurotransmitters, ranging from the slow-onset, long-acting neuropeptides to the fast-acting amino acids, such as glutamate, which universally stimulates almost any neuron, and GABA (gamma-aminobutyric acid), which universally inhibits almost any neuron.

Advanced clinical psychopharmacology consists of developing a rationale for specific multiple drug use based on multiple transmission factors. Using drugs with multiple mechanisms or multiple drugs in combination will be the therapeutic rule rather than the exception (Stahl, 2008).

Medication Management

The remainder of this chapter is devoted to expanding on and synthesizing the information on medications given in preceding chapters. The accompanying charts and graphs will guide clinicians in choosing the best course of treatment for their patients.

Antidepressants and Other Medications for Depression

All antidepressants work by altering neurochemicals, primarily serotonin, norepinephrine, and dopamine, in and around the synapses in one of several ways. Some antidepressants increase neurochemicals by blocking their absorption (reuptake blockade); others act for a neurotransmitter (agonist effects) or against a neurotransmitter (antagonistic effects); still others block metabolism of the neurotransmitters or modulate messages inside the cells (second-messenger effects). The antidepressant classes are based on their actions and their side effect profile (Marangell et al., 2003).

With minor exceptions, all antidepressants are equally effective, differing primarily by their side effects and potency. Almost 70% of depressed patients respond (have a 50% reduction in symptoms) to an antidepressant within 4–6 weeks (Andreasen & Black, 2006). Only one third of patients will have an absence of depressive symptoms during their initial treatment (remission). Those patients who respond to treatment will relapse at a rate of 50% within 6–12 months if their antidepressant is stopped (Stahl, 2008).

Most patients begin to respond to antidepressants within the first 2 weeks of treatment. If the patient has failed to respond to the medication in 4 weeks, the dose should be increased, or the patient should be switched to a different class of antidepressants. Response (or failure to respond) to antidepressants mandates augmentation by adding other medications to get the patient to full remission. After complete remission of symptoms, the medications should be continued for at least 6 months to prevent relapse.

Tricyclic Antidepressants

The three-ringed compounds—tricyclic antidepressants—were developed in the 1950s when investigators serendipitously discovered that imipramine, being investigated as a treatment for schizophrenia, elevated mood but did

	TABLE 15-1		
Key Features of Tricyclic Antidepressants			
MEDICATION	**STARTING DOSE**	**THERAPEUTIC DOSE**	**SPECIAL USES AND SIDE EFFECTS**
Elavil (amitriptyline)	50 mg	100–300 mg	• Highly Anticholinergic • Highly Sedating • Irritable bowel syndrome
Anafranil (clomipramine)	25 mg	100–250 mg	• Obsessive-compulsive disorder
Tofranil (imipramine)	50 mg	100–300 mg	• Panic, enuresis
Norpramin (desipramine)	50 mg	100–300 mg	• ++ Anticholinergic • ++ Sedating
Pamelor (nortriptyline)	25 mg	50–150 mg	• Neuropathic pain • Migraine headache
Vivactil (protriptyline)	10 mg	20–60 mg	• Activating
Asendin (amoxapine)	50 mg	100–400 mg	• Metabolite has antipsychotic properties

nothing to relieve psychosis. Soon, more than half dozen tricyclics were being used to treat depression.

Elavil (amitriptyline), Tofranil (imipramine), and Sinequan (doxepin) primarily block serotonin uptake, while Norpramin (desipramine), Pamelor (nortriptyline), and Vivactil (protriptyline) primarily block norepinephrine reuptake. Clomipramine, primarily a selective serotonin reuptake inhibitor (SSRI), is used to treat obsessive-compulsive disorder (OCD) **(Table 15-1)**.

The tricyclic antidepressants are contraindicated in patients with prostate hypertrophy, closed-angle glaucoma, and heart disease. All tricyclics prolong cardiac conduction. Orthostatic hypotension is a serious complication in the frail and elderly. Dry mouth, sedation, weight gain, blurred vision, urinary hesitation, and constipation are common side effects. Although these medications are relatively inexpensive, side effects and potential for death in overdose designate them as third-line antidepressants reserved for those patients who fail to respond to other treatments.

Monoamine Oxidase Inhibitors

About the same time that the tricyclic antidepressants were being developed, psychiatrists began using monoamine oxidase inhibitors (MAOIs) to treat depression. The MAOIs work by preventing the metabolism of neurotransmitters dopamine, norepinephrine, and serotonin. They also prevent the metabolism of stimulants and a toxic amino acid, tyramine. Eating tyramine containing foods in conjunctions with taking MAOIs can produce dangerously high levels of tyramine resulting in myocardial infarction or stroke (Rea & Kilgus, 2009).

There are two types of MAOIs: Type A, found in and outside of the brain, is responsible for metabolizing tyramine (a MAOI prevents this metabolism, causing life-threatening effects); Type B, only found in the brain, produces psychotropic effects (Rea & Kilgus, 2009). Currently there are three MAOIs available in the United States (Rea & Kilgus 2009).

MAIOs With Type A and B Effects

- Nardil (phenelzine) with an initial dose of 15 mg three times daily orally that can be increased to up to 30 mg three times daily orally has both A and B effects.
- Parnate (tranylcypromine) with an initial dose of 10 mg three times daily orally that can be increased to very slowly to maximum dose of 20 mg three times daily orally has both A and B effects, with type B effects only in low doses; in antidepressant, doses above 10/mg daily orally may a also have Type A effects (Stahl, 2005).
- Eldepryl (selegiline) with an initial dose of 2.5 mg twice daily orally that can be very gradually increased to 30–60 mg orally in divided doses. Antidepressant doses may be 30 mg or higher (Stahl, 2005).
- The MAOI transdermal Emsam (selegiline) provides several unique properties over typical MAOIs. Because Emsam primarily affects MAO-B, there is little need to follow a strict tyramine-free diet (Andreasen, Black 2006). Because it is applied to the skin (every 24 hours), Emsam avoids first pass metabolism. The 6-mg patch is 10 times more potent than 10 mg of oral Eldepryl and generally requires no dose increase to be effective (Goodnick, 2007).

The MAOIs seem to work more efficiently in individuals with an unusual cluster of depressive symptoms (Andreasen & Black, 2006). These symptoms include:

- Depression associated with acute panic attacks, post-traumatic stress disorder (PTSD), or phobias.
- Depression associated with a great deal of physical complaints such as headaches, backache, and musculoskeletal pain.
- Atypical depressive features such as weight gain and hypersomnia.
- Depression associated with rejection sensitivity—those patients easily hurt by slights or rejections.

Four decades ago, case reports by Blackwell et al. (Amsterdam & Shults, 2005) made the connection among the tyramine-containing foods, MAOIs, and hypertensive crises. Eventually, a whopping 70 food items found their way onto lists restricting their use in conjunction with MAOIs. Systematic evaluations of hypertensive crises have reduced the list considerably **(Table 15-2)**.

In addition to the potential of creating a hypotensive crisis, other side effects of MAOIs include sedation, fatigue, tremor, nausea, dizziness, abdominal pain, dry mouth, headaches, dyskinesia, confusion, constipation, orthostatic hypotension, and agitation.

Selective Serotonin Reuptake Inhibitors
Pharmaceutical companies soon began looking for medications that were just as effective as the tricyclics and MAOIs but with fewer side effects. The

TABLE 15-2	
Foods and Drugs Disallowed and Allowed With MAOIs	
FOOD/DRUGS TO AVOID WITH MAOIs	**FOOD ALLOWED WITH MAOIs**
Matured or aged cheese	Processed cheese, mozzarella, ricotta cheese, cottage cheese, and yogurt
Fermented sausage, pepperoni, salami	Commercial chain-restaurant pizzas prepared with cheeses low in tyramine
Improperly stored meat, fish, pickled herring	Fresh meat, poultry, or fish
Banana peels Broad bean pods	All other fruits and vegetables (except broad bean pods and banana peels)
All tap beers	No more than two domestic bottled or canned beers; no more than one 4-fluid-ounce glass of red or white wine
Concentrated marmite (yeast), sauerkraut, soy sauce, soybeans	Brewers yeast, Baker's yeast
Tegretol; Trileptal; cold medications containing pseudoephedrine, ephedrine phenylephrine, phenylpropanolamine; amphetamines; anesthesia products	Fresh milk products (ice cream, sour cream, and yogurt) that have been stored properly; soy milk
Antidepressants, methadone, and Darvon should be avoided for 1–2 weeks because of potential serotonin syndrome	

TABLE 15-3

Selective Serotonin Reuptake Inhibitors (SSRIs)

BRAND NAME (GENERIC NAME)	SPECIAL PROPERTIES	DAILY DOSE
Prozac (fluoxetine)	Activating SSRI.	20–60 mg
Paxil-CR (paroxetine)	Sexual side effects common.	25–50 mg
Zoloft (sertraline)	Also boosts dopamine in high doses; Sigma-1 action may make Zoloft useful as an adjunct in treating psychotic depression.	50–200 mg
Celexa (citalopram)	Favorable properties for treating the elderly.	20–40 mg Inconsistent therapeutic benefits at the lower doses.
Lexapro (escitalopram)	Best-tolerated SSRI.	10–20 mg
Luvox (fluvoxamine)	Used primarily to treat OCD.	200–300 mg in divided doses.

first serotonergic agent, Desyrel (trazodone), was released in 1981, but because it produced extreme somnolence in therapeutic doses, the search for an improved antidepressant continued. The release of Prozac (fluoxetine) to the U.S. market in 1988 introduced a new class of antidepressants, the SSRIs. The ease of use and safety of the SSRIs has vaulted antidepressants to some of the most commonly prescribed drugs in the United States **(Table 15-3)**.

In addition to antidepressant effects, the SSRIs have been approved for treating panic disorder, social phobia, generalized anxiety disorder (GAD), PTSD, and OCD. Indeed, the SSRIs may be better anxiolytics than antidepressants. SSRIs appear to be relatively ineffective in perimenopausal and menopausal women who are not taking supplemental estrogens (Stahl, 2008).

Side effects, transient and dose related, include mild nausea, diarrhea, restlessness, tremor, headache, sedation, insomnia, and increased sweating. Some patients complain of weight changes, vivid dreams, or lack of motivation. Inderal (propranolol) in doses of 10–30 mg three times daily orally may alleviate tremor, and Trazodone will aid sleep.

Sexual dysfunction may be the most troubling side effect. Both men and women complain of decreased libido. Because men complain of ejaculatory delay, the SSRIs can be used to treat premature ejaculation. Women may experience anorgasmia. Wellbutrin (bupropion) or Viagra may help, as might lowering the dose or switching to another class of drugs.

Because the SSRIs inhibit cytochrome P450 isoenzymes, they may induce an increase in the blood levels of drugs that are dependent on these isoenzymes for their clearance. Celexa and Zoloft are least likely to cause drug interactions (Andreasen & Black, 2006).

Serotonin discontinuation syndrome develops after abrupt discontinuation of an SSRI. Symptoms include dizziness, malaise, nausea, paresthesias, tremor, ataxia, confusion, myoclonus, anxiety, and vivid dreaming. Symptoms usually develop 48 hours after the last dose, peak around day 4–5, and can last as long as 2 weeks. Treatment consists of restarting the medication and tapering slowly.

Serotonin syndrome, characterized by delirium, autonomic instability, myoclonus, hyperreflexia, nystagmus, akathisia, and muscle rigidity, has been reported with use of the SSRIs. Treatment begins with discontinuing the medication. The benzodiazepines and Inderal may be useful in treating serotonin syndrome.

Wellbutrin

Serotonin, the "star" neurotransmitter—the one most written about, the one most commonly known, the one impacted by the SSRIs—while decreasing anxiety, agitation, sleep disturbance, obsessions, traumatic dreams, and panic attacks, also has terrible consequences. Serotonin dampens passion, dulls the senses, decreases drive, and makes the world seem dull, stale, flat, and unprofitable.

Dopamine can, in many ways, be thought of as the counterbalance of serotonin. Dopamine, our endogenous "love potion," enhances libido, increases motivation, improves concentration, and focuses attention. Dopamine release from the presynaptic neurons during cocaine and amphetamine use produces an addicting euphoria that eventually depletes the dopamine stored in the central nervous system (CNS), leading to profound depression. Likewise, stress, a genetic predisposition, or a combination of both can produce a dopamine deficiency.

While the SSRIs are the medications of choice to increase serotonin, bupropion (Wellbutrin) boosts dopamine. The well tolerated extended release product, Wellbutrin XL, a norepinephrine dopamine reuptake inhibitor commonly prescribed for major depressive disorder, bipolar depression, attention deficit disorder, sexual dysfunction, and nicotine addiction (under the trade name Zyban), boosts neurotransmitters norepinephrine and dopamine by blocking their reuptake in the presynaptic neuron. Wellbutrin can be added to SSRIs to reverse SSRI-induced sexual dysfunction or SSRI-induced apathy. One popular combination known colloquially as "Well-oft" blends Wellbutrin with the SSRI Zoloft. This amalgamation makes pharmacological sense because in high doses Zoloft has some ability to block dopamine reuptake, giving a boost to the Wellbutrin effects.

The starting dose for Wellbutrin L is 150 mg each morning orally. After 2 weeks, the dose can be increased to 300 mg. After a month with partial response, the dose can be increased to 450 mg each morning.

Wellbutrin can activate bipolar disorder but is less likely to produce hypomania than other antidepressants. The most common undesirable side effects include insomnia, tremor, agitation, headache, and dizziness. Side effects caused by norepinephrine blockade include dry mouth, constipation, nausea, anorexia, and sweating. Most side effects go away with time. Wellbutrin may be the safest antidepressant to use during pregnancy, but the benefits of the medication must outweigh the hazards to both mother and child.

Very rarely, seizures can occur. The medication should be used cautiously in alcoholics, anorexics, and bulimics because of increased seizure risk in these patients.

Remeron

Remeron, an alpha-adrenergic receptor blocker with specific action on serotonin-2 and serotonin-3 receptors, has special advantages for a subset of the population. Because the medication causes sedation and weight gain, it is a perfect medication for nervous, sleepless, and underweight depressed patients. Remeron has fewer sexual side effects than most other antidepressants and improves normal sleep. Remeron in combination with Effexor gives a quadruple boost in serotonin and norepinephrine while double-boosting dopamine, an action that Stephen Stahl (2009) called "California rocket fuel" **(Table 15-4)**.

Serotonin-Norepinephrine Reuptake Inhibitors

Because of their effects on serotonin and norepinephrine, the SNRIs (serotonin-norepinephrine reuptake inhibitors—Effexor, Cymbalta, Pristiq) have become the drugs of initial choice in treating depressive disorders. In addition to serotonin-norepinephrine effects, the SNRIs increase dopamine in the prefrontal cortex. Recurrence prevention studies with Effexor showed low rates of recurrence (Stahl, 2008). Effexor seems to have an advantage in treating pre- and postmenopausal depressed women (Stahl, 2008).

The dual-mechanism antidepressant Effexor targets only serotonin at doses below 150 mg/day and begins to affect norepinephrine (and serotonin) at doses above 150 mg/day. Higher doses promote dopamine in the prefrontal cortex. Because of dose-dependent increases in blood pressure in about 3% of patients, blood pressure monitoring is recommended.

After the patient has been on Effexor for at least 6 months following full

TABLE 15-4			
Third Generation and Special Antidepressants			
BRAND NAME (GENERIC NAME)	**HOW THE DRUG WORKS**	**SPECIAL USES**	**DAILY DOSE**
Desyrel (Trazodone)	Serotonin 2 antagonist.	Soporific	50–600 mg
Effexor (venlafaxine)	Boosts serotonin and norepinephrine (in doses greater than 150 mg).	Energizing antidepressant; generalized anxiety; chronic pain.	75–300 mg
Cymbalta (duloxetine)	Boosts serotonin and norepinephrine in equal amounts.	Peripheral neuropathy, fibromyalgia, chronic pain, stress, urinary incontinence	60 mg
Wellbutrin XL (bupropion)	Boosts dopamine and norepinephrine.	Activating antidepressant, useful in cocaine-induced depression, improves cognitive slowing, reverses SSRI-induced sexual dysfunction, reduces craving during smoking cessation.	150–450 mg
Remeron (mirtazapine)	Blocks alpha 2 adrenergic presynaptic receptors; blocks $5\text{-}HT_{2A}$, $5\text{-}HT_{2C}$, $5\text{-}HT_3$ serotonin receptors.	Boosts usefulness of Effexor; improves appetite, insomnia, and anxiety; antiemetic.	15–45 mg

remission, a gradual reduction in the dose of Effexor is recommended rather than abrupt cessation to avoid the occurrence of discontinuation symptoms.

The expense of Pristiq (desvenlafaxine), a metabolite of Effexor, fails to justify its use until more clinical data has been collected and analyzed.

Almost 60% of patients with major depression have at least one painful physical symptom, including limb pain, backaches, joint pain, and headaches (Blumer & Heilbronn, 1984). Abnormalities of serotonin and norepinephrine contribute to an increase of painful response in depressed patients. Painful stimuli are more actively conducted up the nociceptive neurons of the spinal cord in depressed patients. In addition, the descending neurons of the spinal cord responsible for diminishing pain reception fail to work efficiently in depressed patients (Stahl, 2008). Studies have shown that the SNRIs are effective in treating certain pain syndromes that may or may not be associated with major depression. Cymbalta shows relatively equal affinity for binding to both serotonin and norepinephrine across the entire dosage range. This equal affinity for serotonin and norepinephrine seems to enable Cymbalta to be effective in treating a wider range of pain syndromes and has a more rapid onset of action than previous antidepressants.

Cymbalta appears to have several unique characteristics:

- It is a rapid-onset antidepressant.
- It seems to be an energizing antidepressant.
- It is more likely to induce full remission of symptoms rather than the partial treatment response more commonly produced by other antidepressants.
- It apparently treats pain syndromes unassociated with depression (Frampton & Plosker, 2007).

The usual starting and maintenance dose is 60 mg given in the morning. Beginning with 30 mg and taking Cymbalta after breakfast can reduce the risk of nausea, a mild side effect most commonly cited during the first week of treatment. Other side effects include insomnia, headaches, somnolence, dry mouth, and sweating. Some men taking Cymbalta have more difficulty reaching orgasm. The agent is contraindicated in those patients taking MAOIs and those with narrow-angle glaucoma, hepatic insufficiency, and end-stage renal disease. Studies have shown that Cymbalta contributes to liver disease more dangerously than Effexor, and for that reason Effexor is the drug of choice in treating depression associated with chronic pain and liver disease.

Choosing an Antidepressant

Currently three neurotransmitters—serotonin, norepinephrine, and dopamine—have been implicated as the most important neurotransmitters in depression. Depletion of these neurotransmitters causes specific symptoms that can help the physician choose which antidepressant would be the first choice for each patient. SSRIs are indicated for depression associated with anxiety syndromes; Wellbutrin is appropriate to improve motivation and pleasure. When the choice of antidepressant is in doubt, Effexor in generic form is the drug of choice, followed closely by Cymbalta, with the advantage of simple dosing but the disadvantage of higher cost (**Table 15-5, Table 15-6**).

Management of Treatment-Resistant Depression

Thirty to forty percent of depressed patients fail to achieve complete remis-

TABLE 15-5		
Symptoms of Neurotransmitter Depletion		
SEROTONIN LOSS	**NOREPINEPHRINE LOSS**	**DOPAMINE LOSS**
Anxious depression	Lethargic depression	Joyless depression
Waking during night	Restless sleep	Sleeping too much
Panic symptoms	Worry	Apathy
Obsessions and compulsions	Feeling tired all the time	No motivation
Anger, irritability	Lethargy	No pleasure
Traumatic dreams	Run down feeling	Decreased sexual drive and function
Flashbacks	Chronic pain symptoms	Poor concentration and attention

sion of depressive symptoms following adequate dosing of antidepressant medication **(Table 15-7)**.

Several treatment approaches may be effective for treatment-resistant depression (Stahl, 2008):

- If a patient has been started on an SSRI and given an adequate trial (2–4 weeks), switching to Effexor or Cymbalta to increase norepinephrine (as well as serotonin) at the synapse may induce remission. Switching to Wellbutrin SR may prove effective by increasing dopamine at the synapse.
- A combination of Effexor plus Remeron boosts antidepressant effects. Combining Effexor with Remeron often reduces the weight gain associated with Remeron.
- The combination of an antidepressant and antipsychotic significantly improves the response rate.
- The psychostimulants, such as Adderall and Ritalin, are useful in boosting the effectiveness of antidepressants.
- The mood stabilizers (lithium or Lamictal) also effectively boost the response rate to antidepressants. Lithium has been shown to reduce suicide attempts.

- Combining Effexor with Wellbutrin produces single-boost serotonin increase and a double boost of norepinephrine and dopamine.
- An antidepressant plus thyroid medication can produce remission in treatment-resistant depression.
- Estrogen replacement helps in perimenopausal and menopausal women.
- Many psychiatrists are using Provigil to augment antidepressant medications in the treatment of depression. Some are using Provigil to help treat dysthymia, a chronic low-grade depression **(Table 15-8)**.

Benzodiazepines and Other Treatments for Anxiety

The benzodiazepines work by facilitating GABA, the major soothing transmitter in the brain. The benzodiazepines attach to chloride ion channels near the GABA receptor, helping GABA open the chloride ion channel, decreasing neuronal excitability (Stahl, 2008).

Benzodiazepines, highly effective antianxiety agents, possess anticonvulsant and muscle relaxant properties. Benzodiazepines are useful in the

TABLE 15-6		
Specific Medications That Primarily Work on the "Big Three" Neurotransmitters		
SEROTONIN	**NOREPINEPHRINE**	**DOPAMINE**
Prozac	Effexor, a "pure" serotonin medication at doses below 150 mg daily; in doses higher than 150 mg, increases norepinephrine.	Wellbutrin (also boosts norepinephrine).
Paxil	Cymbalta (boosts serotonin and norepinephrine in equal amounts).	Some tricyclic medications (Vivactil).
Zoloft	Some tricyclic medications, especially Pamelor.	Effexor at the higher end of the dosage range increases dopamine in the prefrontal cortex.
Celexa	Wellbutrin.	Cymbalta increases dopamine in the prefrontal cortex.
Lexapro		Zoloft at higher doses.

TABLE 15-7

Medications to Augment Antidepressants

BRAND NAME (GENERIC NAME)	HOW THE DRUG WORKS	SPECIAL USES	DAILY ORAL DOSE
Eskalith (lithium)	Boosts the actions of monoamines.	Bipolar depression, mania	450 mg twice daily
Armour thyroid	Increases T_3 (triiodothyronine) and T_4 (thyroxine).	Hypothyroidism	Starting dose 30 mg; usual dose 60–120 mg
Estrace (estradiol)	Regulates the trimonoaminergic neurotransmitter systems.	Perimenopause and menopause symptoms	Standard dose 1 mg
Risperdal (risperidone)	Alpha 2 antagonist properties may contribute to anti-depressant actions.	Schizophrenia, psychosis, bipolar disorders, impulse control disorders	0.5–6 mg
Lamictal (lamotrigene)	Blocks sodium channels, inhibits release of glutamate.	First-line treatment option for bipolar depression	25–400 mg
Provigil (modafinil)	Enhances activity in the hypothalamic wakefulness center.	Narcolepsy, shift work sleep disorder, sleep apnea, fatigue, attention deficit disorder	200 mg once or twice daily
Adderall	Enhances dopamine actions.	Attention deficit disorder	20–60 mg

treatment of generalized anxiety, panic, social phobia, alcohol withdrawal, insomnia, acute stress, and anxiety that complicates depression. Because these medications cause drowsiness and reduce motor coordination, patients are cautioned not to drive or use dangerous machinery, especially when starting them. Alcohol potentiates the effects of the benzodiazepines. Although apparently safe in pregnancy, the benzodiazepines are secreted in breast milk, restricting breast-feeding. Abuse and addiction usually occur when these medications are used in combination with other drugs of abuse. Possessing a high index of safety, benzodiazepines rarely, if ever, prove fatal unless they are combined with alcohol or other medications in a suicide

Complete Mental Health

attempt. Rapid discontinuation of benzodiazepines mimics alcohol withdrawal.

Rebound Anxiety and Withdrawal

Benzodiazepines differ in their rate of elimination. Rebound anxiety and nervousness are more likely with the benzodiazepines with a short half-life. Patients using Xanax, for example, can experience acute anxiety between doses **(Table 15-9)**.

Abruptly discontinuing benzodiazepines results in a withdrawal syndrome characterized by acute anxiety, agitation, tremor, confusion, delirium, or convulsions. Discontinuation of Xanax must be done slowly. The withdrawal rate should be no faster than 0.5 mg every 2–3 weeks. Withdrawal from high doses of benzodiazepines may take several months.

There are few clinical reasons to taper benzodiazepines rapidly, but sometimes patients requiring surgery must temporarily discontinue taking their medications. Patients taking medications with a short half-life like Xanax and who have been placed on oral restriction can be given 1–2 mg Ativan intramuscularly every 6 hours until the patient's oral benzodiazepine can be resumed.

TABLE 15-8	
Side Effects of Selected Antidepressants	
CLASS	**SIDE EFFECTS**
Tricyclic antidepressants	Dry mouth, constipation, blurred vision, orthostatic hypotension, urinary hesitation, weight gain, heart block, lowered seizure threshold.
MAOIs	Hypertensive crisis.
SSRIs	Diarrhea, retarded ejaculation, impaired sexual satisfaction, apathy, decreased libido.
Effexor (venlafaxine)	Sexual impairment, diarrhea, dose-dependent elevation in diastolic blood pressure, withdrawal symptoms if discontinued abruptly.
Cymbalta (duloxetine)	Erectile dysfunction, delayed ejaculation, liver impairment, orgasmic dysfunction.
Remeron (mirtazapine)	Weight gain, somnolence.
Wellbutrin (bupropion)	Lowered seizure threshold.

TABLE 15-9			
Medication Half-Lives and Potency			
MEDICATION	**POTENCY**	**HALF-LIFE**	**USES**
Valium	Low	Long	Chronic anxiety in patients who fail all other treatments.
Klonopin	High	Long	First choice for panic disorder.
Librium	Low	Long	Alcohol withdrawal syndrome.
Ativan	High	Short	Acute agitation usually in combination with Risperdal (e.g., 2 mg Ativan and 2 mg Risperdal).
Xanax	High	Shortest half-life	Can cause breakthrough anxiety and acute withdrawal syndrome.

Therapeutic Dependency

The benzodiazepines are extremely effective anxiolytics and can be used effectively to treat a variety of anxiety syndromes. Concerns about dependency are sometimes overemphasized. There exist three types of dependency. *Psychological dependency* is taking a drug for the pleasure the drug gives; *physiologic dependency* is taking the medication to prevent the discomfort of withdrawal symptoms; and *therapeutic dependency* is taking the medication to mitigate symptoms.

The diabetes/insulin example can be used to better explain therapeutic dependency. A diabetic patient who has failed to respond to dietary restrictions and oral medications will require insulin to control blood sugar levels. After the insulin is adjusted, the patient begins to have normal glucose readings. If the patient stops the insulin, the blood sugars rise to dangerous levels. Is the patient addicted to insulin? Yes—the patient is *therapeutically* addicted to insulin because insulin is required to maintain health **(Table 15-10)**.

Likewise, patients who take benzodiazepines to control symptoms of anxiety or panic can be therapeutically addicted to the medication. Take away the medication and the symptoms return. Benzodiazepines can be used safely by following these guidelines:

- Avoid benzodiazepines in patients who are abusing alcohol or other substances.

- Warn about the sedating properties of the benzodiazepines.
- Document the reason for using benzodiazepine.
- Write the prescription for the exact number of pills to take the patient through the month with no more than two refills.
- Examine the patient and document findings every 3 months along with the reasons to continue using the medication.
- Once the correct dose has been determined, if the patient desires to increase the dose, slowly discontinue the benzodiazepine and treat with another medication.
- If a patient reports "losing" a prescription, accidentally flushes the medication down the commode, has the medication stolen, or the like, discontinue the medication and treat with another agent.

Benzodiazepines for the Treatment of Generalized Anxiety Disorder

Because GAD has common characteristics with other anxiety disorders and depressions, first-line treatment for GAD includes the SSRIs, SNRIs, and benzodiazepines. In the ideal world, a patient can begin, concurrently, on a benzodiazepine and an SSRI or SNRI. Because the anxiolytic effects of the antidepressant may take 6 weeks or longer to become manifest, the patient is kept on the benzodiazepine for this length of time. Then, the benzodiazepine can be tapered and discontinued. In the meantime, the patient is taught relaxation techniques and begins psychotherapy to deal with underlying emotional conflicts contributing to the anxiety.

To diminish the possibility of abuse, one of the longer-acting benzodiazepines—Valium or Librium—would be the best choice for the benzodi-

TABLE 15-10	
Dependence Potential of Benzodiazepines	
TYPE OF DEPENDENCE	**COMMENTS/EXPLANATION**
Therapeutic dependence	The medication treats clinical manifestations of panic disorder, just as insulin treats diabetes.
Psychological dependence	There is craving for the pleasurable experiences that the drug arouses. There is a compulsion to take a drug for enjoyment and emotional gratification.
Physical dependence	Physiologic symptoms occur when the drug is withdrawn: tremor; increased vital signs; acute, almost incapacitating agitation and anxiety; and, in severe cases, delirium.

azepine. A good starting dose for Valium is 5 mg twice daily orally. Lexapro, because it has the lowest side effect profile of the SSRIs, is a good choice for the anxiolytic effects of an SSRI. Lexapro started at 10 mg daily orally may need to be increased to 20 mg daily orally after 1 month to get full anxiolytic benefits.

Some patients with GAD fail to respond to the SSRIs/SNRIs. In those cases, a long-acting benzodiazepine can be used alone, or BuSpar, a partial serotonin agonist, can be tried, but in my experience BuSpar is little better than a placebo.

Benzodiazepines are contraindicated in patients with a history of substance abuse/addiction. There are several choices for those who abuse alcohol or other drugs. Trazodone (50–450 mg) can be used for sleep. The sedating antidepressant Remeron (15–30 mg at bedtime) may be helpful. The antiepileptic Neurontin (300 mg three times daily) can be tried. The antihistamine Vistaril (50–100 mg four times daily) is another choice. Sedating tricyclic antidepressants can be used **(Table 15-11)**.

Benzodiazepines for the Treatment of Panic Disorder

Again, a benzodiazepine in combination with an SSRI/SNRI is the treatment of choice for panic disorder. Although psychiatrists differ in their particular choices for these classes of medications, I like to begin the patient on Klonopin (0.5 mg two times daily) and Zoloft (50 mg daily orally). Although Klonopin is a rather long-acting benzodiazepine, indicating that twice-daily dosing would be sufficient, some patients have breakthrough panic if the drug is given less than three or four times daily. In intractable cases, the dose may need to be increased to 1–2 mg three or four times daily orally. Zoloft can be increased by 50-mg increments each month as long as the physician is alert to the activating properties of higher doses of Zoloft. Usually, 100 mg daily is sufficient.

After 6 weeks, Klonopin can be very slowly tapered and discontinued. Reducing the total daily dose by 0.25 mg each week is a good idea. Some patients will begin to have panic attacks again. In those cases, Klonopin can be continued and Zoloft gradually discontinued.

Treatment-resistant cases may require augmentation with atypical antipsychotics or mood stabilizers. Because of the strong possibility of breakthrough anxiety that is difficult to distinguish from a panic attack, Xanax is best avoided. The MAOIs can be used instead of the SSRI/benzodiazepine combination in those patients who abuse alcohol and other substances.

Medications for Social Anxiety, PTSD, and OCD

The SSRIs/SNRIs are the first-line treatment for social anxiety. Aggressive marketing has made Paxil the drug of first choice, although the other SSRIs

	TABLE 15-11		
	Medication Treatment for Anxiety Disorder		
MEDICATION	**EFFECTIVENESS**	**DOSE**	**PROBLEMS**
Benzodiazepines	Very effective for generalized anxiety disorder and panic disorder.	Depends on medication.	Can produce physiologic dependency and breakthrough anxiety, especially Xanax.
Effexor	First-line treatment for generalized anxiety; start with 75 mg daily.	Start with 75 mg daily; work up to 150–300 mg as needed.	Takes 2–4 weeks to begin working.
Paxil	First-line treatment for social anxiety.	20–40 mg daily.	Takes 2–4 weeks to begin working.
Luvox	OCD	200–300 mg daily in divided doses.	May require augmentation with mood stabilizers, antidepressants, or antipsychotics.
All of the SSRIs	Equally effective in treating anxiety disorders.	Depends on medication.	Choose by side effect profile and special properties.
Remeron	Sedating antidepressant.	15–30 mg at bedtime.	Especially useful in chronically anxious, sleepless, and thin worriers.
BuSpar	Several research studies have shown efficacy.	Start with 5 mg three times daily, work up to 20 mg three times daily.	In the real world, little better than placebo; high dropout rate, especially if patient has taken benzodiazepines in the past.

and Effexor work just as well. Benzodiazepines are a third-line choice for social anxiety.

Clinical trials failed to support the use of benzodiazepines in the treatment of PTSD (Stahl, 2008). Anger and aggression may increase when patients with PTSD take benzodiazepines. Because of their disinhibiting properties, benzodiazepines are generally contraindicated in PTSD.

Because of a strong marketing push, the SSRI Luvox seems to be the first line treatment for OCD although any SSRI works as well. The tricyclic antidepressant Anafranil is the second choice, followed by a SNRI or a MAOI. Antipsychotics and mood stabilizers can also be used in augmentation. Benzodiazepines are rarely used.

Antipsychotics

Antipsychotics are useful in the treatment of schizophrenia, brief psychotic disorder, delusional disorder, manic episodes, delirium, major depression with psychotic features, and aggressive behavior in a variety of syndromes **(Table 15-12).**

A discussion of the treatment of schizophrenia must begin with the dopamine pathways in the brain (Stahl, 2009):

- The mesolimbic dopamine pathway has a role in pleasurable sensations, the euphoria induced by drugs of abuse, and the delusions and hallucinations of psychosis.
- The mesocortical dopamine pathway involves the cognitive and affective symptoms of schizophrenia.
- The nigrostriatal dopamine pathway, part of the extrapyramidal system, controls motor function and movement.
- The tuberoinfundibular dopamine pathway controls prolactin secretion.

TABLE 15-12
Common Uses of Antipsychotics
Schizophrenia
Schizoaffective disorder
Psychotic depression
Mania and bipolar disorder
Delusional disorders
Brief psychotic disorders
Flashbacks in post-traumatic stress disorder
Aggression in mental retardation
Agitation in delirium or dementia
Tourette's disorder to diminish tics
Drug-induced psychosis
Aggression in autistic patients
Aggression in borderline personality disorders

The leading theory of schizophrenia contends that dopamine will enhance positive psychotic symptoms (delusions and hallucinations) and drugs that decrease dopamine will decrease positive symptoms. The modern designation of this theory is the "mesolimbic dopamine hypothesis of positive symptoms (delusions and hallucinations) of schizophrenia" (Stahl, 2008). An increase of dopamine activity in the mesolimbic dopamine neurons may cause aggression and hostile symptoms. Hyperactivity of the mesolimbic dopamine pathway also accounts for the hallucinations and delusions in other psychotic disorders, such as drug induced psychosis, manic psychosis, and psychotic depression, psychosis associated with dementia (Stahl, 2008).

A *deficit* of dopamine activity in projections of the mesocortical dopamine pathways may cause the negative symptoms (affective blunting, anhedonia, asociality, alogia, avolition) of schizophrenia. Theoretically *increasing* dopamine in the mesocortical dopamine pathways may improve the negative symptoms of schizophrenia (Stahl, 2008).

Deficiency in the nigrostriatal dopamine pathway causes extrapyramidal symptoms (EPS) characterized by tremor, muscle rigidity, akinesia (lack of movement), bradykinesia (slowing of movement), akathisia (motor restlessness), and dystonias. These movements, characteristic of Parkinson's disease, can also be caused by drugs that block dopamine-2 receptors in these pathways (Stahl, 2008).

Prolonged use of dopamine-2 blocking agents can result in a dopamine hypersensitivity that causes contortions of the mouth, tongue, and jaw, a condition known as tardive dyskinesia (tardive = late; dys = bad; kinesia = movements). According to Stahl (2008) about 5% of patients maintained on conventional antipsychotics will develop tardive dyskinesia every year they take the medication. That means that after 5 years of taking conventional antipsychotics 25% of patients will have developed tardive dyskinesia. Based on my experience that figure seems awfully high. Nonetheless, tardive dyskinesia is a viable threat.

Normally, dopamine neurons from in the tuberoinfundibular dopamine pathway inhibit prolactin release. A decrease in the activity of dopamine neurons cause prolactin levels to rise so that lactation occurs.

The conventional antipsychotics also called neuroleptics (because they produce motor slowness), first-generation antipsychotics, or typical antipsychotics (Haldol, Trilafon, Stelazine, Prolixin, Thorazine, Navane), work primarily by blocking the dopamine receptors in the mesolimbic pathway to reduce psychotic symptoms, but they also block dopamine throughout the brain, causing EPS, lactation, and, because they block the pleasure areas of the mesolimbic areas, worsen apathy, anhedonia, and lack of motivation.

TABLE 15-13

Typical Antipsychotic Medications

MEDICATION (GENERIC NAME)	DOSAGE RANGE (MG/DAY)
Thorazine (chlorpromazine)	200–800 orally
Prolixin (fluphenazine)	1–20 orally; decanoate = 12.5–62.5 mg IM every 2 weeks
Trilafon (perphenazine)	16–64 orally
Stelazine (trifluoperazine)	15–20 orally
Navane (thiothixene)	15–30 orally
Haldol (haloperidol)	1–40 orally; decanoate 50-200 IM every four weeks

Blocking D-2 receptors in the mesocortical pathway adds to the worsening of negative symptoms (Szabo, Gould, & Manji, 2006).

The serotonin-dopamine antagonists (SDAs), the so-called atypical antipsychotics, have largely replaced the dopamine receptor antagonists because of the multiple adverse effects produced by the typical antipsychotics. The potential for most of the SDAs to induce metabolic syndrome may encourage another look at the much less expensive conventional antipsychotics, because we are trading one set of side effects for another. A large clinical trial comparing four serotonin dopamine antagonists (SDAs) with the typical antipsychotic, Trilafon, showed little difference between the two classes (Lieberman et al., 2005) **(Table 15-13)**.

Nonetheless, the atypical antipsychotics appear to have several advantages. Both types of antipsychotics decrease the positive symptoms of schizophrenia (hallucinations, delusions, agitation), but the SDAs seem to improve socialization, pleasure, memory, and attentiveness more than the typical antipsychotics **(Table 15-14)**.

The SDAs, weaker D-2 receptor antagonists than the conventional antipsychotics, are robust serotonin-type receptor antagonists. This combination appears to expand the effects of the SDAs and reduce motor side effects, lactation, and an exacerbation of negative symptoms caused by the conventional antipsychotics (Andreasen & Black, 2006) **(Table 15-15)**.

Scientists, looking for more effective medications with fewer side effects, thought they had found the panacea with the discovery of Clozaril (clozap-

Complete Mental Health

TABLE 15-14

Atypical Antipsychotics

MEDICATION (GENERIC NAME)	DOSAGE RANGE (MG/DAY)
Clozaril (clozapine)	200–600 orally
Risperdal (risperidone)	2–6 orally; Consta = 12.5–50 mg IM every two weeks
Zyprexa (olanzapine)	5–30 orally
Seroquel (quetiapine)	300–600 orally
Geodon (ziprasidone)	80–240 orally
Abilify (aripiprazole)	5–30 orally

TABLE 15-15

Motor Side Effects of Conventional Antipsychotics

TERM	DESCRIPTION
Acute dystonic reaction	Idiosyncratic drug reaction that causes acute involuntary muscle spasms such as tongue retraction, upward eye roll, facial grimacing, muscle rigidity, and body arching.
Parkinsonian-like symptoms	Fixed facial stare, slow positional changes and body movements, shuffling gait, tremors.
Akathisia	Restlessness, fidgeting, rocking from foot to foot, pacing, inability to sit still.
Akinesia	Reduced body movements.
Tardive dyskinesia	Involuntary movements of the tongue, mouth, and occasionally the arms and trunk.

The Uses and Abuses of Pyschiatric Medications

ine), the first SDA. Certainly, the drug had remarkable effects. Patients who had been in the back wards of psychiatric units became well enough to go home and care for themselves. Unfortunately, the miracles brought misfortune. A certain number of patients (0.8%) developed a life-threatening agranulocytosis, the inability of the bone marrow to produce white blood cells, demanding assessment of a blood count each week. Almost all of the patients developed massive weight gain and drooling. Since then, other SDAs have been developed, all with their own unique problems and advantages.

Considerable evidence indicates that certain SDAs can produce rapid weight gain. At 10 weeks of therapy, weight gain for some of the SDAs can be as high as more than 10 pounds. Almost all of the weight gain is fat. The binding affinities of these drugs, especially histamine-H^1 receptors, have been implicated in weight gain by increasing hunger and decreasing satiety (American Diabetes Association, 2004) (**Table 15-16**).

Data consistently show an increased risk for diabetes in patients taking Clozaril or Zyprexa. While some studies showed a risk for diabetes with Risperdal and Seroquel, some did not. Abilify and Geodon showed no increased risk for diabetes. Clozaril and Zyprexa, which produce the greatest weight gain, are associated with the highest increase in low-density lipoprotein (LDL) cholesterol, total cholesterol, and triglycerides. Even with the increased risk of metabolic syndrome with some of the SDAs, the benefits of these medications sometimes supersede the hazards (American Diabetes Association, 2004).

Given the possibility of these adverse side effects, patients taking the SDAs merit baseline screening and ongoing monitoring. The Consensus Confer-

TABLE 15-16			
Metabolic Risk of Antipsychotic Medication			
DRUG	**WEIGHT GAIN**	**DIABETES RISK**	**INCREASED LIPIDS**
Clozaril	Very high potential	High potential	High potential
Zyprexa	Very high potential	High potential	High potential
Seroquel	High potential	Equivocal findings	Equivocal findings
Risperdal	Moderate potential	Equivocal findings	Equivocal findings
Geodon	None	None	None
Abilify	None	None	None

	Baseline	4 Weeks	8 Weeks	12 Weeks	Every Quarter	Every Year	Every 5 Years
TABLE 15-17							
Monitoring Protocol for Patients on Atypical Antipsychotics							
Personal and family history	✓					✓	
Weight	✓	✓	✓	✓	✓	✓	
Waist circumference	✓					✓	
Blood pressure	✓			✓		✓	
Glucose	✓			✓		✓	
Lipid profile	✓			✓			✓

ence (American Diabetes Association, American Psychiatric Association, American Association of Clinical Endocrinologists, North American Association for the Study of Obesity, 2004) recommended the following baseline information:

- Personal and family history of obesity, diabetes, dyslipidemia, hypertension, or cardiovascular disease.
- Weight and height to calculate the body mass index (BMI).
  - BMI of 25–29.9 = overweight
  - BMI of 30 or above = obese
- Waist circumference at the level of the umbilicus.
- Blood pressure.
  - 140/90 or greater = hypertension
- Fasting plasma glucose.
  - 100–125 mg/dL = prediabetes
  - 126 mg/dL and higher = diabetes
- Fasting lipid profile.

Obese patients or patients with hypertension, prediabetes, diabetes, or dyslipidemia merit a referral to the appropriate health care professional **(Table 15-17)**. If any of these conditions occur with follow-up monitoring, these patients should be switched to Geodon or Abilify and referred to the appropriate specialist for treatment. In switching antipsychotics, it is best to taper off the offending medication slowly while ramping up the new medication.

The following is a summary of the SDAs (J. I. Walker, 2008b):

- Clozaril (clozapine)
  - This is the breakthrough medication that led to the development of SDAs and has greatly changed the way we treat patients with psychosis.
  - Limiting factors are agranulocytosis and massive weight gain.
  - Although this medication is clearly the most effective SDA, because of serious side effects, it should be used only after the patient has failed to respond to all other medications.
- Risperdal (risperidone)
  - Risperdal is atypical at lower doses, conventional at higher doses.
  - EPS can occur if the dose is too high.
  - It elevates prolactin even at low doses.
  - Higher doses cause a decrease in therapeutic effectiveness.
  - It is a good starting medication for psychotic patients.
  - The usual dose is 1–4 mg, lower in the elderly.
  - Zyprexa (olanzapine).
  - A weight gain of 20–30 pounds is a limiting factor.
  - It may contribute to metabolic syndrome.
  - It is effective in psychotic depressions (especially in the elderly).
  - Although very effective, side effects limit its usefulness except in thin, malnourished, or anorexic patients who are depressed or psychotic.
  - Start dosage with 5 mg, lower in the elderly.
- Seroquel (quetiapine)
  - Seroquel has virtually no EPS at any dose.
  - Sedation and orthostatic hypotension are major side effects.
  - It decreases aggressiveness, hostility, and anger.
  - It is the drug of choice for those patients who have experienced EPS with other medications.
  - It is an excellent sleeping medication in low doses but is very expensive for a sleeping aid.
- Geodon (ziprasidone)
  - It causes minimal weight gain and metabolic syndrome problems.
  - It inhibits both serotonin and norepinephrine uptake, indicating usefulness in depression.
  - Its unusual side effect profile causes agitation or akathisia in some patients, sedation in others. The patient profile fails to predict side effect profile. Dose may be as high as 160–240 mg daily. Paradoxically, higher doses may reduce side effects.

- It is a versatile medication that can be used for a variety of syndromes.
- Abilify (aripiprazole)
    - Its mechanism of action is unrelated to other antipsychotics.
    - Although listed as an SDA, it is actually a third-generation antipsychotic.
    - Partial D^2, D^3, and serotonin 1^A agonist and serotonin 2^A antagonist.
    - It is a dopamine-serotonin system stabilizer.
    - It causes minimal weight gain and metabolic syndrome problems.
    - Dopamine saturation is reached at lower doses than original research indicated.
    - It can cause akathisia and agitation.
    - Usually, 5–15 mg is the correct dose to prevent agitation.
- Invega (paliperidone)
    - This is the active major metabolite of Risperdal.
    - Clinical trials lasted 6–11 weeks.
    - It is provided as an extended release tablet.
    - The dose is 3–12 mg daily.
    - It is excreted by the kidney; thus a lower dose may be given in kidney impairment.

Choosing an Antipsychotic

As an initial choice for treatment of schizophrenia or acute psychosis due to other disorders, the clinician *might* consider starting patients with 5–10 mg of Haldol at bedtime because it is so inexpensive (around 10 cents a pill). The dose may be increased to no more than 40 mg orally. Seroquel is a good choice if the patient has difficulty sleeping and is agitated. As with all these medications, deciding on the initial dose is difficult and is based on age, weight, general health, and the amount of agitation. A general starting dose for Seroquel may be 100 mg at bedtime orally working up to about 300 mg at bedtime, watching out for hypotension or excessive daytime sleepiness. The dose can be split and given 2–4 times daily depending on symptoms. An alternative to Seroquel is Risperdal, starting with 2 mg at bedtime and increasing, if necessary, to no more than 6 mg. At doses higher than 6 mg orally there is danger of excerbating psychotic symptoms. To prevent metabolic syndrome or weight gain, Geodon or Abilify may be the drugs of first choice. For Geodon, begin with 40 mg twice daily and work up to 120–240 mg. The neurochemical actions of Geodon make it an extremely attractive medication, but the dose is very difficult to regulate. Generally, the higher the dose the fewer the side effects. For withdrawn psychotic patients, Abilify is

TABLE 15-18	
Treatment of Acute Agitation in Psychotic Patients	
GEODON IM	**HALDOL IM**
Use in milder cases of agitation.	Use in severe agitation.
Dose = 10–20 mg IM.	Dose = 2–10 mg IM (lower in the elderly).
Ativan unnecessary.	Give in combination with 1–2 mg of Ativan.
Calms without obtunding.	Sedates out-of-control patients.

appropriate. Begin with 5 mg daily and work up to 15 mg. Rarely, the dose can be increased to 30 mg to control psychotic symptoms.

Mood stabilizers can help with augmentation. Rarely, a combination of antipsychotics is needed.

Agitated and out-of-control patients require high doses of Haldol combined with Ativan (try Haldol 5 mg IM and Ativan 2 mg IM). Some patients may require higher doses. The medication should be repeated every 1 to 4 hours until agitation is controlled. For less-severe agitation, Geodon 20 mg IM is an exellent choice and given every twelve hours as needed. **(Table 15-18)**.

Chronic psychotic disorders require long-term maintenance because, well, they are chronic illnesses. Most experts would agree that the risk of medication side effects is less important than the risk of relapse. Undermedicated individuals with schizophrenia risk the possibility of social deterioration with each additional relapse. (Baseline functioning gets further and further away with each relapse.)

For noncompliant patients, long-acting antipsychotic medications are recommended. Haldol decanoate 50–200 mg IM can be given once monthly; Prolixin decanoate 12.5–62.5 IM every 2 weeks. Risperdal Consta 25–50 mg IM every 2 weeks is an extremely expensive choice (about $300 per injection compared to a few dollars per injection of long acting Haldol or Prolixin).

Treatment of Antipsychotic Side Effects
Normal motor functioning requires equilibrium of dopaminergic and cholinergic neuronal activity. Antipsychotic medications cause a relative increase in acetylcholine by decreasing the action of dopamine. This acetylcholine/dopamine imbalance results in extrapyramidal symptoms (EPS). EPS

include Parkinsonian-like symptoms, acute dystonic reactions, akathisia, akinesia, and tardive dyskinesia. First-line treatment consists of reducing the dose of the medication or switching to an atypical antipsychotic, especially Seroquel, which is least likely to cause EPS **(Table 15-19)**.

The low-potency antipsychotic Thorazine can cause anticholinergic side effects such as blurred vision, dry mouth, urinary retention, and constipation. Orthostatic hypotension can occur especially with Thorazine and to a lesser degree with the SDA Seroquel, but can occur with any antipsychotic. The treatment involves lowering the dose or switching to another antipsychotic.

Neuroleptic malignant syndrome, a potentially fatal delirium characterized by the triad of symptoms of altered level of consciousness, muscular rigidity, and autonomic instability that includes hyperthermia, tachycardia, labile blood pressure, diaphoresis, incontinence, and occasional dysphagia and bowel obstruction, can be complicated by rhabdomyolysis and renal failure. Associated findings include elevated creatine phosphokinase (CPK), increased white blood cells (WBCs), and metabolic acidosis. Treatment consists of discontinuing the offending agent and transferring to the intensive care unit, where supportive care includes rehydration and cooling. Medications to treat neuroleptic malignant syndrome include benzodiazepines; bromocriptine, 100–300 mg/day orally; Dantrolene, given intravenously or orally, starting with 2–3 mg/kg divided three times a day, or amantadine, 100 mg twice a day orally.

TABLE 15-19
Treatment of Antipsychotic Side Effects

SIDE EFFECT	TREATMENT
Tardive dyskinesia	After stopping offending agent, a 3-month trial of 1,600 IU/day vitamin E.
Parkinsonian-like symptoms	Reduce dose; switch to SDA; anticholinergic medications.
Acute dystonic reaction	50 mg IM Benadryl, then 2 mg Cogentin orally twice daily for 2 weeks.
Akinesia	100–300 mg Amantadine daily (potentiates the release of dopamine in the basal ganglia, restoring the dopamine/acetylcholine balance).
Akathisia	10–20 mg propranolol three or four times daily.

The Uses and Abuses of Pyschiatric Medications

Mood Stabilizers

The following mood stabilizers are discussed next: lithium, Depakote, Lamictal, Tegretol, and other drugs for bipolar illness.

Lithium

Lithium is considered the "gold standard" for treating mania and is useful in bipolar maintenance and unipolar depression. Lithium is less effective in treating mania associated with dysphoria or mixed states and for treating patients with rapid-cycling bipolar disorder (Bowden, 1995). Lithium probably alters sodium transport across cell membranes. It also alters metabolism of serotonin and norepinephrine and reduces protein kinase C activity, which possibly affects gene expression (Stahl, 2008).

Measuring blood levels is necessary to regulate doses of lithium. Levels around 0.5 to 0.8 mEq/L may reflect the most effective dose. Levels higher than 0.8 mEq/L may cause side effects that lead to increased dropout rates (Vestergaard et al., 1998). A major problem with lithium has to do with toxicity. The therapeutic effects of the medication are close to the toxic effects. Levels above 1.6 mEq/L can cause a coarse tremor, slurred speech, staggering gait, nausea, vomiting, and dizziness. The following list summarizes information from several sources. Most of the information can be found in *Stahl's Essential Psychopharmacology: The Prescriber's Guide* (2005):

- Acute phase of illness = 600 mg three times daily to achieve level of 1–1.2 mEq/L.
- Maintenance treatment = 300 mg three times daily to achieve level of 0.5–0.8 mEq/L.
- Reaches steady-state blood level in 5 days.
- Half-life = about 24 hours.
- Kidney function tests, complete blood count (CBC), and thyroid-stimulating hormone (TSH) level initially and annually.
- If weight gain greater than 5%, evaluate blood glucose and lipids.
- Mild tremor and leukocytosis (very common).
- 20–40 mg propranolol orally two or three times daily for mild tremor.
- Euthyroid or hypothyroid goiter in 3% of patients.
- T-wave flattening and inversion.
- Severe tremor, vomiting, ataxia, slurred speech, or memory problems indicate toxicity.
- Toxicity levels (about 1.6 mEq/L or above) close to therapeutic level **(Table 15-20)**.

	LITHIUM	DEPAKOTE	LAMICTAL
TABLE 15-20			
Common Mood Stabilizers			
Indications	Acute manic episodes; bipolar depression; maintenance treatment for recurrent unipolar depression; augments antidepressant medications in the treatment of depression.	Mania, bipolar maintenance especially in mixed states or rapid cycling; agitation and aggression; migraine prophylaxis; alcohol withdrawal; may retard return to drinking.	More effective in treating depressive episodes than manic episodes; maintenance treatment for bipolar disorder.
How it works	Exact mechanism unknown; alters sodium transport and second-messenger systems.	Increases GABA, a calming neurotransmitter.	Inhibits release of glutamate, an activating neurotransmitter.
Laboratory evaluation	Kidney function, TSH, CBC.	Liver function.	None.
Blood levels	1.0–1.2 mEq/L for acute episodes; 0.5–0.8 mEq/L for maintenance.	100–125 mg/mL for acute episodes; 75–100 mg/mL for maintenance.	Not available.
Usual dose	1,800 mg acutely orally; 900 mg orally for maintenance.	10–30 times body weight acutely; 750–3,000 mg orally for maintenance.	25 mg orally for 2 weeks, 50 mg orally for 2 weeks, 100 mg orally for 2 weeks, 100–300 mg orally for maintenance.
Side effects	Mild tremor; weight gain; goiter (3% of patients); toxicity indications are nausea, vomiting, diarrhea, slurred speech, delirium.	Sedation, tremor, dizziness, ataxia, abdominal pain, nausea, vomiting, weight gain, alopecia.	Nausea, tremor, sedation, headache; rare multiorgan failure associated with Stevens-Johnson syndrome.
Other features	Reduces suicide risk.	Reduces aggression.	May take several weeks or months to optimize effects.
Treatment of side effects	Inderal for tremor.	Zinc and selenium for alopecia.	Fewer side effects than lithium or Depakote.

Depakote

Depakote (valproate), a first-line treatment option for bipolar disorder that may be best for patients with mixed states of bipolar disorder (patients who simultaneously show signs of depression and mania) or for patients with rapid-cycling bipolar disorder, is a versatile anticonvulsant that is useful in treating a wide assortment of illnesses, such as mania; bipolar disorder; migraines (for prophylaxis); complex partial seizures/atypical seizures; as adjunctive treatment in psychosis, agitation and aggression secondary to dementia; intermittent explosive disorder; mood disorder secondary to closed head injuries; aggression/agitation in personality disorders; and alcohol withdrawal symptoms. In addition, Depakote possibly delays return to drinking in chronic alcoholics.

- It increases brain concentrations of GABA, a calming neurotransmitter.
- For mania, the usual starting dose for Depakote ER is 10 times body weight (a patient weighing 150 pounds would require a starting dose of 1,500 mg).
- If necessary, the starting dose may be repeated two times within the first 24 hours of treatment for a maximum dose 30 times body weight.
- Maintenance doses to achieve stability of mood vary widely, often between 750 and 3,000 mg/day.
- Plasma drug levels range from 50 to 125 mg/mL.
- Depakote ER has fewer gastrointestinal and alopecia side effects and thus is preferred over immediate release divalproex or generic valproate.
- Side effects include sedation, tremor, dizziness, ataxia, abdominal pain, nausea, vomiting, diarrhea, and reduced appetite.
- Alopecia is a bothersome side effect in about 7% of patients; multivitamins fortified with zinc and selenium may help reduce alopecia.
- It is contraindicated in pancreatitis, liver disease, thrombocytopenia.
- Be alert for symptoms of hepatotoxicity: malaise, lethargy, edema, jaundice.
- It can cause pancreatitis marked by abdominal pain, vomiting, and anorexia.

Lamictal

Lamictal (lamotrigine), an anticonvulsant, has emerged as a popular medication for treating bipolar disorder, probably because this medication has fewer side effects than the traditional medications used to treat bipolar illness.

- Lamictal is more effective in treating depressive episodes than manic episodes.

- It inhibits the release of glutamate, an activating neurotransmitter.
- The usual dose for bipolar disorder is 100–300 mg daily.
- The dose in combination with Depakote is 100 mg daily.
- Very rarely, it causes multiorgan failure associated with Stevens-Johnson syndrome.
- To prevent Stevens-Johnson syndrome, gradually increase to therapeutic levels: 25 mg daily for 2 weeks; 50 mg daily for 2 weeks; 100 mg daily for 1 week, then taper upward as necessary.
- Because Depakote increases blood levels of Lamictal, give Lamictal every other day during titration when using both medications.
- Side effects are benign rash (found in approximately 10% of patients, as opposed to the Stevens-Johnson rash, which is exceptionally rare), nausea, vomiting, abdominal pain, constipation, sedation, blurred or double vision, dizziness, ataxia, headache, tremor, and insomnia.

Tegretol

Tegretol (carbamazepine), an anticonvulsant used in the treatment of bipolar illness, has, with the extensive use of Depakote and Lamictal, waned in popularity.

- Tegretol is generally used when the patient has failed to respond to Depakote and lithium.
- It is useful in rapid-cycling bipolar disorder.
- The starting dose is 200 mg twice daily.
- The therapeutic dose usually ranges from 600 to 1,600 mg daily to maintain blood levels of 8–12 mg/mL.
- Leukopenia and, rarely, aplastic anemia mandate periodic measurements of CBC, which limits the popularity of Tegretol.
- Watch for hyponatremia.

Other Medications for Bipolar Illness

The atypical antipsychotics have Food and Drug Administration approval for treating bipolar syndromes. The calcium channel blocker Verapamil can be useful in treating mania. The dosage that is most effective ranges from 360 to 480 mg daily in divided doses. The most common side effects are dizziness, skin flushing, and tachycardia due to its vasodilatory properties (Bigger & Hoffman, 1991).

Slightly less than 10 g/day of omega-3 fatty acids provided longer periods of remission than did placebo-controlled groups (Stoll et al., 1999). Treatment with omega-3 fatty acids should be considered experimental until more studies can be done.

A Final Word

Given inappropriately and indiscriminately, any drug is harmful. Administered appropriately, however, the benefits of medications far outweigh the hazards. Drug therapy is not the entire answer. While levels of neurotransmission can be altered with medications and thus improve neurochemical function of cells, psychotherapy is important to help patients adjust to illness and to make social and personal advances. Although medications can stabilize erratic behavior, they do little or no good for most "neurotic" behavior and personality disorders and will not help with the everyday problems of living.

TABLE 15-21				
Approved Antipsychotic Use in Bipolar Disorder				
MEDICATION	**MAINTENANCE**	**BIPOLAR MANIA**	**BIPOLAR DEPRESSION**	**MIXED SYMPTOMS OF DEPRESSIONS AND MANIA**
Risperdal		Yes, in combination with lithium or valproate.		
Risperdal Consta	Yes			
Invega				
Zyprexa	Yes	Yes	Yes, in combination with Prozac (known as Symbyax).	Yes, in combination with lithium or valproate.
Geodon		Yes		Yes
Seroquel	Yes	Yes	Yes	
Seroquel XR	Yes, with lithium or valproate	Yes		Yes
Abilify		Yes		Yes, in combination with lithium or valproate.

Data collected by Stephen Ingram, RPh, BCPP, Clinical Pharmacy Specialist in Psychiatry, July 2009.

TABLE 15-22

Summary of Medication Treatment of Bipolar Disorders

MEDICATION	SPECIAL BENEFITS OR CHALLENGES
Lithium carbonate	Mood stabilizer; useful in augmenting effects of antidepressant medication; reduces suicide attempts; close relationship exists between the therapeutic and toxic dose of the medication.
Depakote	Effective in acute mania; decreases irritability in a variety of illnesses; weight gain and hair loss are the chief side effects; scant evidence that Depakote is useful in treating depression.
Lamictal	Most effective in bipolar depression; rarely can cause a fatal rash (Stevens-Johnson syndrome).
Atypical antipsychotics	Useful as primary or adjunctive medications in treating bipolar illness.
Antidepressants	Have a high potential for inducing manic episodes in patients with bipolar illness.

CHAPTER 16

Psychotherapy
Mending Shadows

Thought field therapy (TFT) is one of several unusual psychotherapies that have witnessed rapid growth despite the absence of scientific support (Gaudiano & Herbert, 2000). TFT is a kind of psychological acupuncture in which therapists instruct their clients to tap on different body parts while thinking about their problems to relieve psychological distress. TFT is part of a larger rise in the so-called "power, energy, or neoteric therapies." These therapies share extraordinary claims of effectiveness for a wide range of psychological problems that greatly outstrip their empirical support.

On the other hand, hundreds of well-designed clinical studies have demonstrated the effectiveness of mainstream psychotherapy for a wide range of psychiatric illnesses, including depression, anxiety, post-traumatic stress disorder, substance abuse, obsessive-compulsive disorder, gambling addictions, and sexual dysfunctions **(Table 16-1)**.

Characteristics of Psychotherapy

Psychotherapy has been facetiously defined as an imprecise procedure applied to vague emotional problems with inconsistent results—mastery of this skill demands meticulous preparation. Psychotherapy, a generic term for "talking cures," is best thought of as a teaching process that helps a person learn better ways of handling life's challenges.

TABLE 16-1		
Major Schools of Psychotherapy		
TYPE OF THERAPY	**CAUSE OF CONFLICTS**	**TREATMENT STRATEGIES**
Cognitive-behavior therapy	Conflicts result from improper thinking	Change thought patterns.
Psychoanalytic therapy	Conflicts result from unconscious sexual and aggressive impulses	Relieve conflicts by discovering how unconscious impulses developed.
Insight-oriented psychotherapy	Current problems are caused by childhood emotional experiences	Understanding how past traumas are connected to present feelings and concepts.
Interpersonal therapy	Poor self-esteem causes problems in relationships	Improve self-esteem and resolve interpersonal conflicts.
Behavior therapy	Behavior patterns are conditioned by past experiences	Use reconditioning techniques to change behavior.
Short-term therapy for conflict situations	Situational crises or maladaptive personality patterns cause inter-personal difficulties	Examine personal responses and change approach to stressful situations.
Group therapy	Poor social skills	Learn and practice improved interaction with others.
Supportive therapy	Current situations that are difficult to resolve	Advice and encouragement.
Couple therapy	Distorted expectations or inappropriate behavior	Identify and alter specific target behaviors.
Family therapy	Family dysfunction	Improve communication, clarify expectations, correct inappro-priate behavior problems.

Although the various forms of psychotherapy differ in their conceptual framework, most legitimate psychotherapies have 10 elements in common that produce emotional change:

- The therapist–patient relationship—trust and rapport between physician and patient ensures a good working relationship. Truax and Carkhuff (1962) found that a favorable outcome in psychotherapy correlates with the therapist's empathy, nonpossessive warmth (caring without controlling), and honesty. The patient must be motivated to change, actively participate in the treatment process, and make reasonable sacrifices in time and fees.

- Release of tension—the opportunity to talk to an authority figure about individual frustrations and concerns contributes to emotional relief through an unburdening process that arouses hope for improvement.
- Insight—understanding the source of the problem leads to change. The therapist helps the patient clarify problems, confronts the patient concerning self-defeating behavior, maps out a plan of action to change the behavior, and encourages the patient as those changes are made.
- Reinforcement—the therapist gives positive feedback when appropriate behavior patterns are tried. Implicitly and explicitly approving productive behavior and disapproving maladaptive behavior acts as a conditioning response to change.
- Corrective emotional experience (Alexander & French, 1946)—the therapist's accepting, tolerant, and understanding attitude can counteract angry, rejecting, and demeaning parental attitudes, enabling the patient to gradually develop a better self-concept. The therapist's belief in the patient's worth as a person, what Rogers (1975) called "unconditional positive regard," enhances the patient's self-esteem and strengthens self-confidence. The therapist must walk a fine line because although the patient benefits from warm understanding and unwavering respect, overkindness and sympathy are detrimental to the patient's development of independence.
- Identification—patients tend to model themselves, consciously and unconsciously, after their therapists; thus, therapists who behave maturely set standards with which patients can identify.
- Hope and encouragement—the assurance and authority of the therapist inspires the patient's belief in the treatment process. Therapists provide encouragement through a quiet confidence, a calm resolve, and an appeal to both emotion and logic.
- Teaching—therapists teach the five ways to deal with stress known as the mature defense mechanisms:
  - Suppression—the purposeful, conscious avoidance of particular memories, desires, regrets or resentments until they can be dealt with properly (as opposed to repression, which is an unconscious concealment of problems that cause anxiety).
  - Sublimation—turning aggressive and unacceptable impulses into productive work and creativity.
  - Anticipation—being able to predict an emotional response to trigger situations so that maladaptive responses can be proactively replaced with healthier alternatives.

- Altruism—unselfish concern for the welfare of others through an emotional understanding and empathy for another person's suffering or behavior.
- Cosmic humor—the ability to laugh at life's absurdities and to take oneself less seriously.
- Practice of new coping techniques—just as it takes many hours of practice to correct an errant golf swing, correcting old patterns of personal behavior requires repetition before new techniques can be mastered.
- Experiencing success—succeeding at new ways of behaving leads to more victories in dealing with problems in the future **(Table 16-2)**.

Behavior Therapy

Behavioral therapy, derived from laboratory investigations of learning, focuses on modifying behavior by manipulating the environment (Berkowitz, 2003). Behavioral therapists believe that the environment can be shaped to change behavior, and they believe that giving rewards for good behavior in progressively small steps causes deviant behavior to disappear. As the patient begins to act differently, feelings and attitudes will subsequently change. The primary viewpoint driving this model of therapy is that *feelings follow actions.*

TABLE 16-2	
Characteristics of Good Therapists and Good Patients	
TRAITS AND QUALIFICATIONS OF A THERAPIST	**EXPECTATIONS OF THE PATIENT**
Is empathetic.	Is actively seeking help and is not forced, cajoled, or tricked into therapy.
Is emotionally warm.	Is willing to communicate openly.
Is honest.	Tells the truth.
Has a noncontrolling attitude.	Keeps appointments.
Is licensed by the state.	Is punctual.
Identifies their areas of expertise.	Pays for therapy at the time of the visit (this indicates that the patient values the therapy and is dedicated to the therapeutic process).
Has a degree in their particular field of therapy.	Follows through with assigned homework.

Or, as they say in east Texas, "You've got to put wood in the fireplace and light it before you get heat." The emotional rewards the patient obtains by achieving goals will provide the motivation he or she needs to continue the good behavior.

A behavior is something that we do, some action that we take—walking, running, talking. Thinking also can be considered a behavior because we are actively engaging the mind when we think (even those of us who do not think straight). Aside from the very few human instinctual behaviors (e.g., sleeping), most behaviors are learned, and because they are learned they can be manipulated or shaped.

A new, unfamiliar action can be learned when that action is paired with an instinctually motivating stimulus. For example, horses do not instinctively approach humans, but offering a horse a handful of corn will teach the horse to approach a human.

When learning new behavior, there are two types of motivation: to approach something desirable and to avoid something painful. In other words, motivation can be positive or negative and can be used as punishment or reward. In learning theory, approach motivations are known as reinforcing, and avoidance motivations are known as punishing (or negative reinforcements).

Behavior therapy focuses on observable actions and uses conditioning techniques to change behavior. These conditioning techniques are based on two principles:

- Classical conditioning—ring a bell each time a dog eats meat, and the dog will eventually learn to salivate with the sound of the bell even when there is no meat present.
- Operant conditioning—behavior is shaped by consequences. Reward a behavior, and it will increase; punish a behavior, and it will decrease; ignore a behavior, and it will be extinguished.

Behavior therapy works best for disorders that present with clearly overt actions, such as eating disorders, smoking, sexual dysfunction, compulsions, phobias, and conduct or oppositional disorders of children. There are a variety of behavioral techniques:

- Systematic desensitization—developed by Joseph Wolpe (1958), this technique teaches the patient to confront feared situations in a progressive, systematic manner. Patients are first taught ways of relaxing deeply while imagining the feared object or situation as vividly as they can. Say, for example, that a woman is afraid of driving in automobiles because she has been involved in an automobile accident. She is first taught relaxation techniques and then is asked to imagine seeing an automobile at a distance. The individual then gradually approaches the automobile in her imagination, imagines getting into the car, and finally imagines driving off in the automobile. Whenever the patient becomes anxious, she is asked to divert her attention and relax again. She goes through this hierarchy until she is able to master the imagined scenes without anxiety. Next, the patient goes through the hierarchy in reality. These techniques are practiced until she is actually able to drive in an automobile without fear.

- Flooding—the technique of fully and immediately exposing a patient to the feared stimulus, for example, taking a person with elevator phobia up and down an elevator without first being exposed systematically to a hierarchy of the feared situation. Virtual reality exposure seems to work just as well as the actual feared stimulus.
- Implosive therapy—patients are exposed, in their imaginations, to what they are afraid of, as vividly as they can imagine it.
- Positive reinforcement—rewarding appropriate behavior by praise or attention. This technique can be used to increase medication compliance, improve a child's study habits, or strengthen social behaviors.
- Negative reinforcement—taking away a desired object or situation when an unwanted behavior occurs.
- Extinction—ignoring unwanted behavior until it goes away or eliminating a conditioned behavior by taking away the stimulus. Dogs, for example, that have been taught to salivate when a bell rings can have the salivation extinguished by taking away the meat when the bell rings. Ignoring a child's whining is a practical example of extinction. Attention—even unfavorable attention—may be reinforcing, so to get bad behavior to go away, ignore it.
- Relaxation training—teaching a patient to control his or her emotions by learning to relax the muscles, change the breathing pattern, or meditate on a simple mantra.
- Biofeedback—provides patients with knowledge of internal body processes by using electronic instrumentation. Feedback devices convert information such as heart rate and muscle tone into light or sound signals that can be monitored by the patient. With practice, individuals are able to change autonomic functions of the body by altering feedback signals. For example, biofeedback can help relieve pain by aiding the patient's voluntary control over muscle spasm or blood flow. The bathroom scale is an example of a simple biofeedback machine.
- Modeling—the therapist performs a desired behavior, and the patient imitates the behavior. For example, after the therapist demonstrates how he or she introduces himself or herself to a stranger, the patient

TABLE 16-3

Three Ways of Relating to Each Other

AGGRESSIVE	PASSIVE	ASSERTIVE
Dominance.	Submission.	The middle way.
Imposing a person's will on another.	Fulfilling the desires of the dominant partner.	Use aggression defensively and never offensively.
Disrespect of the partner's personal boundaries.	Disrespect of one's own personal boundaries.	Respect for oneself and respect for others.

pretends the therapist is a stranger and practices introducing himself or herself to the stranger.

- Aversive control—adopted only with the consent of the patient, this technique uses unpleasant stimuli to change inappropriate behavior. For example, a child molester may be placed before a video screen, and as pictures of nude children are flashed on the screen the molester is given an unpleasant electrical shock. This rarely used form of behavior therapy requires supervision by a committee because of the ethical issues it engenders. Likewise, if the punishment fails to control the behavior in a reasonable time, the technique should be abandoned.

- Assertiveness training—a form of behavior therapy in which people are taught appropriate interpersonal responses involving direct expressions of their feelings, both positive and negative. Assertiveness training involves exploring personal preferences, role-playing, practicing using "I" statements with feedback from the therapist or the group, learning self-observation skills, and shaping behavior so that one can become comfortable with saying "no" to projects and people who interfere with one's happiness **(Table 16-3)**.

Here's an example of behavior therapy using several of the techniques described:

Mr. Solitary visits a behavior therapist because he is afraid to ask women out for a date. The therapist asks Mr. Solitary to keep a detailed log of daily activities. The therapist thoroughly studies the diary (attention is motivating, especially to Mr. Solitary who never gets attention). He notices that when Mr. Solitary comes home from work he turns on the television and watches it until he goes to bed at night. On Saturdays and Sundays, he goes fishing alone. The therapist tells Mr. Solitary to call a male friend and ask him to go fishing Saturday. If he gets a refusal, he is to call another friend and a third if necessary. Mr. Solitary says that telephoning people makes him too nervous. The therapist demonstrates how to call someone and ask him to go fishing. He then has Mr. Solitary practice by having Mr. Solitary pick up the telephone and role-play calling the therapist. If Mr. Solitary gets anxious doing this, the therapist teaches Mr. Solitary relaxation techniques. The therapist then helps Mr. Solitary make a list of three people that he thinks are most likely to go fishing with him.

When Mr. Solitary returns for the next visit, he tells the therapist that he was too nervous to follow the assignment. Mr. Solitary and the therapist practice some more and then the therapist assigns Mr. Solitary to make the calls in his presence. Between calls, the therapist helps Mr. Solitary relax. The third call produces a positive response.

On the third visit, the therapist discovers that Mr. Solitary wants a new fishing rod. The therapist establishes that Mr. Solitary will reward himself with a new fishing rod when he becomes involved in three social activities. Together, they decide on the three: Fishing with a friend on Saturday; going to church on Sunday; joining a bowling league. The therapist helps Mr. Solitary develop a detailed plan of action and has Mr. Solitary visualize the steps of attending church (where he will sit, etc.) and joining a bowling league. When Mr. Solitary has earned his new fishing rod, his next assignment is to call a woman to ask her out on a date. The reward for getting a date would be a new bowling ball. This task is rehearsed and practiced until it is mastered.

Cognitive-Behavior Therapy

Cognitive-behavior therapy (CBT), one of the most common psychotherapy techniques used in treating depression, has also been found effective in treating anxiety, eating disorders, and personality disorders. The goal of CBT is to shape a person's *thinking*, subsequently leading to behavior change. Notice the contrast with strict behavior therapy, which hypothesizes that a change in *actions* stimulates behavioral improvement.

Research studies have shown that CBT is just as effective as antidepressant medication in mild-to-moderate depression, and that CBT augments the effectiveness of antidepressant medication in severe depression (Elkin et al., 1995). Cognitive therapy also seems to prevent relapse (Fava, Rafanelli, Grandi, Conti, & Belluardo, 1998).

Each person has a particular set of cognitive patterns—the way we think and react to situations (Beck, Rush, Shaw, & Emery, 1979). Due to erroneous thinking, some of these patterns are detrimental. These patterns include:

FIGURE 16-1

Think Like a Stoic; Live a Contented Life

CBT is associated with the concepts of the Stoic philosophers who lived around the beginning of the first millennium 2000 years ago—Marcus Aurelius, Seneca, and Epictetus. The essence of CBT was summed up by these philosophers who believed they could be content whatever the circumstances: whether well fed or hungry, whether living in plenty or in want; whether admired or scorned.

- Personalization—relating negative events to oneself when there is no basis. John doesn't acknowledge Mary's greeting in the hallway. She immediately concludes John doesn't like her instead of considering he might be having a bad day or was deep in thought about something else.
- Polarized thinking—seeing things in extremes. Bumstead gets passed over for a promotion. He sees only two choices: ask for a transfer or quit. He fails to see other options, such as asking his boss for ways he can improve in his job, getting advice from a trusted friend, or seeking guidance from the human relations department.
- Selective abstraction—focusing only on a negative aspect of the situation. Webster, who is trying to make the college debate team, participates in a practice debate. At the critique, she gets many positive responses. Her professor makes a suggestion for one way to improve her closing statement. Webster ignores the positive feedback and dwells on this one comment.
- Magnification—distorting the importance of particular events. Homer is an 11th-grade center fielder who wants to earn a college athletic scholarship. He has a batting average of .340 but gets no hits during the state championship semifinal. He becomes demoral-ized and thinks his baseball career is doomed.

FIGURE 16-2

Two Fundamental Truths

- Not everything that makes us feel better is good for us.
- Not everything that hurts is bad for us.

FIGURE 16-3

Examples of the Cognitive Triad of Depression

A negative view of oneself:
"No one likes me because I'm not funny."

A negative view of the world and the environment:
"Everyone cheats."

A negative expectation of the future:
"No matter what I do, I won't succeed."

- Overgeneralization—Punch can't remember Judy's name. Punch overgeneralizes and says he can never remember anyone's name.

These cognitive structures are shaped by past and present successes and failures, our childhood emotional experiences, and our interpersonal interactions. Aaron Beck (Beck et al., 1979) identified three cognitive errors that occur in depressed people, which he called the cognitive triad of depression: a negative view of oneself, a negative view of the world and the environment, and a negative expectation of the future (**Figure 16-3**).

The goal of CBT is to identify distorted negative thinking and change the way we talk to ourselves (Wright, Beck, & Thase, 2003). Therapists can challenge destructive thought patterns by asking clarifying questions and by teaching patients to avoid negative self-talk, especially when the patient habitually overgeneralizes by peppering his speech with "shoulds," "oughts," and "musts."

Questions Cognitive-Behavior Therapists Ask
- Every time?
- Who specifically?
- Where did you hear that?
- What makes you think that?
- When will that happen?
- How do you know?
- Are your feelings based on fact?
- Will your thinking help protect your life and health?
- Will your thinking help you achieve your goals?
- Will your thinking help you avoid interpersonal conflicts?
- Will your thinking help you feel the emotions you want to feel?

FIGURE 16-4

Challenging Shoulds, Oughts, and Musts

What is the evidence for should, ought, or must?
(There is no evidence.)

How is should, ought, or must true?
(They are entirely false.)

Where is should, ought, or must etched in stone?
(They are not carved indelibly anywhere.)

CBT also incorporates treatment techniques of behavior therapy. Cognitive therapists teach patients to shape their thinking by asking them to perform the rational "ABCDs," wherein A is the activating event, B is the belief about the event, C is the consequences of the belief (not the consequences of the event), and D is the doing—the action that results from the belief. The therapist teaches the patient: "You cannot change events, but you can change your belief about the event, consequently having positive feelings and appropriate actions" **(Figure 16-5, 16-6)**.

Psychoanalytic Therapy

Psychoanalysis, based on the theories of Sigmund Freud, seeks to remove symptoms, alter maladaptive personality traits, and improve the patient's relationships with others by helping patients uncover unconscious conflicts (Ursano & Silberman, 2003). Freud found that if a patient talks in an uncontrolled and spontaneous manner (which he called *free association*), it enables the patient to become aware of unconscious thoughts and feelings. To encourage free association, the patient lies on a couch. The analyst, seated behind the couch and out of sight of the patient, limits his or her input to merely pointing out resistances that the patient uses to prevent remembering emotional conflicts from childhood. The inactivity of the analyst encourages development of a transference, in which the patient reacts to the analyst based on feelings the patient had for parents and other important people in childhood. Working through the transference material and confronting resistances gradually results in an understanding of the patient's unconscious conflicts.

Merely remembering the experiences is not enough; the patient must reflect, repeatedly thinking about the past and reliving the past during the analytic hour. The analytic setting encourages reexperiencing the fantasies, dreams, and realities of childhood with very strong emotions so that what was once emotionally harmful can be safely relived and understood.

FIGURE 16-5

Irrational Beliefs and Actions

A = **A**ctivating event—a man is about to leave for a romantic liaison. He sees a snake blocking the door of his automobile.

B = **B**elief—the snake is a cobra. If he tries to get into the car, he believes the cobra will bite him and he will die.

C = **C**onsequence of the belief—fear.

D = **D**oing—he stays at home, never consummating the relationship. He dies a lonely old man.

Psychoanalysis is lengthy (four 45-minute sessions weekly for 3 to 5 years or longer) and costly. Nevertheless, it is of benefit to psychologically minded patients who have the capacity to form relationships with other people but are overanxious, oversensitive, or obsessive about everyday things in life. In other words, individuals who need psychoanalysis the least can benefit from it the most.

The old joke goes that becoming an analyst is easy: the first year of training, you learn to say, "hmmmm." The second year, you add the phrase, "my, my." And before you graduate, you must master "tell me more." Actually, to be a psychoanalyst in the United States, one must first have an M.D., or occasionally another advanced degree, and take extensive coursework to learn the analytic process. The coursework includes a personal analysis and direct

---

FIGURE 16-6

Rational Beliefs and Actions

A = **A**ctivating event—man sees snake.

B = **B**elief—the snake is a harmless grass snake.

C = **C**onsequence of the belief—no fear.

D = **D**oing—he gets into the car and consummates his romantic liaison, eventually marrying the woman of his dreams.

Psychotherapy

supervision by a practicing analyst on four controlled cases. It generally requires the candidate to have 8 to 10 years of training following medical school before certification by an analytic institute.

Insight-Oriented Psychotherapy

Insight psychotherapy, psychodynamic therapy, psychoanalytically oriented psychotherapy, and uncovering psychotherapy are all modalities of psychotherapy based on psychoanalytic theory, but the approach differs greatly (Ursano & Silberman, 2003). Guided by the therapist, the patient gains understanding about factors affecting his or her behavior and acquires wisdom for improvement.

Typically, the patient will sit on a chair facing the therapist. The therapist talks more and is much more active than in classical psychoanalysis. There is more give and take, and the sitting position encourages conscious rather than unconscious processes. Psychotherapy tends to focus on how attitudes and behavior are related to childhood conflicts and experiences of the past. This understanding, along with the nine other elements of psychotherapy defined in this chapter, can help change behavior.

> PATIENT: I hate my job. It's just not working out. But I'm scared to try something different. Every time I try something new, I get scared, my hands sweat, and I get shaky. I'm getting nervous just thinking about going on interviews for a new job.
>
> THERAPIST: Can you remember a time in the distant past when you felt the same way?
>
> PATIENT: Let's see . . . Ahh . . .
>
> THERAPIST: Something that scared you when you were a boy, maybe?
>
> Patient: Yes. Well, . . . I remember . . . yes, when I played Little League baseball. Whenever I got up to bat, I would get real scared.
>
> THERAPIST: What were you scared of?
>
> PATIENT: Striking out.
>
> THERAPIST: How would that cause you to get anxious?
>
> PATIENT: I was afraid my father would scream at me. He always yelled at me and lectured me when I struck out.
>
> THERAPIST: Well, that explains in part why you get anxious when you try something new. You are afraid of failure and the perceived punishment you will receive if you do fail.
>
> PATIENT: Yeah. . . . Well I guess that might be right, but how does that help me now? I still get nervous when I try something new.
>
> THERAPIST: Let's look at failure through a different lens. Do you know who Babe Ruth is?
>
> PATIENT: Yes. He was the home run hitter for the Yankees. I used to remember my dad talking about him when he yelled at me.

THERAPIST: Did your dad tell you that Babe Ruth struck out more times than anyone else in the whole era of his time?

PATIENT: No. He probably didn't know about the strikeouts . . . but still I don't see how that's going to help me.

THERAPIST: Well, it may not, right away, . . . that is until you begin to look at failure in a different way. If fear keeps you from swinging you won't hit any home runs, and if you don't swing you are going to strike out with the bat on your shoulder and your dad would still yell at you. Would you rather swing or just stand there and strike out? Would you rather try something new or stay in the old job that you hate?

PATIENT: Well, I do hate my job, but I get so anxious about going through interviews for a different one . . . it would be hard to do.

THERAPIST: Yes, it will be. It will be very hard for you to do until you begin to look at failure in a different way. Somebody once said, "Failure is the successful identification of what doesn't work." What does that mean to you?

PATIENT: Well, I guess it's okay to fail if you learn from it. Do you think I can get over being scared?

THERAPIST: Certainly you can. It's just a matter of relearning and practicing—swinging repeatedly until you hit the ball. The more you swing, the less anxious you get.

PATIENT: Getting up to the plate is my problem [laughing].

THERAPIST: [Laughing.] Yes, . . . but you'll get there. This has been very interesting and helpful to me because we know in part what causes your reluctance to try something different. I hope it has been an encouragement to you, too. Think about what we discussed today and reevaluate your view of failure. We'll talk about this more during your next visit, and I'm sure we will uncover some other issues that will help you deal with your fear of trying new things. There's a lot more we can do to help you. In the meantime, keep swinging.

Patient: Thanks, doc . . . for the encouragement and all . . . I think I'm beginning to understand what you are talking about . . . maybe I can do better.

PATIENT: I know you can. See you next week. Hey [patting the patient on the back] . . . keep swinging.

Patients with a wide range of conflicts, situational crises, or maladaptive personality patterns causing interpersonal difficulties can benefit from psychotherapy. Both patient and clinician share the responsibility to maximize the efficiency and effectiveness of therapy.

Time limit and frequency of visits should be strictly followed; additional contacts (telephone calls, emergency visits) should be discouraged. If they do occur, the therapist should take care of the immediate problem but should avoid lengthy involvement to discourage more of these "emergencies." To avoid missed appointments, indicating unconscious resistance to treatment, patients should be aware that they will be charged for last-minute cancellations unless the cancellations are caused by circumstances clearly out of the patient's control. If the therapist fails to consistently set limits, the patient's goals can unconsciously be diverted from a potentially productive effort to overcome symptoms to a futile attempt to fulfill dependency needs.

Similarly, effective psychotherapy obligates the therapist to see patients punctually and to give the patient undivided attention during the sessions. Except for extreme emergencies, all interruptions should be deferred.

Several types of insight-oriented psychotherapy exist. A few of the more common modalities are described next.

Interpersonal Therapy

Interpersonal therapy (IPT), a time-limited, manual-based psychotherapy that was developed for research in the treatment of depression, proved so successful that it is being tested for the treatment of other disorders as well. Initially, IPT was limited to psychotherapy research, but now training programs are available through continuing education courses and professional workshops (see the *Clinician's Quick Guide to Interpersonal Psychotherapy* by Myrna Weissman, John Markowitz, and the late Gerald Klerman [2000]).

IPT is based on the assumption that depression generally occurs during life transitions or social conflict—divorce, loss of job, move to a new city, death of a loved one, retirement, graduation, a relationship breakup, a dispute or lawsuit, a promotion or a demotion. Helping the patient work through these conflicts is the essence of IPT (Markowitz, 2003).

The IPT therapist divides depression into three parts: symptoms (sleeping and eating disturbances, guilt, indecisiveness, loss of pleasure), social and interpersonal stressors, and enduring personality patterns of behavior. The IPT therapist avoids treating personality traits, past problems, or childhood conflicts but instead aims to understand the context in which the depressive symptoms appeared and how those symptoms relate to the current social and personal situation. The goals of therapy are to help the patient deal with the current stressors, reduce the symptoms of depression, and deal with the people and life situations that precipitated the depression.

Initially, the therapist gives a formal diagnosis, educates the patient about depression, identifies the major problem areas, informs the patient that the focus of therapy is on the current problem, discusses the goal of therapy as symptom relief rather than character change, and establishes a time limit for the therapy.

The middle phase of therapy uses specific strategies for treating the current causes of depression. These strategies help the patient cope with, work through, and resolve current problems. Four treatment situations commonly occur:

- Grief—treatment aims to facilitate the grieving process, help the patient accept the loss, and encourage the development of new relationships.
- Role disputes—treatment helps the patient manage expectations about a relationship, focusing on understanding the nature of the disagreement, clarifying current communication difficulties, and changing or expanding communication strategies.
- Role transition—treatment helps the patient give up the old role and take on a new one by encouraging the expression of emotions about the loss and facilitating the development of skills necessary for the new role.
- An interpersonal deficit (no active life event)—treatment corrects deficits in social skills, including initiating and sustaining relationships, improves communication skills (often by role-playing with the therapist), and helps the patient develop new relationships.

On termination of IPT, the therapist consolidates the strength, stability, and depth of the patient's improvement, gives suggestions on how to manage situations that require more improvement, discusses relapse prevention, and processes emotions related to the completion of therapy **(Table 16-4)**.

Short-Term Therapy for Conflict Situations

Short-term psychotherapy is ideal for helping patients work through temporary crisis situations but can also be used for a wide variety of problems, conflicts, and difficulties. Candidates for short-term conflict resolution do best when they possess the following traits:

- Normal intelligence.
- A history of work.
- The capacity to trust others.
- The ability to form a positive relationship with the therapist.
- The ability to connect symptoms with psychological causes.
- The capacity to express feelings.
- A motivation to change.
- A core conflict—difficulty with peer relationships, difficulty dealing with authority figures, excess competition, fear of success, dependence-independence conflicts, personality issues causing distress, situational crises, and the like.

TABLE 16-4		
Similarities and Differences Between CBT and IPT		
SIMILARITIES	**COGNITIVE-BEHAVIOR THERAPY**	**INTERPERSONAL THERAPY**
Time limited and last about the same number of weeks.	Addresses distorted, negative thinking.	Addresses stressful social and interpersonal conflicts.
Focus on current issues.	Relates emotions to thoughts.	Relates emotions to life events.
Can be combined with antidepressant medication.	Homework assignments can be given.	Assigns no explicit homework.
Can involve role-playing.	Focuses on thoughts.	Focuses on feelings.

At the conclusion of the first diagnostic interview, the therapist can summarize what is seen as the core conflict and establish a goal of 6 to 10 sessions, with an average visit lasting 45 minutes, to work through the conflict. Weekly sessions are appropriate for most problems; sessions that are more frequent risk development of dependency, and less-frequent sessions impair continuity.

It is essential that the therapist persistently link specific stress factors in the patient's present situation to thoughts and feelings the patient has about the core conflict. In helping the patient deal with conflict situations, the therapist employs several therapeutic techniques:

- Clarification—the therapist summarizes and sharpens the methods and techniques the patient can use to resolve the conflict. For example, the therapist might say, "During the first session, we discussed the difficulties you are having with your boss. I think that part of the reason you have difficulty getting along with him is because you considered your mother bossy, and your father seemed to want to control your every move. That is bound to affect the way you react to authority figures. We can discuss this further and see if we can figure out better ways to deal with these authority figures, your boss in particular."
- Facilitative remarks—the therapist asks insightful questions to streamline the progress of therapy, forcing the patient to think through the core issues:
    - "What ideas have occurred to you about this?"
    - "Can you be more specific?'
    - "Please give me an example."

- "In what way?"
- "Tell me more about this."
- "Can you clarify that?"
- "Is there anything else that causes you to feel that way?"
- "Compared to what?"
- "Really?"
- What, where, when, why, and how questions.

- Interpretation—ties the core conflict with the patient's personality patterns or habitual methods of dealing with stress. For example, the therapist may say, "It seems to me that your difficulties with your boss have to do with your view of authority figures—your mother and father, for example. Let's talk more about some of the other authority figures in your life and how you reacted to them." Later, the therapist might say, "You know, I'm an authority figure, too, but you treat me differently. I wonder why?"
- Dealing with resistance to change—missed appointments, intellectualization, forgetting what was said in the previous session, and silence all indicate the patient's fear and reluctance to change. The therapist can help the patient understand that no matter how stressful the current situation, learning to handle crises in a different way causes a great deal of anxiety. Helping the patient understand and deal with the anxiety can move the therapy along. For example, the therapist can say, "You know it is best for you to tell your boss exactly what will help you do better at work, but it makes you nervous to do so because you think he won't appreciate your honesty about improving your performance. What do you think he would do if you discussed this with him? What are some of the other reasons you get anxious when you try to change your behavior? What are some of the ways you can deal with that anxiety?"
- Confrontation—the therapist empathetically, warmly, and perhaps with humor challenges the patient's statements with facts that have been previously elicited. "Well, let me see . . . you told me your boss was very controlling, but in the situation you just mentioned he gave you a great deal of freedom to establish your work goals. I wonder if there is another dimension to your boss's character that we haven't yet discussed."
- Transference interpretations—patients often develop feelings about the therapist based on perceptions of significant people in their past or current situation. To confront this, the therapist can say, for example, "It seems to me that you sometimes act as if I were the high school principal who is going to punish you if you don't follow my suggestions. Do you think that is correct? Can you discuss those feelings?"

Psychotherapy

To prevent incapacitating dependence, therapy should be terminated after the core conflict has been resolved or after 10 sessions, whichever comes first. By the seventh session, the patient can be reminded that therapy will end after three more sessions. The termination of therapy can be worked through along with the core conflict by tying the patient's reaction to ending therapy to the current crisis. If the patient fails to improve following 10 sessions, a consultation for a second opinion should be sought.

Group Therapy

A limitless number of variations of group therapy are possible, including cognitive-behavior groups, dual-diagnosis groups, substance abuse groups, parenting groups, interpersonal groups, eating disorder groups, social skills training groups, supportive groups, self-help groups, cancer support groups, diabetes education groups, families of Alzheimer's patients groups, medication education groups, encounter groups, sensitivity training groups, analytically oriented groups, transactional groups, and behavioral groups. The primary thrust of Alcoholics Anonymous (AA) is group therapy. Psychiatric hospitals and community mental health centers use group therapy as one of their main therapeutic modalities.

Psychotherapy groups can be divided into three basic models (Vinogradov, Cox, & Yalom, 2003):

- Therapy by means of the group—focuses on the whole rather than on specific individuals. This type of group therapy is considered experimental and helps explain institutional dynamics and organizational change. It is rarely used in practical situations.
- Therapy in the group—focuses on one patient at a time, placing little or no emphasis on group process and group interactions. Behavior therapy groups are included in this type of group therapy.
- Therapy with the group—also known as interpersonal group therapy or interactional group therapy, therapy with the group focuses both on individual concerns and group dynamics. Interactional group therapy offers the individual a chance to examine interpersonal interactions with the help of group members and the group leader. The individual is able to learn and practice techniques for successfully relating to others and simultaneously explore intrapsychic issues. In addition, interactional group psychotherapy offers a model of self-disclosure, contact, and intimacy and allows an individual to learn that others also have fear, anger, wishes, impulses, and frustrations.

An advantage of group therapy is that it allows confrontation of character defenses by group members, while the therapist remains therapeutically

TABLE 16-5

Advantages of Group Therapy

ADVANTAGE	EXPLANATION
Improves social skills	Therapist teaches patients how to communicate more clearly and interact more effectively.
Uses modeling	Watching others interact with each other helps the patient discover which social interactions do and do not work.
Increases feedback	Getting different perspectives from several other people in a supportive environment promotes growth and change.
Uses sharing	Patient feels less isolated when others share similar feelings and behaviors.
Is safe	Therapist provides an atmosphere in which thoughts and feelings can be expressed much more easily than outside the group.
Teaches empathy	Seeing emotional pain in others allows patients to identify with those who suffer—"They feel just like I do."
Teaches the value of praise and encouragement	Seeing self-esteem grow in others when they are commended reinforces the positive aspects of honest compliments.
Improves assertiveness	The patient learns to ask directly and specifically for what is wanted.
Is less expensive	Group therapy costs a fourth to a third of individual therapy.

allied with the patient. The patient's distorted views of others are more obvious and more clearly challenged in a group **(Tables 16–5, 16-6)**.

Most groups meet once weekly for an hour to an hour and a half. The optimal number of group members is generally felt to be seven or eight patients. Group therapy is the most practical and least expensive form of psychotherapy.

Psychotherapy

TABLE 16-6

Indications, Contraindications, and Requirements for Group Therapy

INDICATIONS	CONTRAINDICATIONS	REQUIREMENTS
Personality problems	Dementia	Some degree of impulse control
Extreme dependency	Psychosis	Motivation to change
Passive-aggressive tendencies	Antisocial personality disorder	Enough reality testing to make sense of the group activity
Hostile reactions to authority figures	Extreme somatization	Empathy
Depression or anxiety (not so severe that it prevents interaction with others)	Acute mania	Psychologically minded— believes that behavior, in part, is motivated by learned emotional and cognitive reactions
Self-centered behavior	Severe narcissism	The ability to trust

Family Therapy

In the first sentence of *Anna Karenina*, Tolstoy wrote, "All happy families are alike; each unhappy family is unhappy in its own way." Likewise, family therapy, although applying common therapeutic techniques, differs for each family dynamic depending on the presentation of each case.

Family therapy was defined by Pinsof and Wynne as "any psychotherapy that directly involves family members in addition to an index patient and/or attends to the interaction among family members" (1995, p. 586). A variation of family therapy is couple therapy, an updated term for marital therapy, which includes committed unmarried couples, live-in partners, and gay and lesbian partners as well as heterosexual couples (Pinsof, Wynne, & Hambright, 1996).

Couple or family therapy (CFT) aims to open up communications and teach healthy interactions to the family. Dysfunctional communication patterns can be identified, and family members can be taught how to listen, ask questions, and respond nondefensively. Family therapy can also help when a member suffers from a chronic illness, and this illness tears apart the emotional fabric of the others, creating turmoil and hostility **(Table 16-7)**.

Complete Mental Health

Goals of CFT include:

- Building a treatment alliance with the family.
- Creating a favorable climate for change.
- Improving the empathy of each family member.
- Reframing family members' dysfunctional attempts to deal with problems as well intentioned.
- Inquiring about each family member's understanding of each other's motives.

TABLE 16-7	
Indications and Contraindications for CFT	
INDICATIONS	**CONTRAINDICATIONS**
CFT is requested.	The family denies having any family problems.
The presenting problem involves two or more family members.	The presenting problem does not have an effect on the family.
There is a sexual problem.	One partner is unwilling to stop or discuss an affair.
A family crisis is causing disruption in the family.	Crucial members of the family refuse to be or cannot be included.
A child or adolescent is the presenting problem.	Severe parental pathology is present.
An adult is being treated for a severe psychiatric illness.	One family member is paranoid, manic, psychotic, overtly aggressive, hostile, or agitated.
There is relationship disharmony.	A patient is only motivated to be treated alone.
Family caregivers for dementia patients are involved.	There are strongly held beliefs against outside intervention in the family.
Alcohol and drug abuse problems are present.	CFT is used to deny individual responsibility for personal problems.

Adapted from L. Fields, T. L. Morrison, & C. C. Beets (2003).

Psychotherapy

- Teaching observation skills.
- Teaching communication skills.
- Helping family members express feelings appropriately.
- Reducing hostility, frustration, and dejection.
- Working with individual challenges in the context of the family.
- Understanding how past relationships and events have an impact on the individual's and the family's current behavior.
- Inspiring hope.
- Teaching the traits that all happy families possess.

According to Kuzma (1992), the essential traits of a strong, happy family include:

- Commitment—putting the family first. Despite struggles, frustrations, and individual differences and desires, the marriage is rock-solid stable. In addition, in a committed family, each family member helps others in the family reach their potential.
- Appreciation—treating each other as special. Here are some words that convey appreciation:

  - I really like the way you ...
  - One of the things I like best about you is ...
  - You make me happy when you ...
  - You have a real talent for ...
  - I love you because ...
  - You make me proud when ...
  - You make me feel wonderful when you ...

- Time together—happy families don't let jobs, school, or activities steal time from the family. Schedule time together and keep it.
- Meaningful communication—spending time each day talking directly to each other.
- Religious faith—worshipping together creates family bonds.
- Playing and laughing together.
- Sharing responsibility—members can all contribute to getting the work done around the house. Caring, empathy, and emotional support can help family members get through the roughest days.
- Common interests—tennis, hiking, camping, and learning something new are just a few examples.
- Serving others—helping others less fortunate than your family can make daily personal problems seem insignificant.
- Admitting to and seeking help with problems—happy families are not problem free. We all have problems, but we shouldn't ignore them.

Complete Mental Health

Dealing with issues when they come up by listening and responding without blaming or excuse-making can prevent a communication cancer from growing. If the problem can't be solved within the family structure, happy families seek professional help.

Simple actions on the part of the therapist can make a vast difference in improving family interaction. A good therapist notices and calls attention to behavior and speech patterns that the family often overlooks. For example, a therapist noticed that when a teenager talked to his father, the father looked down, picked at his hand, or adjusted his watch. Every other sentence or two, the teenager would say, "Listen to me, Dad." The therapist intervened and asked the father to look the patient directly in the eye. Later, the teenager was asked how this direct eye contact affected him. Reasons for not looking his son in the eye (anger, insecurity) were explored with the father. As the father gradually began to feel comfortable looking his son in the eye, communication between father and son improved.

Family therapists often use creative approaches to help family members better understand one another. For example, during a session a daughter may be asked to assume the role of the mother, while the mother takes the daughter's role. These acted-out role changes help each family member empathize more with the others as they begin to experience a new set of responsibilities and difficulties. A mix of psychoeducation, insight-oriented psychotherapy, interpersonal theory, and behavior techniques are often employed in family therapy to deal with problems.

Scooter's hyperactivity required a great deal of attention from Mom and Dad that led to his 12-year-old sister, Harmony, feeling lonely and unloved. Harmony, previously studious and dependable, started wearing seductive clothes and outlandish makeup and began to neglect her studies. A crisis ensued when Harmony insisted on getting a tattoo. Family therapy resolved the issue when Mom and Dad realized that they had been so busy dealing with Scooter that they had neglected Harmony. Feelings were expressed, and specific plans were outlined to actively involve Harmony in family activities. As Harmony began getting more attention, Scooter's hyperactivity increased. This issue was dealt with by teaching the parents how to appropriately set limits on Scooter's behavior, to stop treating him like a sick child and instead treat him as a child who could learn more appropriate behavior through rewards and negative reinforcement.

Supportive Therapy

Supportive therapy involves three broad goals: reduction of suffering, improvement in social functioning, and development of the patient's work and daily living skills. The purpose of supportive therapy is not to radically change the patient's character but rather to help the patient cope with an ongoing psychiatric illness or an emotionally distressing event. Indications for supportive psychotherapy include

- A stressful event such as loss of a loved one, a serious illness, or any major loss.
- Severe anxiety.
- Severe depression.
- Persistent somatic complaints.
- Medication checks.
- Psychosis.
- Social skills training.

Because most patients in supportive therapy are taking medication (with the exceptions of social skills training and grief reactions), physicians are the therapists of choice. A great deal of the time in therapy will be spent evaluating the effects of the medication, monitoring the proper dosage, and encouraging the continued use of medication until the medication is no longer necessary. Often, medication checks can be supplemented with psychotherapy sessions generally managed by a nonphysician therapist. Psychotherapy can assist the patient in eventually being able to discontinue medication.

Supportive Therapy for Grief or Loss
Encouraging the patient to talk about regards, regrets, and resentments in an empathetic, relaxed atmosphere helps the patient work through the stages of grief or loss: denial, anger, bargaining (looking at other alternatives or possibilities encompassing the loss), depression, and acceptance.

Supportive Therapy for Anxiety
Supportive therapy for anxiety generally consists of teaching the patient relaxation techniques or autohypnosis. When the patient has learned these relatively simple procedures, the physician can help the patient identify situations that produce anxiety and can offer suggestions for managing stress-producing situations. Having the patient imagine an anxiety-producing situation while relaxed can build a resistance against anxiety.

With concurrent psychotherapy aimed at resolving the cause of anxiety, most patients can discontinue medication after working through the primary problems. A certain subset of the population does well on lifetime benzodiazepine therapy. These patients have chronic anxiety that fails to respond to therapy. Usually, these patients are lower-functioning individuals.

Supportive Therapy for Depression

Supportive therapy for patients suffering from depression consists of a combination of drug therapy and explanations. The patient can be told about the biological causes of depression and how antidepressants work. The psychological causes or contributors of depression can be discussed, and the patient can be encouraged to get back into a regular routine. "Activity cures misery" is a good aphorism.

Once-weekly sessions are established to regulate the medications, then the patient can be seen monthly until stable and then every 3 months to monitor progress. A challenge for the physician is to make certain the patient remains on medications for at least 6 months after remission of first-time symptoms and then for a lifetime if the patient has had two or more bouts with depression.

Persistent Somatic Complainers

The goal of therapy when working with persistent somatic complainers is not to cure but to help the patient avoid hospitalization and needless surgeries and procedures and reduce the amount of medication that the patient takes. Patients with multiple physical complaints should be seen weekly; 15-minute sessions are appropriate. Vital signs should be taken and heart, lungs, and reflexes evaluated. This "hands-on-approach" indicates to the patient that the physician takes the complaints seriously.

Once a trusting relationship develops, the patient can be encouraged to talk about positive situations rather than focus on physical symptoms. The opportunity to talk to an authority figure about challenges and successes contributes to emotional relief through the release of tension. The patient will particularly benefit from a physician who provides an unconditional positive regard for the patient and a corrective emotional experience. Identification with a physician who models a relaxed approach to problems can be helpful, as can encouragement to try new ways of approaching chronic interpersonal conflicts.

Because patients with somatic complaints are persistently negative, the physician must remember that family and neighbors rarely like these patients. The physician must find something in the patient's character to admire, manage the patient with equanimity, and realize that the patient has a chronic condition that is difficult to change. Approaching the patient's presentation armed with cosmic humor can help the physician support the patient's slow progress without becoming discouraged or negative.

Supportive Therapy for Psychotic Patients

The goal of supportive therapy for psychotic patients is to help the patient maintain the highest level of functioning outside the hospital. Appointments should last for no longer than 15 minutes and should be scheduled at regular intervals, varying from once or twice weekly to once or twice monthly, depending on the severity of the condition. Fifteen minutes is generally sufficient to evaluate the patient's adjustment and to offer help with any current problems. Because the psychotic patient requires structure, sessions should always begin and end on time.

Compliance to medication is essential and often is the focus of the session. The patient's resistance to taking medication can be explored, and the reason for taking medication can be explained. A simple explanation is often very helpful: "Your symptoms indicate that you have too much dopamine in the brain. That's why you hear voices. This medicine helps lower the dopamine and will help get rid of some of your troubling symptoms and keep you out of the hospital."

Social Skills Training

For patients with schizophrenia and other severe mental illnesses, community mental health teams can be helpful by visiting the patient at home to ensure medication compliance and to assist in improving activities of daily living. Patients may initially need help with grooming and hygiene—bathing, brushing teeth, washing clothes, wearing clean clothes, and eating regular, healthy meals. Sometimes, a mental health worker can help with cleaning and cooking, take the patient shopping, or assist the patient in keeping appointments with the doctor. The physician can learn about the patient's abilities and skill development by talking with the mental health worker during the patient's visit for a medication check.

Later, basic social skills can be taught—how to introduce themselves to others and talk with them appropriately, how to get along with those of the opposite sex. Many patients need basic help in learning how to manage money and government checks. As functioning improves, the patient can be taught how to establish appointments for job rehabilitation, how to apply for a job, and how to get along with others at work.

For Patients: How to Make Psychotherapy Work for You

Although no aspect of psychotherapy is easy, picking the right therapist is probably the hardest part. Choosing a therapist from the yellow pages could be hazardous to your mental health. The best way to pick a therapist is to be well informed about the various schools of psychotherapy and the variety of psychotherapists. The next thing you should do is talk to someone who has benefited from psychotherapy and ask your family physician to recommend a few therapists. Then, you need to consider exactly what you want to work on, how much time you want to spend in therapy, and how much money you can afford to pay.

If you have the time, visit with several therapists before you choose one. When selecting a therapist, look for affirmative answers to these important criteria:

- Is the therapist professionally trained and certified?
- Does the therapist demonstrate empathy and emotional warmth?
- Is the therapist trustworthy and honest?

From the very beginning of therapy, you must be completely honest in your presentation of thoughts and problems. The therapist must agree to protect the confidentiality of your revelations. In addition, stipulations of the treatment process need to be established from the onset. You need to have a clear understanding of the times that you will meet and the cost of therapy. You should also have a rough grasp of how long the therapy is going to take.

Keep your appointments. Most therapists will charge for unexcused missed appointments unless they have been caused by circumstances clearly out of your control. There are a couple of reasons for doing this. In the first place, the therapist expects to get paid—after all, this is how he or she makes a living. In the second place, therapy can be emotionally upsetting, and it is understandable to want to miss some meetings. Knowing that you are going to have to pay for missing a meeting will probably inspire you to attend even though you would rather be doing something else. Attending when you don't want to will help you see positive changes more quickly.

Likewise, you should expect that your therapist see you punctually and give you undivided attention during the sessions.

It is essential that both you and your therapist try to focus on your major conflict. It is easy to digress and talk about things that really don't bother you too much. Because you are paying for the therapy, you should try to get the most out of it by staying on the subject of your problem. Of course, this is a major part of the therapist's job—he or she will help you deal with your resistance to talk about those things that are bothering you. The therapist will assume the responsibility of helping you overcome resistance to improvement, and you will assume the responsibility to improve.

During the course of your therapy, you will invariably ruminate over things that really aren't important, forget appointments, forget what was said in previous sessions, become silent, and so forth. Don't worry about this. The therapist will nonjudgmentally point out these resistances to change and try to find out what is causing them.

Transference is another inevitable phenomenon of therapy. You can expect to develop feelings about your therapist based on reactions that you had for significant people in childhood. Thus, if you felt criticized in your childhood, you will perceive the therapist as critical. Anger, fear, affection, and sexual attraction may be a result of transference distortion. The therapist's task is to recognize these transference phenomena and interpret them to you.

When the time comes to end therapy, you will be surprised how difficult it will be to give up the therapeutic relationship. You may not end your therapy abruptly, but over the course of time, you will gradually work through what it will mean to be on your own.

Complete Mental Health

CHAPTER 17

Overcoming Emotional Illness

Making Change

The Lower Ninth Ward in New Orleans experienced calamitous flooding from Hurricane Katrina in 2005 as violent currents smashed homes and ripped them from their foundations. The storm became the costliest natural disaster in U.S. history. At least 1,836 people lost their lives in Hurricane Katrina, and many more thousands were rendered homeless (Graumann et al. and Houston, 2006).

When Katrina hit, we lived not far from Houston, Texas, an area where many refugees were being relocated. My wife volunteered to help feed and care for the victims who were temporarily housed in a local church. She recalleds commiserating with one of the Hurricane evacuees:

"That must have been the most terrible thing that ever happened to you. You lost your home. You lost your clothes and all of your possessions. You have no money. You can't get in touch with your relatives. Your friends have been displaced. What a tragedy. How will you ever recover?

The evacuee replied:

"Surely that storm was a terrible thing. I was scared and pretty well knew I was going to die. Then a boat came, and they took us to the Superdome, and it was like the devil himself had come down and was torturing us. We were all crowded together and squashed-up. People were yelling and crying. It was hot and dirty. And we all got thirsty and hungry. It smelled bad, and it seemed there was no hope for any of us. But somehow, we got rescued and taken care of. And now here I am in this nice church. We have food. And water. And air conditioning. And good people are helping us and looking after us.

Yes, that hurricane was a horrible thing, and I never want to go through anything like that again. But, you know, that hurricane—no matter all the bad things that happened—was the best thing that ever happened to me, and I am thankful for it.

I'm not discounting the bad things that happened to so many people and all the dead people and people who never will find their families, but for me that hurricane was good. If it hadn't been for Katrina, I would have been trapped in the Lower Ninth Ward for life. Before the hurricane, I had nowhere to go. I had no idea how to go. I had no money to go. I was just there, and that was my life. But the big wind came and blew me to a better way of looking at things. And now I have a new life, a new start on life. I've got possibilities. Yes, thank God for Hurricane Katrina. I've got hope."

My wife listened with tears in her eyes, marveling at this woman's perspective. The dozens of other evacuees who surrounded them in the church gym sat with their heads in their hands, despair and hopelessness etched on their weary faces. All the victims had endured the same horrific suffering, yet here was one woman who chose to think differently from the rest. Forced to change her whole life by circumstances beyond her control, she chose to embrace the future rather than wallow in misery and self-pity.

The Tragic Failure to Change

Most people aren't forced to drastically change their lives by hurricane-force winds. Conversely, they get stuck in a rut, a routine way of life that is comfortable and easy to maintain. Unfortunately, this "rut" often includes self-destructive behaviors that need to be eliminated.

Change is difficult. Some people have trouble changing because they are caught in financial, physical, or geographical traps. Let us consider those people, however, who have every opportunity to change but nonetheless continue to engage in self-defeating behavior despite ongoing negative consequences. For example, smoking, obesity, and alcohol abuse can lead to chronic illnesses and premature death. Despite ominous health warnings that are more certain than storm alerts from the National Hurricane Center, surveys by the Centers for Disease Control and Prevention (2009) showed that very few people are willing to stop their self-destructive unhealthy habits:

- 20% of American adults smoke.
- More than 30% of Americans are overweight.
- 15% of Americans are binge drinkers.
- 50–65% of Americans fail to follow their doctors' treatment recommendations.
- 10% of hospital admissions among older adults result from failure to follow doctors' directions.
- Almost one third of patients visiting a physician fail to get their prescriptions filled.
- 70% of patients receiving treatment at a community mental health center dropped out of treatment before the third visit.

Most serious attempts to maintain behavior change are unsuccessful. A University of Scranton study found that only 19% of those who had made a significant change in a problem behavior maintained the change when surveyed 2 years later (Norcross, Mrykalo, & Blagys, 2002). With this daunting news, how can we encourage others—and ourselves—to make positive changes that will last? **(Table 17-1)**.

TABLE 17-1	
Forces That Impede Change	
PSYCHOLOGICAL FORCES	**THOUGHTS AND HABITS THAT LIMIT CHANGE**
Pain versus pleasure.	The immediate pleasure of the habit (gambling) is more powerful than the delayed pain (financial ruin).
Fear of failure.	"If I change, I will feel even worse than I do now."
All-or-nothing thinking.	"I must lose 50 pounds; losing 10 pounds is unacceptable."
Unconscious conflicts—unaware of problems.	We may repeat maladaptive behavior because we fail to recognize the destructiveness of our acts.
Change is unpredictable.	The discomfort of the status quo may be preferred over the anxiety produced by change.
Resisting authority.	"I don't like anyone telling me what to do."
An undesirable habit may provide unmet needs.	Drinking relieves stress. Physical abuse provides attention. Eating fills a psychological void.

A Caveat: We Can't Change Everything
Before going any further, let me add one admonition—we can't change every-thing. For a brilliant discussion on this concept, read Seligman's book, *What You Can Change and What You Can't*. We can't change our genetics, but learned habits are possible to change. That's what this chapter is about—the things about ourselves that we can change.

Why People Change
An age-old concept suggests that two primary motivators facilitate lasting change: pursuing pleasure and avoiding pain.

- Pleasure—Realizing that new behavior patterns will produce more pleasure than maladaptive behavior patterns activates change. Believing that we can have a better life engenders different approaches. The power to visualize a successful outcome gives the courage to try new ways of doing things.
- Pain—Understanding that maladaptive behavior causes intolerable distress causes sufferers to search for alternatives. Drastic environmen-tal consequences may be required before inertia can be overcome. Imprisonment, financial ruin, homelessness, or the threat of death may be necessary before transformation occurs. Suffer may be the best motivator for change.

There are two types of pain (Lassner, Powell, & Rinnegan, 1986): imposed suffering (acts of flood, fire, famine), which comes from outside one's psyche; and elected suffering (a sense of rejection, shame, guilt, loneliness), which people inflict on themselves. Imposed suffering tends to elicit more sympa-thy than elected suffering. Either type of pain can be harvested for change. The key is attitude.

Attitude Is Everything
A familiar motivational story tells of two shoe salesmen who were given a new territory on a Pacific island. Immediately on arrival, the first salesman placed an urgent call to the home office: "Get me out of here. No one on this island wears shoes." The second salesman sent an e-mail request to the fac-tory, "Please put everybody on overtime. Will need as many shoes as you can manufacture. No one on this island has any shoes."

Attitude determines the difference between shoed or shoeless. Attitude is more critical than events. It's more significant than what has happened or what is happening. Attitude is more consequential than the past, than genetics, than education, than money. Attitude is more important than what other people think, say, or do. It is more important than appearance or talent. Attitude will make or break an individual, a home, a company, or a country.

Because attitude determines whether we are happy or unhappy, fulfilled or empty, the positive perspective assures us that we can never truly fail. A hopeful attitude guarantees internal success. Attitude—the internal altitude adjuster—determines whether we fly high or low, crash or soar, glide or slide.

A while ago, I had a pity party. I became upset with everything and everybody. Suddenly, I felt ashamed. I wasn't any better than a spoilsport. I rebuked myself: "Anybody can have a positive attitude when things are going well. It's how you act when things are going badly that determines the strength of your character. An appropriate attitude means feeling hopeful in challenging times. Stop feeling sorry for yourself. Count your blessings. Look for the good."

I shared my insight with a friend who, later that day, gave me an adhesive label to place on my bathroom mirror. Now, whenever I shave, brush my teeth, or comb my hair, I see the message: "Attitude is everything." This little reminder helps me tidy up my point of view.

Do platitudes help us live better? Do bathroom decals influence us? Are positive stories helpful? You bet! Suggestions—both positive and negative—powerfully influence our attitudes. Here's an example:

> A psychologist stood in the produce department of a grocery store. As each customer passed him, the psychologist tested his or her reaction to verbal influence. He declared to one group, "You don't like strawberries, do you?" Ninety percent of the customers agreed with his statement. He offered the next group a basket of strawberries with this assertive query, "You want some strawberries, don't you?" Half of them accepted his strawberries. He asked the third group, "Do you want one or two baskets of strawberries?" Forty percent of these customers took two baskets; 50% took one basket; and only 10% took no strawberries.

What is said to us and what we say to ourselves has a strong impact on our attitude about everything we encounter—from shoes to strawberries. So, tape those aphorisms to your refrigerator door, and, by the way, have you heard? Strawberry-colored shoes are hot items this season.

Practical Methods of Change

There are several practical methods that can be used for change. These are discussed next.

Verbalize the Positive

The mind is like a computer with a keyboard and a storage disk. Sensory input represents the keyboard. Chemical pathways in the brain's unconscious represent the brain's storage disks (Carpenter, 2009). Speaking negative words programs negative data into the storage disk called the unconscious mind. The storage disk (the unconscious mind) is unable to distinguish the truth from a lie. The unconscious believes everything that is put into it. As computer programmers say, "Garbage in, garbage out."

Check yourself. Listen consciously to everything you verbalize. Does most of your self-talk build you up or put you down? Would you type the words you say about yourself into your computer as lifelong directives?

You can reprogram your brain. The chemical pathways in your brain's unconscious can be broken down in about 21 days. Replace negative words with positive words, and the negative chemical pathways—the negative programs—will be destroyed in 21 days. If words are the most powerful destiny shaper that we control—and they are—then by governing the words that come out of our mouths, we can have a better chance of living a fulfilling life.

Learn to see something positive in everything that happens. Speak hopeful words. Never miss an opportunity to praise others. Find and verbalize the good in every situation. Show appreciation at every opportunity. Encourage the timid. Fortify the weak. Use positive words to become all you can be and to help others get the most out of life.

Teach Your Body to Work for You

Because motion creates emotion or, to put the axiom in another way, because physiology creates feelings, teach your body to give you the positive results you want. Smile (even if you don't feel like it), stand erect, walk briskly, speak rapidly, and alter the pitch and tone of your voice. When you change the way you talk, speak, and move, you become more confident, more helpful to others and, yes, happier.

Act as if you already possess the outcomes that you want to realize in your life. If you want to be a successful writer, tell yourself that you are a best-selling author. If you want to lose weight, tell yourself, "I weigh 145 slim, trim pounds."

Plan for Success

Goal-directed planning provides a framework for realizing dreams and for helping others. Goals can be achieved by following the **SMART** acronym:

- Specific goals—Goals must be specific, such as "I will write from 6–7 A.M. Monday to Saturday."
- Measurable—Goals must have a time or number so they can be measured.

- Achievable—Goals must be sensible. Anyone can write an hour daily if motivated.
- Realistic—Establishing a goal to write 8 hours daily is unlikely, unless you are Stephen King, who writes from 8 A.M. to 5 P.M. each day.
- Time oriented—Set a deadline. An absence of a specific time to accomplish your goals makes measuring your progress impossible.

Accept Responsibility

Accepting responsibility for our lives requires continual self-examination. Every time we make a decision, we would do well to ask ourselves, "Will this choice help me grow intellectually, emotionally, and spiritually, and will this choice help my loved ones grow as well?"

While intellectual, emotional, and spiritual growth requires that we assume responsibility for our own behavior, transcendence also demands that we reject responsibility that is not truly ours. We must avoid enabling and attempting to control others. We can throw a rope to a drowning man, but he must grab it himself. An eaglet doesn't learn to fly by riding the back of an eagle. We can control our thoughts and actions, but we cannot control the thoughts and actions of others.

Responsible people learn to delay gratification—put off instantaneous pleasure—to achieve spiritual, emotional, and intellectual growth. Those who have worked for something in which they believe, who have sweated and strived to achieve a task, know that there is joy in the struggle. There is, as Robert Frost wrote, "the pleasure of taking pains." Joy comes when we delay instantaneous gratification and work to become all we are capable of being.

Spiritual Change

Spiritual transformation, essential for lasting change, provides the foundation for ethical living and the modification of a maladaptive lifestyle. Finding meaning and strength beyond willpower enables us to address the difficult questions uneasily answered by science and reason alone.

The purpose of life, I think, is to grow spiritually. As we fade physically, we can grow spiritually. This is encouraging for all of us who have failed to respond to Oil of Olay.

> Though outwardly we are wasting away, yet inwardly we are being renewed day by day. For our light and momentary troubles are achieving for us an eternal glory that far outweighs them all. So, we fix our eyes not on what is seen, but on what is unseen. For what is seen is temporary, but what is unseen is eternal.
>
> —2 Corinthians 4:16–18

Do You Make Appropriate Changes to Your Life?

Make Check Mark (✓) in Appropriate Column	Little of the Time 1 point each ✓	Some of the Time 2 points each ✓	A Lot of the Time 3 points each ✓	Most of the Time 4 points each ✓
When things are terrible, I "hunker down" and ride it out.				
When little things go wrong repeatedly, I stay put.				
The pleasure I get from something that is bad for me is better than the pain it would take to change.				
If I can't change something all at once, I'm not changing.				
When I look back, I see things I could have and should have changed about my life.				
When others tell me I need to change, I resist them.				
I am a creature of habit.				
I am "wishy-washy" about change.				
When making decisions, I get concerned that I might make a mistake or fail.				
I'm afraid to try anything new.				
Multiply ✓ by the value given in each column.				

Add the total for each column to get the **Grand total** = _____

SCORING

10–14 points = Unafraid of change

15–24 points = Change is kind of scary

25–34 points = Turtle

35–40 points = Head inside the shell

A Clinician's Quiz

1. Approximately what percentage of those who had made a significant change in a problem behavior maintained the change when surveyed two years later?
2. What are the two primary motivators that facilitate lasting change?
3. Name two types of emotional pain.
4. Explain how platitudes may help us live better.
5. Name four practical methods of change and discuss each.
6. Goals can be achieved by following the SMART acronym. What word does each letter in the acronym represent?
7. Name 7 forces that impede change.
8. For you personally: Are you taking care of yourself? Are taking time off before you get exhausted? Do you have a hobby or something you look forward to each day? Is work fun for you? Are you learning not to take yourself so seriously? Are you laughing each day?
9. Another personal question: Are you joyful or happy or just getting through the day?
10. Finally: have you made a list of ten things you want to change about yourself and your situation and have you been using the pain/pleasure motivators to make those changes in persistent little steps, enjoying each step along the way?

A personal note to you: As I was looking at those last three questions, I noticed some things I would do well to work toward. So, I'm off to make those changes. See ya . . . and I do hope I will see you somewhere along life's path. Finally, I hope you enjoyed reading the book as much as I enjoyed writing it and that you will benefit from some of the words written here.

References

Abraham K. Notes on the Psychoanalytic Investigation and Treatment of Manic-Depressive Insanity and Allied Conditions. 1911. In *Selected Papers of Karl Abraham.* New York: Basic Books, 1968, pp. 137–156.

Addiction Recovery Basics. Social Drinker, Alcohol Abuse, or Alcoholic: Where do You Fit In? 2008. Retrieved July 24, 2009, from http://addictionrecoverybasics.com/2008/08/06/social-drinker-alcohol-abuse-or-alcoholic-where-do-you-fit-in/

Ader A, Cohen N. Behaviorally Conditioned Immunosuppression. *Psychosomatic Medicine* 37:333–340, 1975.

Akiskal HS. Le Spectre Bipolaire: Acquisitions ET Perspectives Cliniques. *Encephale* 21(Spec No 6):3–11, 1995.

Alcoholics Anonymous World Services (aa.org). The 12 Steps of Alcoholics Anonymous Service material for the general service office. AA World Service New York: Alcoholics Anonymous, 1939. Retrieved October 25, 2009, from http://www.aa.org/en_pdfs/smf-121_en.pdf

Alcoholics Anonymous World Services (aa.org). Alcoholism information. 2007. Retrieved July 24, 2009, from http://www.alcoholism-information.com/Alcoholism_Statistics.html

Alcoholics Victorious. The Impact of Alcohol Abuse on Modern Society. 1994. Retrieved July 25, 2009, from http://www.alcoholicsvictorious.org/faq/impact.html

Alderman CP, McCarthy LC, Marwood AC. Pharmacotherapy for Post-Traumatic Stress Disorder. *Expert Review of Clinical Pharmacology,* February 5, 2009. Retrieved July 24, 2009, from http://www.medscape.com/viewarticle/586385

Alexander J. Alcoholics Anonymous, *Saturday Evening Post,* March 1, 1941.

Alexander F. Emotional Factors in Essential Hypertension. *Psychosomatic Medicine* 1:173–179, 1939.

Alexander F, French TM. *Psychoanalytic Therapy.* New York: Ronald Press, 1946.

Alexander F, Selesnick S. *An Evaluation of Psychiatric Thought and Practice From Prehistoric Times to the Present.* New York: Harper and Row, 1996.

Alexander F. *Psychosomatic Medicine: Its Principles and Applications.* New York: W. W. Norton, 1950.

Altman N. *Hypochondriasis in Psychological Care of the Medically Ill: A Primer in Liaison Psychiatry.* Edited by Strain JJ, Grossman S. New York: Prentice Hall, 1975.

2009 Alzheimer's Disease Facts and Figures. *Alzheimer's & Dementia* 5(3):234–270, May 2009.

Ambrose SE. *Undaunted Courage.* New York: Simon & Schuster, 1996.

American Diabetes Association, American Psychiatric Association, American Association of Clinical Endocrinologists, North American Association for the Study of Obesity. Consensus development conference on antipsychotic drugs, obesity, and diabetes. *Diabetes Care* 27(2):596–601, 2004.

American Psychiatric Association. *Diagnostic and Statistical Manual of Mental Disorders, Fourth Edition.* Washington, DC: American Psychiatric Association, 1994.

American Psychiatric Association. *Diagnostic and Statistical Manual of Mental Disorders, Fourth Edition, Text Revision.* Washington, DC: American Psychiatric Association, 2000.

Amsterdam J, Shults J. MAOI efficacy and safety in advanced stage treatment-resistant depression—a retrospective study. *Journal of Affective Disorders,* 89(1):183–188, 2005.

Anderson J. Alcoholics Anonymous. *Saturday Evening Post,* March 1, 1941.

Andreasen NC. Negative versus positive schizophrenia: definition and validation. *Archives of General Psychiatry* 39:789–794, 1982.

Andreasen NC. The Diagnosis of Schizophrenia. *Schizophrenia Bulletin* 13:9–22, 1987.

Andreasen NC. Positive and Negative Symptoms in Schizophrenia: A Critical Reappraisal. *Archives of General Psychiatry* 47:615–621, 1990.

Andreasen NC, Black DW. *Introductory Textbook of Psychiatry, Fourth edition.* Washington, DC: American Psychiatric Publishing, 2006.

Angst HS. Epidémiologie du spectre bipolaire. *Encephale* 21(Spec No 6):37–42, 1995.

Aserinsky E, Kleitman N. Regularly Occurring Periods of Eye Motility and Concomitant Phenomena During Sleep. *Science* 118:273–274, 1953.

Barkley RA. *Attention Deficit Hyperactivity Disorder: A Handbook for Diagnosis and Treatment.* New York: Guilford, 1990.

Barrie JM. *Peter Pan.* New York: Viking, 1991.

Beck AT, Rush AJ, Shaw BF, Emery G. *Cognitive Therapy of Depression.* New York: Guilford, 1979.

Becker JV, Johnson BR. Sexual and gender identity disorders. In *Textbook of Clinical Psychiatry, Fourth Edition.* Edited by Hales RE, Yudofsky SC. Washington, DC: American Psychiatric Publishing, 2003, pp. 743–764.

Beattie M. *Codependent No More.* Center City, Minnesota: Hazelden, 1992

Berkowitz RI. Behavior therapies. In *Textbook of Clinical Psychiatry, Fourth Edition.* Edited by Hales RE, Yudofsky SC. Washington, DC: American Psychiatric Publishing, 2003, pp. 1225–1244.

Benson H. *The Relaxation Response.* New York: HarperCollins, 2000.

Berman JR, Berman LA, Lin H, et al. Effect of Sildenafil on Subjective and Physiologic Parameters of the Female Sexual Response in Women with Sexual Arousal Disorder. *Journal of Sex and Marital Therapy* 27:411–420, 2001.

Biederman J, Faraone S. Attention-Deficit Hyperactivity Disorder. *Lancet* 366:237–249, 2005.

Bigger JT, Hoffman BF. Antiarrhythmic drugs. In Goodman and *Gilman's The Pharmacological Basis of Therapeutics, Eighth Edition.* Edited by Gilman AG, Rall TW, Nies AS, et al. New York: Pergamon, 1991, pp. 840–873.

Bigger JT, Hoffman BF. Antiarrhythmic drugs. In Goodman and *Gilman's The Pharmacological Basis of Therapeutics, Eighth Edition.* Edited by Gilman AG, Rall TW, Nies AS, et al. New York: Pergamon, 1991, pp. 840–873.

Biology Online. Sleep and Dreams—Neurology. 2000. Retrieved July 25, 2008, from http://www.biology-online.org/8/6_sleep_dreams.htm

Blazer DG. Psychopathology of Aging. *American Family Physician,* June 1977.

Bleuler E. *Dementia Praecox or the Group of Schizophrenias.* Translated by Zinken J. New York: International Universities Press, 1950. (Original work published 1911)

Blumer D, Heilbronn M. Antidepressant Treatment for Chronic Pain: Treatment Outcome of 1,000 Patients with the Pain Prone Disorders. *Psychiatric Annals* 14:796–800, 1984.

Bourgeois JA, Seaman JS, Servis ME. Delirium, Dementia, and Amnestic Disorders. In *Textbook of Clinical Psychiatry, Fourth Edition.* Edited by Hales RE, Yudofsky SC. Washington, DC: American Psychiatric Publishing, 2003, pp. 259–308.

Bowden CL. Predictors of Response to Divalproex and Lithium [review]. *Comprehensive Psychiatry* 56(Supp 3):25–30, 1995.

Bowden CL, Brugger AM, Swann AC, et al. Efficacy of Divalproex Versus Lithium in the Treatment of Mania. The Depakote Mania Study Group. *Journal of the American Medical Association* 2171:918–924, 1994.

Braslow JT. *Mental Ills and Bodily Cures Psychiatric Treatment in the First Half of the Century.* Los Angeles: University of California Press, 1997.

Bridge JA, Iyengar S, Salary CB, et al. Clinical Response and Risk for Reported Suicidal Ideation and Suicide Attempts in Pediatric Antidepressant Treatment: A Meta-Analysis of Randomized Controlled Trials. *Journal of the American Medical Association* 297:1683–1696, 2007.

Brown SL, Steinberg RL, van Praag HM. The Pathogenesis of Depression: Reconsideration of Neurotransmitter Data. In *Handbook of Depression and Anxiety.* Edited by den Boer JA, Sitsen JMA. New York: Dekker, 1994, pp. 317–347.

Burt VK, Hendrick VC: Women's Mental Health. In *Textbook of Clinical Psychiatry, Fourth Edition.* Edited by Hales RE, Yudofsky SC. Washington, DC: American Psychiatric Publishing, 2003, pp. 1511–1533.

Cable News Network. Sleep Deprivation as Bad as Alcohol Impairment, Study Sug-

gests. September 20, 2000. Retrieved July 28, 2009, from
http://archives.cnn.com/2000/HEALTH/09/20/sleep.deprivation/

Canfield J, Hansen MV. *Chicken Soup for the Soul.* Deerfield Beach, Florida: Health Communications, Inc., 1993.

Cannon WB. *Bodily Changes in Pain, Hunger, Fear and Rage: An Account of Recent Research Into the Function of Emotional Excitement, Second Edition.* New York: Appleton-Century-Crofts, 1929.

Carey G, DiLalla DL. Personality and Psychopathology: Genetic Perspectives. *Journal of Abnormal Psychology* 103:32–43, 1994.

Carnegie D. *How to Win Friends and Influence People.* New York: Simon and Schuster, 1938.

Carpenter R. The Hippocampus and Cortex and Their Relationship to Computing. *Computational Brain,* 2009. Retrieved July 29, 2009, from
http://www.cs.utexas.edu/~dkit/Winner2.doc

Carper Jean. *Your Miracle Brain: Maximize Your Brainpower, Boost Your Memory, Lift Your Mood, Improve Your IQ and Creativity, Prevent and Reverse Mental Aging.* New York: Harper, 2001.

Cassano GB, Akiskal HS, Musetti L, et al. Psychopathology, Temperament, and Past Course in Primary Major Depressions, 2: Toward a Redefinition in Bipolarity with a New Semistructured Interview for Depression. *Psychopathology* 22: 278–288, 1989.

Centers for Disease Control and Prevention. Suicide Facts at a Glance. 2005. Retrieved June 4, 2009, from http://www.cdc.gov/injury

Centers for Disease Control and Prevention: National Center for Injury Prevention and Control. Suicide Facts at a Glance. 2007. Retrieved July 20, 2009, from http://www.cdc.gov/ncipc/dvp/suicide/SuicideDataSheet.pdf

Centers for Disease Control and Prevention. FastStats. 2009. Retrieved July 29, 2009, from http://www.cdc.gov/nchs/fastats/default.htm

Centers for Disease Control and Prevention. Alcohol use. n.d. Retrieved July 24, 2009, from http://www.alcoholism-information.com/Alcoholism_Statistics.html

Cline F, Fay J. *Parenting with Love and Logic (updated and expanded edition).* Colorado Springs, Colorado: NavPress Publishing, 2006.

Cheney M. *Tesla: A Man Out of Time.* New York: Simon and Schuster, 1981.

Children and Adults With Attention Deficit Hyperactivity Disorder. Understanding AD/HD—treatment. Children and Adults With Attention Deficit/Hyperactivity Disorder CHADD. 2008. Retrieved July 17, 2009, from
http://www.chadd.org/Content/CHADD/Understanding/Treatment/default.htm

Comfort A. *The Joy of Sex.* London: Mitchell Beazley Octopus Publishing Group, 2004.

Cousins N. *Anatomy of an Illness.* New York: W. W. Norton, 1979.

Cox JL, Murray D, Chapman G. A Controlled Study of the Onset, Duration, and Prevalence of Postnatal Depression. *British Journal of Psychiatry* 163:27–31, 1993.

Cozza SJ, Crawford GC, Dulcan MK. Treatment of Children and Adolescents. *In Textbook of Clinical Psychiatry, Fourth Edition.* Edited by Hales RE, Yudofsky SC. Washington, DC: American Psychiatric Publishing, 2003, pp. 1399–1453.

Criss T, Kilgus M. Mood disorders. In *Essential Psychopathology and Its Treatment.* Edited by Maxmen JS, Ward NG, Kilgus M. New York: W.W. Norton, 2009, pp. 331–337.

Davies LM, Lewis S, Jones, PB et al. Cost-effectiveness of First- *v.* Second-generation Antipsychotic Drugs: Results From a Randomized Controlled Trial in Schizophrenia Responding Poorly to Previous Therapy. *British Journal of Psychiatry* 191:14–22, 2007.

Department of Health and Human Services. Office of the Surgeon General. The Obesity Crisis in America. U.S. Department of Health and Human Services 2007a. Retrieved July 25, 2009, from http://www.surgeongeneral.gov/news/testimony/obesity07162003.htm

Department of Health and Human Services. Office of the Surgeon General. Overweight Children and Adolescents. U. S. Department of Health and Human Services 2007b. Retrieved July 25, 2007, from http://www.surgeongeneral.gov/topics/obesity/calltoaction/fact_adolescents.htm

Depression-guide.com. What role does genetics or family history play in bipolar disorder? n.d. Retrieved July 22, 2009, from http://www.depression-guide.com/bipolar-disorder-history.htm

Depression-help-resource.com. Famous Depressed People: You're in Good Company. Retrieved October 18, 2009 from http://www.depression-help-resource.com/articles/famous-depressed-people.htm

Dickerson FB, Lehman AF. Evidence-based Psychotherapy for Schizophrenia. *Journal of Nervous and Mental Disease* 194:3–9, 2006.

Dossey L. *Space, Time, and Medicine.* Boston: Shambahala, 1982.

Douglas VI. Cognitive Deficits in Children with Attention Deficit Hyperactivity disorder: a long-term follow-up. *Canadian Psychology* 46:23–31, 2004.

Dubovsky SL, Davies R, Dubovsky AN. Mood disorders, In the *American Psychiatric Publishing Textbook of Clinical Psychiatry, Fourth Edition.* Edited by Hales RE, Yudofsky SC. Washington, DC: American Psychiatric Publishing, 2003.

Dubovsky SL, Murphy J, Christiano J, Lee C. The Calcium Second Messenger System in Bipolar Disorders: Data Supporting New Research Directions. *Journal of Neuropsychiatry and Clinical Neurosciences* 4:3–14, 1992.

Dubovsky SL, Thomas M. Psychotic Depression: Advances in Conceptualization and Treatment. *Hospital and Community Psychiatry* 43:1189–1198, 1992.

Dunbar F. *Emotions and Bodily Changes, Third Edition.* New York: Columbia University Press, 1947.

Duvall S, Delquadri J, Ward L. A Preliminary Investigation of the Effectiveness of Home School Instructional Environments for Students with Attention-deficit/Hyperactivity disorder. *School Psychology Review* 33:140–158, 2004.

Dweck DS. The Secret to Raising Smart Kids. *Scientific American Mind,* November

28, 2007. Retrieved July 10, 2009, from http://www.scientificamerican.com/article.cfm?id=the-secret-to-raising-smart-kids

Eaton DK, Kann I, Kinchen SA, et al. Youth Risk Behavior Surveillance—United States, 2005. *Morbidity and Mortality Weekly Report* 55(No. SS-5):1–108, 2006.

Edman I. *Introduction to Don Quixote*. Translation by Ormsby J. Norwalk, CT: Easton Press, 1979.

Elkin I, Gibbons RD, Shea MT et al. Initial Severity and Differential Treatment Outcome in the National Institute of Mental Health Treatment of Depression Collaborative Research Program. *Journal of Consulting and Clinical Psychology* 63:841–847, 1995.

Elkin I, Sea MT, Watkins JT, et al. National Institute of Mental Health Treatment of Depression Collaborative Research Program: General Effectiveness of Treatments. *Archives of General Psychiatry* 46:971–982, 1989.

Endler NS. The Origins of Electroconvulsive Therapy. *Convulsive Therapy* 4:5–23, 1988.

Etherington-Smith M. *The Persistence of Memory: A Biography of Dali*. New York: Da Capo Press, 1995.

Ewing JA. Recognizing, Confronting, and Helping the Alcoholic. American Family Practice 18:107–114, 1978.

Fava GA, Rafanelli C, Grandi S, Conti S, Belluardo P et al. Prevention of Recurrent Depression with Cognitive Behavioral Therapy. *Archives of General Psychiatry* 55:861–820, 1998.

Fields L, Morrison TL, Beels CC. Couple and Family Therapy. *In Textbook of Clinical Psychiatry, Fourth Edition*. Edited by Hales RE, Yudofsky SC. Washington, DC: American Psychiatric Publishing, 2003, pp. 1373–1398.

Fitzgerald FS, Wilson E. *The Crack-Up (reissue)*. New York: New Directions, 2009.

Frampton JE, Plosker GL. Duloxetine: A Review of its Use in the Treatment of Major Depressive Disorder *CNS Drugs* 21(7):581–609, 2007.

Frankl VE. *Man's Search for Meaning*. Washington, DC: Square Press, 1964.

Friedman M, Rosenman RH. *Type A Behavior and Your Heart*. New York: Knopf, 1974.

Gabriel G: Hans Selye. *The Discovery of Stress*. BrainConnection.com. Retrieved October 23, 2009 from
http://brainconnection.positscience.com/topics/?main=fa/selye2

Gaudiano, BA, Herbert JD: Can We Really Tap Our Problems Away? A Critical Analysis of Thought Field Therapy. *Skeptical Inquirer* 24:4, July-August 2000. Retrieved October 31 from
http://www.csicop.org/si/show/can_we_really_tap_our_problems_away_a_critical_analysis_of_thought_field_th/

General Service Office of Alcoholics Anonymous. World Services Comments on AA's Triennial Surveys. December 1990. Retrieved July 24, 2009, from
http://www.aa.org/lang/en/subpage.cfm?page=222

Gershon ES. *Genetics in Manic-Depressive Illness*. Edited by Goodwin FK, Jamison KR. New York: Oxford University Press, 1990, pp. 373–401.

Gilbreth DA, Carey EG. *Cheaper by the Dozen*. New York: HarperTorch, 2003

Goleman D. *Emotional Intelligence: Why It Can Matter More Than IQ.* New York: Bantam, 1995.

Goleman D. *Working with Emotional Intelligence.* New York, Bantam, 1998

Goodnick PJ. Selegiline Transdermal System in Depression. *Expert Opinion on Pharmacotherapy* 8(1):59–64, 2007. Retrieved June 6, 2009, from http://www. Selegiline.com/transdermal-review.html

Goodwin DW. Genetic Determinants of Reinforcement from Alcohol. *In Why People Drink: Parameters of Alcohol as a Reinforcer.* Edited by Cox WM. New York: Gardner Press, 1990, pp. 37–50.

Goodwin DW. *Psychiatric Diagnosis.* New York: Oxford University Press, 1996.

Gottesman II. *Schizophrenia Genesis: The Origins of Madness.* New York: Freeman, 1999.

Graumann A, Houston T, Lawrimore J, et al. National Climatic Data Center. National Oceanic and Atmospheric Administration. Hurricane Katrina, A Climatological Perspective. Presented in Asheville, NC, October 2005, updated August 2006. Retrieved July 25, 2009, from http://www.ncdc.noaa.gov/oa/reports/tech-report-200501z.pdf

Grossberg GT, Lake JT. The Role of the Psychiatrist in Alzheimer's disease. *Journal of Clinical Psychiatry* 59(Suppl 9):3–6, 1998.

Hadjipavlou G, Mok H, Yatham LN. Bipolar II Disorder: An Overview of Recent Developments. *Canadian Journal of Psychiatry* 49:12, 2004.

Hales RE, Yudofsky SC (editors). *Textbook of Clinical Psychiatry, Fourth Edition.* Washington, DC: American Psychiatric Publishing, 2003.

Halmi KA. Eating Disorders: Anorexia Nervosa, Bulimia Nervosa, and Obesity in Infancy, Childhood, or Adolescence. In *Textbook of Clinical Psychiatry, Fourth Edition.* Edited by Hales RE, Yudofsky SC. Washington, DC: American Psychiatric Publishing, 2003, pp. 1001–1020.

Helpguide. Relaxation Techniques for Stress Relief. n.d. Retrieved July 24, 2009, from http://helpguide.org/mental/stress_relief_meditation_yoga_relaxation.htm

Henry O. *Best Short Stories.* Mineola, NY: Dover, 2002.

Ho BC, Black DW, Andreason NC, Schizophrenia and Other Psychotic Disorders. In *Textbook of Clinical Psychiatry, Fourth Edition.* Edited by Hales RE, Yudofsky SC. Washington, DC: American Psychiatric Publishing, 2003, pp. 379–438.

Hogshire J. Opium: Poppy Cultivation, Morphine, and Heroin Manufacture. 2009. Retrieved July 24, 2009, from http://opioids.com/jh/index.html

Hollander E, Simeon D. Anxiety Disorders. *In Textbook of Clinical Psychiatry, Fourth Edition.* Edited by Hales RE, Yudofsky SC. Washington, DC: American Psychiatric Publishing, 2003, pp. 379–438.

Holmes TH, Rahe RH. The Social Readjustment Rating Scale. *Journal of Psychosomatic Research* 11:213–218, 1967.

Hornek D. Franz Kafka Biography. 2005. Retrieved July 25, 2009, from http://www.kafka-franz.com/kafka-Biography.htm

Ibsen H. *A Doll's House and Other Plays, First English Edition.* New York: Lovell, 1889.

Ingram, Stephen, personal communication.

Jamison KR. *Touched With Fire: Manic-Depressive Illness and the Artistic Temperament.* New York: Free Press, 1994.

Jamison KR. Manic-Depressive Illness, Genes, and Creativity. *In Genetics and Mental Illness: Evolving Issues for Research and Society.* Edited by Hall LL. New York: Plenum, 1996, pp. 111–132.

Jennings P, Brewster T. *The Century.* New York: Doubleday, 1998.

Jordan A. Academic Success Strategies for Adolescents with Learning Disabilities and ADHD. *Child Language Teaching and Therapy* 20:322–323, 2004.

Kadesjo B, Gillberg C. The Comorbidity of ADHD in the General Population of Swedish School-Age Children. *Journal of Child Psychology and Psychiatry and Allied Disciplines* 42:487–492, 2001.

Kaplan HS. *The New Sex Therapy: Active Treatment of Sexual Dysfunctions.* New York: Brunner/Mazel, 1974.

Kilgus M, Adams F. Disorders Usually First Diagnosed in Infancy, Childhood, or Adolescence. In *Essential Psychopathology and Its Treatment. In Essential Psychopathology and Its Treatment.* Edited by Maxmen JS, Ward NG, Kilgus M. New York: W.W. Norton, 2009, pp. 583–662.

Kilgus M. Factitious disorders. In *Essential Psychopathology and Its Treatment.* Edited by Maxmen JS, Ward NG, Kilgus M. New York: W.W. Norton, 2009, pp. 438–443

Kim-Miller M. Hydration and Dementia. LightBridge Health Care Research, January 31, 2000. Retrieved October 25, 2009, from http://www.lightbridgehealthcare.com/2303.xml

King 3A. Pain disorders. In *Textbook of Clinical Psychiatry, Fourth Edition.* Edited by Hales RE, Yudofsky SC. Washington, DC: American Psychiatric Publishing, 2003, pp. 1023–1043.

Knowles JA. Genetics. In *Textbook of Clinical Psychiatry, Fourth Edition.* Edited by Hales RE, Yudofsky SC. Washington, DC: American Psychiatric Publishing, 2003, pp. 3–65.

Knutson KL, Ryden AM, Mander BA, Van Cauter E et al. Role of Sleep Duration and Quality in the Risk and Severity of Type 2 Diabetes Mellitus. *Archives of Internal Medicine* 166:1768–1774, 2006.

Koenigsberg HW, Kaplan RD, Gilmore MM, Cooper AM. The Relationship Between Syndrome and Personality Disorder in DSM-III Experience with 2,462 Patients. *American Journal of Psychiatry* 142:207–212, 1985.

Kolb LC. *Modern Clinical Psychiatry.* Philadelphia: Saunders, 1977.

Kraepelin E. *Manic-Depressive Insanity and Paranoia.* Translated by Barclay RM. Edinburgh, UK: Livingstone, 1921.

Kripalani S, Henderson L, Chiu EY, et al. Predictors of Medication Self-

Management Skill in a Low Literacy Population. *Journal of General Internal Medicine* 21(8):852–856, 2006.

Kulkin S. *The DISC Personality System: Enhance Communication and Relationships.* New Castle, PA: Institute of Motivational Living, 2002.

Kuzma K. What Makes a Strong, Happy Family?—Essential traits for happiness. *Vibrant Life,* January–February 1992. Retrieved July 4, 2009, from http://www.highbeam.com/doc/1G1-11702650.html

Lachar BL. Coronary-Prone Behavior: Type A Behavior Revisited. *Texas Heart Institute Journal* 20:143–151, 1993.

Lassner J, Powell K, Rinnegan E. *Social Group Work: Competence and Values in Practice.* New York: Haworth Press, 1986.

Leamon MH, Feldman MC, Scott CL. Factitious Disorders and Malingering. *In Textbook of Clinical Psychiatry, Fourth Edition.* Edited by Hales RE, Yudofsky SC. Washington, DC: American Psychiatric Publishing, 2003, pp. 691–703.

Levenson J. Psychological Factors Affecting Medical Conditions. *In Textbook of Clinical Psychiatry Fourth Edition.* Edited by Hales RE, Yudofsky SC. Washington, DC: American Psychiatric Publishing, 2003, pp. 631–657.

Levenson H, Butler SF, Bein E. Brief Dynamic Individual Psychotherapy. *In Textbook of Clinical Psychiatry Fourth Edition.* Edited by Hales RE, Yudofsky SC. Washington, DC: American Psychiatric Publishing, 2003, pp. 11151–1175.

Licht RW. Drug Treatment of Mania: A Critical Review. *Acta Psychiatrica Scandinavica* 97:387–397, 1998.

Lieberman JA. Comparative Effectiveness of Antipsychotic Drugs: Commentary on Cost Utility of the Latest Antipsychotic Drugs in Schizophrenia Study: Clinical Antipsychotic Trials of Intervention Effectiveness (CATIE). *Archives of General Psychiatry* 63:1069–1072, 2006.

Lieberman JA, Stroup TS, McEvoy JP, et al. Effectiveness of Antipsychotic Drugs in Patients with Chronic Schizophrenia. *New England Journal of Medicine* 353:1209–1223, 2005.

Lijffijt M, Kenemans JL, Verbaten MN, et al. A Meta-Analytic Review of Stopping Performance in Attention-Deficit/Hyperactivity Disorder. *Journal of Abnormal Psychology* 114:216–222, 2005.

Lilly J. *The Deep Self: Profound Relaxation and the Tank Isolation Technique.* New York: Simon and Schuster, 1977.

Linehan MM. *Cognitive-Behavioral Treatment for the Borderline Personality Disorder.* New York: Guilford, 1993.

Longo LP, Johnson B. Addiction: Part I. benzodiazepines—side effects, abuse risk, and alternatives. *American Family Physician,* April 1, 2000.

Longo LP, Parran T, Johnson B, Kinsey W. Addiction: Part II. Identification and Management of the Drug-Seeking Patient. *American Family Physician,* April 15, 2000.

Lorenz EN. Deterministic Non-periodic Flow. *Journal of the Atmospheric Sciences* 20:130–141, 1963.

Lorenz EN. *The Essence of Chaos.* Seattle: University of Washington Press, 1996.

Luciano J. *Al Capone: A Biography.* Westport, CT: Greenwood Press, 2003.

Mace NL, Rabins PV. *The 36-Hour Day: A Family Guide to Caring for Persons With Alzheimer's Disease, Related Dementing Illnesses, and Memory Loss in Later Life, Fourth Edition.* Baltimore, MD: Johns Hopkins University Press, 2006.

Mack AH, Franklin JE, Frances RJ. Substance Use Disorders. *In Textbook of Clinical Psychiatry, Fourth Edition.* Edited by Hales RE, Yudofsky SC. Washington, DC: American Psychiatric Publishing, 2003, pp. 309–377.

MacKinnon RA, Michels R. *The Psychiatric Interview in Clinical Practice.* Philadelphia: Saunders, 1971.

MacQueen G, Young T. Bipolar II Disorder: Symptoms, Course, and Response to Treatment. *Psychiatric Services* 2:3, 2001.

Marangell LB, Silver JM, Goff DC, et al. Pharmacology and Electroconvulsive Therapy. In *Textbook of Clinical Psychiatry, Fourth Edition.* Edited by Hales RE, Yudofsky SC. Washington, DC: American Psychiatric Publishing, 2003, pp. 1047–1149.

Marilynvossavant.com. The Ask Marilyn Daily Diet. *Parade Magazine,* November 21, 2004. Retrieved July 26, 2007, from http://www.marilynvossavant.com/articles/diet_print.html?f=4

Markowitz JC. Interpersonal Psychotherapy. *In Textbook of Clinical Psychiatry, Fourth Edition.* Edited by Hales RE, Yudofsky SC. Washington, DC: American Psychiatric Publishing, 2003, pp. 1207–1223.

Marston WM. *Emotions of Normal People.* New York: International Library of Psychology, 1928.

Maslow A. *Motivation and Personality.* New York: Harper, 1954.

Masters WH, Johnson VE. *Human Sexual Inadequacy.* Boston: Little, Brown, 1970.

Mayes R, Rafalovich A. ADHD and Paediatric Stimulant Use, 1900–80. *History of Psychiatry* 18:435–45, 2007. Retrieved July 17, 2009, from http://hpy.sagepub.com/cgi/reprint/18/4/435.pdf?ck=nck

Mayo Clinic. Social Anxiety Disorder (Social Phobia). n.d. Retrieved July 24, 2009, from http://www.mayoclinic.com/health/social-anxiety-disorder/DS00595/DSECTION=treatments-and-drugs

Mays R, Bagwell C, Erkulwater J. *Medicating Children: ADHD and Pediatric Mental Health.* Unpublished manuscript. Cambridge, MA: Harvard University Press, 2009. Retrieved July 17, 2009, from http://www.hup.harvard.edu/pdf/MAYMED_excerpt.pdf

McClure AK. *"Abe" Lincoln's Yarns and Stories: A Complete Collection of the Funny and Witty Anecdotes That Made Lincoln Famous as America's Greatest Story Teller.* New York: International Publishing, 1901.

McDaniel JS, Musselman DL, Proter MR. Depression in Patients with Cancer. *Archives of General Psychiatry* 52:89–99, 1995.

McNeil H. *Emily Dickinson.* London, UK: Virago Press, 1986.

McPherson J. *Battle Cry of Freedom: The Civil War Era.* New York: Oxford, 1988, p. 588.

MedlinePlus. Somatization Disorder. 2008. Retrieved July 25, 2009, from http://www.nlm.nih.gov/medlineplus/ency/article/000955.htm

Merkel L. The History of Psychiatry. PGY II Lecture University of Virginia Health Systems. September 18, 2003. Retrieved July 10, 2009, from http://www.health-system.virginia.edu/internet/psych-training/seminars/history-of-psychiatry-8–04.pdf

Mitchell M. *Gone With the Wind*. Norwalk, CT: Easton Press, 1968.

Morihisa JM, Cross CD, Price S, et al. Laboratory and Other Diagnostic Tests. In *Textbook of Clinical Psychiatry, Fourth Edition*. Edited by Hales RE, Yudofsky SC. Washington, DC: American Psychiatric Publishing, 2003, pp. 219–256.

Mueser K, Glynn S. *Behavioral Family Therapy for Psychiatric Disorders*. Boston: Allyn and Bacon, 1995.

Nasar SA. The Lost Years of a Nobel Laureate. New York Times on the Web, November 13, 1994.

Nasar SA. *A Beautiful Mind: A Biography of John Forbes Nash, Jr. Winner of the Nobel Prize in Economics, 1994*. New York: Simon and Schuster, 1998.

National Center for Posttraumatic Stress Disorder. Empirical Evidence Regarding Behavior Treatments for PTSD. United States Department of Veterans Affairs, 2007. Retrieved July 24, 2009, from http://www.ncptsd.va.gov/ncmain/ncdocs/fact_shts/fs_empiricalinfo_treatment_dis.html?opm=1&rr=rr129&srt=d&echorr=true

National Institute on Drug Abuse: NIDA InfoFacts: Inhalants, June 2009. Retrieved October 24 from http://www.nida.nih.gov/Infofacts/Inhalants.html

National Institute of Mental Health. U.S. Department of Health and Human Services. Mental Health: Schizophrenia: A Report of the Surgeon General. Rockville, MD, 1999. Retrieved July 24, 2009, from http://www.surgeongeneral.gov/library/mentalhealth/chapter4/sec4.html

National Institute of Mental Health. Generalized Anxiety Disorders. 2007. Retrieved July 24, 2009. http://www.nimh.nih.gov/health/publications/anxiety-disorders/generalized-anxiety-disorder-gad.shtml

National Institute of Mental Health. Attention Deficit Hyperactivity Disorder. NIH Publication No. 08–3572, 2008. Retrieved July 17, 2009, from http://www.nimh.nih.gov/health/publications/attention-deficit-hyperactivity-disorder

National Institute of Mental Health. Antidepressant Medications for Children and Adolescents: Information for Parents and Caregivers. July 15, 2009. Retrieved July 20, 2009, from http://www.nimh.nih.gov/health/topics/child-and-adolescent-mental-health/antidepressant-medications-for-children-and-adolescents-information-for-parents-and-caregivers.shtml

National Institute of Mental Health. What Are the Risk Factors for Bipolar Disorder. April 15, 2009. Retrieved October 20, 2009, from http://www.nimh.nih.gov/health/publications/bipolar-disorder/what-are-the-risk-factors-for-bipolar-disorder.shtml

National Institute of Neurological Disorders and Stroke. Asperger Syndrome Fact Sheet. NIH Publication No. 05–5624, 2005. Retrieved July 17, 2009, from http://www.ninds.nih.gov/disorders/asperger/detail_asperger.htm

National Institute of Neurological Disorders and Stroke (NINDS). National Institutes of Health. Restless Leg Syndrome Fact Sheet. National Institute of Health Publication No. 01–4847, May 15, 2009. Retrieved July 25, 2009, from http://www.ninds.nih.gov/disorders/restless_legs/detail_restless_legs.htm

National Survey on Drug Use and Health. Results from the 2007 National Survey on[JW1] Drug Use and Health: National Findings. Department of Health and Human Services Substance Abuse and Mental Health Services Administration, Office of Applied Sciences Retrieved October 18, 2009, from http://www.oas.samhsa.gov/nsduh/2k7nsduh/2k7results.cfm#Ch7

National Vital Statistic Report 50:15. 2002. Leading Causes of Death in the United States. Retrieved July 24, 2009, from http://www.the-eggman.com/writings/death_stats.html

Neylan TC, Reynolds CF III, Kupfer DJ. Sleep disorders. *In Textbook of Clinical Psychiatry, Fourth Edition*. Edited by Hales RE, Yudofsky SC. Washington, DC: American Psychiatric Publishing, 2003, pp. 975–1000.

Noga JT, Kilgus M. Schizophrenia and Related Disorders. *In Essential Psychopathology and Its Treatment*. Edited by Maxmen JS, Ward NG, Kilgus M. New York: W.W. Norton, 2009, pp. 290–330.

Norcross JC, Mrykalo MS, Blagys MD. Auld Lang Syne: Success Predictors, Change Processes, and Self-Reported Outcomes of New Year's Resolvers and Nonresolvers. *Journal of Clinical Psychology* 58:397–405, 2002.

O'Conner LE, Berry JW, Weiss D. Guilt, Fear, Submission, and Empathy in Depression. *Journal of Affective Disorders* 71:19–27, 2002.

O'Hara MW. *Postpartum Depression: Causes and Consequences*. Edited by O'Hara MW. New York: Springer-Verlag, 1995, pp. 168–194.

Oates, SB. *With Malice Toward None: The Life of Abraham Lincoln*. New York: Harper and Row, 1977.

Palmer LF. What You Need to Know Now about Feeding a Premature Baby. Babyreference.com. 2004. Retrieved July 25, 2009, from http://babyreference.com/FeedingPreemieForBestSurvival.htm

Paris J. Personality Disorders: A Biopsychosocial Model. *Journal of Personality Disorders* 7:255–264, 1993.

Peto R, Lopez AD, Boreham J, Thunham M, Heath C Jr et al. Mortality From Tobacco in Developed Countries: Indirect Estimation From National Vital Statistics. *Lancet* 339:1268–1278, 1992.

Phillips KA, Yen S, Gunderson JG. Personality disorders. *In Textbook of General Psychiatry, Fourth Edition*. Edited by Hales RE, Yudofsky SC. Washington, DC: American Psychiatric Publishing, 2003.

Pinsof WM, Wynne LC. The Efficacy of Marital and Family Therapy: An Empirical

Overview, Conclusions, and Recommendation. *J Marital and Family Therapy* 21:585–613, 1995.

Pinsof WM, Wynne LC, Hambright AB. The Outcomes of Couple and Family Therapy: Findings, Conclusions, and Recommendations. *Psychotherapy* 33:321–331, 1996.

Poland RE, McCracken JT, Lutchmansingh P, et al. Differential Response of Rapid Eye Movement Sleep to Cholinergic Blockade by Scopolamine in Currently Depressed, Remitted, and Normal Control Subjects. *Biological Psychiatry* 41:929–938, 1997.

Popper CW, Gammon GD, West, SA, et al. Disorders Usually First Diagnosed in Infancy, Childhood, or Adolescence. In *Textbook of Clinical Psychiatry, Fourth Edition.* Edited by Hales RE, Yudofsky SC. Washington, DC: American Psychiatric Publishing, 2003, pp. 833–974.

Psychiatric-disorders.com. Causes of Schizophrenia: Genetics, Environment, and Dopamine. n.d. Retrieved July 24, 2009, from http://www.psychiatric-disorders.com/articles/schizophrenia/schizophrenia-causes.php

Rea WS, Kilgus M. Psychopharmacology. *In Essential Psychopathology and Its Treatment.* Edited by Maxmen JS, Ward NG, Kilgus M. New York: W.W. Norton, 2009, pp. 124–171

Rea WS, Kilgus M. Substance-Related Disorders. *In Essential Psychopathology and Its Treatment.* Edited by Maxmen JS, Ward NG, Kilgus M. New York: W.W. Norton, 2009, pp. 241–289.

Raskind MA, Peskind ER, Kanter ED, et al. Reduction of Nightmares and Other PTSD Symptoms in Combat Veterans by Prazosin: A Placebo-Controlled Study. *American Journal of Psychiatry* 160:371–373, 2003.

Raspe RE. *The Surprising Adventures, Great And Imminent Dangers, Miraculous Escapes, And Wonderful Travels Of The Renowned Baron Munchausen (1802).* Republished by Whitefish, Montana: Kessinger Press, 2009.

Read Print Publishing. *Biography of JM Barrie.* 2009. Retrieved July 17, 2009, from http://www.readprint.com/

Rechtschaffen A, Gilliland MA, Bergmann BM, Winter JB. Physiological Correlates of Prolonged Sleep Deprivation in Rats. *Science* 221:182–184, 1983.

Reid TR. *National Geographic* 20(1):23–48, January 2005.

Rogers C. *Client-Centered Therapy: Its Current Practice, Implications and Theory.* London, UK: Constable, 1951.

Rogers CR. The Necessary and Sufficient Conditions of Therapeutic Personality Change. *Journal of Consulting and Clinical Psychology* 21:459–461, 1975.

Rosenhan, Seligman, Walker EF. *Abnormal Psychology, Fourth Edition.* New York: W. W. Norton, 2001.

Ross PE. The Expert Mind. *Scientific American Magazine,* August 2006. Retrieved July 10, 2009, from http://www.scientificamerican.com/article.cfm?id=the-expert-mind&page=4

Rutledge G. Understanding Sleep. Mysleepcentral.com. 2009. Retrieved July 27, 2009, from http://www.healthcentral.com/sleep-disorders/c/68/?ic=4019

RxList. Chantix (varenicline) Tablet—Warning. 2009a. Retrieved July 25, 2009, from http://www.rxlist.com/chantix-drug.htm

RxList. Requip. 2009b. Retrieved July 25, 2009, from http://www.rxlist.com/requip-drug.htm

Sabbatini RME. The History of Shock Therapy in Psychiatry. Retrieved July 10, 2009, from http://www.cerebromente.org.br/n04/historia/shock_i.htm#jauregg

Sadock BJ, Sadock VA. *Kaplan and Sadock's Pocket Handbook of Clinical Psychiatry, Fourth Edition*. Philadelphia: Lippincott Williams and Wilkins, 2005.

Sahelian R. *Mind Boosters: A Guide to Natural Supplements that Enhance Your Mind, Memory, and Mood*. New York: St. Martin's Griffin, 2000.

Salerian AJ, Vittone BJ, Geyer SP, et al. Sildenafil for Psychotropic-Induced Sexual Dysfunction in 31 Women and 61 Men. *Journal of Sex and Marital Therapy* 26:133–140, 2000.

Schatzberg AF, Cole JO, DeBatista C. *Manual of Clinical Psychopharmacology, Sixth Edition*. Washington, DC: American Psychiatric Publishing, 2007.

Schmahl C, Bremner JD. Neuroimaging in Borderline Personality Disorder. *Journal of Psychiatric Research* 40:419–427, 2006.

Schulberg HKW. Epidemiology of Depression in Primary Care. *General Hospital Psychiatry* 14(4):237–247, 1992.

Seligman MEP. *Helplessness: On Depression, Development, and Death*. San Francisco: Freeman, 1975.

Seligman MEP. *What You Can Change and What You Can't*. New York: Random House, 1993.

Seligman MEP. *Learned Optimism: How to Change Your Mind and Your Life*. New York: Vintage Books, 2006.

Seligman MEP, Walker EF, Rosenhan DL. *Abnormal Psychology, Fourth Edition*. New York: Norton, 2001.

Selye H. *The Stress of Life*. New York: McGraw-Hill, 1956.

Selye H. *Stress Without Distress*. Philadelphia: Lippincott, 1974.

Selye H. *The Stress of Life, Revised Edition*. New York: McGraw-Hill, 1976.

Shankle WR, Amen DG. *Preventing Alzheimer's*. New York: Penguin Group, 2004.

Shirer WL. *The Rise and Fall of the Third Reich*. New York: Simon and Schuster, 1960.

Shorter E. *A History of Psychiatry*. New York: Wiley, 1997.

Siever LJ, Davis KL. Overview: Toward a Dysregulation Hypothesis of Depression. *American Journal of Psychiatry* 142:1017–1025, 1985.

Spillane JF. *Cocaine: From Medical Marvel to Modern Menace in US 1884–1920*. Baltimore: Johns Hopkins University Press, 1990.

Spock B. *Common Sense Book of Baby and Child Care*. New York: Duell, Sloan and Pearce, 1946.

Stahl SM. *Essential Psychopharmacology: The Prescriber's Guide.* Cambridge, UK: Cambridge University Press, 2005.

Stahl SM. *Stahl's Essential Psychopharmacology: Neuroscientific Basis and Practical Applications, Third Edition.* New York: Cambridge University Press, 2008.

Stern A. Borderline Group of Neuroses. *Psychoanalytic Quarterly* 7:467–489, 1938.

Stigler JW, Hiebert J. *The Teaching Gap: Best Ideas From the World's Teachers for Improving Education in the Classroom.* New York: Free Press, 1999.

Stoll AL, Severus WE, Freeman MP, et al. Omega-3 Fatty Acids in Bipolar Disorder: A Preliminary Double-Blind, Placebo-Controlled Trial. *Archives of General Psychiatry* 56:407–412, 1999.

Sturgis ET, personal communication.

Substance Abuse and Mental Health Services Administration, Office of Applied Studies. Results from the 2007 National Survey on Drug Use and Health: National Findings. NSDUH Series H-34, DHHS Publication No. SMA 08–4343, 2008. Rockville, MD. Retrieved July 24, 2009, from http://www.oas.samhsa.gov/NSDUH/2k7NSDUH/2k7results.cfm

Szabo ST, Gould TD, Manji HK. Neurotransmitters, Receptors, Signal Transduction, and Second Messengers in Psychiatric Disorders. In *Textbook of Psychopharmacology, Third Edition.* Edited by Schatzberg AF, Nemeroff CB. Washington, DC: American Psychiatric Publishing, 2006, pp. 3–52.

Thase ME. Relapse and Recurrence in Unipolar Major Depression: Short-Term and Long-Term Approaches. *Comprehensive Psychiatry* 51(Suppl 26):51–57, 1990.

Thase ME. Long-Term Treatments of Recurrent Depressive Disorders. *Comprehensive Psychiatry* 53(Suppl 9):32–44, 1992.

Torrey EF. *Surviving Schizophrenia.* New York: HarperCollins, 2001.

Treatment for Adolescents With Depression Study (TADS) Team. Fluoxetine, Cognitive-Behavioral therapy, and their Combination for Adolescents with Depression: Treatment for Adolescents with Depression Study (TADS) Randomized Controlled Trial. *Journal of the American Medical Association* 292(7):807–820, 2004

Trinkle DB, Downs DA, Kilgus M. Delirium, Dementia, Amnesia, and Other Cognitive Disorders. In *Essential Psychopathology and Its Treatment.* Edited by Maxmen JS, Ward NG, Kilgus M. New York: W.W. Norton, 2009, pp. 209–240.

Trinkle DB, Kilgus, M. Sleep Disorders. In *Essential Psychopathology and Its Treatment.* Edited by Maxmen JS, Ward NG, Kilgus M. New York: W.W. Norton, 2009, pp. 495–532.

Truax CB, Carkhuff RR. *Toward Effective Counseling and Psychotherapy: Training and Practice.* Chicago: Aldine, 1962.

U.S. Department of Health and Human Services. Mental Health: A Report of the Surgeon General—Anxiety Disorders. Rockville, MD: U.S. Department of Health and Human Services, Substance Abuse and Mental Health Services Administration, Center for Mental Health Services, National Institutes of Health, National

Institute of Mental Health, 1999. Retrieved July 24, 2009, from http://www.surgeongeneral.gov/library/mentalhealth/chapter4/sec2.html

U.S. Drug Enforcement Administration. The Controlled Substances Act: Drugs of Abuse. Washington DC, U.S. Drug Enforcement Administration, US Department of Justice, 2005. Retrieved October 25, 2009, from http://www.usdoj.gov/dea/pubs/abuse/1-csa.htm#Formal

U.S. Drug Enforcement Administration. Stats and Facts. n.d. Retrieved July 24, 2009, from http://www.usdoj.gov/dea/statistics.html

Ursano RJ, Silberman EK. Psychoanalysis, Psychoanalytic Psychotherapy, and Supportive Psychotherapy. In *Textbook of Clinical Psychiatry, Fourth Edition.* Edited by Hales RE, Yudofsky SC. Washington, DC: American Psychiatric Publishing, 2003, pp. 1177–1206.

Vaillant G. Alcoholism and Drug Dependence. In *The Harvard Guide to Modern Psychiatry.* Edited by Nicholi AM. Cambridge, MA: Harvard University Press, 1978.

Vaillant GE. Ego Mechanisms of Defense and Personality Psychopathology. *Journal of Abnormal Psychology* 103:44–50, 1994.

Valenstein ES. *Great and Desperate Cures: The Rise and Decline of Psychosurgery and Other Radical Treatments for Mental Illness.* New York: Basic Books, 1986.

Vasudeva S, Kilgus M. Anxiety Disorders. *In Essential Psychopathology and Its Treatment.* Edited by Maxmen JS, Ward NG, Kilgus M. New York: W.W. Norton, 2009, pp. 373–415.

Vestergaard P, Licht RW, Brodersen A, et al. Outcome of Lithium Prophylaxis: A Prospective Follow-up of Affective Disorder Patients Assigned to High and Low Serum Lithium Levels. *Acta Psychiatrica Scandinavica* 98:310–315, 1998.

Vinogradov S, Cox PD, Yalom ID. Group Therapy. *In Textbook of Clinical Psychiatry, Fourth Edition.* Edited by Hales RE, Yudofsky SC. Washington, DC: American Psychiatric Publishing, 2003, pp. 1333–1371.

Walker A. *Vivian: The Life of Vivian Leigh.* New York: Grove Press, 1987.

Walker JI. *Clinical Psychiatry in Primary Care.* Menlo Park, CA: Addison-Wesley, 1981.

Walker JI. Older Medications May Trump the New Psychotropics. *Psychopharmacology Update* 6:10, 2006.

Walker JI. Older Medications May Trump the New Psychotropics. *Psychopharmacology Update* 1:1 2008a.

Walker JI. Overview of Atypical Antipsychotics. *Psychopharmacology Update* 8:3, 2008b.

Walsh JJ. Bedlam. *The Catholic Encyclopedia.* New York: Appleton, 1907. Retrieved July 11, 2009, from http://www.newadvent.org/cathen/02387b.htm

Warshaw MG, Dolan RT, Keller MB. Suicide Behavior in Patients with Current or Past Panic Disorder: Five Years of Prospective Data from the Harvard Brown Anxiety Research Program. *American Journal of Psychiatry* 157:1876–1878, 2000.

WebMD.com. Children's Health: Thumb-sucking—Topic Overview. September 12,

2008. Retrieved October 25, 2009, from http://children.webmd.com/tc/thumb-sucking-topic-overview

Weisman MM, Bland RC, Canino GJ, et al. Cross-National Epidemiology of Major Depression and Bipolar Disorder. *Journal of the American Medical Association* 276:293–229, 1996.

Weissman MM, Markowitz JC, Klerman GL. *Comprehensive Guide to Interpersonal Psychotherapy*. New York: Basic Books, 2000.

Whybrow PC, Akiskal HS, McKinney WT. *Mood Disorders: Toward a New Psychobiology*. New York: Plenum, 1984, pp. 21–42.

Wing L. Asperger Syndrome: A Clinical Account. *Psychological Medicine* 11(1):115–29, 1981.

Wisner KL, Wheeler SB. Prevention of Recurrent Postpartum Major Depression. *Hospital and Community Psychiatry* 45:1191–1196, 1994.

Wolfe MS. Shutting down Alzheimer's: New Research Reveals Strategies for Blocking the Molecular Processes that Lead to this Memory-Destroying Disease. *Scientific American*, April 23, 2006.

Wolff HG. Life Stress and Bodily Disease—A Formulation. *In Life Stress and Bodily Disease*. Edited by Wolf HG, Itase CC. Baltimore: Williams and Wilkins, 1950.

Wolpe J. *Psychotherapy by Reciprocal Inhibition*. Stanford, CA: Stanford University Press, 1958.

Wright JH, Beck AT, Thase ME. Cognitive Therapy. *In Textbook of Clinical Psychiatry, Fourth Edition*. Edited by Hales RE, Yudofsky SC. Washington, DC: American Psychiatric Publishing, 2003, pp. 1245–1284.

Yutzy SH. Somatoform Disorders. In *Textbook of Clinical Psychiatry, Fourth Edition*. Edited by Hales RE, Yudofsky SC. Washington, DC: American Psychiatric Publishing, 2003, pp. 659–690.

Zanarini MC, Frankenburg FR, Dubo ED, et al. Axis I Comorbidity of Borderline Personality Disorder. *American Journal of Psychiatry* 155:1733–1739, 1998.

Zebro GW, Kilgus M. Somatoform Disorders. *In Essential Psychopathology and Its Treatment*. Edited by Maxmen JS, Ward NG, Kilgus M. New York: W.W. Norton, 2009, pp. 416–437.

Index

nail biting, 213
nightmares and excessive fears,
210–11
oppositional defiant disorder, 21,
203–4
parenting skills to prevent or manage, 214–18
pervasive developmental disorders,
21, 204–6
post-traumatic stress disorder, 214
psychotherapy, 213–14
sleep terror, 264
sleepwalking, 264
stuttering, 211–12
suicide risk, 207
thumb sucking, 212–13
tic disorders, 211
see also attention deficit/hyperactiv-
ity disorder; conduct disorder;
development
chlorpromazine (Thorazine), 83–84,
297
chronic pain disorder
behavior therapy, 141–42
clinical conceptualization, 24, 139
pharmacotherapy, 139–41
prevalence, 139
psychotherapeutic interventions, *143*
Cialis, 241
cigarette smoking, 121–22
cingulate gyrus, 155
circadian rhythm sleep disorder, 27,
262–63
Cline, F., 204
clomipramine, 272
clonidine, 199
clozapine (Clozaril), 290–92, 294
Clozaril. *see* clozapine
cocaine, 181, 184–85
codeine, 185–86
cognitive-behavior therapy
applications, 311
behavioral techniques in, 314
for depression in children and adolescents, 208
depression treatment, 35, 49, 50–51
effectiveness, 311
goals, 311, 313
interpersonal therapy and, *320*
maladaptive cognitive patterns,
311–13
obsessive-compulsive disorder treatment, 103
post-traumatic stress disorder treatment, 102

schizophrenia treatment, 86–87
therapist questions in, 313
cognitive functioning
alcohol-induced disorders, 175–77
DSM diagnostic classification, 22–27
elements of emotional intelligence, 9
exercises to prevent Alzheimer's disease, 236, 237–38
magnification of significance of
events, 312
overgeneralization, 313
polarized thinking, 312
preventing psychosomatic illness,
124–26
rational versus irrational, *315*
selective abstraction, 312
self-knowledge, 9
somatization disorder manifestations, 133
theory of depression, 43
see also dementia
cognitive therapy
bipolar disorder treatment, 67
depression treatment, 49
panic disorder treatment, 97
see also cognitive-behavior therapy
Cohen, N., 113
Coleman, Leonard, 91–92, 105
Comfort, A., 239
communication, interpersonal, 245–46
communication disorders, 21
complementary medicine, Alzheimer's
disease treatment, 232–34
compliance
patterns, 268
schizophrenia treatment, 85
strategies for improving, 269–70
conditioning
aversive control techniques, 310
chronic pain management, 142
conceptual basis, 142, 308
psychosomatic illness as, 120–21
reinforcement in, 309
sleep patterns, 255
see also behavior therapy
conduct disorder
attention deficit/hyperactivity disorder and, 197, 198, 202
causes, 202
clinical features, 202
comorbidity, 202
course, 202
DSM diagnosis, 21
parental role in, 202
pharmacotherapy, 202

Complete Mental Health

dopaminergic system
  antipsychotic drug effects, 289–90
  in attention deficit/hyperactivity disorder, 199
  bipolar disorder and, 63
  cognitive function, 259
  in depression, 44
  functions, 276
  neurotransmitter depletion, *280*
  in schizophrenia, 78, 288–89
  structure and function, 288
  in substance use and abuse, 180–81
doxepin, 272
dreams, 253–54, 257, 264
Dubovsky, S. L., 36
Dunbar, F., 117
dyspareunia, 240, 242
dyssomnias, 255. *see also specific disorder*
dysthymia, 23, 31, *33*, 36, *37*

eating disorders, 21–22, 209
Ecstasy, 182, 184
Edison, Thomas, 252
Effexor, 207–8, 277–78, 279
Elavil, 140, 272
Eldepryl, 273
elimination disorders, 22
emotional functioning
  capacity for fun, *128*
  causes of anxiety, 92
  control, 9
  developmental significance, 8–9
  dopamine effects, 276
  emotional intelligence, 9–10
  love, 246
  preventing psychosomatic illness, 123
  psychoneuroimmunology, 114
  schizophrenia manifestations, 75–76
  serotonin effects, 276
enuresis, 212
environmental conditions
  alcohol abuse risk, 172
  determinants of behavior, 3–4
  personality disorder risk, 150
  see also family functioning; sociocultural context
erectile dysfunction, 241
erotomania, 82
estradiol, 237
Exelon, 232
exercise, to prevent Alzheimer's disease, 235–36
exposure-response prevention, 103

extrapyramidal symptoms, 296–97
eye-movement desensitization and reprocessing, 102

factitious disorder, 25, 142–44
family functioning
  conduct disorder management, 202
  good qualities, 326–27
  intervention with member with personality disorder, 163–64
  parenting assessment, *219–21*
  parenting skills, 214–18
  parenting techniques for child with attention deficit/hyperactivity disorder, 201–2
  sexual abuse, 243
  strategies for maintaining marriage, 244–45
  structural changes related to divorce, 239
family therapy
  for child and adolescent problems, 214
  definition, 324
  goals, 324–26, 327
Fay, J., 204
Fields, W. C., *170*
fight-or-flight response, 92
Fitzgerald, F. Scott, *170*
flexibility, *12*
flooding, 309
fluoxetine, 208, 275
Ford, C.V., 137
Freud, S., 314
Friedman, M., 117–18
function theory of behavior, 7–8

gamma-aminobutyric acid
  bipolar disorder and, 63
  in depression, 44
  neurotransmitter action, 271, 281
  in sleep, 260
gender identity disorder, 239–40
generalized anxiety disorder
  clinical features, 94
  definition, 23
  drug therapy, *95*, 285–86
  prevalence, *93*
  substance use and, 94
genetics
  alcoholism risk, 172
  Alzheimer's disease, 230–31
  bipolar disorder risk, 63, *64*
  borderline personality disorder and, 155–56

Lamictal. *see* lamotrigine
lamotrigine (Lamictal), 65–66, *299*,
    300–301
learned helplessness, 42
learning disorders, 21
Leigh, Vivian, 54
Lewis, Meriwether, 54
Lexapro, 286
Librium, 285–86
librium, 178
life change units, 116
Lincoln, Abraham, 169, *254*
lithium, *299*
    applications, 298
    bipolar disorder treatment, 65
    conduct disorder treatment, 202
    mechanism of action, 298
    prescribing practice, 298
locus coeruleus, 96
London, Jack, *170*
loss
    depression and, 41
    supportive psychotherapy, 328
LSD, 184
Luvox, 287
Lyrica, 140

major depression, 23, 31, *33*, 34–35, *37*
malingering, 142–43
marijuana, 181, 183
Markowitz, J., 318
marriage
    communication in, 245–46
    divorce patterns and trends, 239
    romance in, 246–47, *250*
    sexual dysfunction and, 244
    sexual intimacy in, 247
    strategies for maintaining, 244–45
Marston, W. M., 4
Maslow, A., 2, 10
Master, W. H., 239
maturity, self-assessment, *13*
McPherson, James, 169
medical conditions
    alcohol-induced, 173–77
    behavioral risk factors, *120*, 121–23
    bipolar symptoms arising from, 62
    factitious disorders versus, 142–43
    psychiatric symptoms related to, 27
    psychological factors in course of,
        112–14, *115*
    somatization disorder versus, 132–33
    somatoform disorder versus, *133*
    see also psychosomatic illness
meditation, 105

memory
    diagnostic categories of dysfunction,
        22
    exercises to improve and maintain,
        237–38
mental health practitioners
    equanimity in clinical setting, 105–7
    relationship with patients with
        somatoform disorder, 130, 131,
        134–35
    therapeutic alliance in treatment of
        substance abuse, 190
    types of, *26*
messenger RNA
    bipolar disorder and, 64
    depression and, 44
methamphetamine, 182, 184
methylphenidate, 198, 199
Minpress, 102
modafinil (Provigil)
    hypersomnia treatment, 259
    narcolepsy treatment, 260–61
    side effects, 259, 261
modeling, behavior, 309–10
monoamine oxidase inhibitors
    food interactions, 273, 274
    indications, 48, 273
    mechanism of action, 273
    prescribing practice, 273
    side effects, 48, 274
mood stabilizing drugs
    bipolar disorder treatment, 65, 68
    personality disorder treatment, 165,
        166
    post-traumatic stress disorder treat-
        ment, 101
    see also specific drug
morphine, 185–86
motivation
    for behavior change, 308
    persistence, 10
    productive action, 9
multiple personality disorder, 104
Munchausen's by proxy, 144–45
Munchausen syndrome, 144

nail biting, 213
naltrexone, 177
Namenda, 232
narcissistic personality disorder,
    157–58, 161, 162
narcolepsy, 25, 260–61
Nardil, 273
Nash, John, 74, 87
neurobiology

Complete Mental Health

psychotherapy, 85–87
residual, 80
social skills training, 330
as spectrum disorder, *82*
treatment outcomes, 87
types, 79–80
undifferentiated, 80
viral infection theory, 78
schizophreniform disorder, 22
schizotypal personality disorder, 153, 161, 162, 165–66
Schumann, R., 15
second messenger system
bipolar disorder and, 64
depression and, 44
selective serotonin reuptake inhibitors
anxiety disorder treatment, 105, 286–87
applications, 48, 275, 279
bupropion and, 276–77
discontinuation syndrome, 276
drug interactions, 276
effects on dreaming, 264
historical development, 274–75
obsessive-compulsive disorder treatment, 103
panic disorder treatment, 97
post-traumatic stress disorder treatment, 101
side effects, 48, 275–76
somatization disorder treatment, 135
use by children and adolescents, 207–8
selegiline, 273
self-beliefs
body dysmorphic disorder, 138–39
borderline personality disorder, 155
causes of depression, 41–42, 43
self-esteem, 10
self-knowledge, 9
Seligman, M. E. P., 336
Selye, H., 113
separation anxiety, 22, 210
Seroquel, 292, 294, 295
serotonergic system
in bipolar disorder, 63
in borderline personality disorder, 166
in depression, 44
functions, 276
neurotransmitter depletion, *280*
in obsessive-compulsive disorder, 103
serotonin-dopamine antagonists, 290–95

serotonin-norepinephrine reuptake inhibitors, 48, 101, 277–79
serotonin syndrome, 276
sexual disorders
diagnostic classification, 25, 239–40. *see also specific disorder*
female arousal disorder, 240, 241
female orgasmic disorder, 240, 241–42
hypoactive, 240, 241
male anorgasmia, 240, 242
male erectile disorder, 240, 241
painful intercourse, 240, 242
premature ejaculation, 240, 242
premenstrual dysphoric disorder, 240, 242–43
sexual dysfunction
causes and contributing factors, 240–41
clinical features, 240
definition, 239
marital status and, 244
prevalence, 239, 240
sexual abuse and, 243–44
SSRI side effects, 275–76
sexual intimacy in relationships
assessment, *249*
good qualities, 247
see also sexual disorders; sexual dysfunction
shift work sleep disorder, 263
Sinequan, 272
sleep
biological function, 252–53
conditioning, 255
disorders. *see* sleep disorders
dreams, 253–54, 257
neurobiology, 260
normal, 252–53
self-hypnosis for, *267*
sleep apnea, 25, 261–62
sleep disorders
breathing-related. *see* sleep apnea
causes, 255
circadian rhythm, 262–63
diagnostic classification, 25–27, 255
dyssomnias, 255
hypersomnia, 259
jet lag, 263
mental disorders associated with, *256*
narcolepsy, 260–61
nightmares and sleep terror, 27, 264
parasomnias, 264
prevalence, 255